Praise for

PRODUCT LAUNCH THE MICROSOFT WAY

"Mastan's detailed and pragmatic approach to teaching launch concepts and techniques based on his extensive Microsoft experience really nails the topic. Fills a significant gap in marketing and product launch knowledge."

-Pam Radford, Group Account Director, McCann Relationship Marketing (MRM) Worldwide

"In *Product Launch the Microsoft Way* James Mastan provides a holistic perspective on successfully taking a product to market based on his extensive experience at Microsoft, one of the world's foremost marketing companies. A must-read for both experienced marketers and those less-experienced marketers who want to learn what it really takes to launch a product."

-Cathy Pricco, Senior Strategy Consultant, West Monroe Partners

"James Mastan has successfully captured the unique blend of artistry and discipline needed for a successful product launch in a powerful easy to read and use guide."

-John Zagula, former Microsoft head of Global Campaigns, author of *The Marketing Playbook*, and partner at Ignition Partners

"*Product Launch the Microsoft Way* offers a unique, valuable, and practical perspective to help companies learn effective product launch techniques."

-Peter Gavalakis, former Product Marketing Manager, Intel Corporation

PRODUCT LAUNCH

The Microsoft Way

PRODUCT LAUNCH

The Microsoft Way

James Mastan

Commercio Press, LLC
New York • London • Rome

Published by Commercio Press, LLC, New York 10019

Direct inquiries for reproduction, permissions, or content usage to *permissions@commerciopress.com.*

Printed in the United States of America
16 15 14 13 12 11 10 09 08 1 2 3 4 5

Library of Congress Cataloging-in-Publication Data

Mastan, James P.
Product Launch the Microsoft Way / James Mastan.—1st ed.
p. : ill. ; cm.
Includes index

ISBN-13 978-0-6152-0946-3

1. Marketing 2. Strategic Planning 3. Product Launch I. Title

Library of Congress Catalog Card Number: 2008928828

First Edition

Product Launch the Microsoft Way is an independent book publication and is not affiliated with, nor has it been authorized, sponsored, or otherwise approved by Microsoft Corporation.

Contents

Acknowledgments

This book would not have been possible but for the excellent review feedback and assistance from a number of people. I would like to thank Commercio Press, LLC, for their excellent assistance in getting this book published. My editor, Robyn M. Fritz, turned my original content into a well-written work that I can be proud of. She also kept me on track and was excellent on the project management aspects of getting the book completed on time and on budget. Jenn Cassie and Kyra Freestar are excellent copyeditors and proofreaders and did great work. Bob Lanphear handled the book layout and the cover design, doing a great job. I highly recommend their services. To contact them please email editorial@commerciopress.com.

A number of colleagues reviewed chapters and gave feedback on the content, providing a sanity check and their expert insight on what I was writing. These included (in alphabetical order) Chris Bryant (Microsoft), Will Cousins (Twisted Pair Solutions), Piyush Dogra (Microsoft), Peter Gavalakis (Intel), Anne Hamilton (Microsoft), Cathy Pricco (West Monroe Partners), Pam Radford (McCann Relationship Marketing), Abhijeet Rane (9th Point), and John Zagula (Ignition Partners). Thanks to all of you for generously donating your time and thoughts to help make this book the best it could be. You are all highly competent and smart professionals. I'm extremely grateful for your help and support.

Preface

Most companies create and sell products, and bringing these products to market requires that they be launched. Unfortunately, there are few if any comprehensive or high-quality resources on how to effectively plan and execute a product launch from a business and marketing perspective. *Product Launch the Microsoft Way* fills this knowledge gap by conveying the details of proven Microsoft launch methodologies and concepts. This book consolidates, expands upon, and conveys my knowledge of important aspects of the product launch, business, and marketing strategy experience that I've acquired after 14 years as Director of Marketing at Microsoft, and over 20 years of industry experience.

The activities and concepts Microsoft uses to launch a product are applicable to a broad range of product types and industries beyond software or high-technology (although they are perfectly applicable to those industries!). Because Microsoft has excellent, highly developed marketing skills and competencies, and is so successful with product launches, the knowledge of how they do launches is immensely valuable to other firms.

Most marketers, if they are lucky enough to participate in a launch at all, generally are only involved in one slim piece of the overall launch activities. They just don't get a chance to see or participate in the big picture. This leaves little room for increasing marketing skill levels that would permit taking on a broader marketing role. This book attempts to provide a holistic perspective and lessons about a launch from beginning to end. Learning and internalizing these lessons will provide a quantum leap in your knowledge and expertise.

This book is for those who want to understand core product launch concepts, best practices, and tactical execution activities from a business and marketing perspective. Various audiences will find this information informative and enlightening, including:

Experienced Marketers: If you have marketing experience, and possibly launch experience, you will learn how Microsoft does it and pick up a few pointers that can refine your skills and thinking. There are some advanced concepts in the book that you may not have been exposed to, even if you're experienced.

Less-Experienced Marketers: For those who are new to marketing, have limited experience, or have participated in a product launch but were exposed to only a small portion of the overall launch process, this book will train you and provide the knowledge and expertise to take your skills to a higher level.

Technical or Non-Business Folks: If you are on the technical or engineer product development side of creating and launching products, you likely have never been exposed to what the marketing and business folks must do to take a product to market. Understanding this can help you work more effectively with marketing on a launch and possibly help your career—at some point, if you wish to advance in the management hierarchy, you'll need to have a firm grasp on the business and marketing side of a launch in addition to the product development side. A well-rounded and knowledgeable person will be a much more desirable candidate for management roles.

Product launches entail both risk and cost. For any marketer, a few things learned, or a couple of insights gathered from these chapters, could end up saving huge amounts of time or money for a company planning a launch or currently executing one.

There are numerous marketing and business activities required to successfully launch a product. This book covers many of them, but one book cannot cover everything in exhaustive detail. I've chosen to focus on a comprehensive set of topics that are the most important for a launch. However, it was necessary to gloss over or not cover some topics in order to dive a bit deeper into some important areas that are generally not covered.

For example, there is good information available about how to price a product, so I did not cover pricing in depth. Product planning, product development process checkpoints and gating milestones, and setting the right reseller channel margins are other topics I touched on but did not deeply discuss. Chapter 9 discusses post-launch sustaining marketing and provides concepts and structures for planning post-launch marketing activities and staying on top of the business. However, given book size limitations, I was forced to leave out content on drill-down marketing tactics, metrics on response rates, and marketing mix optimization, among others. Even so, this book offers a wealth of useful, actionable, and comprehensive information for you to learn and put into action at your company. The concepts and tactics conveyed here are not solely meant for medium or large size companies, or large-scale product launches. A smaller firm can apply these concepts and improve their launch effectiveness—simply take the concepts and tactics provided and scale them up or down to meet your budget and launch needs.

Finally, I am always open to input. If you have feedback, suggestions for new topics, ideas for expanding the coverage or depth of certain topics, or anything else regarding the book, please email me at **bookfeedback@bluerainmarketing.com**. I'm happy to have a dialog with you regarding your ideas. Until then, enjoy the book.

James Mastan, May 2008

1

The Road to Launch

Launching a new product can be one of the most exciting company activities. The energy level is high, the work comes fast and furious, and expectations of a successful launch abound. Taking a new product to market can be a great experience, especially if the launch team is composed of high-quality, motivated people who communicate well and enjoy working together. It also helps if they know what they are doing.

Product Launch the Microsoft Way distills the broad experience I've acquired leading or participating in many product launches during my 14-year tenure as Director of Marketing at Microsoft. Microsoft is known for its marketing prowess, and for good reason. After taking thousands of products to market, Microsoft has refined the product launch process to focus on the most important elements and steps to efficiently and effectively take a product to market.

This book covers product launch in the approximate launch process order. For example, you need an in-depth understanding of the target customers (Chapter 2) to build a launch plan (Chapter 3). Then development of positioning and messaging (Chapter 4) and the acquisition of any key or required partnerships (Chapter 5) can begin. Following this, awareness creation via public relations and analyst outreach can start (Chapter 6) parallel to planning and developing important customer and partner pre-launch programs (Chapter 7). As these programs are executing, the core block and tackle marketing launch activities are planned and executed, ending with the launch itself (Chapter 8). Following the launch and product general availability, the launch process does not end, and sustaining post-launch marketing activities must be put into place to ensure that business goals are met (Chapter 9).

WHAT TO EXPECT DURING A LAUNCH

Nothing is static during a launch process; change is the rule, not the exception. The launch environment, or state of things, will change significantly throughout the launch process. The level of clarity and available information to enable informed decisions will also fluctuate. At the start, the product's specific feature and functionality definition will be hazy. Folks will have a concept or vision of what the product should be, but it typically will exist only in a PowerPoint document as vaporware—a term used in the software industry to connote a product that does not yet truly exist. This is a time during which the product concept's rationale and fit within the overall corporate strategy are being debated. Initial budget investments and headcount resource asks are also being made.

Assuming there is positive corporate sponsorship a small group will be formed and chartered to further investigate and build a viable business plan based on the existing level of knowledge and information available. Even with the best data, ambiguity abounds at such an early point in a product launch cycle. Many assumptions about the product, market, and customers will be made, validated, and invalidated. The product development team will attempt to define the initial core product functionality and features. Potential target customers will be approached to provide validation for the product concept and their needs regarding product features. Potential key business partners must be contacted to assess interest and willingness to invest in the product; some will get on board and others may become competitors. Internal political battles will be fought as various factions maneuver to retain or take power and control during the launch process. Competitive and market sizing analyses will be performed to estimate market opportunity potential, reachable market share, and potential revenue. Until these types of activities resolve themselves, ambiguity will rule the early launch environment. People who do not deal well with ambiguity may not be the best fit to become involved in a product launch, especially at the very beginning.

As the launch process progresses, things tend to become more clear and structured. Note I did not say "clear and structured," but "more clear and structured." After a viable business plan is created, the beginnings of clarity and structure start to emerge, although future change will still be in the air. A business plan is (or should be) a living document that adapts to newly acquired information and can accommodate the changes a launch process surely will bring. However, once an initial business plan is in place and approved, along with allocated start-up funding and headcount resources, the launch process can kick into high gear.

This means converting the business plan and strategy into an actionable rollout plan that encompasses all the functional groups that must be involved to drive a successful launch from the business perspective. The engineering staff can then create more detailed product planning, product definitions, and specifications in coordination with continually discovered market and customer requirements. Initial key functional group personnel, beyond the original small team, can now be hired. Typically, these initial hires will be the functional team managers, such as sales, marketing, business development, and lead engineers. These folks can begin to create the specific launch plans for their functional roles and then staff up as necessary for the launch.

From the marketing perspective, this is the time when things start to get very interesting. With high-level business plans in place, the marketing team can get started defining and implementing the myriad activities needed for a successful launch.

THE PRODUCT LIFE CYCLE

Figure 1-1 summarizes at a high level the parallel processes of the engineering/product development and business launch activities. Neither the product development nor marketing groups can successfully take a product to market alone. Both groups are critical to a successful launch process.

From a product development perspective, Figure 1-1 identifies what is known as the product life cycle. This is not the broader product market life cycle typically defined as the stages of product development, introduction, growth, maturity, decline, and obsolescence. This product life cycle focuses primarily on those efforts and milestones that occur during the product development process leading up to the product launch. Admittedly, the product life cycle shown in Figure 1-1 is software specific; it is used as a placeholder for conceptually similar product development processes and milestones that must occur at any firm developing and shipping a product, whatever the industry.

Using the software product life cycle model as an example, the cycle is divided at a high level into the activities that occur around the current product in development ("v-current," or the current version) before the launch, and those that happen afterward. Before the launch takes place, the product vision must be conceptualized and specifications created through a product planning process. The product planning process continues through

FIGURE 1-1: Product Launch Cycle Alignment

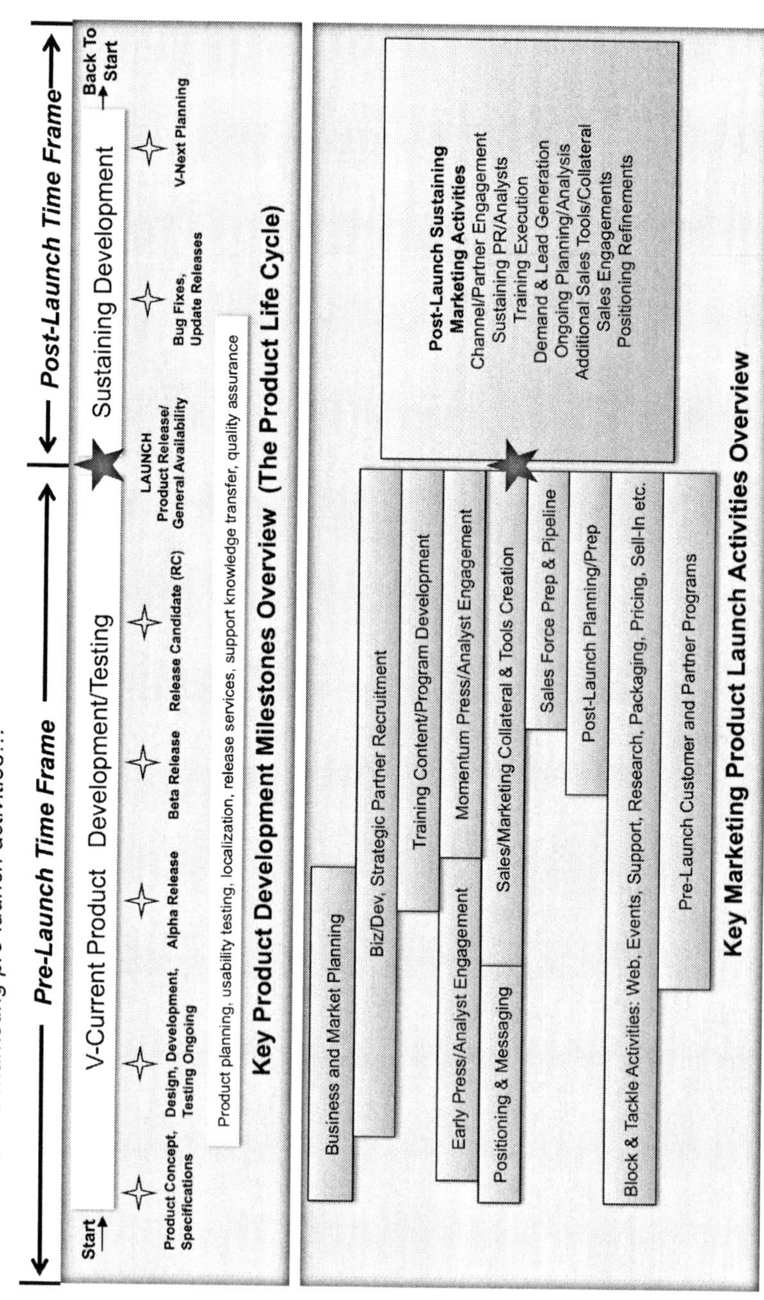

the pre-launch time frame until at some point the product features are considered final, and the product planning focus shifts to the next version or iteration of the product. Once the initial product planning is done and specifications are created, the product design and development begins. Product design involves designing the product's underlying technical architecture and feature set and the user interface or user experience design.

At some point as the product is designed, developed, and tested it is considered stable and complete enough to be the first true version of the product. In the software industry, this is known as the "Alpha" release. It is generally an internal-only release, or is made available only to a small number of important partners involved with the product from a technical perspective. Product stability is quite uncertain at this point. As testing and refinements to the product continue, eventually the product achieves a "Beta" release status. At this point, the product is relatively stable and mostly feature complete, and is typically made available via a "Technical Beta" to a broader number of partners or early-adopter customers to test and evaluate.

Finally, after incorporating feedback from partners and customers participating in the technical beta, a "Release Candidate" of the product is produced. This is the product version that is the first candidate to become the final product that will be released to market and into general availability. Quality assurance kicks in heavily at this point, and goals are set around reducing the number of bugs, or product errors. These errors are generally categorized as Priority One, Two, Three, and, sometimes, Four level errors.

Priority One level errors are significant and serious enough that a product will not be released and shipped until they are all corrected. Priority Two level errors are still significant, and most likely should be fixed before shipping. Levels Three and Four errors may or may not be fixed. The product development team undergoes a process called "triage" to classify the various product defects into the error-level categorization. Resource, time, and error-correction investment trade-offs must be made at this point.

It is unlikely that any product, software or otherwise, ever hits the market in perfect shape. It would be economically unrealistic to strive for perfection. So a line is drawn at some point, with the "must fix" problems above the line, and the "we can live with these issues in the current release" defects below the line. This draws the line for an achievable end to the product development and testing process and enables the product to achieve final release status and hit the market. At the end of the process, when the product is approaching completion, product release services are initiated to handle moving the product into the mainstream processes of the company, including preparing part numbers, manufacturing specifications, and production forecasts.

As each of the product development milestones are achieved, various levels of product usability testing and assessment occur in parallel to ensure the product is actually usable and intuitive and product features are discoverable. In addition, technical knowledge is transferred to the product support team that will provide customer support services after the product is released. If the product is intended for delivery to non-English-speaking customers in various countries, the product is "localized" once the final version is released. Among other things, localization involves ensuring that the product user interface and supporting documentation appears in the local language (e.g., French, German, Italian, Mandarin) and that any product changes legally required by the countries receiving the product are incorporated.

Once the final product is released, product development does not stop, but moves into a sustaining product phase where post-release product issues are designed and fixed, and any product updates are made available. This is also when the planning for the next version of the product kicks into high gear, starting the product cycle all over again, with the "v-next" product vision and specification planning efforts getting under way.

In parallel to all that product development activity, the business and marketing efforts to launch the product are underway. These activities comprise this book's core focus. Some of these activities are tightly tied to the development milestones, while others are relatively independent. Early in the cycle, when the product concept and vision are being developed, planning to create a business plan and fully understand the market opportunity and landscape is occurring. Strategic partners, both technical and business focused, are engaged and recruited. Product positioning and messaging are created, and public relations efforts and outreach begin. Customer and channel partner programs tied to the alpha, beta, and other development milestones are defined, put into place, and executed against.

In the mid to later stages of the product cycle, product training programs are developed and sales and marketing materials created. Important block and tackle marketing activities are defined and implemented, such as the creation of the external product website, industry or internal launch events, packaging creation, and pricing finalization.

Finally, the direct sales force and resellers channels are prepped and trained, and product distribution sell-in activities can occur. At the same time, marketing and sales plans are being created that will acquire customers and revenue in the post-launch time frame after the product becomes generally available. Post-launch, the product is "real" and requires classic marketing and sales activities to create demand, build and manage customer lead pipelines, work with and manage channel partners, continue to build momentum and awareness through PR, and other activities. This is the sustaining marketing phase of a product launch, and is where the rubber hits the road in driving and determining whether or not business goals (revenue/profit/market share) will be met.

Regardless of the specifics of a given product development process, the point remains valid—engineering can't launch a product on their own, and the business side can't launch a product on their own, so defining, aligning, and coordinating a joint go-to-market process is the only way to make a launch happen successfully.

Chapters 2 through 9 focus on the marketing and business launch activities. These chapters describe and hone in on the specific launch planning and tactical activities required to actually take a product to market based on the Microsoft model. However, there is more to a successful launch than planning and tactics. Without a proper understanding and great execution of the more qualitative aspects of a launch, the tactical launch activities have a much higher chance of failing or being poorly executed.

THE QUALITATIVE ASPECTS OF A SUCCESSFUL LAUNCH

It's possible that it can take years to fully complete the product launch cycle. Of course, the actual time will depend on the particular product or industry, the team's experience, the scope of the product, and so on. During this time there are intangible qualitative aspects of the launch process that can make or break a launch, and are important to a successful launch. Think of these as necessary to form the core foundational elements of a successful launch culture among the launch team(s) and other key stakeholders. The most important of these cultural foundational elements are as follows:

Strong Leadership: Strong, focused, and motivational leaders are required to drive the launch process forward at every stage. Not everyone can lead, but almost everyone can be focused and motivated to succeed. During a product launch, the ambiguity and frenzy that will most likely surface at times will require steadfast leadership to guide the launch team through these periods, keeping the team together, focused, and on track.

A product launch leader does not necessarily need to be appointed or to be the most senior employee in the group, but can easily emerge from the rank and file. This person will likely be passionate about the product, completely believe in the vision and mission, maintain focus on delivering value to the core target customer, understand both the business needs and product features, and have a personality that works effectively with the engineering/product development staff, senior management, and business teams. In essence, this person is the product launch champion, willing to step up, make hard calls, take a position (even an unpopular one), defend their point of view successfully, and independently take ownership of difficult issues and drive for resolution and clarity. A launch can happen without a champion, but a champion is required to create an excellent product launch.

Adequate Sponsorship: Without executive sponsorship, a product launch is doomed to wallow in ambiguity and will likely fail. Given the cross-group politics and siloed nature of many organizations, it's important to make sure that a quorum of senior executives across the company are aware of and support the product launch. They must be convinced that launching this particular product will be good for the company and for them and their particular area of ownership. Acquiring this buy-in and support before getting too far down the path of the launch is always a good idea.

Securing Adequate Resources: While not entirely qualitative, this is important. Although gaining adequate levels of buy-in and sponsorship can green light a launch process, that doesn't mean that the sponsors are necessarily aware of the true level of investment required to make the launch successful. This awareness of the appropriate investment levels and the investment timing must be made clear up front and agreement to invest must be secured. While investing cautiously is often prudent ("here's some start-up funding and a couple of heads, show me results, then we can investigate and discuss further investment"), the initial investment needs to be substantial enough to achieve those early results, and a true willingness to cough up more dough and headcount later on needs to actually exist, or the team will suffer through an agonizing launch process.

Solid Planning and Foresight: Good planning makes for good results. Poor planning … well, you already know what the rest of the sentence should read! Developing solid plans for all aspects of the launch requires discipline and foresight. However, investing in robust up-front launch planning will pay dividends as the launch progresses. Those on the team with prior launch experience will likely be able to provide some foresight, but that does not mean they are good planners. Someone, or some team, with good planning skills needs to own the all-up launch planning process. This does not mean that these folks must create every plan for every functional area, but they need to be able to drive and foster the development of functional launch plans across the organization and ensure that these plans are cohesive and support each other when rolled up at the high level. This book can help provide some foresight for what activities need to be planned and considered, but only your organization can take that knowledge and translate it into specific plans for your firm's product.

Skillful Prioritization: A launch plan can easily grow to incorporate many possible activities. The problem is that many times some of the listed activities fall into the "nice-to-have" category. Throughout the launch, consistently reviewing the plans and prioritizing activities relative to the business goals and the existing situation is key to an efficient launch process that maximizes the return on the applied human and capital resource investments. It is not easy to make the hard prioritization calls to stop an ongoing activity, or to take a different approach, especially if the true priorities do not line up with what the majority of the launch team thinks. Hopefully, that kind of situation will be the exception, but it does take diligence to keep on top of the various ongoing launch activities and prioritize them to help ensure the optimal path to launch.

Excellent Communication: Solid and effective communication is a core underpinning for a successful launch. There are so many groups involved, with so many plans and activities that need to be coordinated, synchronized, and reviewed, that any launch will fall apart without an effective communication process (both formal and informal). The incremental level of communication required for a launch will depend on what existing communication mechanisms and processes currently exist and how effective they are. If your firm has a well-structured and adhered-to communication process that functions effectively, fantastic. If not, this is the time to ensure that the core launch team and all stakeholders across the organizations are clear on what the communication processes will be and on their role in making them effective.

Teamwork: Team dynamics can be tight-knit and fluid or broken and dysfunctional. Given the various groups that are involved in a launch—including sales, marketing, engineering, support, legal, finance, and manufacturing operations—creating a solid foundation that fosters cooperative cross-group teamwork can make the launch process proceed smoothly. One method to improve successful cross-group collaboration and teamwork is to align the objectives and priorities of the team leaders. If the leader of each stakeholder group has an annual review objective making the product launch success one of their top priorities, this should align the leaders and trickle down to their subordinates' objectives and priorities, helping to create cross-group alignment.

This alignment should be one result of gaining executive sponsorship across the company. Teamwork within the core launch team is also important, from alignment of objectives to being willing to be a good team member, which can be a function of personality types, team morale, perception of reward for a job well done, or simply the leadership skills of the team's manager. A cohesive launch team whose members like one another and can maintain complementary skill sets and personalities that do not conflict can really help a launch go smoothly. To get this team, hiring the right people is critical, especially for the early hires that will set the tone for those that follow.

Accommodate Flexibility and Adaptability: The norm for a launch process is change and ambiguity. The launch team and stakeholders must be flexible to accommodate change and be willing to modify plans and activities according to the changing dynamics of the launch. Adapting to these changes in a positive manner will help maintain a strong and focused launch team.

Perseverance and Stamina to Do Whatever It Takes: Ambiguity and constant change can cut into anyone's ability to persevere. The crushing workload that a launch process brings can do the same. This is where leadership by example can play a key role in moving the launch process forward, by stepping up to do whatever it takes to get the job done. "Whatever it takes" means that organizational roles and seniority levels take a backseat to pitching in on any activity to make it happen. It also means that if weekend or late-night work is occasionally required to achieve important goals, then so be it—just do it. The people you want on a launch team either have these personality traits or can be motivated to develop them.

Keeping the Customer First: As the launch proceeds, and tasks and activities begin to pile up, it is important to always keep the customer top of mind. It's sometimes easy to forget that all the launch activities should be focused on creating and releasing a great product for the target customer so your firm can generate a lot of revenue and profit. Step back on occasion to regularly ensure that decisions and activities are being pursued in line with customer needs.

Having Fun and Keeping Up Morale: If the team is not having fun and morale is low a product launch process can be agonizing. Taking fun breaks is always a good idea; however, a better idea is to bake fun into the process. Fun does not have to be structured, formally planned events. The teams that have the most fun and the highest morale are those that do little things all the time to make the work enjoyable. Think of ways to bake fun into the process, and the team will deliver beyond expectations!

Given the context of the product launch cycle, the overview of the parallel business and marketing activities required, and some qualitative criteria that can help make a launch successful, it's time to get into the details. The first stop on the road to launch begins where all good business and marketing planning should start—with the customer.

2

You Better Know Your Target Customers

Before you can start writing a rollout plan for launch, begin creating positioning and messaging statements for your product, or execute planned launch activities, it is important to create a clear target customer definition. You need to develop a crisp and detailed understanding about who your target customers are, including what their needs are, what motivates them to purchase, and how and where they purchase. Knowing this allows you to paint a clear and actionable picture of your targeted customers.

Why is it worth putting time and money into understanding your customers? Figure 2-1 illustrates the answer—your customer definition is at the core of all your launch and marketing activities and will drive and shape the go-to-market strategies and execution tactics for your launch. If you get the customer definition wrong, paint an incorrect picture, or lack a detailed understanding of your target market's attributes, there is a knowledge gap that will flow through all your product development and go-to-market activities and significantly weaken your launch efforts and post-launch business success.

THE BENEFITS OF CLEARLY DEFINING YOUR TARGET CUSTOMER

Clearly identifying, describing, and understanding your target customers enables you to accurately formulate plans around fundamental go-to-market options and considerations that should feed into your rollout plan (see Chapter 3).

FIGURE 2-1: The Importance of Target Customer Definition

Customer definition drives core marketing launch activities…

A crisp definition of your target customer will ensure you can do the following things:

Determine the Size of Your Potential Market: You can't accurately estimate the overall market potential for your product unless you can clearly and accurately identify the intended target market to size the opportunity in terms of units and revenues.

Understand Customer Needs and Frustrations: Addressing specific customer needs and frustrations ("pain points") is the core focus of product development, value proposition creation, and messaging. Without a crisp customer definition, you cannot effectively address these needs and frustrations.

Identify the Relevant Distribution Channels: It's important to understand the purchasing patterns of the intended target market. Not every potential customer purchases through the same channels. To effectively deliver the product to the targeted customers, you need to understand which channels are important and how product typically flows through them. For example, you may learn that your target customers typically purchase similar products through systems integrators, to benefit from their product deployment and integration service offerings. If you had intended to sell your product only through retail channels (e.g., Wal-Mart) you would have created a mismatch with your customers' buying practices.

Resolve and Determine Proper Pricing: How you determine pricing depends on the situation. A complex server software product that is highly customizable will be more difficult to price than a pre-packaged, off-the-shelf consumer software application. Pricing will also be driven by various stock keeping unit (SKU) offerings you choose to deploy. Low-end SKUs with lower functionality will likely be less expensive than high-end SKUs with full functionality. The key point is that by knowing your customers you will be able to determine what they pay for similar products (if they exist), identify which existing transaction models are acceptable, understand price sensitivity, and discover what percentage of their budget they will allocate for products like yours. You cannot properly price your product without this type of information, and you can't get the information unless you know who to ask (i.e., your clearly defined target customer).

Effectively Drive Product Feature Input or Required Service Offerings: One of the best ways to improve your product is to ask those who are using it or intend to use it for feedback on the product feature set. The proposed product feature set is a natural outgrowth of your work on understanding customer needs and frustrations. Your target customers can provide a wealth of information to fine-tune your product, identify significant gaps in functionality or usage capabilities, and understand what services customers need.

Identify Key Value Propositions and Positioning: It is crucial to communicate your product's proper value propositions as they relate to meeting customer needs. Your key communication, marketing, and sales messages will flow through all of your out-bound communication vehicles (see Chapter 4). To create the right messages, you must have a clear understanding of your specific customer target's needs and pain points. A poor understanding will produce the wrong messages, resulting in ineffective marketing.

Understand Which Reach and Awareness Mechanisms Will Best Market the Product: Having a clear target customer definition lets you determine the best marketing vehicles to leverage that will best communicate your messages, e.g., identifying the magazines they read, what websites they visit, what newsletters they subscribe to, what analysts are credible to them, and what events they attend.

UNDERSTANDING YOUR STRATEGIC INTENT STARTING POINT

When creating launch plans you should start with a broad perspective to define the high-level landscape. Planning around customer definition is no different, and first assessing the high-level situation relative to your customers and the product you are launching is a useful conceptual exercise. Figure 2-2 describes a framework for this.

Understanding where your situation falls in the Figure 2-2 grid is a start toward fully understanding your target customers and implies the amount of marketing effort you must provide to clearly identify and understand your customers and rollout the product.

For example, from Figure 2-2, determine which quadrant describes your situation:

FIGURE 2-2: Strategic Intent

Strategic intent drives customer focus...

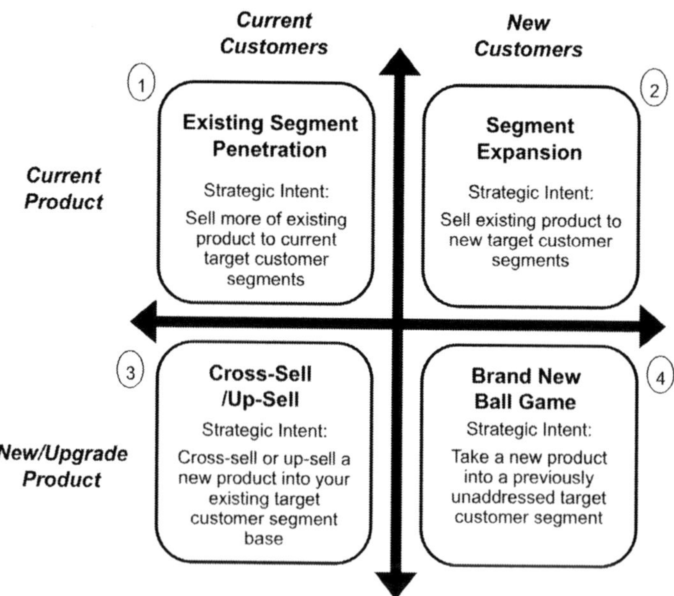

- **Quadrant 1—Existing Segment Penetration:** You are essentially launching or re-launching your current product to existing customers, although you may be reaching more broadly and expanding into new customer accounts (e.g., focusing on Fortune 100 today, expanding to Fortune 1000 with the launch or re-launch). Lowest launch marketing effort required relative to other quadrants.
- **Quadrant 2—Segment Extension:** You are extending, or adding, new customer targets. In essence, you are launching your existing product into a new category of customer not previously addressed. Moderate level of launch marketing effort required.
- **Quadrant 3—Cross-Sell/Up-Sell:** Here you are developing a new product (could be brand new, could be upgrade, or next version) and want to launch it into your existing customer target base. Significant level of launch marketing effort required.
- **Quadrant 4—Brand New Ball Game:** In this most radical quadrant you have a brand new product and are focusing on a completely new set of customers. Considerable marketing and launch work is required.

Understanding your goals and intent relative to the Figure 2-2 grid can help you focus on what you intend to achieve with your launch. This level of focus can also help ensure that relevant stakeholders across the organization (technical, business, operations, etc.) are on the same page.

Although it is quite possible your intentions may fall within multiple quadrants of the grid, the most relevant ones for a new product launch will likely be Quadrants 3 and 4, where you are taking your soon-to-be-launched product into your existing customer base or into new market segments. A typical new product launch scenario for companies with existing products in-market is to go after a cross-sell/up-sell scenario into your current customer base while also attempting to move into new customer segments with the new product.

This is a fine strategy, but it requires that the appropriate marketing program development, funding, customer understanding, and resource/level of effort prioritization and trade-offs are explicit and rational. Typically a "one-size-fits-all" approach leads to mediocre results within both scenarios. You need to design your go-to-market plans and post-launch sustaining market plans to address the unique requirements of each scenario (or quadrant you are addressing) or risk failure.

The required marketing effort will vary somewhat depending on the quadrant addressed. Essentially, each quadrant presupposes a different level of customer knowledge and places you at a different starting point from a launch perspective. Any launch, by default, requires a significant amount of work and some basic must-do activities. However, starting with significant clarity about who your target customers are gives you a leg up in the launch process and removes some level of effort.

For example, in a Quadrant 1 scenario, you likely already have some understanding of and data about your customers, access to prior sales information, existing marketing collateral, current product messaging, and are executing ongoing demand generation programs. However, in Quadrant 4, you have nothing—no customer data and no direct prior customer knowledge. Everything must be created from scratch, including developing positioning and messaging, creating brand new collateral, developing new partnerships, and understanding and describing your customer attributes.

Regardless of which quadrant you fall into, let's assume that you don't have a clear definition or understanding of your target customer, whether you have a new product to launch or an existing product in market. This is a valid assumption—it is never a bad idea to review and rethink existing assumptions about how you currently define your customers and your true level of customer knowledge and understanding. Regularly challenging your assumptions and continuing the learning process around your customer attributes, needs, and profile will help refine and improve your marketing and sales activities.

Your task then is to figure out who are or should be the correct target customers and to make sure all the internal stakeholders in your company are brought into this focus. Multiple customer segments could be candidates for your attention to ensure a successful product launch. However, each potential target segment may differ in relative importance regarding their need for the product, influence in the purchase decision cycle, or budgeting and spending authority. Some customer segments may be harder or more expensive to reach than others, and you must make appropriate trade-offs. It's important to clearly identify exactly who you are reaching out to in your launch and subsequent marketing campaigns given your starting point.

There are three specific actions you must take to achieve clarity and definition around your target customers:

- Define and segment your customers.
- Understand these customers and their attributes in depth.
- Describe the customer persona and usage scenarios in detail.

DEFINING AND SEGMENTING YOUR CUSTOMERS

Customers can be defined and viewed from various perspectives. A critical aspect to defining your target customers is to ensure that how you define them is actionable. Actionable means that you as the product marketing stakeholders have the ability to specifically identify and reach your target audience through various marketing reach mechanisms at your disposal. If your definition is not actionable, you may not be successful in launching or marketing your product. A simple way to reality check your customer definition is to ask yourself, "Can I get a mailing list of these customers for a direct mail campaign?" This forces you to identify your customers in a discrete and specific manner. The answer will also help determine how tactically effective you might be as you rollout your launch activities and begin communicating with potential customers. The more specific and actionable you are at defining your target customer the better you will penetrate your customer base and the more effective your marketing dollar spend will be.

For example, Figure 2-3 indicates various ways that one could define customer segments: by company size, by vertical market, via demographics, etc. Some of these definitions are more actionable than others. At a conceptual and strategic level it may be correct to segment your audience by age or gender. If you are selling Modern Maturity Lipstick, you may narrow in on women ages 50-79 as one definition of your target customer segment. In applying our reality check question, we see that it may be difficult to get a mailing list where women list their age, because women are not generally predisposed to let others know their age! Of course, you can assume that a magazine called For Women Over 50 Only would likely be reaching your market, but the chances are remote that this specific type of magazine exists, and if it did, it would likely reach only a small fraction of your target audience. Or take the horizontal segmentation with customer service departments within an organization as the target. This is also vague—are you defining the IT group in the customer service department, the line managers supervising in-bound call agents, or the agents themselves?

The point is that although you can choose any of these perspectives to define your target customers, they alone may not provide an actionable segmentation for you. A better way may be to merge multiple views to provide a more optimal segmentation perspective.

FIGURE 2-3: Target Customer Segmentation

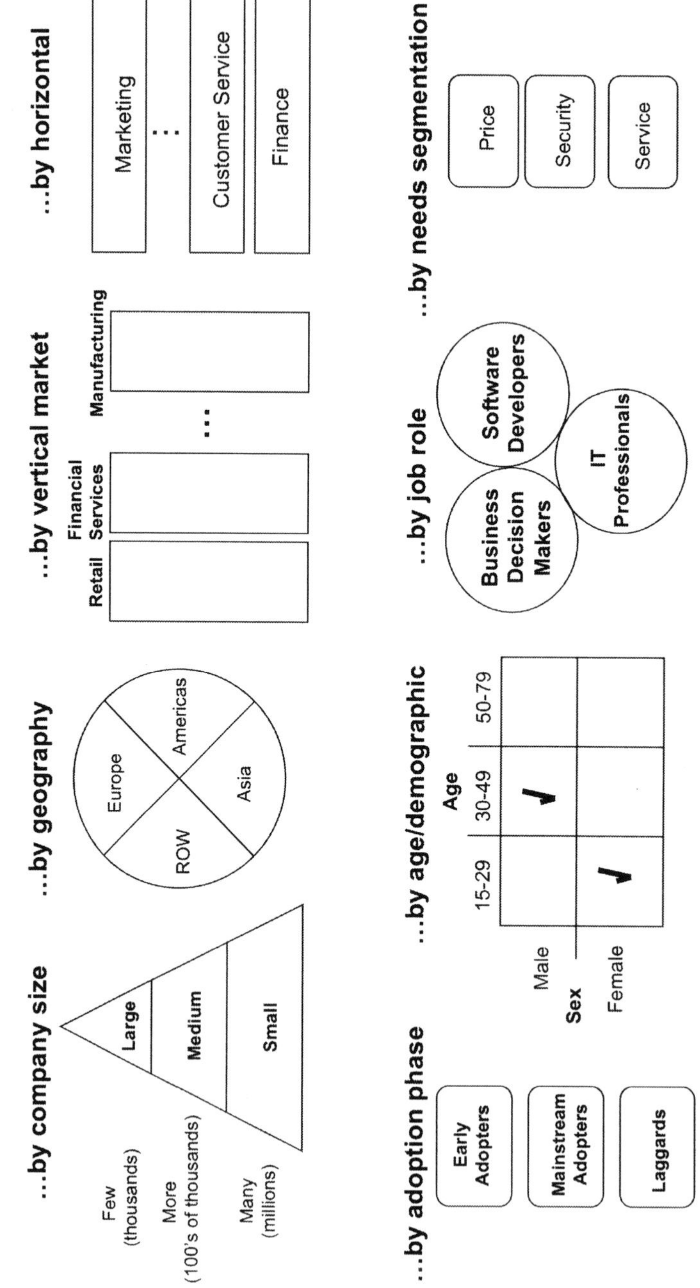

Defining Actionable Segments by Combining Views

A traditional textbook approach to determining customer segments is via needs-based statistical segmentation research using cluster analysis and factor analysis. In this approach, a statistically representative sample of the target market is polled on various questions about important purchase criteria for them, including why they need the product, what business problems the product solves, and what their most important needs are. The answers are then statistically modeled so that related customers are clustered in groups. For example, the needs segmentation example shown in Figure 2-3 might be an output of this process. This output shows three specific segment clusters, where a certain percentage of the target market is driven by price as the most important purchase need driver, while the other two segments rank security and service as the most important needs which all in each cluster group share in common.

This is great information for your positioning and messaging, but it does you absolutely no good if you want to actually talk to these folks. How do you find all the IT Professionals who believe price is the most important purchase criteria for a product like yours? The answer is you cannot. There is no list you can buy that will have anything close to this information, so this type of segmentation *alone* is not actionable. Needs-based segmentation is, however, the best type of segmentation you can produce, and when used in conjunction with other views it provides a powerful perspective into your target market. One way to do this is to combine or merge the various potential customer segment views provided in Figure 2-3 to generate a more optimal and actionable segmentation.

Figure 2-4 illustrates one example of combining these views. It is crystal clear in this case who the exact customer target is, i.e., IT decision makers who base their applications on Windows and use Visual Studio development tools in large financial and healthcare companies. In fact, you actually can pull mailing lists for this target customer down to the "using Windows and Visual Studio" level.

The final criteria of cost and security are key needs and value propositions that you must determine through your customer research process. These are the outputs of a needs-based customer segmentation study and, combined with other customer segmentation perspectives, can provide a clear and actionable customer segment definition. These segment priority needs will feed into the key messaging and positioning marketing statements you communicate via your marketing communication vehicles and campaigns. So when you pull your mailing list for "financial/healthcare vertical market

FIGURE 2-4: Actionable Customer Definition

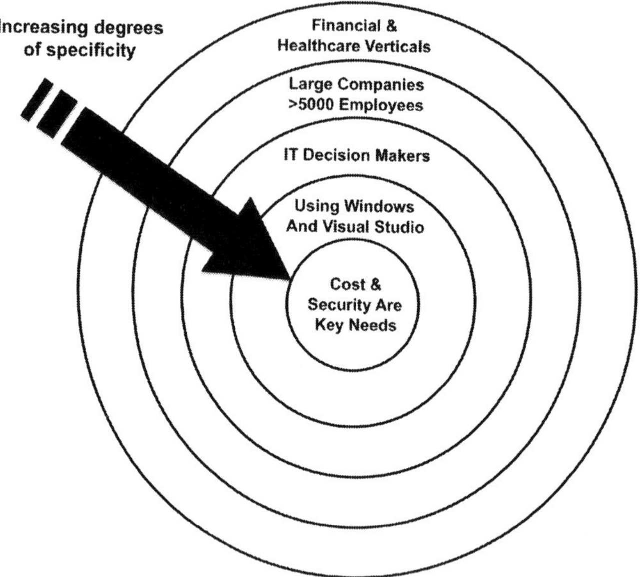

folks with VP or Director of IT job titles who have purchased Windows and Visual Studio," your marketing copy should focus on playing up the cost and security benefits and value propositions of your product.

Target Segment Focus May Shift Through Launch

Your customer target may change in different phases of the pre- and post-launch life cycle. This may be due to the nature of the product itself or as a consequence of the purchase decision making process within your target customer's organizations. Windows Server (or any software server product for that matter) is an example of a product where the customer target focus and emphasis varies as the launch progresses, which Figure 2-5 illustrates.

Specifically, early in the cycle professional developers are a core target audience, as this customer segment enables the Windows team to test development tools for the next version of Windows and to encourage either new or ported applications to be made available on the new version immediately at launch. The focus on developers for a particular version of

FIGURE 2-5: Shifting Customer Focus

Customer focus may shift by launch phase...

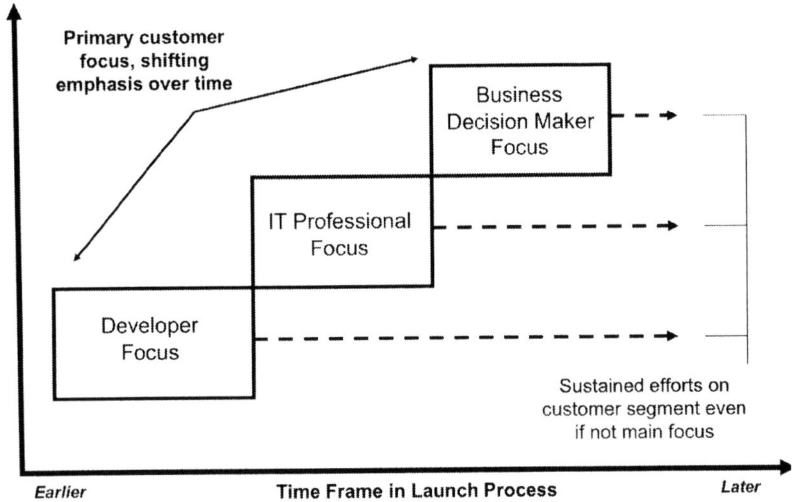

Windows can start years before the actual ship date. Although the efforts around developers never actually stop, at some point during the launch cycle the primary focus shifts to IT Professionals, the key customers who will purchase, deploy, and manage Windows Server in their companies. Finally, as the launch progresses, the top business decision makers (CxO level) are engaged via marketing activities.

As you shift your customer focus, you are focusing the marketing mix elements for the intended target audience using different messaging and different reach techniques. For example, a great way to reach developers is via developer-focused websites, which developers use daily. The huge investment Microsoft has made into the MSDN (Microsoft Developer Network) online presence is a testament to that fact. Business decision makers, however, don't use the web as extensively in the normal course of their work as developers do. In-person meetings and seminars could be a more appropriate way to engage these folks. And be aware that for both audiences the messaging can be quite different, e.g., developer messaging could likely focus on productivity and ease-of-development for your product, while business decision maker messaging might focus more on return on investment (ROI) and total cost of ownership.

Assessing Customer Segment Viability

After defining a number of potential addressable market segments, you may realize that going after all of them may not be the best approach given the level of resources available. It is always better to optimize and do a great job in the most important, strategic, and highest ROI segments than to do a mediocre job attempting to address all possible segments. For your product and your organization it's critical to not only understand which segments you are targeting but also to clearly identify those you are explicitly not targeting.

You must make trade-offs on which segments to pursue. Figure 2-6 provides some specific criteria that you may wish to consider as filters applied to the segment choice decision. Some criteria are qualitative in nature, and some are quantitative.

For example, you must make monetary investments to acquire a new customer, whether it's sales, marketing, channel, or other investments. These costs and the number of customers you can get with this money will indicate the cost to acquire a new customer. For example, if you spent $100 in marketing and acquired 10 new customers, that is $100/10 = $10 cost per new customer acquisition. This seems fine, but if the product you are selling nets you only $5 in revenue, that's a problem—this segment is too expensive for you to pursue.

Cost to reach can be looked at in a similar manner: if your segment is a highly niche segment, or is an extremely broad consumer segment, the amount of money you must spend to reach this audience and create awareness about your product may be cost-prohibitive. Assuming it is cost-effective to reach and acquire a customer in a particular segment, you need to be able to manage these customers post-purchase and provide service and support. Are your company infrastructure and resources in place, trained, and able to provide this level of post-purchase service? Can you afford the cost of such activities?

Other key segment assessment criteria include how competitive the particular segment is and the feature/functionality fit of your product into that segment. If all the competition is focused in the financial vertical market, is that really where you want to enter with your product? Should you instead go after the healthcare vertical where the competition is lower and the probability of success is higher, and where your product may better fit customer needs?

Finally, a sometimes overlooked element of segment selection criteria is the sales cycle length for purchase. Some segments will have much shorter

FIGURE 2-6: Criteria to Assess Customer Segment Viability

Understanding important customer segment characteristics can help determine which segments to address…

Ability and Cost to Acquire
- ✓ Organizational/skills/resources enabled to acquire customer (e.g., sales and technical sales support investment/skills)
- ✓ Investment required to acquire a customer (e.g., $500 per customer acquisition cost)

Ability and Cost to Reach
- ✓ Organizational/skills/resources enabled to reach (e.g., appropriate marketing investment/skills)
- ✓ Investment required to reach a customer (e.g., appropriate channel/distribution investments)

Ability and Cost to Keep/Manage
- ✓ Organizational/skills/resources enabled to keep and manage a customer once acquired (e.g., loyalty programs, communication)
- ✓ Investment required to keep a customer (e.g., discounts, rebates, special offers, satisfaction drivers)

Ability and Cost to Service/Support
- ✓ Organizational/skills/resources enabled to support (e.g., local/regional/national support centers)
- ✓ Investment required to support a customer (e.g., appropriate support personnel/training/skills investments)

Competitive Dynamics
- ✓ Little or much competitive activity?
- ✓ Ability to win vs. competition in the segment?

Product Fit to Customer Needs
- ✓ Fit to needs alignment good/average/limited in segment?
- ✓ Cost/ability to increase fit?

Segment Market Opportunity
- ✓ Revenue/unit/share potential high?
- ✓ Profitability of transactions high?

Sales Cycle Length
- ✓ Lengthy or short sales/purchase cycles?
- ✓ Ability to support/weather length of sales cycle?

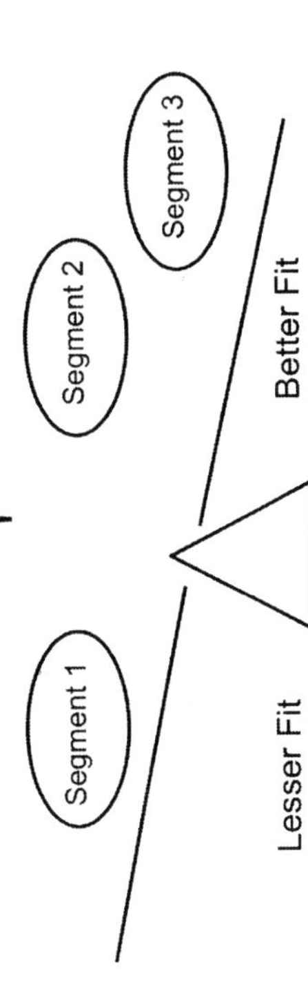

Assessing and balancing various viability criteria against the potential segments

purchasing turnaround times than others, helping to generate quicker sales and accruing revenue faster post-launch. This could be because customer decision makers in those segments have prior experience with similar products, a stronger or more urgent need, or other factors.

In many launches I have witnessed post-launch dissension when sales were just not happening fast enough, causing angst and doubts about the product and the people involved. The issue was not that the sales were not happening fast enough—they were actually happening at a rate that was typical for those customers and industries. The real problem was that the true sales cycle rate was not identified clearly during the strategy planning phases of the launch, thus setting incorrect expectations for deal acquisition—and causing the ensuing angst. Bottom line: to set proper expectations, understand the sales cycle length for the segments you choose to pursue.

There may be additional evaluation criteria at your firm, but you should at least apply the Figure 2-6 criteria against the different potential segments to help decide which segments are best pursued given your strategic goals and resource capabilities.

Describing the Segment Financial Opportunity

The work isn't over once you've created your actionable target customer segment definitions. You may have the greatest segmentation definition the world has ever known, but if you have no idea about how much potential revenue you might derive from each segment your efforts are in vain.

That said, segment financial potential is a major input factor to consider when evaluating your customer segmentation and determining which segments you will actively address and market. For each segment under consideration, you should have a best estimate as to the segment financial opportunity and the share of that opportunity you can take. Chapter 3 details the product rollout planning process and provides some frameworks on how to calculate market financial opportunities. You can also apply these frameworks to a segment sizing exercise.

Assuming you have done so and sized the market and the segments for revenue opportunity, a great way to view, evaluate, and make trade-offs about taking action on a potential customer segment is to create an opportunity map to paint a picture of the overall opportunities.

Figure 2-7 illustrates one format for an opportunity map. In essence, you are attempting to consolidate many key factors, both qualitative and

FIGURE 2-7: Illustrative Opportunity Map

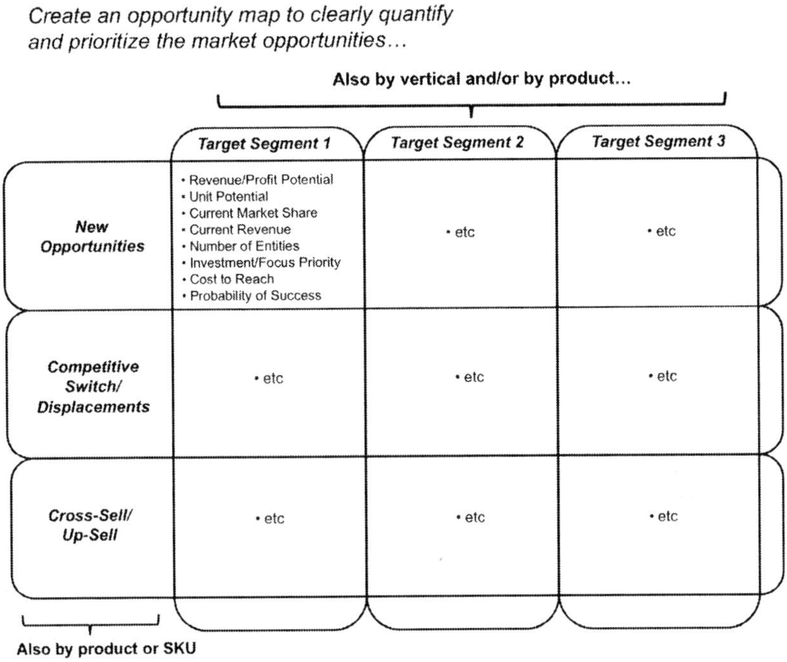

Create an opportunity map to clearly quantify and prioritize the market opportunities…

Also by vertical and/or by product…

	Target Segment 1	*Target Segment 2*	*Target Segment 3*
New Opportunities	• Revenue/Profit Potential • Unit Potential • Current Market Share • Current Revenue • Number of Entities • Investment/Focus Priority • Cost to Reach • Probability of Success	• etc	• etc
Competitive Switch/ Displacements	• etc	• etc	• etc
Cross-Sell/ Up-Sell	• etc	• etc	• etc

Also by product or SKU

quantitative, into one chart that overviews your revenue opportunities and the associated attributes for each opportunity. This example shows the potential actionable target customer segments as the columns, and a perspective on new, competitive switching, and cross-sell/up-sell opportunities as the rows. At each intersection of segment and opportunity type, similar information is presented:

- What is the revenue and profit potential?
- What is the unit potential?
- What is the current or anticipated market share?
- If there is current revenue, how much?
- How many customers are there?
- What is the level of strategic priority?
- How much is willing to be spent?
- How much will it cost to reach the market (some may be easier/cheaper to reach than others)?

FIGURE 2-8: Quantifying Market Growth and Share

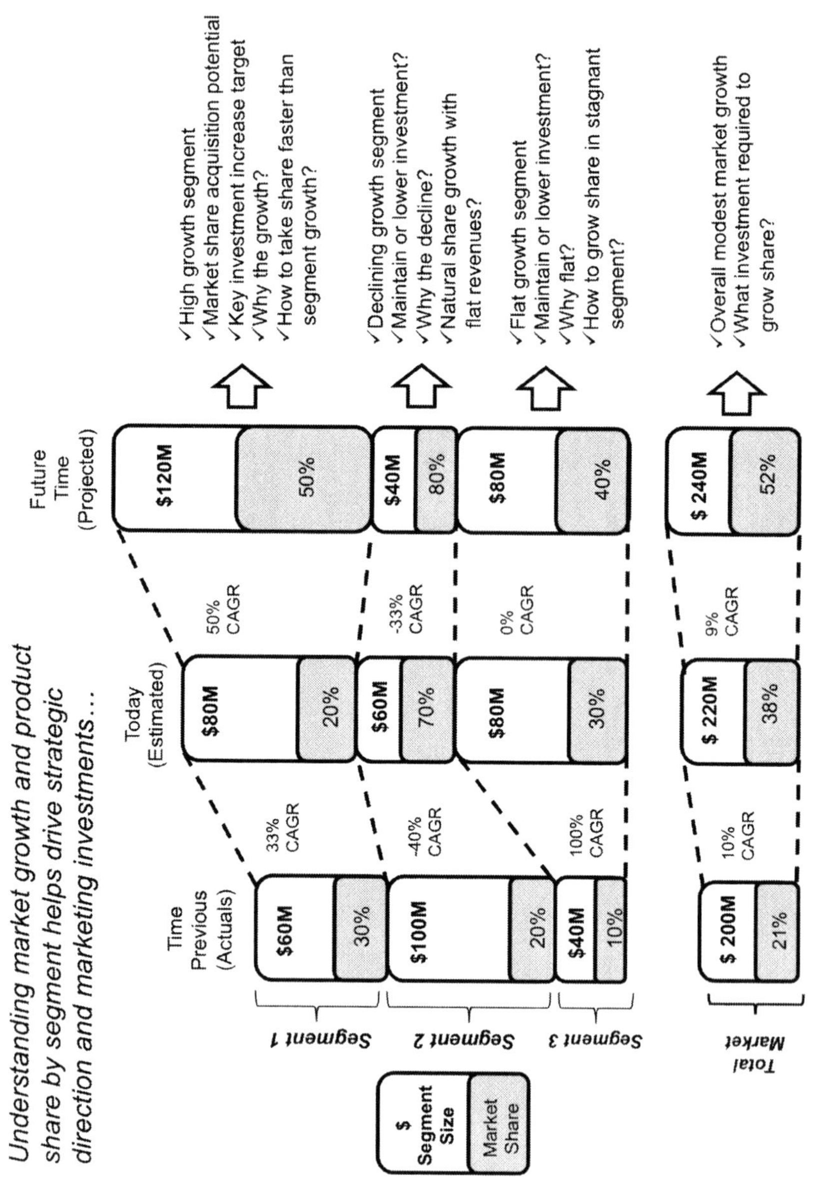

- Given existing resources and organizational attributes, what is the probability of successfully achieving stated goals?

Answering these types of questions on such a map can provide good insight into the potential opportunities and also enable proper trade-offs to be made. For example, one segment/opportunity combination may have a lot of revenue potential but be cost-prohibitive to effectively go after. Another may promise less revenue, but given your organizational strengths, might be more easily obtainable and the goals more successfully achieved.

Finally, you can also view such a map with different axes, such as the rows being product type or SKUs, and the columns being other types of customer segment views such as vertical markets, or even have products or SKUs as the columns. Playing with different variations of an opportunity map will help you narrow in on the correct choices.

Along with an opportunity map it is always a good idea to understand market growth by segment. It is fine to have a static understanding of your potential revenues by segment, but it is better to have a time-based perspective, as shown in Figure 2-8.

Gathering or producing the data to build a chart like Figure 2-8 can also help you make the correct segment targeting decisions. In the example it is clear that Segment 1 is the high growth segment, with a 50% compound annual growth rate, and offers the largest revenue opportunity in the future at $120M. This segment currently accounts for 20% of the overall market, but is anticipated to grow over time to be 50% of the overall market revenues. Given this, should you be targeting this segment? Why is it growing much faster than other segments? Can you grow with the market if you launch your new product, or can you actually grow faster than the market segment growth?

At the same time, Segment 3 is a flat growth segment. Why? If you are launching into this segment, how do you intend to grow share in a static segment? Answer: you must take competitive share! Looking at the market this way and understanding the segment financial growth dynamics while using this information with the opportunity map and your segment definitions can provide immensely valuable perspectives and insights into making the correct segment investment choices.

Given that you have decided on your segmentation strategy, and have decided which segments to address given the segment viabilities, the opportunity map, and the financial opportunity, you need to drill-down into these segments and paint a clear picture of the customers.

UNDERSTANDING YOUR CUSTOMERS

The challenge now is to have a clear, in-depth understanding of the target customers across various descriptive attributes to ensure you can make the correct business and marketing decisions during your product launch. You've already identified the "who"; now you need to dive into the "what" aspects of these customers. What channels do they purchase from? What role do they play in the purchase process: decision maker or influencer? What role do they have regarding budgets: decision making or recommending? These and many other questions must be answered for you to paint a solid and detailed picture of your customer.

Using Research to Provide Customer Data

Using planned, structured research is an excellent way to acquire customer data that will help you better understand your target customers. There are a number of research methods that can facilitate a good understanding; two are qualitative and quantitative primary research. Qualitative research typically consists of information acquired from a limited number of customers and is used for directional purposes. It can help you with general insights and trends within your target audience, e.g., customer perspectives on product features, needs, and messaging. This information points you in the generally correct direction but does not provide statistically accurate data, e.g., the numeric size of the target market.

Primary qualitative research can include activities such as:

- Structured and facilitated focus groups
- Structured and facilitated one-on-one meetings
- Direct informal customer interviews or discussions
- Channel partner input from round table discussions or one-on-one discussions

Secondary sources for qualitative input may also be available. Some good sources include existing third-party qualitative research and published trade magazine or web articles.

Quantitative research captures statistically significant data from large numbers of customers. These methodologies provide specific and statistically accurate answers to key questions. For example, creating precise market segmentation, determining price elasticity of demand, and quantifying a market opportunity or size generally require quantitative research to get statistically accurate results. Quantitative research includes primary research activities such as large sample surveys conducted online, by mail, or via telephone. Existing secondary quantitative research sources such as third-party research from analysts may also be available.

The information that you capture and internalize from your research, whether qualitative or quantitative, will help you make the correct decisions during your product launch. It is incorrect to assume the only method of understanding your customers is via structured research. Getting out there and actually talking to customers and partners should be on your agenda.

One of the first activities that Microsoft executives undertake when they move to a new group or job is a road trip across the country to talk with as many customers and partners as possible. You'll also find regular customer or partner "round table discussions" on their schedule, or informal meet-and-greet discussions to stay in touch. In addition, most executives will take every opportunity to learn from customers, whether that is a formally scheduled process or walking around the trade show floor, talking with folks after a presentation, having dinner with customers or partners, or inviting customers or partners to the corporate facility to further engage with them. There is no better education than talking directly with your key constituencies to rapidly understand your target audience's issues, concerns, and needs. Some Microsoft folks have even taken part-time jobs (usually without pay) at a target customer business to experience firsthand the needs and pains these customers experience.

However, there is also the reality of limited time constraints for the majority of us who aren't free to roam around the country visiting customers. A time-efficient way to fill in customer knowledge gaps is through a dedicated research process.

Important Pre-Launch Structured Research

Structured research is an excellent way to learn about your customers. Microsoft performs a huge amount of research every year and drives a good amount of planning and decision making from it.

When launching a product, there are a number of basic research projects necessary to help paint a complete customer picture. Important pre-launch research projects include the following:

- **Needs Research:** Fundamental research to determine a customer's key needs, the underlying reasons for why the needs exist, how or if the needs are currently being met, or if unarticulated needs exist.

FIGURE 2-9: Customer Research Methodologies

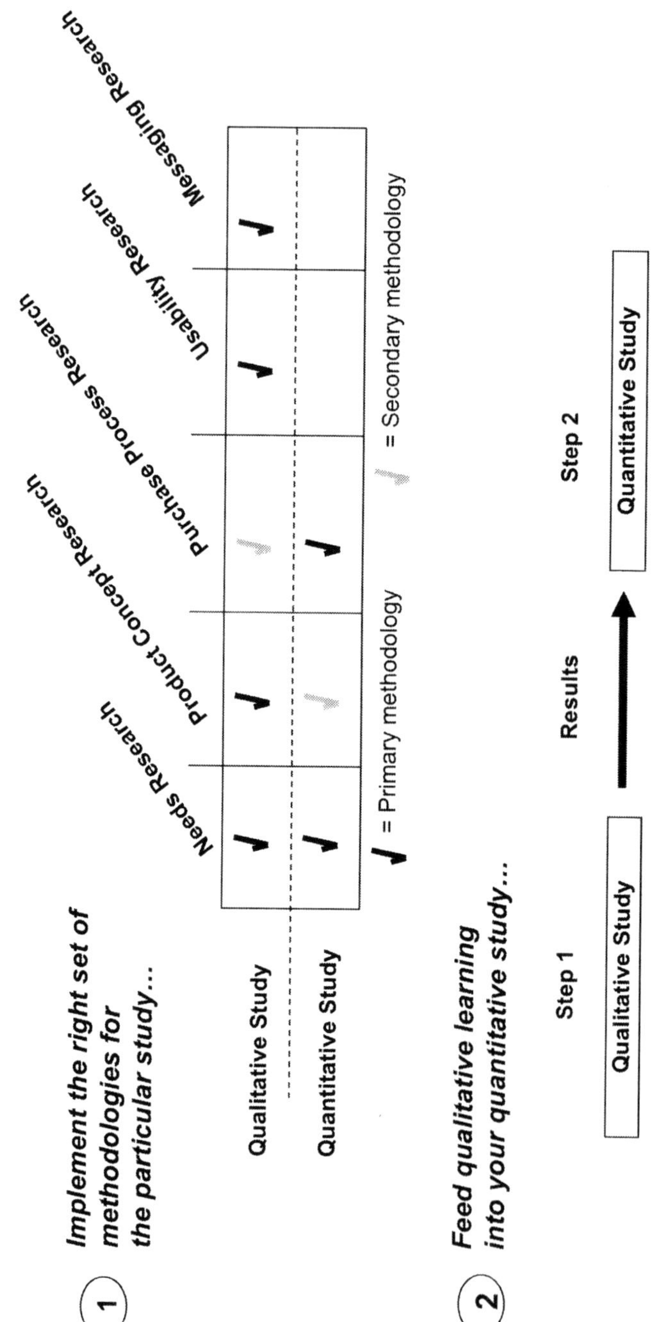

- **Product Concept Research:** Research that helps determine, at a high level, the interest in your product, where it fits well and what needs it serves, and where the product might be missing the mark.
- **Usability Testing:** When you have a prototype of your product ready, you'll want to bring customers into your lab to test it. This research evaluates users as they install and actively use the product. Can the customers effectively use the product features? Are the features easily discoverable? Is it intuitive?
- **Positioning and Messaging Testing:** Once you go through the process of identifying the key positioning statements and messages for your product, you should test your work with customers. How well do the messages resonate with the customers? Which are most critical? Which are most persuasive and effective? Are there any credibility problems with what you are saying?
- **Purchase Decision Making Research:** An overview research project paints the big picture of the customer, the elements that make up purchase decisions, and how they are made. Identifying channels, purchase decision making criteria, decision makers and influencers, and budgets are key objectives.

These research projects will help you make the correct decisions during your launch. There are particular methodologies that work best for each type of research. Figure 2-9 provides a guideline for each of these research projects and the most appropriate methodology. You can apply either qualitative or quantitative research methods to any of these studies. Studies that generally will benefit most from qualitative research are those that require significant interaction with the customer, that are about complex topics, that are tactile in nature (i.e., require using a gaming console, or holding/using the product), or require significant amounts of probing to acquire the data you need. If you need statistically relevant data via large numbers of customers, your only choice is quantitative research methods.

Conducting Qualitative Research

Focus groups or one-on-one interviews (in-person or by phone) are two of the most popular types of qualitative research. As you implement these forms of research after talking to 20-30 customers you will generally see repetitive patterns of information that will assure you that you are getting consistent and accurate information.

IMPLEMENTING FOCUS GROUPS

For focus groups, you'll want to set up 4-6 separate meetings, each with 8-10 of your target customers and a moderator to lead each group through a series of discussions. This total number of participants (32-60) will provide you with a large enough sample size to enable reasonable, directional decisions for your launch planning.

The focus group conversation is driven by a moderators guide, a predetermined guide outlining the issues you want to understand during the research. Typically, the customer participants do not know who has sponsored the research, which helps remove any bias. There are various facilities around the country that can host focus group research. They'll set you up behind a one-way mirror so you can observe the discussion in-person.

You can set up and run these groups yourself informally, but I recommend that you engage a professional firm and moderator to help you implement the focus group process. Each group you hold will cost from $7k-$15k, so worst case is you would spend about $90k on six groups. Before you engage a research firm, create a document that exactly outlines your expectations. This will make sure you get what you want and provide proper direction to your research vendor—and ensure you have thoroughly thought through the research process. This document should include elements such as:

- The key purpose(s) of the focus groups, detailing the key data you intend to discover via the research.
- The definition of the target audience and profile of customers you want in the groups.
- The number of groups and their locations. Typically you'll want to ensure that you are talking to enough customers to get good data and that you have adequate geographic representation (this means holding the groups in 2-3 cities across the country).
- The format and timing for the groups, such as whether you want to video the groups, include any props or survey handouts, or hold the groups in the morning, afternoon, or evening.
- The specific dates you want to run the sessions.
- The screening criteria to be used to recruit the groups. The research vendor will use this information to make phone calls to recruit participants to attend your groups and ensure they are getting the right target customers (and weed out the rest).

- The key questions for the moderators guide. These will be the basis of the discussion the moderator will have with customers and for the discussion flow. The questions should be focused on uncovering the information you want. The guide should be broken into sections that indicate how much time should be spent on each section or question area. This keeps the discussion moving and ensures that all the important questions are asked.
- Incentives to entice target audience members to attend the groups. Typically you will need some incentives to get people to attend your group. Generally this will be a monetary incentive, although I have known beer companies that hold focus groups and the incentive is to sample new beers. No money needed to get some folks into a group like that!

This document can be as short or as long as you need. Just make sure you capture the salient points at the level of detail required to make your research successful.

There are a few tips that can help make a focus group research project go more smoothly; these are indicated in Figure 2-10. In general, the more involved you are in the research project details, the more successful the research will be. Simply handing off the project to a vendor and waiting for the results is risky.

CONDUCTING ONE-ON-ONE INTERVIEWS

Direct customer interviews are another approach you can take either standalone or in conjunction with other research. In-person customer visits or telephone interviews are two rewarding approaches. In-person visits will take a bit more time and effort to set up than telephone interviews.

Customer interviews, like focus groups, require similar preparation, i.e., specifying the screening criteria, developing your list of questions, and addressing a variety of customer scenarios. You can adapt the example provided for focus groups for direct customer interviews. Structure the discussion as you would structure your focus group, following the moderators guide or the list of questions you have prepared in advance. Whether you hold in-person or telephone meetings, you should:

- Have someone schedule the meetings for you well in advance and send a reminder email/phone call the day before the interview is scheduled.
- Have several people do the interviews in parallel. This increases your efficiency and lets you get more interviews done in less time.

FIGURE 2-10: Focus Group Tips

Following are a few key tips that can make the focus group process proceed more smoothly and ensure good results...

Video the Groups Videotape the groups and have the tapes transcribed verbatim. Permits double checking research firm conclusions. Also excellent source for customer sound bites for presentations or other uses.	**Over Recruit** Not everyone who agreed to attend your groups will actually show up—you'll likely have a drop-off rate of at least 20%. Signing up more than required will help cushion the drop-off and ensure a full group.
Pass Questions to the Moderator Don't be afraid to send in questions to the moderator during the groups. Clarification of points will be necessary. Questions can be delivered as the group discussion progresses, or set up a predetermined time when the moderator will step out of the group to receive your questions.	**Align the Incentive Amount to the Audience** Make sure the incentive amount is right for your audience. Higher-level executives will require more money to attend than consumers or lower-level employees. Some categories of customers are likely to be contacted many times about attending focus groups and thus may need a higher incentive.
Avoid Career Attendees Some folks make a mini-career out of attending focus groups to pocket extra money. Try to identify and avoid these folks. When recruiting, put a screening criteria that limits your attendees to those who have not attended a group in the past six months.	**Video Teleconference the Groups (VTC)** Not all the stakeholders at your firm will be able to attend the groups in person. Video teleconferencing is the next best way to enable them to participate real time during the groups. Have a phone available to those attending the groups so the remote folks can call in questions.
Help Develop the Moderators Guide Be heavily involved in creating the moderators guide. You know your business, the data you need, and the customers better than the moderator ever will. Your direct involvement will shape a more effective guide.	**Maximize Time and Data Collection** Ask respondents to arrive at the focus group facility 15–30 minutes in advance to sign in and take care of any administrative tasks. Have them fill out a short written survey that could augment the data collection from the discussion. And use written surveys during the group discussion. This helps maximize the data collection process and the research investment.
Hold Groups in the Evening Evening groups generally draw best. Particularly true if targets are busy professionals. For some audiences mornings may be best, such as for stay-at-home spouses.	**Research Deliverables** Make sure vendor deliverables and reports are scheduled to meet your timing needs (e.g., draft report due one week after last group, final report two weeks later).
Use Tight Screening Criteria Tight screening criteria can help identify the correct candidates and high-quality respondents. Start with tight screening criteria and loosen up gradually if you are not getting the quantity of respondents you need or if the cost appears too high because you are screening out most of the candidates.	**Own the Project** It's your money and your project—don't feel intimidated or shy about giving direction to the moderator as you see fit. They are experts in research, so taking their advice is generally warranted, but you know your business better than they do. A successful research project is one where you walk away satisfied with the process and the results: don't let a bossy moderator walk all over you and ruin the experience.

- Have a structured form everyone uses to gather the information. When you consolidate everyone's interview results it's a lot easier to collate and analyze the information collected if it was captured in a structured manner.
- Limit your phone interviews to a maximum of one hour and send the questions to the customer in advance. Many phone interviews will be much shorter. Lawyers, doctors, and other busy professionals will generally only give 10-15 minutes of their time for such calls, even with an incentive.
- Limit in-person meetings to two hours, and don't have more than two people at the customer site or research facility for the visit.

Your partners are another source; gather their perspectives. Telephone or in-person meetings work fine with partners. Focus group formats will also work if you manage any competitive dynamics as the group discussion proceeds.

Implementing Quantitative Research

When you need to scale up and get a statistically valid sample size and responses for your information needs, you need to implement quantitative survey research. Generally you have three choices: online surveys, telephone surveys, or paper-based surveys.

The grid provided here compares the various survey types to some research attributes.

	Online	**Telephone**	**Paper**
Cost	Low	High	Medium
Ability to reach targeted segments	Moderate	Very high	High
Flexibility	High	Medium	Low
Time to develop	Moderate	High	Moderate
Time to results	Instant	Two weeks	Many weeks
Complexity	Low	Medium	Low

If you want the least expensive, quickest answers to your research with a reasonable degree of accuracy, and you are focusing on a primarily technical audience, choose an online survey method. If you want a slightly higher degree of accuracy, and need to reach a very targeted set of customers with a high degree of selection or screening criteria, go with a telephone survey.

The last resort is a paper survey and is not recommended because it takes too long and has no significant benefits over either telephone or online methods.

For telephone surveys, you can purchase lists of potential respondents from third-party list brokers or magazines that target your audience, or supply your own internal customer lists. Online surveys offer similar choices for lists. For an online survey you must determine the specific online methodology, or combination of methodologies, to acquire respondents. Three popular methods for acquiring respondents for online surveys are:

- **Pop-Up Surveys:** On websites that you feel might be visited frequently by your target audience, pop-up windows are generated randomly to site visitors asking them to opt-in and participate in the survey.
- **Web Links:** You place a link or web ad onto a likely website and hope that visitors will click through and take your survey.
- **Email:** By acquiring email lists through third parties or using your own internal lists, you email the list with a request to do the survey, including a link driving the respondent back to a website that hosts your survey.

Any of these methods is fine for online research, although I have found that you can be more targeted with an email approach—it's a bit less random.

Consider hiring a research company to help you implement either online or telephone surveys. Vendors can take the load off you for survey design, execution, and reporting. In fact, you'll likely need to hire a research vendor if you want to do large-scale telephone surveys. For online surveys, there are many self-service online survey companies that provide easy to use and inexpensive web-hosted applications that you can leverage with internal staff to perform your research.

If you hire a vendor you don't need to know statistics to do the research, as your research vendor will be adequately prepared. As a general rule you want to shoot for a 95% confidence level and an accuracy of +/- 3% for your results, which means that there is a 95% chance that the answers to your questions will be a statistically significant accurate result within +/- 3%. You may want to go higher than 95% and tighten the accuracy. If so, you will need to significantly increase the sample size of your respondent base, which will significantly drive up your research costs. I wouldn't bother doing this on the types of research we are discussing. For purchase process studies or other kinds of business research, 95% at +/- 3% accuracy is more than adequate.

When you complete a study, you should communicate the results to the stakeholders in the organization. Sometimes you can get the research vendor to come in and present the results in lieu of doing it yourself. Having the vendor do it might lend third-party credibility, but if you do the presentation you are taking ownership of the results, showing your depth of knowledge, and implicitly taking responsibility to drive action based on these results. On balance, you should take ownership and do the internal results presentation yourself.

Important Customer Attributes to Identify

Your overall output from the investigations into understanding your customers should paint a complete picture of the important customer attributes that will inform your planning. Figure 2-11 shows some of the key attributes that will help flesh out the descriptive details of your target customer segments and some of the important questions to consider. It may be cost-prohibitive for you and your firm to invest in research that would cover all of the factors shown here. However, you will still need to form some understanding of these attributes to maximize your chances of a successful launch and to meet your post-launch revenue goals. At the least, you and your colleagues should spend time with customers whenever you can to get some indication of the answers to the questions posed around the attributes—a little directional data is better than no data at all.

All of the customer attributes listed in Figure 2-11 will in some way affect your rollout planning process (see Chapter 3). For example, you will find it difficult to enter into relationships with channel partners unless you know which channels your customers purchase from. Your marketing communications, positioning, and messaging will suffer if you do not understand the key customer needs and pain points, or through which vehicles customers acquire information about products like yours. Sales will suffer if you have little or no knowledge as to what the key purchase triggers are that incent a customer to act and make the purchase decision.

Once discovered, the important customer attributes must then be organized into a consumable form for use by others during the launch.

DESCRIBING YOUR CUSTOMERS

After having clearly defined your customer targets and done the due diligence to understand their needs and paint the customer picture through your research, you must provide this information in an easy-to-understand format that can be communicated to stakeholders in your organization

FIGURE 2-11: Understanding Key Customer Attributes

Important customer attributes...

Customer Needs/Pains
- ✓ What are the key customer needs & pain points?
- ✓ Which are the most/least important?
- ✓ Which can your product effectively address?

Purchase Channels
- ✓ How do customers purchase similar products today?
- ✓ What purchase channels do they use?
- ✓ Why do they purchase from these channels?

Purchase Influencers
- ✓ Are there other important influencers in the purchase decision making process (e.g., analysts, press, co-workers, managers)?
- ✓ What role do these influencers play in the purchase process?
- ✓ Why are these influencers important?

Purchase Process
- ✓ What is the flow of the purchase process?
- ✓ What are the steps involved in the purchase process?
- ✓ What are the most/least important steps?

Purchase Triggers
- ✓ What are the key needs or pains that trigger purchase?
- ✓ What are the key incentives or offers that trigger purchase?

Information Sources
- ✓ What are the key sources customers use to learn about products such as yours?
- ✓ Which are the most/least influential sources?

Perceived Substitutes
- ✓ What products would customers consider as solving the same problem or need as your product?
- ✓ Why are they considered substitutes?
- ✓ Strengths/weaknesses of these substitutes?

Perceived Competitors
- ✓ What other companies are perceived as offering similar solutions?
- ✓ What is the customer perspective on these firms: good, bad, indifferent?

Target Customer Attributes... Painting The Customer Picture

Budget & Spending
- ✓ What is the overall budget for your product category?
- ✓ Is spend planned to increase/decrease/stay the same?
- ✓ Can your product effectively take budget share?

Current Product Ownership
- ✓ What similar products have customers purchased?
- ✓ Is there an opportunity to replace or augment with your product?
- ✓ Why did they buy the similar product? What needs is it fulfilling?
- ✓ What is the satisfaction level with their existing products?

Product Usage Scenarios
- ✓ What are the usage scenarios for the customer with your product?
- ✓ Which scenarios are the most/least important?
- ✓ What are the important problems/needs the usage scenario solves?

Perception of Risk
- ✓ What are the risks associated with purchasing your product?
- ✓ Which risks are the most/least important?

Price Sensitivity
- ✓ How sensitive are customers to price in your product category?
- ✓ What is the impact on potential customer demand driven by price?

Perceived Product & Business Value
- ✓ What is the perceived value your product can deliver to the customer?
- ✓ What are the core product value propositions?
- ✓ Any gaps in required vs. provided product value?

Demographics
- ✓ What industries, vertical markets, age groups define your customers?
- ✓ What are the typical number of employees, branch offices/locations, revenues?
- ✓ What are the typical titles/job roles?

Decision Making
- ✓ Who are the key purchase decision makers?
- ✓ What is the scope of their decision making: workgroup/departmental/enterprise?
- ✓ Who has final purchase decision authority vs. recommendation?

for their use in product planning, marketing, documentation, sales, engineering, and for other launch activities.

Creating Personas

A key format used at Microsoft to present this information in an easily understandable form is called a Persona, because it personifies your customer. It is a descriptive tool that allows everyone in the organization to get on the same page regarding who the specific target customer is for your product.

A Persona essentially paints a relatively detailed yet easily understandable picture of the target customer. A key point is that the Persona is created based on real customer data, not assumptions or guesses about the customer. As you continue to learn about your customers it is important to keep the Persona as current as possible.

Figure 2-12 provides an example of a Persona that can serve as a template for creating your own Personas. This Persona is named "Johnny" and is based on a decision maker in a call center—it's an example of a target customer within the horizontal call center segment.

As you can see, the Johnny Persona concisely describes the target customer and is an easily used high-level tool to help all stakeholders in your organization understand the customers you are targeting. The Persona can be used as an input to your positioning and messaging development, for product feature prioritization, for sales collateral and selling tools, and much more.

You would typically create a Persona for each targeted customer type in each targeted customer segment. These Personas could have many similarities, but will also likely have many differences. For example, if you are targeting IT Professionals in the healthcare and financial vertical markets some of their key tasks may be similar, but the specific pain points may vary, such as business planning (different business needs and problems in different vertical markets) or technology infrastructure planning (perhaps different vertical industry regulations drive varying infrastructure planning needs).

Describing the Customer Problem and Usage Scenarios

There is another lens to apply to describing your customer along with the key attributes and the Persona. The primary value your product can bring to the customer is the solution to an important problem, issue, or

FIGURE 2-12: Creating a Persona

Name	Johnny: Call Center Business Decision Maker	
Persona Description	Johnny is the key business and strategic direction setter in the call center. He manages a team of front line-of-business operational managers that manage the call center agents. He also manages the call center technology group that implements the key IT systems that host both internal Line of Business applications and external customer accessible customer service applications. He reports to the Chief Operating Officer of his company.	
Persona Quota	"Help me reduce operating costs in my call center."	
Company Taxonomy	Large- and medium-size organizations having large call centers with more than 250 agents.	
Key Responsibilities	Manage overall call center operations Determine business strategy and technology strategy for the call center Increase operating efficiencies and drive out costs in the call center	
Important Skills	Business thinking and strategy High-level understanding of technology In-depth understanding of call center operations and management	
Johnny wears a number of hats in his job.		
Hat	**Key Tasks**	**Pain Point**
Business Planning	Define call center business strategy relative to corporate business strategy Determine performance metrics for organization Increase customer satisfaction	Inability to attain expected ROI on customer-facing projects Rising operating expenditures Reduced customer satisfaction Difficulty differentiating service levels
Technology and infrastructure planning	Define call center technology strategy relative to corporate technology direction and call center business needs Drive implementation of technology projects to lower costs and increase efficiencies	Pressure to reduce IT budget costs while IT expenditures are increasing Inability to manage growth due to technology churn Integration with existing systems is difficult Unable to support user needs for service and application availability
Managing day-to-day call center operations	Overall management of call center agent representatives Ensuring adequate staffing levels Training of call center agents Management reporting across the organization	Call volume forecasting inaccuracies while call volumes are increasing Turnover of agents high Inadequate reporting capabilities Staffing levels inadequate to handle call volume leading to long delays for customers and decreasing customer satisfaction

need. Whether your product focuses on core technology in the enterprise like technology infrastructure needs (e.g., server products), desktop productivity needs (like Microsoft Office), or some non-software/non-technology need, the product should be solving the customer problem and meeting the need, or I'm not sure you should actually be launching and shipping the product!

Your rollout plan (see Chapter 3) should summarize this problem (or problems) at a high level to set the basis and context for why you are launching your product. The more explicit you can be about the specific customer problem, and how your product and rollout plan is solving the customer problem and reaching the target customers, the better positioned your product will be in the market when it launches. Clarity in this area will also help you as you are selling your plan throughout the organization, and provide the backdrop for the rest of the rollout plan elements.

So how do you identify the key customer problem(s) and product usage scenarios? This information is an outcome of your customer research and customer discussions, as discussed earlier in this chapter. By going through that customer knowledge acquisition process you have identified core customer needs, segmented your market, and profiled the customer via the Persona. You need to communicate a succinct summary of this information in your rollout plan so that it is clear to all who you are going after and what specific customer scenarios your product is addressing.

A great way to augment this summary and make it real to those that read your plan is to include an example customer scenario that typifies your product's usage in the real world. Presumably, these types of usage scenarios have been identified through your product planning research and activities. Include a couple of the important targeted usage scenarios in the rollout plan. In the Microsoft parlance, these scenarios are sometimes known as "workloads," which means the types of specific customer tasks that the product enables (and are needed) for the customer's business.

Figure 2-13 is an example of the level of detail you should strive for; it uses an example product (a server operating system) that illustrates the high-level customer problems it solves and corresponding customer usage scenarios.

You see that these are succinct summaries. Yet, once created, they very clearly lay out the customer situation you plan to address with your product. They can also be used to help drive your product features and functionality as part of your product planning efforts.

Using the scenarios in conjunction with your Persona, customer attributes, and segmentation paints a crystal clear picture of your target

FIGURE 2-13: Defining Customer Scenarios

Your Product:

A server operating system (i.e., the product you are launching)

Customer Problem Statement:

The target customer needs to overcome issues that limit their ability to simultaneously serve up information to a large number of users, on a common and consistent technology infrastructure (vs. a multitude of differing non-interoperable platforms), and work in an environment where they require network connectivity for users and devices. The server operating system should solve these problems for the customer and their users.

Specific Key Customer Problems the Product Addresses:

- Allows a large number of users to simultaneously access and store information, content, and applications.
- Provides a common platform for building and deploying necessary software applications.
- Enables network connectivity for a number of heterogeneous client devices, e.g., PCs, mobile devices, and printers.

Example Customer Usage Scenario 1: Core Technology Infrastructure

- *Customer Scenario/Workload:* File storage, printer, and network device management, firewall/security.
- *Customer Pain Point:* Multiple server operating systems (OSs) are difficult and costly to deploy, manage, and support. Users are confused when they try to save files to servers with different interfaces and don't have a consistent way to add printers or access other devices on the network, like copiers. Controlling network security is a nightmare with the differing operating systems and configuration settings.
- *Market Situation:* Server OS consolidation gaining traction in the market. Fragmented supplier situation exists. UNIX and Windows customers seeking alternative solutions.
- *Your Product's Solution:* Enables server consolidation through "gee-whiz" server engine technology. Provides automated replacement of existing OSs, and auto-replicates to each hardware server. Customer-validated easy-to-use standard interface to store files and access/use and set up network devices. Customer-validated network-wide security administration console simplifies, standardizes, and automates network security settings across all servers.

Example Customer Usage Scenario 2: Mobile Access to Network

- *Customer Scenario/Workload:* Accessing files and information when not in office, synching mobile devices for network access.
- *Customer Pain Point:* Difficult or impossible for customer to access network files and information or synchronize mobile devices while on the road due to differing server connection protocols and bandwidth requirements, and varying/limited mobile device support.
- *Market Situation:* Mobile worker population dramatically increasing. Types of mobile devices rapidly growing. No common interface, protocol, or API for mobile device network access.
- *Your Product's Solution:* AutoConnect and Autosynch features enable one-step network access, authentication, and synchronization for both laptops and a variety of mobile devices. Standard interface/protocol/API serves all devices. Easily extensible to newly emerging mobile devices.

audience, their problems, and the solution via your product. This level of customer knowledge now enables you to begin creating the rollout plan for your product launch.

3

And You Better Have a Rollout Plan

It may be stating the obvious, but having a solid business plan is a must-have prerequisite to successfully launching a product. Exactly how a business plan is defined is subject to interpretations that can vary from company to company and person to person. Some call a marketing or sales plan a business plan, which they are not. Others consider a business plan complete at a couple of pages in length, while others require a 200-slide PowerPoint deck. And the elements and topics for inclusion in a business plan can vary as well. For example, different executives may have specific items or analysis they always want included in a business plan, or there may be a required company business plan template. For others, it's a free-for-all with no particular required elements demanded of the plan (not a good approach).

The key issue is not so much how the plan is physically structured and delivered, any individual content preference variations, or the extent of the plan content. Rather, it is making sure that all the important considerations are thought through and described in the plan, that it hangs together holistically, and that the plan communicates the Who, What, Where, When, Why, and How in its final form.

Generally, for moderate to large firms, a company will have in place an overall corporate business plan that describes at a high level the strategy and direction the firm will take. This plan then drives individual business unit strategic plans. Within the context of those plans, the product launch plan lives.

The key conceptual elements and focus areas described in this chapter are a good start to structuring a launch plan. Aligned to the higher-level plans, a launch plan takes high-level business planning from a conceptual exercise to an actionable output. Think about the launch plan as a "rollout" or "go-to-market" plan that provides both a context and an execution framework for the product launch within the larger corporate scheme of things; in essence it describes the implementation of the business strategy as it relates to the specific product being launched. Developing the plan with this perspective in mind will make the tactical details more concrete and executable.

DEVELOPING A PRODUCT LAUNCH ROLLOUT PLAN

This chapter will explain and overview some key focus areas and concepts to address while planning and developing a rollout plan. They can then be fine-tuned with specifics for your company, market, and business situation. Appropriately addressing them can assist in creating an *actionable* plan instead of an output that is too high level and "strategic," and ultimately not actionable.

Actionable means that the rollout plan should address all required high-level directional thinking required to enable functional, tactical launch plans to be generated as the next level of detail. The rollout plan should, at a high level, impart to readers a cohesive and comprehensive perspective of the go-to-market strategy. To do so, consider addressing the following foundational elements:

- **The Customer Problem, Scenarios, and Segmentation:** Communicate a clear description and definition of the targeted market segments being addressed and the customer problems and pain points solved with the product. Include at least a summary of the target market customer usage scenarios (Chapter 2). Including these items will help set context around the launch in the plan.
- **Key Go-To-Market Strategies:** Describe what is/are the key go-to-market strategy(ies) and business goals being addressed.
    - Identify the key business goals accomplished by each strategy.
    - Identify the key top-level tactics to successfully implement each strategy.
    - Paint a clear (and succinct) vision defining "what success looks like" for each strategy.
- **Product and Pricing:** Articulate the planned product offering in detail.
    - The core product value proposition
    - What SKUs will be shipped

    - SKU pricing and pricing strategy
    - Key feature/benefit differentiation between SKUs and relative to competition
    - Product naming and branding
- **Market Opportunity:** Quantitatively define the market opportunity, growth rates, and your firm's potential piece of the revenue pie.
- **Channel Strategy:** Outline the high-level go-to-market channel strategy and requirements around any required channel partners and channel models, including breadth channel partners and important key partners.
- **Licensing/Transaction Model:** Define the product licensing or transaction model(s).
- **Competition:** Identify the key competitors and how your firm wins against them.
- **Sales Model:** Articulate the high-level sales model and sales execution strategy.
- **Support Model:** Define the basics of the product support strategy.
- **Risks:** Identify any key risks associated with the plan including:
    - Resource or investment gaps
    - Competitive issues
    - Internal or organizational impediments or interdependencies
    - Legal issues
    - External risks and dependencies

Additional elements may be specific to your unique situation, including resource investments for launch budgets or headcount, organizational structure, and third-party investment funding usage. If your firm has successfully launched other products, it may be possible to leverage their launch plans to provide incremental ideas and directions for the current launch and to offer other suggestions for what to include in your plan. You should include whatever else is required; at a minimum include the above foundational elements in the rollout plan.

Marketing is not included as an item above because the marketing elements of a launch cut horizontally across all of the indicated rollout plan elements and constitute the implementation (or, more specifically, actualization) of these launch elements. The rest of the book will provide the important concepts enabling the high-level rollout plan elements to convert into actionable marketing launch activities.

As you develop and evangelize the rollout plan throughout your firm (as you should), the overall story described in the plan must fit together to garner the buy-in necessary from other stakeholders. It is therefore critical that each element of the plan cohesively integrate and tie together. Figure 3-1 illustrates the concept of all plan elements forming an integrated whole, with all elements tied together, dependent, and reinforcing each other. Each element is connected and tightly integrated with the others, and no element is isolated. The Customer Problem, Scenarios, Segmentation, Key Strategies, Target Market, and Market Opportunity & Competition categories set the context for the plan. Then the specific details of Product Features, Pricing, Channel and Licensing Strategy, Sales and Support Models, Risks, and other plan elements can be clearly understood.

Developing a launch rollout plan is analogous to how an architecture and construction firm proceeds to create a skyscraper: first the firm conceptualizes the design for the new skyscraper (what it should look like), then designs and builds the internal framework (the steel skeleton) to support the building, and finally fills in the finishing touches with a skin, flooring, plumbing, and other core infrastructure. The integrated rollout plan is the conceptualization and steel framework, which then drives the specific tactical plans to fill in the framework with the finishing touches and tactical detail for specific functional areas.

FIGURE 3-1: Defining an Integrated Rollout Plan

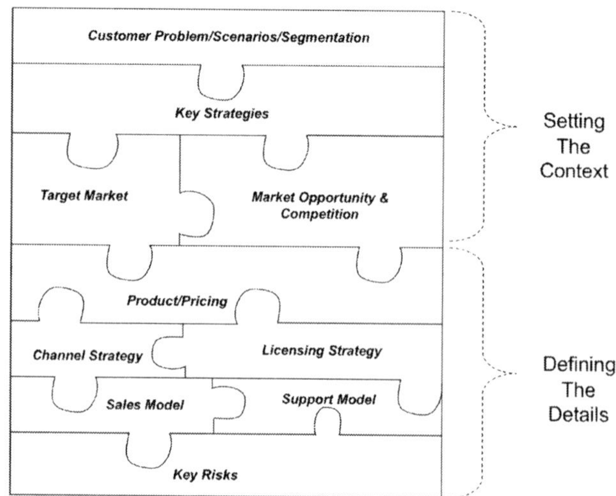

Figure 3-2 illustrates this cascading plan development concept with the overarching rollout plan driving the drill-down tactical marketing, business development, product, and sales plans. It also indicates that for a successful launch alignment is required between the tactical plans. A consistent and integrated rollout plan is critical to enabling aligned tactical plans.

To illustrate good alignment, imagine the rollout plan contemplates taking the product to a new vertical market. You would expect the plan might indicate a need for the development of distribution plans and the cultivation of key distributors serving that new vertical market. The business development activities might be aligned to develop these relationships and sign deals with distributors that serve the targeted vertical market. In addition, the sales force activities to sell into this space might be aligned to manage these distributors and provide for joint-selling activities with the distributor sales force, using vertically aligned marketing sales tools, messaging, and collateral designed by the marketing team.

As a bonus, you would expect the feature set of the product being launched to include special features to serve this particular vertical market. Thus in this one area, the rollout plan has called out and set the direction

FIGURE 3-2: Functional Group Plan Alignment

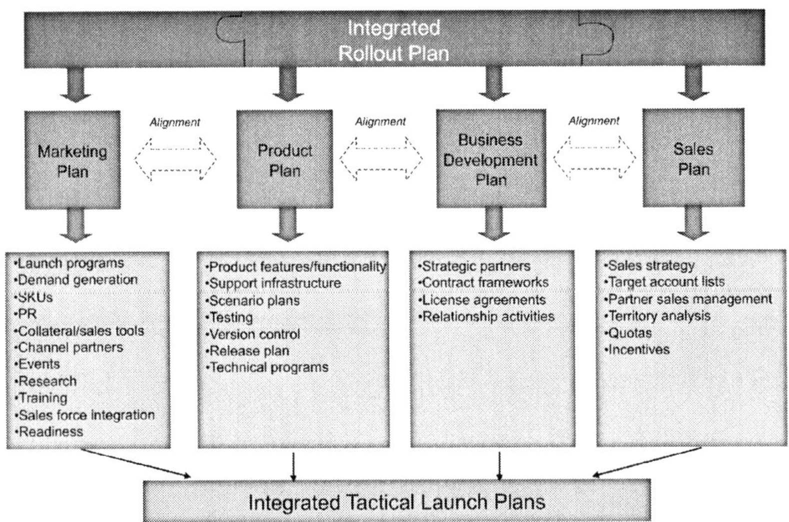

for these activities at a high level (new target vertical market, creation of new distribution channels, product plan supports the market, etc.) that then drives development of aligned drill-down tactical plans. All the key elements of the plan should contemplate this type of alignment and interdependency when laying out the high-level direction.

It is a setup for colossal launch failure if the elements of the rollout plan and the tactical plans do not align. Continuing the example, imagine the business development team signs up a new vertically oriented distributor, but the sales team has not planned for interaction around this new partnership, the marketing team hasn't created the right selling tools to address the new market, or the signed distributors do not have reach into the particular vertical. You thus have misalignment between the rollout plan strategy and direction and the functional, tactical implementation. Clearly, the chances of a successful launch will be lower given such situations. To ensure alignment, it's important to acquire stakeholder buy-in when developing the rollout plan.

Acquiring Stakeholder Buy-In

The rollout plan should provide a comprehensive and detailed perspective that paints a cohesive picture for the product rollout. To successfully get your plan off the ground and moving forward, and to ensure alignment, the plan needs the buy-in and support of key members (stakeholders) of your company. As a stand-alone plan, there should be enough high-level direction and detail indicated to ensure all relevant stakeholders in the organization that the important business elements have been duly considered and thought through, and that they feel the plan is actionable and achievable with their available (or incrementally required and provided) resources. Some of the key stakeholders whose buy-in may be considered crucial include:

- Engineering/product development (including technical development and program management)
- Sales management
- Executive management
- Finance
- Marketing
- Funding partners (venture capital, commercial)

- Board of Directors
- Legal
- Channel management

If there is not consensus and commitment among these key stakeholders your plan is likely doomed to experience great difficulty in execution and approval.

I've also found it to be a best practice to include influential mentors from across the organization when developing a rollout plan. For example, to get a product approved for launch at Microsoft, it's necessary to take the rollout plan through a number of review cycles. Typically, you start the review process within the business or product group where the product has been conceptualized. Once a draft plan is developed, the internal group feedback cycle starts with the various managers and relevant business group stakeholders processing the draft through multiple reviews among themselves and with the business group vice president.

In parallel to these efforts, there are a number of outreach activities and discussions taking place by both the VP and the group managers to acquire plan input from key influential and experienced individuals across the company. There is a dual purpose to these activities. The first is to actually leverage the experience of the influentials to help shape and strengthen the rollout plan. The second is no less important and more political: to gain visible support and buy-in from the influentials so that when the plan is ultimately presented to senior executives for final buy-off, they will see the support for the plan from trusted compatriots. The influentials' support provides credible air cover for the group seeking plan buy-off and helps smooth the approval process.

I am specifically speaking of the business, not the technical, side. However, the outreach concept also applies to the product development and technical sides during the product creation phase. In fact, at Microsoft it is standard to have multiple reviews with key engineering managers across the company during product development. This is especially true during Bill Gates' product review meetings, when the key trusted technical folks in the organization will validate what the presenting group is saying and provide incremental input. To successfully survive those meetings, it's optimal to have previously reviewed the plan and gained at least tacit buy-in and support from other company technical influentials. The same logic applies to business reviews.

Timing to Create a Rollout Plan

At what point in the product life cycle should a rollout plan be developed? This is not always straightforward, as it sometimes depends on the mechanism by which the product has arisen at your company. At Microsoft there are different scenarios by which a product might appear on the launch horizon, including:

- **Top-Down Driven:** Sometimes a product appears via a top-down driven process, i.e., an executive decides to build something and goes ahead and does it ... then tosses it over the wall at marketing to develop a rollout launch plan. Yes, this actually happens.
- **Organically Driven:** Occasionally an employee (usually a developer or program manager at Microsoft) will do a skunk-works project and develop a product on the side. They then present it to their management and the project takes on a life of its own and proceeds to launch.
- **Research Driven:** Usually happens around existing products for upgrades or possible off-shoot products, not net-new products. Customer research and feedback reveals a gap or unaddressed opportunity in the product line or market.
- **Competitive/Strategic Driven:** Product development occurs when management realizes that the competition has a product that could become a serious competitive threat or a big missed opportunity if nothing is done about it. Examples are Google and Yahoo services and advertising offerings driving Microsoft Office Live and Windows Live.
- **Acquisition Driven:** Product or product line is purchased to fill a gap or a market opportunity, typically rebranded, and re-launched. Examples are Microsoft Office Live Meeting (previously PlaceWare) and Microsoft Visio.

In each of these scenarios, the timing within the product life cycle for when a rollout plan needs to be (or actually can be) created can be different. In some of these scenarios the product concept, features, and target market are pretty much pre-determined, requiring rollout planning to occur later in the product cycle. In others, there is an opportunity to affect the product design, feature set, SKUs, and so forth earlier in the cycle, so rollout planning begins earlier.

Each scenario may have additional specific nuances that can affect rollout plan development timing and tactics. For example, in the case of an acquisition, your company may pick up personnel (engineering, sales, marketing, etc.) from the acquired company, intellectual property such as patents or copyrights, or ongoing customer marketing activities and support concerns. You must consider these issues in the go-forward planning processes, but the planned actions taken, and their timing, are likely highly dependent on the specific business situation of the acquirer.

So, the textbook answer to "When should a rollout plan be developed?" is (not surprisingly) at the beginning, before real engineering work takes place, so that the product can be shaped directly for the market specifically targeted, and planning details are thought through before significant product development investment is deployed.

However, the real world answer is that you build the plan as soon as possible given the realities of how the product came to fruition and where it is in the life cycle. I've experienced a number of Microsoft product launches where the product was for the most part engineering driven, designed, and created in the absence of a business or rollout plan—and said plan had to be created and retrofit to the already existing product. Not optimal, but regardless of where the product is in the life cycle, building an actionable rollout plan at any point is far better than having no plan at all. If you don't have the luxury of building a plan at the beginning, you must play the hand you are dealt, so make the most of it regardless of the starting point.

DEFINING THE ROLLOUT PLAN FOUNDATIONAL ELEMENTS

Given an overview of the specific elements of the plan, plan creation timing, the need for stakeholder buy-in, and the requirement to ensure alignment within the rollout plan and between the rollout plan and functional tactical plans, we can now drill-down into the details of each core element that should, at a minimum, be addressed in a rollout launch plan.

Include the Customer Scenarios and Segmentation

It's important to include a description and summary of the key customer usage scenarios the product will address (Chapter 2). Presenting the segmentation and explaining the targeted scenarios will help clearly communicate who the target customers are, what the customer problems and scenarios are, and how the product addresses them. Including these scenarios also helps create context and rationale for the plan, setting the stage for the plan's other elements.

Driving clarity of focus via these scenarios is important; however, they mean nothing absent the context of *why* you are proposing launching the product. It's not enough to state that you have a widget that can do the great things for a customer as indicated in the scenarios if it can't also do great things for your business. Thus, it is also important to supply the "why" of the plan by describing your key business strategies that underlie and drive the launch rationale.

Determining the Core Launch Strategy

The rollout plan should succinctly state the core foundational strategy for the launch, in essence answering the question "Why are we launching this product?" Answer this question in the plan by describing the base strategy taken, the underlying rationale, and the expected business benefit and outcome from pursuing that particular launch strategy. The formation of the core foundational strategy will be based on desire, intuition, market opportunity, and company/business goals. Strategy formulation is always a combination of data-driven and quantitative analysis and an expression of intuition and qualitative thinking. Expect this.

To clearly communicate the foundational strategy, ensure your plan has clear answers to the following questions:

- What are the key strategic and operational goals being pursued? (Why you are doing this launch.)
- What are the key success drivers to meet the strategic and operational goals? (How you expect to achieve success.)
- What does success look like? (The end-game success scenario being pursued.)

There are various levels of strategy—the overall corporate strategy setting high-level direction, the business unit strategy for individual P&L units within a firm, and the product strategy. The strategies at each level must fit together and align. The key strategies referred to here are at the product strategy level—not about specific product features, but about the strategy and strategic *trade-offs* that must be thought through, decided upon, and clearly communicated.

Product launch strategy formulation and desired outcome can be expressed in many different ways. However, a common thread that underlies any product launch strategy is identifying and stating the balance and trade-offs for the product launch strategy between short- and long-term strategic and operational goals for the business (within the context of higher level corporate or business unit strategies), and the time frame to mediate that balance.

Strategic goals encompass the strategic assumptions and aspirations that underlie the ultimate path to what is perceived as success for the product launch, and are generally longer term. For example, perhaps a key strategy is to make a dent in the existing pricing structure of the industry, in effect changing the game for existing competitors and putting your company in a cost-leadership position. Or perhaps the primary strategic rationale is acquiring significant market share.

Both are fine goals to pursue, but they must also be set in the context relative to a business's *operational goals,* such as revenue and profit requirements, or direct vs. channel go-to-market approaches. For example, the goal of changing the game around industry pricing structure must be weighed against the operational goals and the impact to business profitability. The consequences of striving for high-market share over the long term must be weighed against the short-term business revenue growth requirements. A product can be priced really low to gain share, but the lower price can eat into revenue and profitability. Thus a low pricing strategy may not help achieve revenue growth requirements.

FIGURE 3-3: Strategic vs. Operational Goals

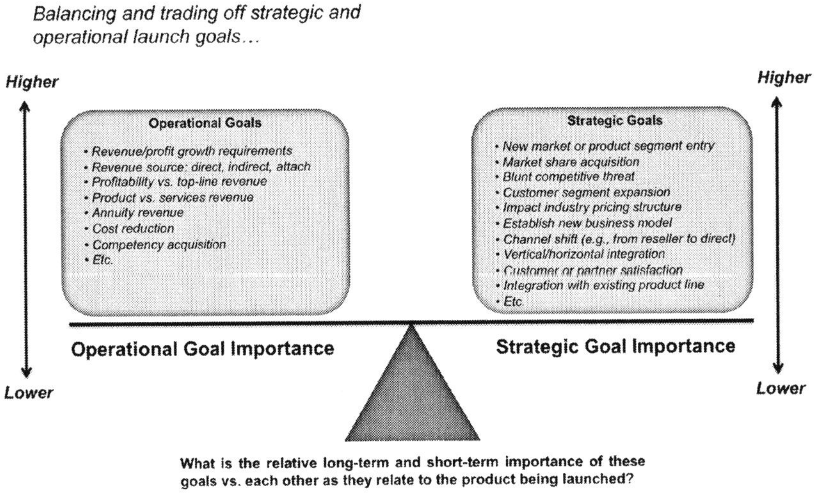

Simply put, there is likely a mix of short- and long-term strategic and operational goals and aspirations regarding the product, and these goals and aspirations must be balanced by investing resources appropriately, at the right time, to ensure success (Figure 3-3). You must quantify and articulate your decisions and thinking around the required balance and trade-offs of these goals to inform the foundational strategy.

Trade-off decisions can take various permutations to shape the foundational strategy. A launch strategy could weigh long-term strategic goals more heavily than short-term operational goals, implying that the product and launch will lay the foundation for monetization in the future at the expense of short-term operational needs. This is a fine approach as long as the risk that the product will fail to be monetized in the longer term is understood and mitigated.

Another possibility is that both strategic and operational goals are highly important, and the focus of the strategy is to balance these needs. Again, the approach is risky; in this case splitting the focus and investments to cover all the bases could result in neither strategic nor operational goals being achieved.

A third possibility is that long-term strategic goals are less important than operational goals or the desired strategic goals have already been met. Then the focus is on meeting operational goals and monetizing the investment immediately. This approach can help maximize near-term revenues, but a reduced focus on strategic goals may also open the door for competitors in the future.

If the product does not help either strategic or operational goals, it should not be launched. While generally a firm will not proceed down the launch path if this is the case, it is entirely possible that as launch activities progress market changes or other significant situational changes can shift the original landscape to one where the product under development no longer meets strategic or operational goals. This mitigates the need for the product and, essentially, ends the launch process.

At Microsoft, trade-offs between strategic vs. operational goals are pervasive. For example, if a Microsoft product group is contemplating launching some sort of new messaging collaboration product (like email or instant messaging), many questions will be asked, including:

- Will it help retain or protect market share?
- Should it be a stand-alone product or integrated with an existing product?
- Does it further particular customer segment goals?

- How does it fit in the product line mix: what is its unique value proposition? Will it add positive value to the brand regardless of financial return?
- Is there a risk of cannibalization? What impact could this have on Windows Live Messenger, Internet Explorer, Outlook, Exchange Server, the Unified Communications platform? Will it negatively impact the market share or revenue of these products? If so by how much, and what is the long-term strategic gain of taking a short-term revenue hit to these key products?
- Is this a share play, competitive parity play, or simply a rounding out of the product line/portfolio? Why choose this approach?
- What's the partner angle? What is the partner value proposition? How do channel partners fit in?

The list of questions in this regard is endless. However, addressing and thinking through the strategic and operational trade-offs in the rollout plan can help prepare cogent answers to them.

For example, assume a strategic play that minimizes the importance of short-term operational goals and elevates the importance of long-term strategic goals is being contemplated (Figure 3-4). In this example, the foundational strategy, the key underlying strategic game plan for the launch, is to pursue a long-term strategic play and forgo short-term revenue gains. The bet is that the company can invest into entering a new market segment and shake things up by changing the segment pricing structure to gain a competitive advantage, to be monetized in the future. Taking a low pricing strategy, the approach is to take market share from the competitors and drive the product (in this case a software platform) to accrue the largest installed base (in units) in the market. To help drive this unit share, in addition to a low price strategy for launch, the plan's success also rests on the ability to recruit and enable a large number of partners to create applications and products on top of the platform, helping to create significant product revenue down the line.

The end result of this foundational strategy occurs when the strategic goal of establishing volume is achieved, a few competitors are knocked out of the market by the low pricing strategy, and the unit share advantage has given the firm control of various key application programming interfaces (APIs) that enables the company to set the future direction for this technology. From that point, the go-forward plan can minimize the focus on strategic objectives and maximize focus on the operational, revenue creation activities, monetizing the now achieved strategic advantage.

FIGURE 3-4: Foundational Launch Strategy

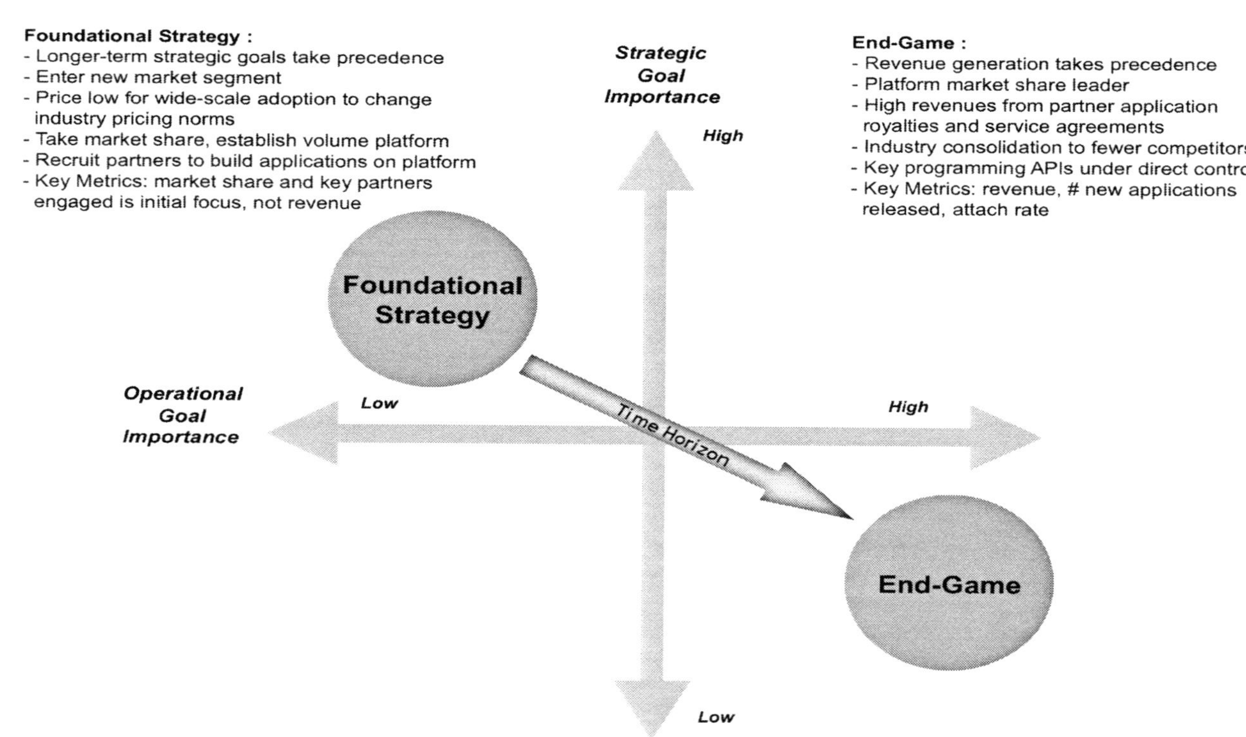

This strategy scenario enables succinct answers to the strategy questions that should be communicated in the rollout plan to explain the "why" for the launch and what the expected strategic results will be:

- What are the key strategic and operational goals being pursued?
    - Expand focus into new market segment
    - Take market share, establish volume platform
- What are the key success drivers to meet the strategic and operational goals?
    - Low price strategy, changing industry pricing paradigm
    - Build large partner application base to help drive platform share
- What does success look like?
    - Market share leader in the new segment
    - Revenue stream from partner royalties and platform revenue
    - Ownership of direction for key industry programming APIs
    - Reduced supplier base because of entry and resulting industry consolidation

This hypothetical strategy is now the summary game plan that should drive the rest of the rollout plan and set the high-level direction drill-down details and key components of tactical plans. In some cases the real strategic intent for a product launch is *not* to directly make money on a particular product. Surprising as that may sound, there are many examples at Microsoft and at other companies where this is true. Examples include a product launched to:

- Meet a strategic goal around industry thought leadership and position the firm as an industry visionary and leader.
- Enhance the corporate brand image.
- Act as a defensive maneuver, blunting a competitive threat and creating fear, uncertainty, and doubt (FUD) in the marketplace.
- Initiate a concerted strategy to drive higher customer satisfaction or post-purchase satisfaction goals for customer support.

There is a presumed (and in some cases a quantified) link between high customer satisfaction and follow-on revenue, based on the assumption that driving up satisfaction creates more loyal and greater numbers of customers willing to continue to spend money on a firm's products or services. Some time ago Microsoft launched a subscription product called TechNet. This product was originally developed to assist IT Professionals with support issues, and was delivered monthly via CD-ROM; it included support information, product information, sample code, tips and tricks, and other information in one convenient package. The product was targeted at IT Professionals to make their lives easier when planning, deploying, and maintaining Microsoft software. It was run on a cost recovery basis not to generate large amounts of revenue but to ensure high satisfaction within this customer segment around past and, hopefully, future purchases of Microsoft technology.

The final take-away here is that it is important to identify in the rollout plan what the key strategic goals and the key success drivers are (the foundational strategy) and to define what success looks like at the finish line post-launch (the end-game).

Target Market Segments, Product SKUs, and Pricing

You must be clear about which customer segments are the primary focus for the product because a targeted and actionable needs-based segmentation underlies most, if not all, of the launch activities. The market segmentation and underlying customer needs have a direct impact on driving the definition (features/functionality) of the product SKUs and pricing. A SKU describes a particular flavor, or variant, of a product. For example, at Microsoft any given product might have multiple SKUs—one targeted at the academic market, another focused at the enterprise market, and another at the small business market. At the core, the product is generally very similar but may have certain feature and pricing differences to effectively address a different market segment.

The product SKUs that are defined and created during the launch process can make or break a product launch. The SKUs are the incarnation and delivery mechanism of the product itself. They are what get promoted and sold to the customer. Creating a SKU that is poorly featured, improperly priced, incorrectly targeted, or competitively mismatched may cause the product to fail in the market, even if it is a good product. Excellent SKU definition is so important to a successful launch that I've drilled-down into it in more detail, starting with some background on the entanglement of customer segments, SKUs, and pricing.

RIDING THE DEMAND CURVE

A reasonable illustration of segment, SKU, and pricing entanglement is illustrated from concepts originating in Economics 101. We all remember the supply and demand curves and the concepts of producer and consumer surplus from school, but in case you have forgotten, very brief and simplified definitions are as follows:

- Supply curve defines the amount of product being produced and available to the market.
- Demand curve defines the relationship of price to quantity demanded by consumers.
- Producer surplus constitutes the delta amount that the manufacturer or product supplier (you and your company) receives between the selling price and the cost to produce. This is the net benefit to producers.
- Consumer surplus is the delta amount a customer is willing to pay for an item above the market price.

The concept of consumer surplus is the crux of the opportunity for the product and business. The consumer surplus essentially amounts to revenue a firm is not accruing—basically giving away revenue and profits by not approaching the market via proper segmentation, pricing, and SKU design. This is bad. Figure 3-5 lays out these economic concepts, showing the consumer surplus area with the "x"s, and the producer surplus with "o"s, overlaid by a hypothetical customer segment map.

In this example, the market price is at $25 and the scenario includes a SKU 3 in the market addressing target customer Segment 3. However, because the upfront segmentation analysis was not carefully done, product SKU 3 is maximizing revenue only from part of Segment 3. This is because a good chunk of Segment 3 customers are willing to pay higher than the current market price of $25 for this SKU (the part of the Segment 3 bubble that bleeds into the Consumer Surplus Area), leaving money on the table. This situation might be an opportunity to revisit the pricing approach and raise the existing SKUs price to capture that extra surplus, or divide Segment 3 into high- and low-end groups, and target the high-end group with a new higher priced SKU.

Another potential opportunity missed in this example is the non-identification, or non-targeting, of Segments 1 and 2, whose constituents might potentially be willing to pay more for a variant of the product currently offered to Segment 3. This is where the confluence of pricing, segmentation, and SKUs actually happens. In the example, you could

FIGURE 3-5: Consumer Surplus

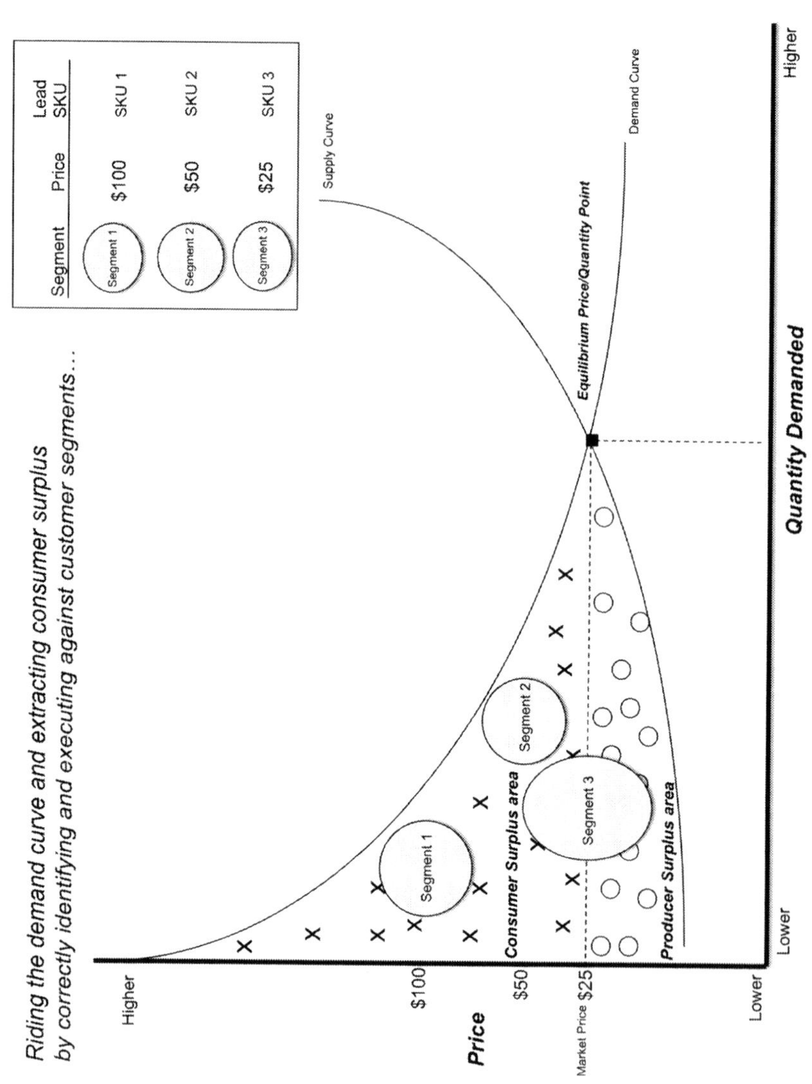

define a new SKU 1 for Segment 1 and price it at $100, and a new SKU 2 targeted at Segment 2 priced at $50, since these segments fall into that consumer surplus sweet spot pricing area on the demand curve.

All these SKUs enable a firm to ride the demand curve with different SKUs and different price points targeted at different customer segments. This provides an example of "scooping up" the available consumer surplus in the marketplace, and expanding the producer surplus opportunity, which in real world terms means you can make more money. But to scoop up the surplus and bring that money into your business, the segmentation must be solid, with the right pricing and SKUs available to fulfill various segment needs.

SKU PLANNING AND DEFINITION

To effectively ride the demand curve and scoop surplus with SKU variants you must keep many considerations in mind when determining exactly how many variants of a particular product to take to market as a SKU. These considerations include:

- There must be valid differentiation between the SKUs, with clearly articulated and differentiated positioning, value propositions, and prices between them.
- The SKUs must address the different customer usage scenarios and segments/segment needs as identified and targeted.
- The SKUs must be competitive relative to market competition and competitive SKUs targeted at the same segment.
- The SKUs must consider revenue maximization via scooping up consumer surplus.
- The SKU strategy must map to and support the partner channel plan and strategy.
- The key sales and marketing strategies and resources must accommodate the defined SKUs.
- SKU planning must minimize support and internal infrastructure costs.

SKU Differentiation: Clearly differentiating between the SKUs is key to an effective strategy. Each SKU must maintain a reasonable differentiation from any other SKU, generally meaning that the features and functionality of the SKUs must be different enough from other SKUs and must deliver

FIGURE 3-6: SKU Differentiation

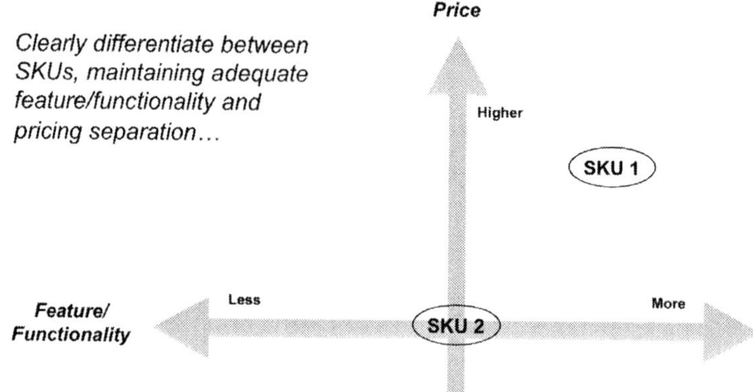

the right value to justify the pricing differential. Figure 3-6 shows a conceptual SKU plan that incorporates adequate feature/functionality and price differentiation.

However, SKU differentiation is not necessarily all about features and functionality. Bundled value-adds from customer loyalty programs, support services, consulting services, integration with other products, licensing terms, and scalability can all play a role in differentiation. An example might be that of a particular software product SKU that enables and supports 100 simultaneous web connections, while a higher priced counterpart SKU handles 10,000 connections and adds a consulting deployment service bundled with purchase. Both SKUs handle the functional checklist feature of "enabling web connections" and meet the customers' core need for this web connection functionality, but they are differentiated by scale and services.

Even if the core customer needs are being met with a particular SKU, if the feature/functionality is too similar to the other SKUs to justify the price differential, that SKU will likely fail. A classic example here was an early Microsoft server product launched with two SKUs—a lower-end Standard Edition (SE) and a higher-end Enterprise Edition (EE).

The SE and EE SKU approach is actually one of the standardized approaches for server SKU definition at Microsoft these days. However, at the time this was not true. They were attempting to increase revenue through the higher priced EE SKU by shifting the unit sales mix from the SE to the EE SKU. The problem was that the EE SKU was not well thought through from a customer value perspective, and thus the incremental feature sets for the EE SKU did not have enough incremental feature/functionality to adequately differentiate it from the SE or to justify the much higher price. There just wasn't enough differentiated value between the SKUs from the customer perspective to justify a move to EE from SE. Needless to say, the hoped-for mix shift did not occur until this situation was rectified some years later by adding more value into the EE SKU and decreasing the price differential.

The Microsoft Office product line offers a current example of SKU differentiation. Figure 3-7 lays out both a generic and the Microsoft Office specific example. The generic example provides a structure by which SKUs, the target customer segment, the SKU price, positioning, and key feature sets are compared. SKU 1 is the most expensive SKU with a complete feature set, covering all features A to F. SKU 2 is the next step down, less expensive, and has only features A to D. SKU 3 is the low-end, least expensive SKU with only a few features. Each SKU targets a separate customer segment or usage scenario, with the relevant positioning reflecting the core customer need(s).

This generic example is then applied to some of the current (year 2007) Microsoft Office SKUs (this is only an illustrative subset of Office SKUs and feature sets). Similar to the generic example, there are three Office SKUs: Enterprise, Professional Plus, and Professional, with the associated pricing, positioning, and feature sets. I have inferred from the positioning verbiage on the Microsoft website which customer segment each SKU targets.

You can see that the high-end SKU, the Enterprise SKU, is the most expensive and has the most complete feature set, the Professional Plus SKU is less expensive and has a slightly smaller feature set, and the regular Professional SKU has the smallest feature set.

So the question is: Are the illustrative Office SKUs adequately differentiated in terms of price and feature/functionality—is there enough perceived "distance" between the SKUs? In the Office example, based on the positioning, the Enterprise SKU seems to be targeted toward enterprise business customers that have a usage scenario around the sharing and collaboration of information among or within teams. This is not too different from the positioning of the Professional Plus SKU, which also

FIGURE 3-7: Illustrative SKU Planning Example

A generic SKU planning example…

SKU	Target Segment	Price	Positioning	Feature A	Feature B	Feature C	Feature D	Feature E	Feature F
SKU 1	Large datacenters	$100	Scalable to meet your every need	✓	✓	✓	✓	✓	✓
SKU 2	Medium datacenters	$50	Meets your critical needs	✓	✓	✓	✓		
SKU 3	Small datacenters	$25	Meets your basic needs	✓	✓				

A Microsoft Office product SKU planning example[1]…

MS Office SKU	Inferred Target Segment	Estimated Retail Price	Positioning	Feature: Word, Excel, PowerPoint	Feature: Outlook email client	Feature: Outlook email client & Business Contact Manager	Feature: OneNote	Feature: Forms, Content Management, Digital Rights Management	Feature: Groove
Enterprise	Information workers at large enterprises with collaboration needs	$584[2]	"Tools for teams to collect, consolidate, organize, access, and share critical information"	✓	✓		✓	✓	✓
Professional Plus	Information workers in enterprises	$478[2]	"Easier to more effectively manage, analyze and share information"	✓	✓			✓	
Professional	Individual information workers in large, medium, and small businesses	$499[2]	"Work more efficiently, manage customer and contact information in one place, develop professional-quality marketing materials and campaigns in-house"	✓		✓			

1) Microsoft SKU information based on public content from www.microsoft.com/office. Not a complete feature list. Illustrative only
2) Pricing from public information on Microsoft.com and February 2007 Directions on Microsoft magazine

pivots around a similar positioning theme about managing and sharing information (i.e., collaborating). So by reading the positioning statements, that aspect of the differentiation between the SKUs is somewhat fuzzy. Looking at the feature set, you can see that the only key feature difference in this example is the inclusion of the Groove functionality in the Enterprise SKU, where Groove is excluded from the Plus SKU.

Given that the products are similarly positioned, enable the collaboration and sharing of information to some level, and target information workers in enterprises, does the Groove functionality in the Enterprise edition carry enough customer value to support a $106 per user price difference to scoop the additional consumer surplus? Does that one feature adequately differentiate the SKUs regardless of the price difference? These same questions can be applied to the difference between the Professional Plus SKU and the standard Professional SKU, where the forms and digital/content management features are the key feature/functionality differences between the SKUs.

An unusual aspect of the Professional Plus SKU and the standard Professional SKU is the price difference—in this case the higher functionality SKU (Plus) is priced lower than the lesser functionality SKU by $21. Why is this? In this case, the Professional Plus SKU is only available via Microsoft's volume licensing program—you can't purchase this product at retail. Volume licensing has discounts unavailable by other purchase transaction methods. So by excluding the Plus SKU from retail, and keeping the value-to-price ratio higher than the standard Professional SKU, Microsoft is likely attempting to shift business purchases of Office to the preferred volume licensing purchase method (because that captures detailed information about the customer that can be used for cross-sell/up-sell purposes, and develops an annuity revenue stream).

Presumably Microsoft has answered these questions diligently and the answer is "yes to all the above." I use this example to stimulate your thinking on the kinds of questions that should be asked when planning the SKU strategy to be communicated in the rollout plan.

SKUs Relative to Customer Usage Scenarios and Segments: Mapping the SKU strategy to the targeted customer usage scenarios and segments is a critical element to defining the correct SKUs (Figure 3-8). You should assume that within a particular target customer segment there are likely multiple usage scenarios. The job is to define those scenarios and ensure that the SKU definitions map to appropriately differentiated scenarios. Chapter 2 had an example of IT Professionals with two server usage

FIGURE 3-8: SKUs Relative to Customer Segment

Defining SKUs relative to the appropriate targeted customer segment...

✓ =Primary target

⋰ =Secondary target

	Customer Segment 1 Or Scenario 1	Customer Segment 2 Or Scenario 2	Customer Segment 3 Or Scenario 3
SKU 1		✓	⋰
SKU 2	✓		
SKU 3		⋰	✓

scenarios: infrastructure and mobility. The implication is that there are potentially two sub-segments of IT Professionals: one which might more highly value feature/functionality to meet their infrastructure needs, and one that more highly values the mobility feature/functionality. This could provide an opportunity for a two-SKU offering, where the lower-priced SKU offers only the infrastructure features, and the higher-priced SKU includes both infrastructure and mobility features. Or, there could be a one-SKU strategy with both feature sets included.

Back to Economics 101, you must determine which is the best way to optimize riding the demand curve and consume the available consumer surplus. Making the right choice will depend on good data and analysis. For example, optimally you would know the size of the sub-segments, the relative value placed on the two key feature differentiators, and the price-elasticity of the two offerings as they relate to the target market sub-segments. This information can help to model out the potential demand for the various SKU configuration potentials and their corresponding revenue or profit opportunity.

If this type of data is unavailable, you can discover it through customer research or make simplifying assumptions (or guesses) about how to define the SKUs. Sometimes the simplest approach is the best: one SKU per scenario or one SKU per market segment depending on segmentation definition.

SKUs Relative to Competition: Competitors are another consideration for SKU plans. If the product is being launched into an established market or one where there are at least a few other competitors, there are competitive SKU models in place for evaluation and to help inform your planning. When purchasing, a customer will likely shop around and compare products and solutions. Taking a SKU approach that is in line with existing industry practice, the product may more likely be placed into the customer consideration process. If the SKU approach taken follows a completely different SKU model than competitors, problems may occur. A totally different model might cause customer confusion from a variety of angles, including an inability on their part to do price or value comparisons.

A safe bet is to follow established industry practice for SKU offerings, but provide a higher SKU value-to-price ratio than the competition. Mapping your firm's proposed product SKU offerings against the relative price and feature/functionality of the competitive SKUs is a good analysis to inform SKU planning (Figure 3-9). To help establish a basis for competitive advantage with a higher value-to-price ratio, strive for least SKU feature/functionality parity. If that is not possible, offset that deficit with incremental SKU value, such as consulting services, support, training,

FIGURE 3-9: SKUs Relative to Competition

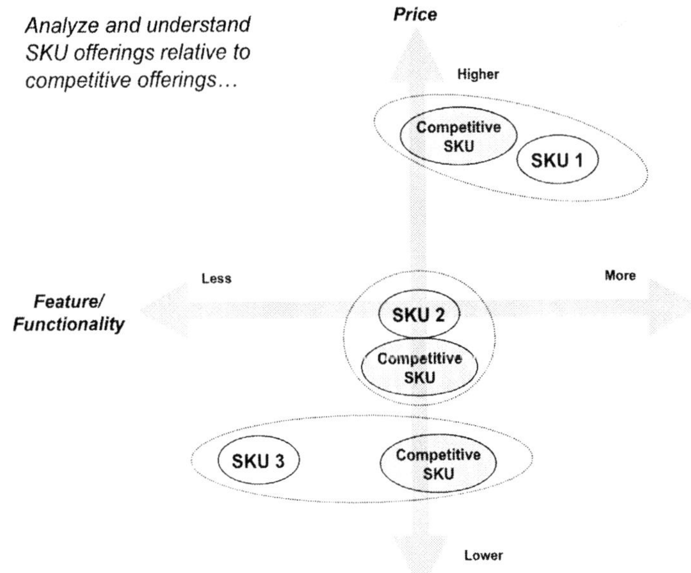

or a lower price. Understanding the competitive SKU landscape and the various value-to-price ratios can help inform product positioning (Chapter 4) and drive the appropriate communication points in marketing and sales materials.

On the other hand, if being disruptive is an option, it is always possible to change things up a bit. In the telephony industry, for example, SKU pricing was, and still is, generally done on a "per port" basis, meaning a cost is charged for each telephone connection supported (one connection equals a "port"). If a SKU was offered and supported 100 telephone connections, a customer pays X dollars times 100 ports. When launching a telephony-focused product some years ago, Microsoft switched this model and charged per processor, meaning that a customer owning the Microsoft SKU could support as many telephone connections as desired for one flat cost, with the number of connections limited only by the processing power of the computer server handling the load.

While this provided a huge benefit to the customers from a value perspective, it also caused confusion for those customers used to a per-port pricing model. Customers were unable to perform a direct comparison between the Microsoft SKU vs. competitive SKU offerings; the resulting confusion was an entré for the competition, causing lost deals for Microsoft. So note that it is possible to gain a competitive advantage by changing industry models to provide increased value for customers, but be prepared to handle the risks and potential issues that can arise from such a change.

SKU Mapping to Partner and Channel Strategy: Another input to consider is the existing or planned partner channel model. Any SKU that will flow through the partner channel must be consumable by the partners. Being consumable means:

- They fit into the selling model of the partners from a sales/marketing perspective.
- They fit from a technology perspective.
- They fit from a packaging perspective.
- They fit from a pricing and licensing perspective.
- They do not cannibalize SKUs in other channels.

Microsoft works with a broad range of channel partners serving a variety of customer segments. This requires a broad and flexible SKU strategy to accommodate the different partner go-to-market models. For example,

Microsoft must consider SKU requirements for the original equipment manufacturer (OEM) channel to pre-load software onto their hardware using different product installation and ID creation features. Similarly, the company must consider SKUs that support the education market (academic) and account for its pricing constraints. Full-package product (FPP) with physical packaging designed for the retail channel drives further SKU needs that must be addressed. Developers and independent software vendors (ISVs) are key target audiences for Microsoft; this sometimes drives the need for a Development SKU. This is a variant of a basic product SKU; the difference is licensing restrictions that limit product usage to development and testing purposes only, not for resale or production deployment at customer locations.

Finally, Microsoft must provide SKUs that are licensing-only for delivery to contract-based volume licensing customers—these SKUs exist only as a part-number in the product SKU database and have no physical packaging other than being shipped via a generic CD bundle.

These different types of Microsoft SKUs are all variants on the basic product SKU, but designed and modified on a pricing, packaging, installation, or licensing basis for a specific channel to consume. Other firms' partner channels may or may not be as complex or diverse as Microsoft's. Regardless, whatever the channel structure, understanding the needs of partners and getting their feedback on the proposed SKU strategy will help inform final SKU definition.

Supporting Sales and Marketing: This may be obvious advice, but ensuring that you can actually market and sell the SKUs you create must be taken into account. It's no use to create an academic flavor of your basic SKU if you do not have the sales, distribution, or marketing wherewithal to go after that market. In addition, you will likely have limited sales and marketing resources to put behind your various product lines and SKUs and will need to prioritize where you put that investment. Spreading your marketing and sales time and efforts trying to sell too many SKUs is a recipe for failure. So if you don't think there are adequate resources behind a particular SKU, don't create it.

Minimizing SKU Costs and Complexity: Large organizations with many products may have a lot of SKUs. As the number of SKUs within a firm grows, it becomes important to take a hard look at the portfolio of SKUs and evaluate whether a SKU is pulling its own weight or is simply adding unnecessary cost and complexity. Every SKU carries both hard and soft costs.

FIGURE 3-10: The Costs of SKU Proliferation

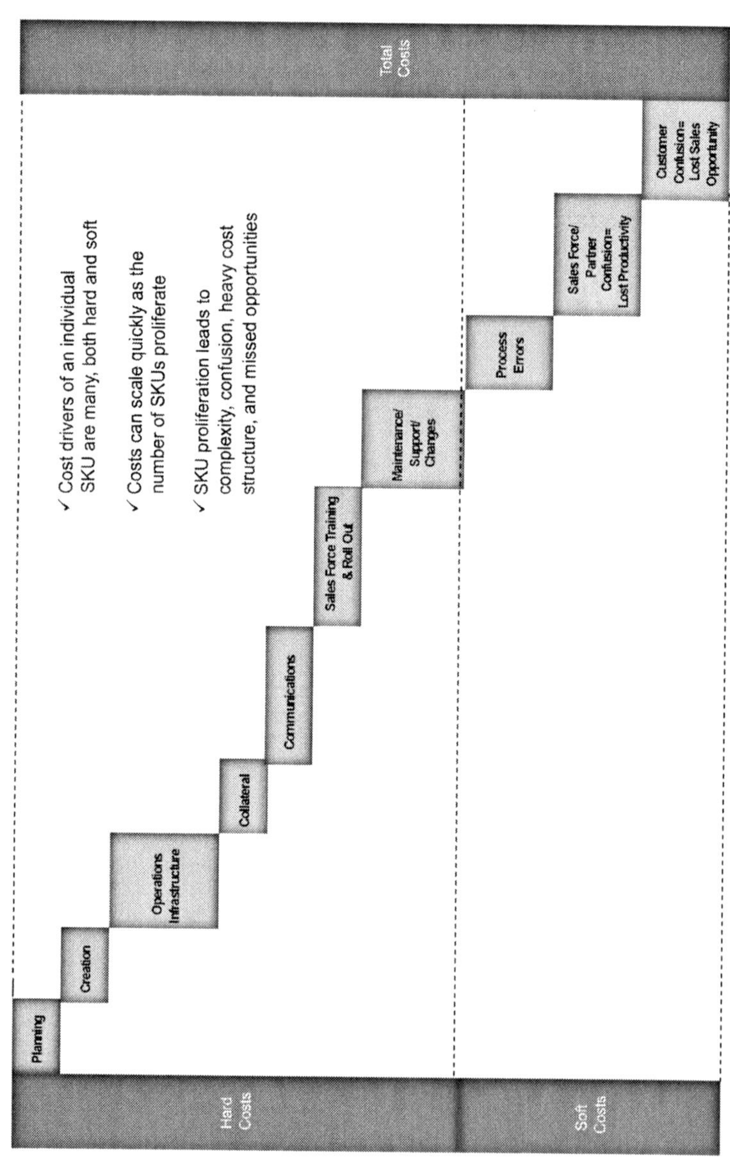

Figure 3-10 indicates some of these costs, including allocated planning costs, communication costs about the SKUs to internal constituents, and costs of printed or web marketing collateral to explain the SKUs. Two large cost drivers need special attention. The first is the operations infrastructure needed to manage and support the SKU data and information, including the databases, personnel to help set up and manage the data, and reporting infrastructure required to feed into your financial systems. The second is the support and maintenance infrastructure needed to manage the information, communicate it, and make changes.

While the exact number can vary for any given company, it can easily cost thousands of dollars per SKU in hard costs to support a SKU. Multiply this by 10, 50, 100, or even thousands of SKUs in market and the costs can be quite dramatic. This does not even account for the soft costs involved.

Besides adding cost, complexity becomes an issue as the number of SKUs rises. This causes errors in processing (mispriced SKU, wrong SKU number in database, etc.), which all tend to create negative downstream issues for the sales force and partners. Decreased sales force and partner productivity or simple ordering errors can occur with too many SKUs—simply determining the correct SKU to use for a particular deal can become a challenge. Proposing the wrong SKU can lead to a botched deal. And the sales force and partners are not the only ones that can be confused.

Customer confusion can run rampant with a high level of SKU complexity. Simply comparing choices between SKUs to determine the appropriate SKU for their needs can be onerous, a pain you do not want to impose on customers. This can create an unnecessary obstacle for customer evaluation and purchase decision making.

Figure 3-11 points out a hidden truth you will likely find at most companies—the 80-20 rule applies to SKUs as it does to so many other things. It will likely be the case that 80% of revenue or profits are generated by only 20% of the SKUs. If so, why continue to carry the costs and deal with the unnecessary complexity of the non-performing SKUs? Of course, the answer is to drop them—get rid of them. It's a relatively straightforward analysis, and requires data at the product and SKU level for revenues, variable costs, and allocated fixed costs by product line and by SKU.

Sizing the Market and Revenue Opportunity

Quantifying the market and revenue opportunity will provide context for the product's potential revenue and profit opportunities. Determining a

FIGURE 3-11: The 80-20 Rule for SKUs

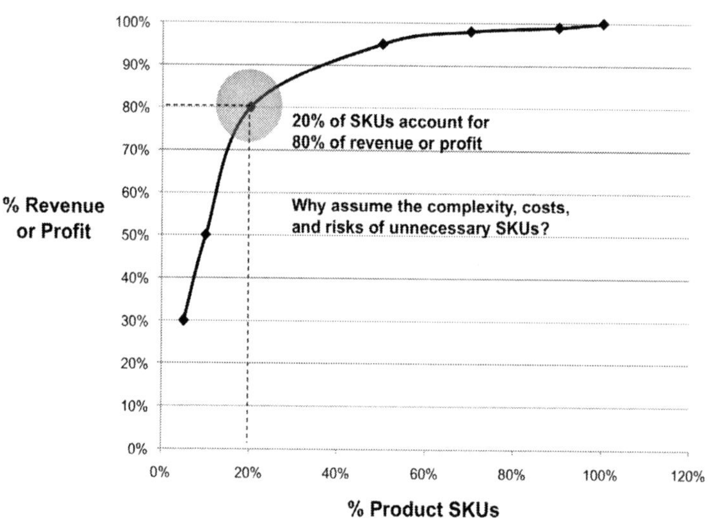

reasonable and supportable estimate of what the true market potential is and a realistic assessment of the product's potential revenue share of that market is the objective here. This is an area where many marketers get bogged down as they try to estimate the market opportunity to the last decimal point. However every market sizing analysis will be based on assumptions and data from internal sources or executive input, analyst reports, primary customer research, or other sources. Each assumption and data point will be estimates that drive such calculations. So don't get bogged down. View the market opportunity analysis results for what they are—a somewhat accurate, best effort portrayal and estimate of market opportunity.

There are three conceptual approaches to quantify a market and revenue opportunity estimate (Figure 3-12):

- A top-down analysis driven by supply-side data
- A bottom-up analysis from a channel capacity perspective
- A bottom-up analysis from an end-customer demand perspective

If possible, it's always a good idea to perform all of these analyses to triangulate and sanity check the final opportunity estimate.

FIGURE 3-12: Market Opportunity Triangulation

Triangulate and sanity check the market opportunity estimate using a number of approaches...

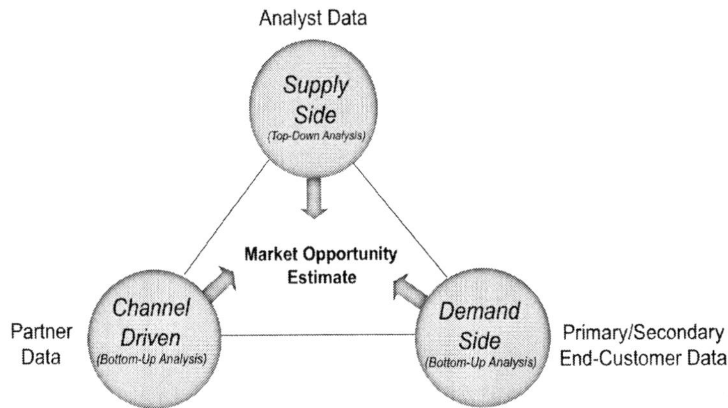

TOP-DOWN REVENUE OPPORTUNITY ANALYSIS

Evaluating a market from the top down involves gathering estimates and supply-side data from various credible sources, then piecing them together to arrive at the estimated overall market opportunity. From that, you can make an educated estimate on what percentage of that market can translate to product revenue.

Getting data on overall market size can be challenging. However, help does exist. For example, in the technology industry, there are various analyst companies (IDC, Frost & Sullivan, Gartner, etc.) that employ their own methodologies to size the various markets. Many industries outside technology will have similar specialty research firms that analyze different markets, providing similar data.

Analyst reports are typically supply-side analyses produced through data collection from companies in a particular industry. Both phone interviews and written questionnaires will be used to gather information that the companies themselves provide about sales, expected deals, market trends, and so on. The analysts then publish market reports using the collected data, adding advice, and modeling out market forecasts. The benefit of such data is it is readily available (for a price) and usually contains associated market analysis that can help inform market opportunity estimates for the product.

The downside is that most of the information originates from existing market suppliers. Although a good analyst firm will attempt to validate the numbers via other sources, the accuracy of such information is never 100%. For example, if an analyst queried a firm on the amount of revenue generated for a particular product and how many actual units were sold, it's possible the firm might not want to provide completely accurate information for competitive, legal, and financial reasons. Information in analyst market reports should be viewed in the context that it is approximate and directional in nature—a starting point.

The first step in developing a top-down supply-side market opportunity analysis is to gather as many analyst reports as possible that cover the product's targeted market and review and compare the assumptions made in each report. How consistent are they? How relevant? Do the analysts differ significantly in assumptions and projections? Are the time frames and manner in which the data is sliced and diced similar enough to enable an apples-to-apples comparison? Does the analysis include the correct or a large enough sampling of industry players? Generally, analyst projections will be in the same general ball park regarding market size and growth, but that ball park can sometimes vary by hundreds of millions of dollars. Figure 3-13 provides an example of various analyst estimates plotted together, enabling a comparison. Three of the analyst firms seem consistent, but one has significantly different projections.

Given the different methodologies and analysis approach each analyst firm may take, some creativity may be required to piece together the various reports. Try to use the data to come up with a consolidated best-guess market opportunity number taking into account all the forecasts you can access. Use a statistical function to find the best-fit approximation among the analyst forecasts, or average the data believed most credible, or simply choose one of the analyst firms in which there is a credibly high degree of confidence. Then use that data as the core dataset for market opportunity size.

Sanity Checking Analyst Estimates

You can use a number of "sanity check" options to augment and validate the analyst input to fine-tune a top-down market opportunity analysis. They range from available competitor revenue numbers to input from channel partners.

Sanity Check Using Revenues of Existing Market Competitors: For any publicly traded competitor, corporate revenue data is available from

FIGURE 3-13: Analyst Market Estimate Comparison

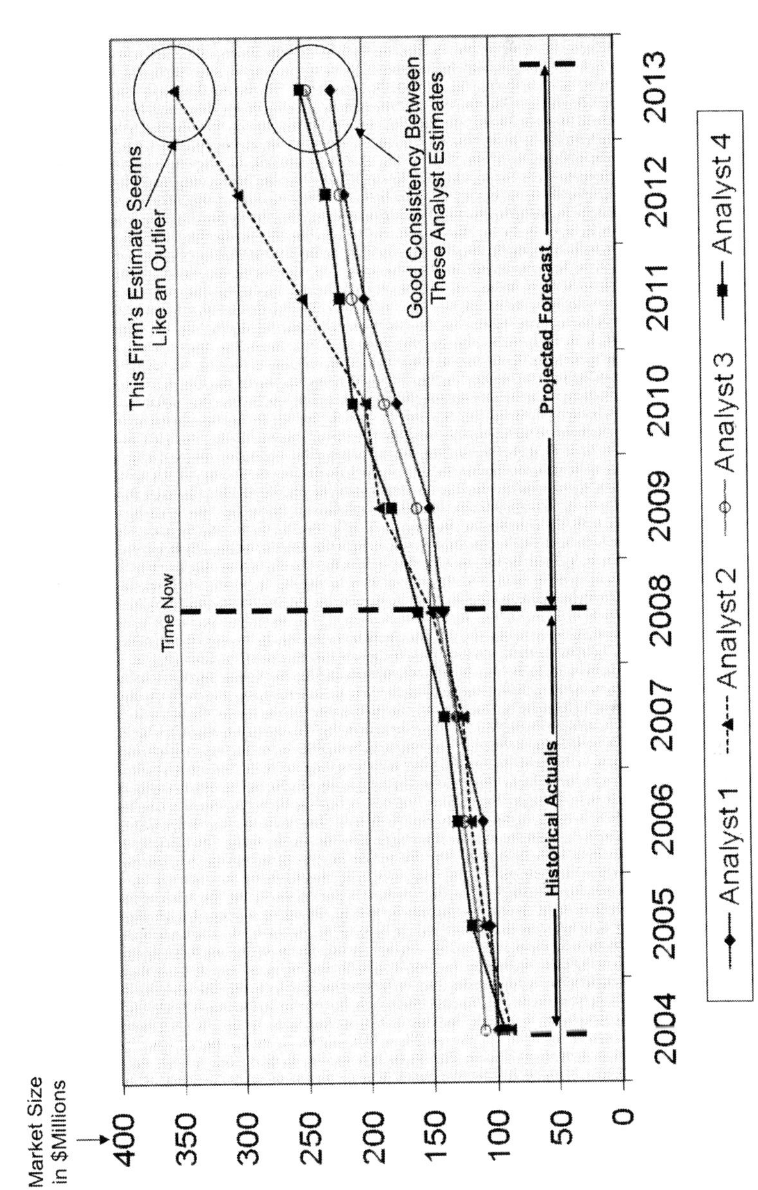

the U.S. Securities and Exchange Commission (SEC) at the SEC website and the Edgar online database. The information includes 10q and 10k reports. Total revenue figures are available, and are sometimes provided by product division, market segment, or product line. For private company information, certain Wall Street firms produce financial reports and analysis on private companies and industries, as does D&B.

The public or private financial information will help assess how accurate the analyst data is. Unless it is highly fragmented, it is not generally difficult to identify the top 10-15 companies in any market that have the majority market share and revenues. Simply add up these revenues to get an approximate market size, comparing them to the analyst data. Hopefully, the numbers will coincide. To analyze financial information for firms of interest, you can "guesstimate" a company's approximate revenues using the following rule of thumb: assume about $100k-$150k of revenue per employee. So a 10-person company would be generating an estimated $1M-$1.5M in revenue.

Sanity Check Using Insider Information: Larger companies generally have employees that have worked for the competition. These employees may have their take on the estimates for your market size or revenue generated by the competitive firm. It is unethical (and possibly illegal) to ask another employee to provide confidential or proprietary information. However, that doesn't mean that they can't sanity check your estimates and indicate if the estimates are really high, really low, or in the ball park. Or, they might point to other sources that can help.

Sanity Check Using Other Government Data: Data from government entities other than the SEC can also be helpful. There are entire branches of the government that produce industry information and data, quantify market revenue and product unit shipments, and provide other industry data points. Examples include the Census Bureau and the Bureau of Labor and Statistics. The information is good and it's free. If the target market is the small business segment, the Small Business Administration produces a large amount of industry data focused on the small business category.

Sanity Check via Correlated Markets: Data which is not directly related to the specific market or product being launched, but is *associated* with that market, can help validate other information sources. An example would be the computer printer market. If a new printer is being launched, printer market analyst reports are likely available and should include printer unit and revenue estimates. Now comes the "associated" part—every printer that ships has a core component inside it, the "print engine," which is the key technology enabling the printer to actually work. Check the "print engine" market data from analysts that track that market—do the sales of printer engines, or the growth rate of printer engine sales, map to the forecasts of the finished goods printer market itself? If they correlate well, that's great and you can feel more confident in the analyst projections of finished goods printer shipments.

Sanity Check With Channel Partners: Partner validation is another avenue to help compile the best possible market size info. Go to partners that have been around for some time in the industry and get their take on the industry size. They may surprise you with their insights and breadth of knowledge into how much and exactly what gets sold in the industry they serve.

Developing the Top-Down Analysis

Once reasonable top-line market opportunity information has been found and settled on as believable, it can be used in a top-down analysis to derive the estimated market opportunity.

Figure 3-14 contains the summary output of an example top-down analysis for a hypothetical product market. The example contains information compiled from the best analyst information, public financial disclosures, and internal sources, indicating a Total Market Potential number of $40M. This number is reduced to $30M, since the hypothetical product is unable to accommodate the needs of certain vertical industries that comprise a portion of the overall market. Thus, the estimated market size of these vertical markets is excluded from the true total potential opportunity. This leaves the $30M as the Product Addressable Market—the market truly available to the product. Since the product is not yet launched, the Served Market (the market revenues the product would be generating if it was already in market) is zero dollars, leaving the final market opportunity at $30M.

With the current market opportunity defined, you can make various estimates regarding projected market growth rates that will change the opportunity potential. You can use market share estimate ranges to see the effect of various share assumptions and their effect on potential product revenue relative to market size.

FIGURE 3-14: Illustrative Top-Down Market Analysis

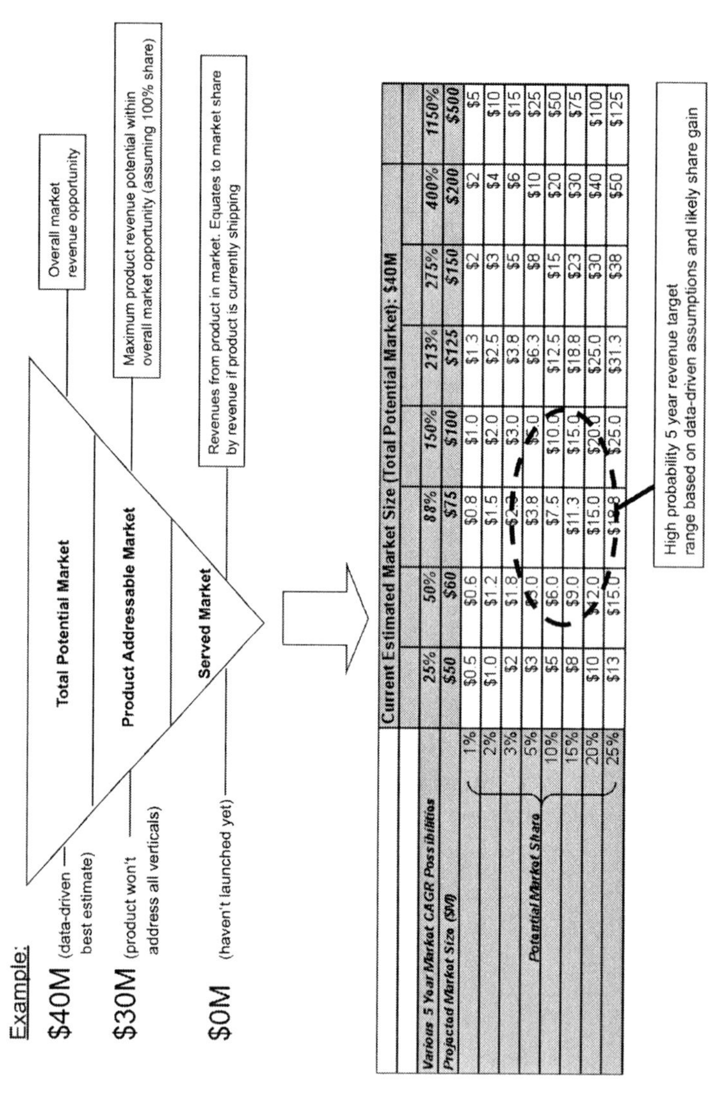

	Current Estimated Market Size (Total Potential Market): $40M							
Various 5 Year Market CAGR Possibilities	*25%*	*50%*	*88%*	*150%*	*213%*	*275%*	*400%*	*1150%*
Projected Market Size ($M)	*$50*	*$60*	*$75*	*$100*	*$125*	*$150*	*$200*	*$500*
Potential Market Share 1%	$0.5	$0.6	$0.8	$1.0	$1.3	$2	$2	$5
2%	$1.0	$1.2	$1.5	$2.0	$2.5	$3	$4	$10
3%	$2	$1.8	$2.3	$3.0	$3.8	$5	$6	$15
5%	$3	$3.0	$3.8	$5.0	$6.3	$8	$10	$25
10%	$5	$6.0	$7.5	$10.0	$12.5	$15	$20	$50
15%	$8	$9.0	$11.3	$15.0	$18.8	$23	$30	$75
20%	$10	$12.0	$15.0	$20.0	$25.0	$30	$40	$100
25%	$13	$15.0	$18.8	$25.0	$31.3	$38	$50	$125

To feel comfortable with the estimates, address the following questions:

- Is there capacity to invest and a will to sustain the required investment for the time required to achieve the share and revenue estimates?
- Do the other elements of the plan (channel strategy, pricing, sales, marketing, etc.) indicate this market share is possible if tactical activities are executed effectively?
- Is there confidence that the product being launched will be competitive in the market vs. direct competition or other alternatives?
- What have been the market share accrual rates of similar or market-related products at the company or by competitors? Do the share accrual estimates and expectations align to these historical realities? If not, why not?
- What is the sensitivity of the estimate to assumption changes?

A top-down analysis is a reasonable approach to assessing market opportunity; however, there are various real world factors that this approach ignores. One is limited channel capacity. There may be a $30M market opportunity to go after, but if there is a dependency on channel partners to sell the product, and there is only one partner selling one unit of the product per year, that's a capacity constraint limiting the ability to access that $30M potential. Another real world factor is the ability to support marketing demand generation activities at the investment levels required to reach the target audience and drive the sales levels to achieve the desired market share. If there are 100,000 customers that make up the target market, but there is only enough money and budget to effectively reach 10 of these customers, it will likely be difficult to get your fair share of the $30M.

There are other constraints as well. It makes sense to check the top-down revenue opportunity with another approach that can factor in some of these real world issues—the bottom-up analysis.

BOTTOM-UP REVENUE OPPORTUNITY ANALYSIS

A top-down approach starts with an estimate of market size and uses assumptions to reduce the market to an estimated share and revenue opportunity. A bottom-up analysis goes the other way, starting with low-level details and assumptions for revenue generation and aggregating that information upward into a final revenue estimate.

Two different approaches for developing a bottom-up analysis are the end-customer demand approach and a partner channel driven approach. The end-customer approach is a demand-side analysis, revolving around estimated customer purchase intent, and does not directly assume any constraints of a partner channel sales model. However, if the product business model at all depends on reseller partners (regardless of partner type), developing a channel-based model to inform the launch plan can be a good idea. Doing so forces an analysis of the actual sell-through capacity of the reseller channel.

Channel Driven Bottom-Up Analysis

Figure 3-15 details a bottom-up approach to estimate potential product revenue opportunity. Implementing such an analysis is relatively straightforward. For each channel the product will flow through, you should estimate the potential revenue given the channel breadth (the number of channel partners selling the product), the channel sales capacity (how many product units each channel partner can sell annually), and any estimated product or services attach revenue expected. Then add up all the potential revenue calculated for each channel, and voila—there is the overall product potential revenue opportunity for the year.

It is then an easy exercise to create a multi-year forecast by changing these key variables to accommodate expected changes in the business. These include a change in the number of partners, increased partner sales driven by training and competency acquisition, acquisition or loss in the number of reselling partners, price changes, and increase or decrease of share in the partner's business.

In this particular example, there is a high-end and a low-end SKU being launched, with different feature/functionality and price points. The key elements driving the analysis are:

- **Average Revenue Per Unit:** the average revenue amount each SKU brings per unit sold
- **Channel Breadth:** the actual number of partners expected to actively sell your product once it is launched
- **Channel Capacity:** a measure of the actual number of product units an average reseller will likely resell based on how many transactions they perform annually, what percentage will include your product, and how many units will be sold in an average transaction

FIGURE 3-15: Illustrative Channel-Driven Bottom-Up Market Analysis

A bottom-up market analysis based on channel capacity is another method to estimate product revenue…

	Product Revenue	***Channel Breadth***	***Channel Capacity***			***Product or Services Attach Revenue***			
	Average Revenue Per Unit (A)	Number of Resellers (B)	Average Annual Transactions Per Reseller (C)	% Transactions Including Your Product (D)	Average Number Product Units Sold Per Transaction (E)	Average Product Attach Revenue Per Transaction (F)	% Transactions In Which Product Is Attached (G)	Average Service Attach Revenue Per Transaction (H)	% Transactions In Which Service Is Attached (I)
Low-end SKU	$100	1000	30	80%	30	$20	30%	$1000	10%
High-end SKU	$200	300	10	30%	5	$50	20%	$3000	50%

✓For each SKU

- **Total Potential Product Revenue= A*B*C*D*E**
- **Total Potential Product Attach Revenue= B*C*D*F*G**
- **Total Potential Services Attach Revenue= B*C*D*H*I**

✓Run the same analysis for each channel product will flow through (e.g., OEM, retail, resellers) and aggregate results for overall annual potential revenue opportunity

✓Change assumptions as necessary for multi-year projections (e.g., number of resellers or capacity grows or shrinks, increase or decrease in attach sales, price increase or decrease)

- **Attach Product and Services Revenue:** an estimate of additional products or services that will be sold with the base SKU in transactions involving the product

Of course, it's simple to say and a bit more complicated to actually complete. Acquiring the necessary data to perform such an analysis can sometimes be challenging. For example, some channel partners may not provide complete visibility about their actual sales results. As well, partners may not want to share information regarding their true selling capacity and how many deals they actually do in a given time frame. Regardless, with a bit of creativity and diligence, you can either get this information or estimate proxies for the key data points to build out your analysis. The results can be assessed relative to the top-down analysis and any significant gaps or differences can be addressed as necessary.

Once again, I caution—don't get caught up attempting to nail down the revenue opportunity to the last decimal place. Be as accurate as possible, but realize that many of the data points will be best guesses (or aspirations).

The final bottom-up method to estimate potential product revenue focuses on the demand side of the market and takes an end-customer perspective to estimate potential product revenue and opportunity.

End-Customer Based Bottom-Up Opportunity Analysis

This analysis starts with the end-customer. The key is to have good data on customer behavior or expected behavior specifically on product purchase likelihood. To estimate revenue potential you must know the percentage of customers indicating they are likely or highly likely to purchase the product post-launch within a given time frame. Some ways to derive this information are:

- **Primary Research:** Conducting a statistically representative, quantitative survey to the target audience to derive likely purchase intent. Primary research is possibly the best source for this data, although it can be expensive. If this is the chosen path, try to piggy-back purchase intent questions with another research project to minimize cost.
- **Secondary Research:** With luck, there may be secondary research from an analyst or other research firm that answers the right questions and provides the purchase intent information. Issues with this stem from the secondary research not exactly matching the product being launched, not asking just the right questions, or being focused on a differently defined end-customer segment.

- **Historical Data:** It may be possible to estimate purchase penetration using historical or actual purchase patterns or adoption curves of products similar to that being launched or from prior versions shipped.
- **Analogous Data:** If there are substitute or similar products currently or previously in the market the adoption rate curves for those products may be available as a guide. There is also a forecasting model called the Bass Diffusion Model which might be applicable.

Conducting an end-customer analysis follows these general steps:

- Identify how large the target customer segment is in terms of the number of customers (e.g., number of key decision makers) or business entities in the market you are targeting (e.g., Fortune 5000 businesses, seven million small businesses).
- Estimate the customer purchase likelihood percentage.
- Based on the number of customers likely to purchase, estimate how many can be converted into actual purchase.
- Calculate the overall estimated revenue from purchasing customers.

Figure 3-16 illustrates one way to approach revenue estimation via the bottom-up end-customer demand perspective. The primary elements of the analysis include:

- **Market Size and Growth:** The number of customers in the target market segment and the growth rates are quantified and broken down into new (greenfield) customers, those currently using competitive products (competitive installed base), and existing customers with older versions of the product being launched. Obviously if any of these scenarios do not apply simply leave it out.
- **Market Demand Projection:** This is the most critical element for the analysis. What is the inclination of your target market to purchase the product you are launching? Again, the example includes new customer purchase intent percentage, the likelihood that a customer with a competitive product will switch, and the likelihood that existing customers will acquire the new product.
- **Sales Conversion:** Based on the number of customers indicating a high likelihood to purchase or switch, an estimate of how many of those customers will actually purchase is made.
- **Market Price Trend:** Product prices rarely remain static over time. An estimation of price changes and trends must be made.

FIGURE 3-16: Illustrative End-Customer Bottom-Up Market Analysis

A bottom-up market analysis taking an end-customer perspective also facilitates product revenue estimates...

		Year 1	Year 2	Year 3	Year 4	Year 5
Market Size & Growth	**Target Customer Segment Annual Growth Rate**	base	5%	7%	9%	12%
	Total Target Customer Segment Size	1,000,000	1,050,000	1,123,500	1,224,615	1,371,569
	Greenfield Opportunities	940,000	987,000	1,056,090	1,151,138	1,289,275
	Competitive Installed Base	50,000	52,500	56,175	61,231	68,578
	Prior Version Installed Base	10,000	10,500	11,235	12,246	13,716
		Year 1	Year 2	Year 3	Year 4	Year 5
Market Demand Projection	**New Customer: Intention to Purchase %**	15%	20%	30%	40%	50%
	Competitive Customer: Willingness to Switch %	1%	2%	3%	4%	10%
	Existing Customer: Upgrade Rate %	5%	10%	15%	20%	25%
		Year 1	Year 2	Year 3	Year 4	Year 5
Sales Conversion	**New Customer Capture Rate %**	3%	5%	8%	12%	15%
	Competitive Customer: Switcher Capture Rate %	5%	5%	5%	5%	5%
	Existing Customer: Upgrade Capture Rate %	80%	80%	80%	80%	80%
	Services Attach Average Rate %	25%	25%	25%	25%	25%
		Year 1	Year 2	Year 3	Year 4	Year 5
Market Price Trend	**Market Bearable Price: % Change Year-Over-Year**	base	-10%	-8%	-5%	-3%
Product/Service Pricing	**Average Product Revenue per Deal/Unit**	$ 150	$ 135	$ 124	$ 118	$ 114
	Average Services Revenue per Deal/Unit	$ 1,500	$ 1,350	$ 1,242	$ 1,180	$ 1,145
Estimated Product Unit Sales	**New Customer: New Purchase Deals**	4,230	9,870	25,346	55,255	96,696
	Competitive Customer: Switcher Deals	25	53	84	122	343
	Existing Customer: Upgrade Deals	400	840	1,348	1,959	2,743
	Total Product Deals	4,655	10,763	26,779	57,336	99,782
Calculated Service Sales	**Total Services Attach Deals (@25% attach)**	1,164	2,691	6,695	14,334	24,945
		Year 1	Year 2	Year 3	Year 4	Year 5
Revenue Estimates	**Total Product Revenue**	$ 698,250	$1,452,938	$ 3,325,905	$ 6,765,131	$ 11,420,038
	Total Services Revenue	$ 1,745,625	$3,632,344	$ 8,314,762	$ 16,912,827	$ 28,550,094
	Total Annual Revenue	$ 2,443,875	$5,085,281	$ 11,640,667	$ 23,677,957	$ 39,970,131
	Cumulative 5-Year Revenue Generated	$ 82,817,912				

With the above information and pricing available, potential revenue opportunity can be calculated.

Determining the Product Launch Channel Strategy

A product can follow various paths to arrive in the hands of an end-customer. Determining and defining which path(s) to take for the product being launched is another core element of the rollout plan. Channel strategy options can be summarized with the following choices (see Figure 3-17):

- Sell only directly to end-customers using a direct sales force.
- Sell only directly to end-customers via the Internet.
- Sell to end-customers through indirect channels only.
- Sell through some combination of the above options.

The choices are straightforward. As the cliché goes—the product will not sell itself. Your firm itself needs to sell the product, get other companies to sell it, or do both. The best channel options to choose will depend on the specific product and SKUs at hand, the target market segment of interest, and the viability and cost of reaching the right customers through a particular channel.

The go-to-market channel choice will play a major role in determining future marketing launch activities, programs, and investments, whether a direct, indirect, or combination channel approach is chosen. High or low product price points, complex or simple installation requirements, customer requirements for direct manufacturer relationships, and the specific business model employed can all impact the correct channel strategy. You choose the right go-to-market channels for the product by understanding target end-customer purchase preferences. As indicated in Chapter 2, answering the following questions as they relate to the target customer segment can aid in the channel decision:

- How do customers currently purchase similar products already in market?
- What purchase channels do the targeted end-customers most often use and prefer?
- Why do they use these channels? What are the underlying drivers?
- What channels do competitors use? Why? How successful are they with those channels?

FIGURE 3-17: Typical Go-To-Market Channel Options

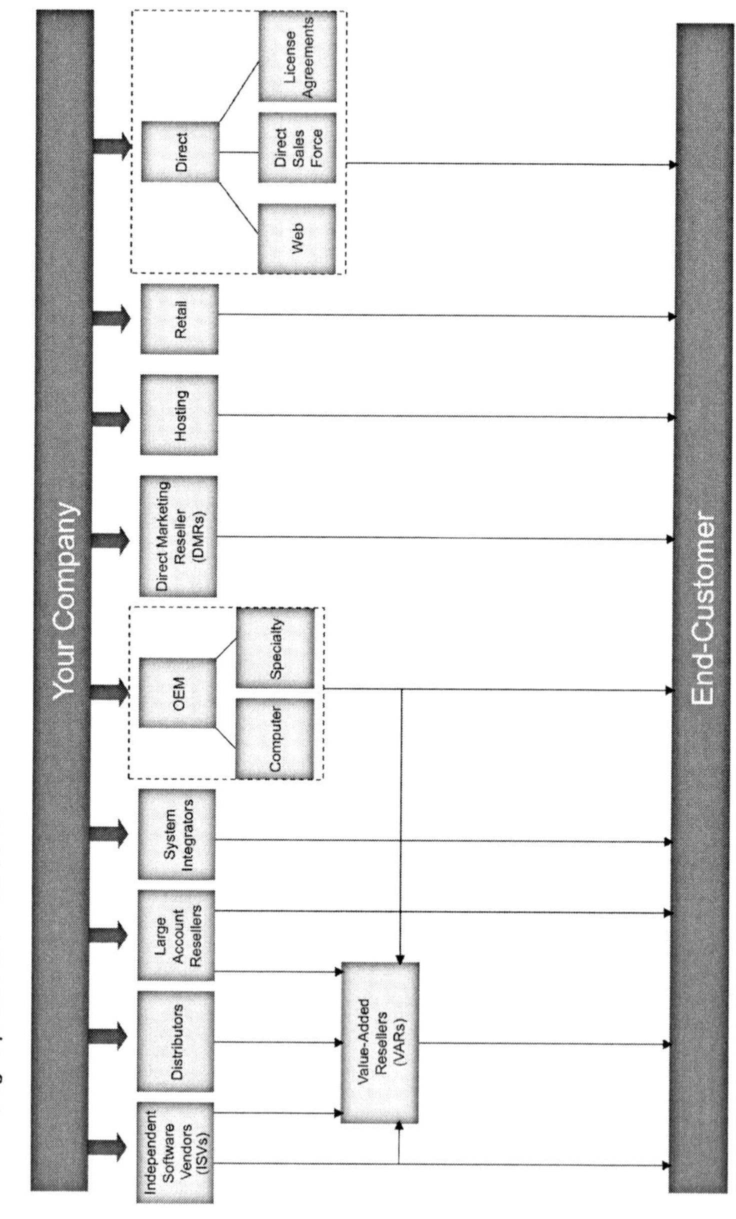

- What is the reach and penetration of a particular channel into the target customer space? What is the channel's share of market in the targeted segments?
- What is the channel growth rate of penetration into the targeted segment?
- What level of priority or focus does a particular channel have on the target segment?

Answers to such questions can help drive the right channel choices. The right choices will naturally align the SKU strategy, channels, and end-customer target segments, as indicated in Figure 3-18.

Given the right data, you can make informed channel selections that permit this alignment. However, there is more to consider. It's great that certain channels have been identified that appear to enable the correct go-to-market strategy, but each possible path to the end-customer may require different types of marketing programs, channel management requirements, or support needs.

Your firm must be able to address these needs with the available resources, both for headcount and budget. A particular desired channel option may carry costs or require resources from your firm that might invalidate the channel as an option. For example, some channels require significant amounts

FIGURE 3-18: SKU, Channel, and Segment Alignment

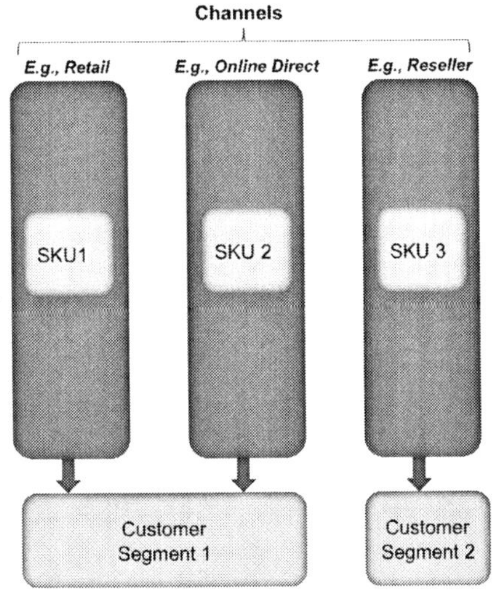

✓SKUs are targeted at a customer segment and are aligned with channels serving that segment

✓SKU packaging and pricing are aligned with customer segment purchase habits, price sensitivities, and channel business model requirements

of money simply to implement basic marketing activities. This means that both the cost of entry and the cost to sustain such a channel relationship could remove that particular channel from the consideration set.

INDIRECT CHANNELS

Figure 3-19 offers another consideration for defining the go-to-market channel strategy. The go-to-market plan should take into consideration whether a depth, breadth, or combination approach is most appropriate given business goals and needs and available resources. Whether one or many different channel types are employed, a breadth strategy focuses on acquiring a large number of channel partners that resell the product. This approach generally requires that some type of programmatic arm's-length channel program be put into place (Chapter 7).

A depth approach involves betting on a smaller number of channel partners from each channel employed, building significant relationships, and focusing most of the sales and marketing time and money aggressively on these channel partners (Chapter 5). A combination approach might also work. Perhaps one channel option has a depth approach employed, while another channel takes a breadth approach.

FIGURE 3-19: Channel Breadth vs. Depth Strategy

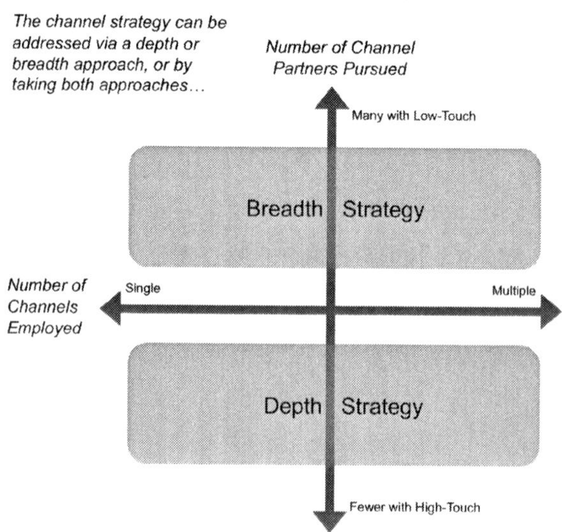

DIRECT CHANNELS

Pursuing an indirect channel model can provide significant opportunities to reach a broad swath of the end-customer targets in a scalable manner. However, if the product or SKUs are not conducive to an indirect model, a direct model can be employed.

Maintaining a direct sales force, or going direct to customers via the Internet, provides both opportunity and challenges. A direct sales force allows the most control over the sales process during a launch. Training can be more easily provided, messaging can be more tightly controlled, and strategies and tactics can be better aligned with an internal sales force—full disclosure and coordination is possible. However, a direct sales force can also be expensive to maintain and scale up. Similar to a service business, a sales force is scaled by adding headcount, which brings direct cost and overhead into a firm. If going direct is the model to pursue, there are only two options to consider:

- Add the product to the quota of the existing sales force leveraging the existing headcount.
- Add headcount to focus on the new product.

Clearly, the benefit of the first option is no additional cost being incurred. On the flip side, the existing sales force must have the selling capacity to take on the product and the skills and knowledge to effectively sell it. There is also the risk that other product sales might suffer if the new product absorbs too much sales time and energy.

The alternative, adding new sales heads, adds increased direct overhead costs. The right number of sales people must be added for this option to work—hiring too few will set the product up for inadequate sales, and hiring too many just increases costs beyond need. One hybrid option that can be implemented to take advantage of both options is a sales overlay approach. In this model, a few new sales heads are added to solely focus on the new product. The existing direct sales force is trained to recognize and canvas for opportunities and leads but does not actually sell the product. When an opportunity is found, the "overlay" sales force is called and works with the customer and account manager on the sale.

The alternative to a direct sales force is, of course, direct sales from the web. Whether this is an option will depend on the product type and price. It's tough to sell bulldozers from a website, but easy to sell trinkets.

MIXING DIRECT AND INDIRECT CHANNELS

Choosing a direct or indirect channel model does not negate the option of also doing both. The primary issue with a mixed channel model is that of channel conflict. This is the situation where the indirect channel considers the direct sales force as taking away business and revenue from their firms. Obviously, this is a bad situation, as at some point the indirect channel will simply stop reselling the product. To avoid channel conflict, there are a number of options to consider:

- Split the SKU mix so that the indirect and direct channels do not sell the same SKUs.
- Focus the direct channel on customer segments that are not the focus of the indirect channel.
- Use the direct channel as a lead generation mechanism for the indirect channel. For example, leads that come in over the web are passed on to the appropriate channel partners to complete the transaction.
- Maintain a direct product price that is always higher than the price through the channel, and be sure that access to a local reseller is readily discoverable on the direct sales website.

Defining the Product Transaction Model

What is the specific business model being pursued? How exactly will a customer be permitted to have the legal right to purchase and use the product? What is the specific transaction model employed?

The rollout plan should be clear on explaining the transaction model planned for the product being launched. The product transaction model will impact the sales process, marketing activities, and even product development. For example, as a purchase condition for a software product, a customer may be required to activate a product on the Internet before use. Or there may be built-in limitations on permitting product usage beyond the original legal purchaser. In either case, you must build features into the product itself to support these transaction requirements, and the requirements must be detailed in sales and marketing collateral and in any product license.

For many products, the purchase transaction may be relatively simple and have no terms, conditions, or restrictions. As products become progressively more complex, the purchase transaction, ownership transfer, and terms of product ownership and usage become progressively more complicated.

Figure 3-20 provides a simple illustration for various industries. There are two ways products or services are generally acquired: either no explicit contract is required or a simple or complex contract is required. For example, when you go to the grocery store, you don't need to sign a purchase contract to buy that loaf of wheat bread and some cheese. There are no terms, conditions, or usage restrictions associated with the purchase. You pay and walk out of the store as owner of the food. However, when you go to the dealer to purchase your new Lexus, a purchase agreement is required containing certain terms and conditions stipulated for that purchase—you don't walk out of the showroom as owner of your car until you sign that agreement. At the upper end of the spectrum are consumer or business high-technology products. For these products, significant contractual purchase agreements may be required, which may include highly complex terms and conditions, and sometimes complicated usage rights.

So depending on what type of product is being launched, significant thought around the purchase transaction model and associated terms and conditions may be required. If the product requires either a simple or complex contract/license for a sale, as likely is the case for most Business-to-Business (B2B) transactions and some Business-to-Consumer (B2C) transactions, the business model and transaction strategy must be fully thought through and aligned with the business objectives of the rollout plan.

A Microsoft example can illustrate this. Generally, transaction strategies are defined with the following in mind:

- The user scenarios the firm *wants* to enable for end-customers.
- The user scenarios that are *demanded by* customers given the way their business functions.
- The *desired* business model being pursued for the product being launched.

Acquiring software from Microsoft, or any large software company for that matter, can be somewhat complicated, and encompasses both B2C and B2B scenarios. In the parlance at Microsoft, and generally in the software industry, purchase terms and conditions are synonymous with the term "licensing." When a product is purchased from Microsoft, a customer is in essence licensing the product to be used and run in certain ways and under certain restrictions. For better or for worse, there are myriad options by which one can license a product from Microsoft, with each option accommodating a different customer or business usage scenario. Figure 3-21 outlines the major licensing mechanisms at Microsoft and the typical distribution mechanisms by which these licenses are sold or executed.

FIGURE 3-20: Purchase Complexity vs. Product Complexity

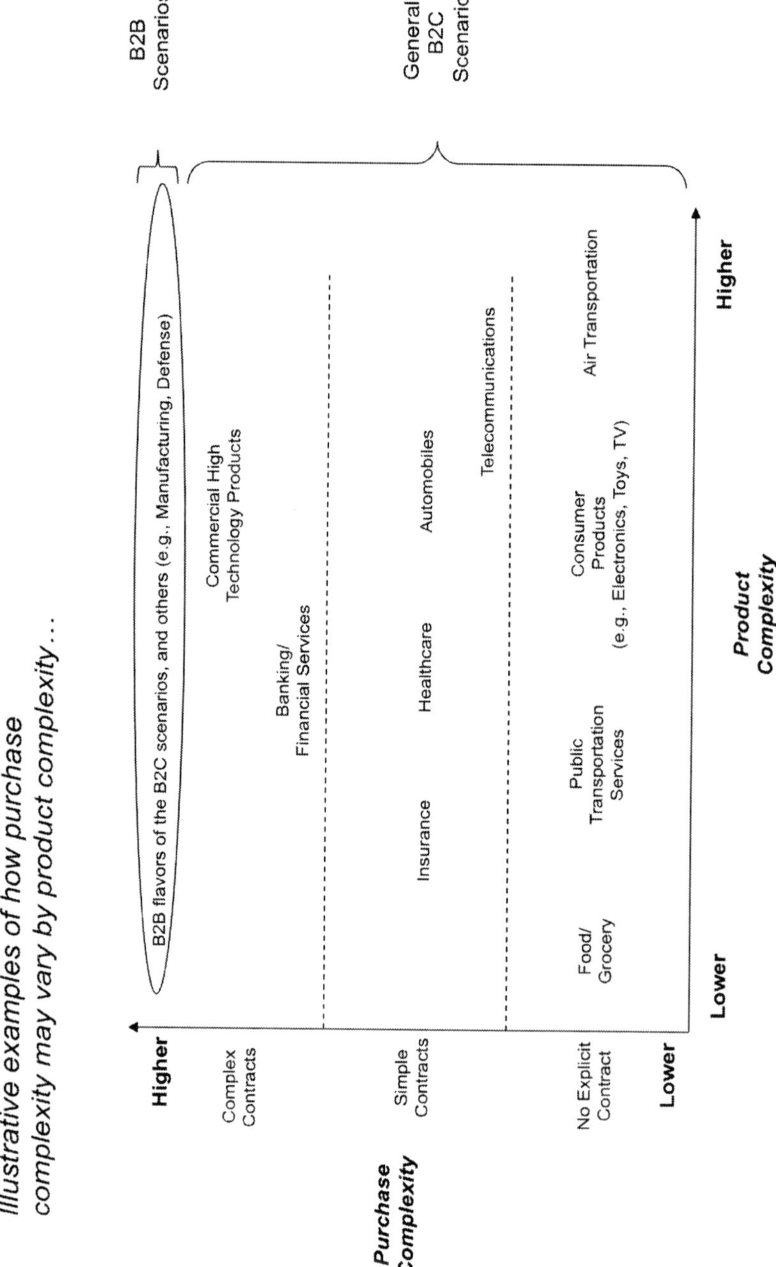

FIGURE 3-21: Illustrative Microsoft Licensing Models

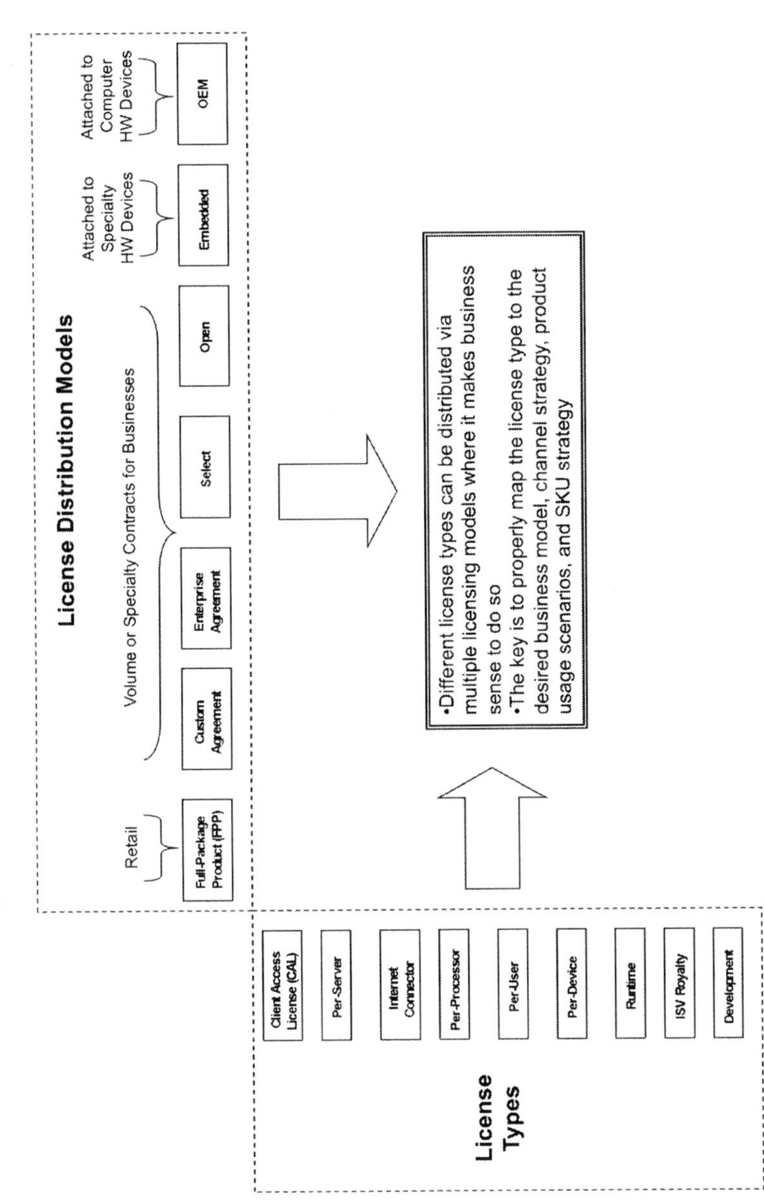

Various Microsoft products can demand or require certain types of licensing models while ignoring others. For example, SQL Server is a database product at Microsoft that takes advantage of a number of the licensing types indicated in Figure 3-21. Why is there a range of license types available for SQL Server? Because licensing type availability is driven primarily by the business or customer usage scenarios required by the customer. Figure 3-22 illustrates example (though not comprehensive) SQL Server usage scenarios and the type of licenses each requires. The core license transaction requirements hinge primarily around whether users are accessing the software from outside of or behind the corporate network firewall. In this example there are three customer usage scenarios accommodated.

- **Per-User Scenario:** This scenario involves users behind the corporate firewall where different users (employees, vendors, contractors, etc.) must access the server with the SQL software and database information. Each of the individual users must have a Per-User Client Access License (CAL) to be authorized to access the SQL software running on the server. As users are added or removed, the number of CALs required can be adjusted by the customer. The server being accessed by the users also must have a license to legitimately install and run the SQL Server software on the server hardware. Requiring both CALs and a server license is typically termed a "Server/CAL" licensing method.

- **Per-Device Scenario:** The Per-Device license type also is useful from within the firewall where corporate devices can be accurately counted. Each device (desktop computer, laptop, handheld device, etc.) that accesses the SQL database must have a license. This is a handy (i.e., less expensive) way to go if the usage scenario in the customer's company is that people share these devices. Maybe one TabletPC is shared by a department or a sales office where multiple sales people share office space and the associated computers. In this case, licensing the smaller number of devices rather than the greater number of users saves money. Again, the customer can manage their costs up or down as they add or remove devices from their company. As in the Per-User scenario, a Server license is needed for the SQL software running on the server hardware being accessed by the devices.

- **Per-Processor Scenario:** Outside the firewall customers may have mobile employees, or their own end-customers, accessing information through the Internet residing on a server that exists behind their firewall. In this usage scenario, it's really impossible to attempt to

FIGURE 3-22: Illustrative Microsoft SQL Server Licensing

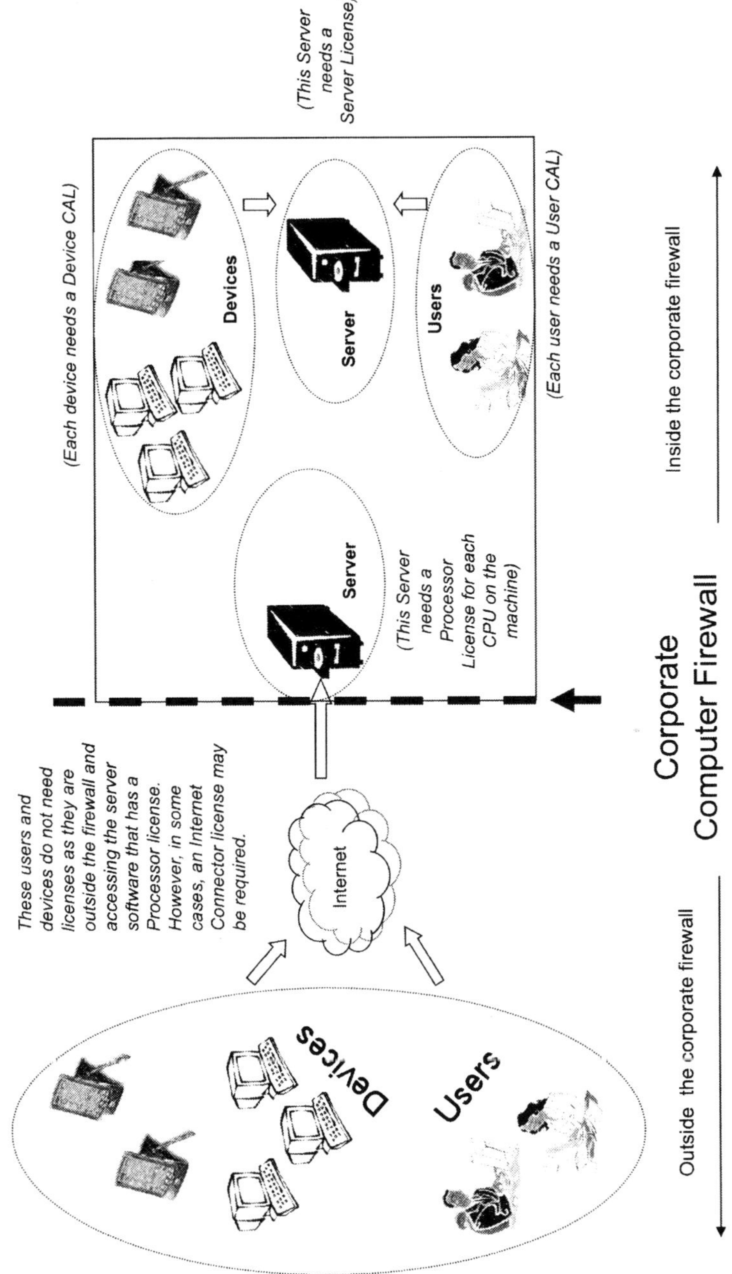

license the number of users or devices coming in from the web because they are generally anonymous users who can't be explicitly identified. To accommodate this usage scenario the license agreement for the SQL software is a Per-Processor license. This means that for each CPU (or microprocessor) installed on the server that is available to the SQL software the customer pays a flat fee (e.g., $5000 per processor). The customer only needs to purchase as many processor licenses that are required to support the processing load placed on the server by the users and devices accessing the server from the Internet. If there are only a small number of accesses coming in through the firewall and they require only simple processing tasks, licensing only one or two processors may suffice. If there are a large number of users requiring computationally intensive activities, more processor licenses may be required to handle the load. An Internet Connector license may also be required in this scenario, but since this is not a Microsoft Licensing 101 course, enough said on that.

Clearly, the methods by which the software is licensed align to the customer's usage scenario and business needs, and are congruent with the Microsoft business model for that type of software.

What is the "firewall" scenario for your business? What kind of customer usage scenarios can your firm enable for your customers as they do business today? What new opportunities can you create for your customers by enabling different scenarios they might not have contemplated? Referring again to Figure 3-20, you can imagine the broad and diverse variation in different industries, products, and associated business models. It would be impossible to go through every potential industry and licensing model—that would take an encyclopedia (and probably not be very interesting, either!). If the product requires a more complex transaction model than buying a loaf of bread, the pre-launch task is to identify the important product usage scenarios, and, while keeping your specific product and target customer segments in mind, think through what is the best transaction model to ensure the model aligns with other pre-launch and post-launch plans. Put the results of this effort into the rollout plan.

Identifying Key Launch Risks

Risks are assumed with any product launch. These risks arise from various factors, both internal and external. The list of possible risks for any given product launch can truly be endless, so it's important to cut through the clutter and really focus in on the key risks that have the broadest potential impact. A risk can be considered a "key risk" if it:

- Can significantly delay or kill the product launch
- Can increase costs beyond acceptable limits (financial costs, organizational costs, resource costs, etc.)
- Can prevent important objectives (operational or strategic) from being met
- Embodies a "single point of failure" dependency

Each of these criteria is fairly self-explanatory; however, the single point of failure dependency deserves a bit more attention. A single point of failure means that the product launch plan or strategy contains an assumption or element that is both unique and required; if it should disappear, the launch fails. One example would be if some highly important product functionality depended on licensed technology from a third-party provider, e.g., if launching a new brand of printer ink cartridges requires licensing a specialized custom ink blend from a sole supplier in India, or if the product is a dictation product requiring a unique speech-recognition engine from a particular speech company. If a poor job was done during the business development deal-making and negotiation (Chapter 5), and the deal falls apart (i.e., you lose the right to use the custom ink blend or the unique speech recognition engine), the launch is hosed. Good advice is that you *don't* put the launch into a situation having a single point of failure—always have a back-up plan (the so-called Plan B) to mitigate critical eventualities. Taking on a single point of failure dependency in a launch is just way too risky.

Other examples of key potential risks to anticipate and plan for during a product launch include:

- Loss of a key executive stakeholder or key technical personnel (loss of executive support and sponsorship can sometimes lead to product cancellation).
- Major engineering challenges (blocking technical issue, overly extended development cycle time frame issues).
- Unanticipated cost issues (product cost issues skyrocket, key supplier raises prices).
- Resource cuts (e.g., incremental expected headcount gets cut, launch budget lowered significantly, or funding dries up).

- Key technology no longer available (e.g., product component supplier goes bankrupt, technology partnership deal with supplier falls apart).
- Competitive threat (unanticipated significant competitor gets to market first with similar product, distribution channels get locked up, competitive pricing response to your product totally undercuts the planned pricing strategy).
- Internal dependencies (technical or business deliverables from another group in your company are not delivered on time or at all).
- Legal or intellectual property issues (risk of being sued for some reason, i.e., antitrust, breach of contract, or patent infringement).

There are likely other possible key risks; some may be specific to your business and the particular product and industry. For example, if a financial accounting tax product is being launched (a software product or a book), it's possible that significant or unanticipated changes in government regulations, tax laws, or IRS rulings could severely impact the product launch should they occur. This unique risk would not be a risk for most products but is an important one for a tax-related product. To identify and mitigate these special risk areas, be aware of the nuances in your industry.

Think ahead and identify the key risks for the launch in advance. Pay special attention to these risks to avoid or mitigate any negative impact to the launch. Make sure the rollout plan includes a section about key risks, the potential impact, and what (if any) workaround or mitigation plans are required.

Accounting for Competitors in the Rollout Plan

Another area that demands focus in the rollout plan is that of competition and the approach to defeat the important competitors. It's important to ensure that key competitors for the product have been clearly identified (with a bull's-eye painted appropriately on their backs) along with the corresponding rationale for why your firm will send them down to flaming defeat! To do so, the rollout plan must clearly identify the key competitors (not every competitor, only those that are truly important), understand the core strategies pursued by these firms in detail, define your firm's corresponding counterstrategy, and identify the specific competitive tactics required to win.

One example of presenting this information is indicated in Figure 3-23. While certainly not the only way to communicate the competitive strategy,

FIGURE 3-23: Competitive Strategy Summary

Summarize the competitive strategy relative to key competitors…

Key competitor(s)	Competitor strategy	How you win vs. competitor	How you lose vs. competitor	Key winning tactics
BigCo	• Dominate IT Professional mindshare • Large direct sales force • Seed product at low-cost, generate revenue on services	• Scale sales reach through broad partner reseller channel • FUD the competition	• If direct customer-to-supplier relationship is key purchase criteria • If switching costs are too high	• Breadth channel program • Reposition competition in customer's mind • Match product pricing and discounts on all competitive deals • Offer low-risk inexpensive departmental pilot programs to gain foothold
MediumCo	• Consultative sales approach: "Business advisor" • Best-of-breed in-person and telephone support services • Customer satisfaction key value proposition	• Low cost strategy: undercut competitive pricing to gain share in segment • Product value-to-price ratio higher than competition. Used as basis for core sales/marketing positioning pitch	• Post-sales support more expensive and fewer services than competition • Partners not skilled in consultative selling	Etc.
VerticalCo	• Depth of specific market knowledge. Vertical is sole focus and they position themselves as industry experts • Broad and varied custom vertical solutions • Tiered pricing structure/ volume discounts	• Develop internal vertical market expertise • Recast generic collateral with vertical market positioning/messaging • Push standard platform advantages over custom solutions	Etc.	Etc.
SpecialtyCo	• Focus solely on platform layer of solution • Best-of-breed technology • Nimbleness and ability to customize deals	Etc.	Etc.	Etc.

the grid succinctly indicates the key competitive information required for a product rollout plan. The example summarizes who the key competitors are, what their core strategies are, how your firm will win against those strategies, and the important tactics that will be deployed. It is worthwhile to consider not just how your firm will win in the market, but also how it might lose. Nothing provides clarity like understanding your own weaknesses and formulating a strategy to overcome them.

When evaluating possible competitive threats within your particular industry, it is important to consider not only those that are clearly existing direct competitors, but also those firms in the industry that are not in the game today but easily could be at some future point. For most product categories, an identifiable list of likely potential competitors can be defined and the threats evaluated. Mergers, acquisitions, and stealthy product development can turn a seemingly non-threatening firm into a viable competitor overnight.

It is always wise to broaden the perspective regarding where potential competitors may originate (Figure 3-24). It is not always the case that new competitors arise from within the market as currently defined. Sometimes competitors can emerge from markets that are adjacent and related to

FIGURE 3-24: Potential Competition Outside the Defined Market

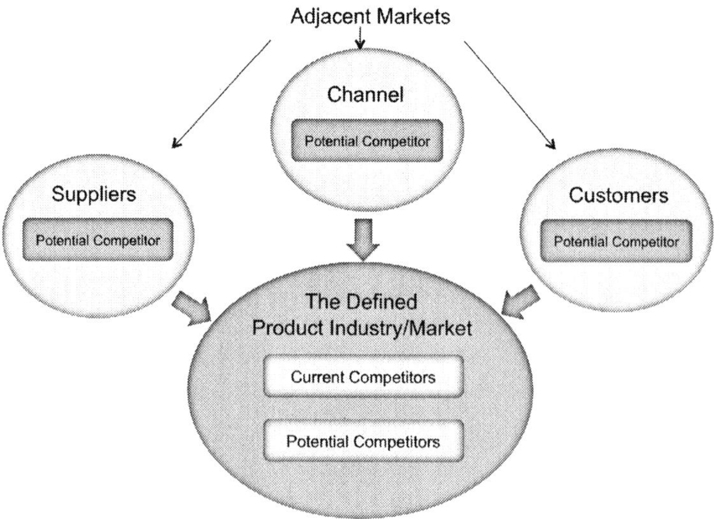

the defined market for the product. Channel partners, suppliers, and even customers in these adjacent markets can turn from being friendly associations to competition. It is worth doing a bit of strategic game playing to assess from which of these adjacent markets and associated organization types a competitor might emerge and under what conditions this might happen. Include the important potential competitors in the rollout plan with the associated probability of occurrence and the appropriate blunting competitive strategy identified.

Finally, any existing competitive offerings should be well understood to formulate a cohesive competitive strategy. In-depth knowledge of the competitive products' strengths, weaknesses, and pricing should be available. A cursory understanding of the competitive products may not be enough to permit the development of a successful sales and marketing effort. And the level of competitive insight should extend beyond the product itself, down to the definition and cost of the overall offering provided by a competitor relative to your own offerings.

Figure 3-25 provides a software industry example of this level of knowledge. In the software industry, the offering is known as a "solution," and together the components required for a complete solution are called a "Solution Stack." In the example, the solution stack is referred to generically

FIGURE 3-25: Illustrative Offer Stack

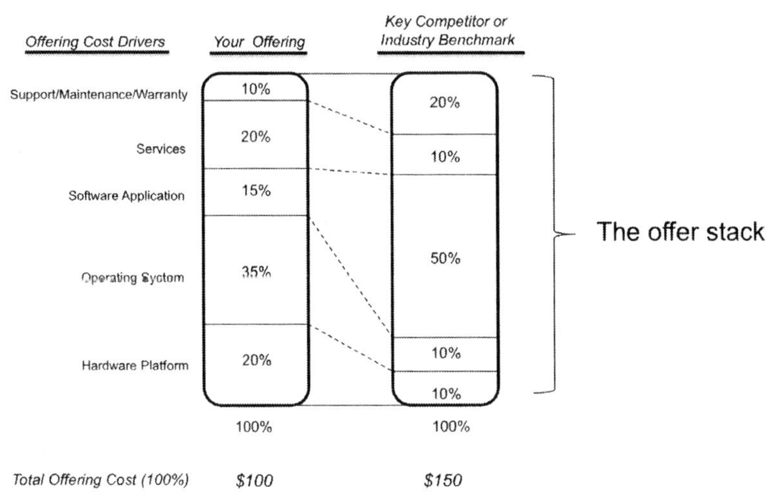

as the "Offer Stack." Understanding the competitive offering costs to this level helps highlight where your firm may either have an advantage or be at a disadvantage. It will illuminate exactly how competitive your firm's offering is relative to the competition from a cost perspective, and where you may need more focus to become competitive.

Support Strategy

The final element of the rollout plan to define is the post-launch support strategy. How exactly will the product be supported once in market? What will the support model and costs be, how will support be provided, and by whom?

Answering these questions and formulating a well-defined product support strategy, before the product hits the market, is a necessary undertaking and should be documented in the rollout plan. Chapter 8 includes more detail on involving support staff in pre-launch rollout activities, and provides an illustrative model for defining product support offerings.

4

Positioning Your Product for Launch

"What we've got here is a failure to communicate."

Cool Hand Luke (1967)

This famous movie line points out that even in a contained environment like a prison communication can break down, be misconstrued, or simply be ineffective. Imagine how communication clarity might become problematic when, in an unconstrained environment (the business market), communications are sent to many at the same time in anonymous manners (advertising, direct mail, PR, etc.)!

The potential for lack of clarity in business and marketing communication, with the associated negative ramifications, underscores the need to get your communication points right from the beginning, as you move your product toward launch, before you begin any large-scale customer communication activities.

Assuming you have done your homework, you should have a solid understanding of your customer targets and segments, including who the product will be designed for and who will be buying it, who influences and decides the purchase, and what their key pain points are. Through your research and interactions with customers, partners, and competitors, you will also likely have some understanding of the key value propositions, features, and benefits that are attractive to customers. Some of this information was discussed in Chapter 2. This chapter assumes that level of customer knowledge is available.

Given this, you need to determine exactly what you will be saying to these potential customers about your product, to whom you will say it, why the customer will care about what you are communicating, and what you want to say about your product relative to the competition. The What, Whom (to customer and against competition), and Why should be completely defined by your positioning messages if you want to be effective in your marketing communications. If you only take away one actionable concept from this book, the positioning and messaging concepts and tools in this chapter will provide you with immediate and tangible value.

PRODUCT POSITIONING DEFINED

Simply stated, product positioning defines the important and differentiated attributes about your product to be communicated to a particular target audience, which places your product and its attributes into context relative to customer needs and to competitive alternatives. The intent is that the customer will understand, internalize, and act upon your positioning in the way you desire. From a business perspective, you typically want positioning to assist in driving product awareness, help to place a product into the consideration set for evaluation and trial, and eventually purchase. Positioning may need to differ somewhat across different target audiences or segments, as each may have different underlying needs or disparate value propositions might appeal to a particular customer group. However, your core product positioning, once developed and finalized, should be viewed as long-term and long-lived, and be relatively stable over time. Any evolution of your positioning, unless there are significant changes to the product or company, should be incremental over a longer time horizon, as opposed to frequent, radical changes over short time periods.

Defining product positioning is a primary product marketing activity and will (and most definitely should) affect and flow into just about every other marketing and launch activity. For clarity, it should be understood that positioning is not the same as messaging or branding. Positioning defines the general and core value propositions you intend to communicate; messaging is the incarnation of that positioning via your communication mechanisms. For example, your positioning statements will flow into and guide clear and on-point messages distributed via your marketing collateral, sales tools, demos, press releases, presentations, website, signage, advertisements, direct mail, videos, and any other out-bound customer, partner, or press communication vehicle you might use, whether written or verbal. Branding, which incorporates and conveys the accumulated experiences and associations a customer has with your product, is not positioning. Excellent branding essentially reflects an excellent execution of your positioning value points.

THE IMPACT OF POOR POSITIONING

Because how you define your positioning essentially affects all communications and launch activities you will pursue while driving the product to a successful launch, it is extremely important to get it right. To understand why, here are some examples of issues (in no particular order—they are all death blows) that will occur if you don't clearly define your positioning, are inconsistent, or just plain get it wrong:

- **You Will Fail to Successfully Engage Your Potential Customers:** If you deliver the wrong message to your customer, or deliver it in a way that doesn't ring true to them, the odds they will act on your message are about nil. That doesn't sound like something you want to happen for a successful launch. Good positioning helps focus communications to the customers using the right and relevant value points, where the focus should be.
- **You and Your Company Lose Credibility:** If you are inconsistent with the messages you are delivering, or you are not presenting well-defined and credible positioning value propositions, you will not be taken seriously and could be perceived as not credible. This is true not only for end-customer perceptions, but also those of press, analysts, and partners. Why should an editor or industry analyst believe you if you are constantly changing your story? Why would a potential partner want to do business with you—do you really understand your customer, the market, and your product's place in that market relative to competition? What do you think the impact of negative credibility will be for your launch?
- **Your Marketing Collateral Is Totally Random and Not Cohesive:** I love to show my clients their competitors' marketing collateral to point out the differing claims and statements made in different collateral pieces and how desperate that seems to make them. Of course, customers will see these inconsistencies as well, which will likely plant seeds of doubt about the competitors' product, as it should. Without consistent positioning points that all your marketing communications materials support and reinforce, your communication points will be random and disjointed.

- **No One Is on the Same Page Internally:** Isn't it great when no one or no group within your organization has a common understanding of your key messages or product value propositions, and everyone has their own pet version of what "really" should be communicated? This situation definitely helps cross-group communication and collaboration, especially if everyone has a different version of what should be communicated. Of course I'm being sarcastic—that situation is the last thing you want during a product launch. To the contrary, agreeing internally about your key messages and positioning statements facilitates working together toward common goals, a common understanding of the customer and market, your product's place in the market, and a constant and consistent reinforcement of these messages and value points externally. Creating agreement internally around positioning forces explicit trade-offs between what your product is, and is not, which is a good thing.

Obviously, you would not want any of the above to occur, since there is typically plenty of work to focus on when driving to launch. So let's discuss what should be done regarding product positioning, and a process for doing it.

POSITIONING ILLUSTRATED

You can perhaps best understand how to successfully position a product by first understanding the context regarding product positioning relative to positioning the business overall, customer needs, and competition. To illustrate, it is necessary to understand there are multiple levels of positioning across a business, and to know how one incorporates customer needs and the competitive product landscape to form the basis for developing successful product positioning.

Positioning Occurs at Multiple Levels in a Business

Positioning is typically required and defined for multiple different levels within a firm and its assets. Positioning the company overall, product segments or product lines within an organization, and a specific product are the primary positioning needs for a company. In the optimal case, as it should be by design, each level of positioning from corporate down to product should be supportive and interlinked. A common mistake when attempting positioning is creating a disconnect between the company positioning and the product positioning, a mistake that undermines the positioning credibility at both levels. Microsoft does a pretty good job attempting to line up the corporate positioning with the core product line brands it sells.

Figure 4-1 outlines the three-tier positioning levels concept from a Microsoft perspective. At the corporate level, Microsoft has evolved its positioning over time with various iterations. Currently, the company positions itself as follows: *"At Microsoft, our mission and values are to help businesses and individuals throughout the world realize their full potential"* (source: Microsoft public website). This is reflected in the current tagline: *"Your Potential, Our Passion."*

Moving down a level to product line brands and positioning, a number of brands at Microsoft require positioning, e.g., the Office system brand. For the Office brand, Microsoft positions the 2007 Microsoft Office system product line and brand as: *"Get ready to save time, organize your workload, manage information, stay connected, and collaborate better with colleagues, family, and friends"* (source: Microsoft public website). The positioning for the Office brand at the product line level supports (albeit somewhat loosely) the corporate positioning of realizing potential through saving time, being more organized, and better collaboration.

As you move down to the product level, the connection to the corporate brand from a positioning perspective becomes somewhat weaker. This is a natural consequence in the difference between positioning a broad corporate brand as an image and positioning specific product features, benefits, and attributes. It is possible to imagine a link between the Microsoft corporate

FIGURE 4-1: Various Levels of Positioning

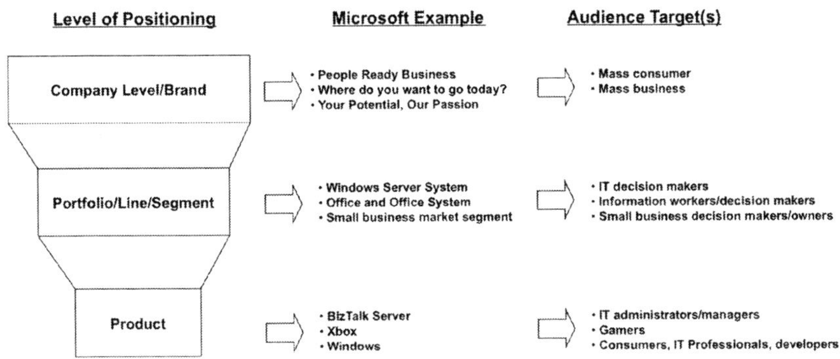

passion and potential positioning and that of the product positioning for the Xbox video game system and gamer audience, but it would likely be a stretch to completely connect the two.

To provide more context to the various ways firms such as Microsoft convey positioning, and to set the stage to get into the details of product positioning, let's look at corporate positioning from other firms in various industries. Positioning the overall company is generally one of the most visible types of positioning, especially when reaching out broadly to the business or consumer audience. This level of positioning is typically associated with positioning the corporate brand image. This corporate "umbrella" positioning should flow down and be reflected in, or at least not contradict, the product positioning. Some examples to illustrate this level of corporate positioning follow.

McKesson Corporation: A U.S.-based healthcare distribution firm dealing with health care systems, medical, and pharmaceutical supplies, McKesson positions itself as follows:

> "McKesson's vision is to help create a healthcare system where quality is higher, mistakes are fewer and costs are lower. By combining its industry-leading technology and scale with unsurpassed clinical knowledge, McKesson is helping healthcare providers deliver better, safer care while reducing unnecessary costs." (source: McKesson public website)

It is clear that using technology and clinical knowledge to make healthcare safer and less expensive is the ground McKesson is staking out to position their company in the healthcare industry.

Cardinal Health, Inc.: Another example from the U.S. healthcare industry provides a different and contrasting approach from McKesson. Cardinal Health positions itself as follows:

> "Focused on the high-growth healthcare market, Cardinal Health has built the industry's broadest suite of products and services that help improve quality, safety and efficiency all along the chain of care. With our unparalleled resources, expertise and proprietary offerings, we deliver integrated solutions that are innovative and practical. To our customers, this means we help them focus on what matters most—improving people's lives." (source: Cardinal Health public website)

While Cardinal Health also includes "expertise" in the positioning, as does McKesson, they clearly pivot more around the breadth of product and service offerings, the depth of their resources, and innovation and practicality as how they wish to be perceived in the marketplace. McKesson takes the positioning high ground around their expertise being "unsurpassed," while Cardinal Health takes the high ground around the "broadest suite of products and services."

Caterpillar, Inc.: A well-known brand and firm in the construction equipment market, Caterpillar positions the firm as follows:

> "In partnership with our worldwide dealer network, we drive positive and sustainable change on every continent. We are the world's leading manufacturer of construction and mining equipment, diesel and natural gas engines and industrial gas turbines." (source: Caterpillar public website)

In this case, technology, expertise, and broad product lines don't play a role in the corporate positioning. Caterpillar positions itself more around the global scope of their dealer, or reseller network, and the claim to be the market leader. They also take on a social responsibility bent in their positioning around driving "positive and sustainable change," as one might imagine that bulldozing trees and creating vast holes in the ground might be objectionable to those with a green or environmentally sensitive attitude.

Intel: One of the leading global hardware and microprocessor manufacturers, Intel has achieved a great deal of brand awareness, primarily from the branding effort they instigated around the "Intel Inside" program logo pasted on just about every personal computer in the world. The issue Intel constantly faced was that their product, while core to the functionality of a computer, was but one component buried inside the machine with little or no visibility on the outside from a branding perspective. The "Intel Inside" campaign changed that forever. Given that the logo created awareness for the company, what did that awareness convey to the consumer? In other words, how does Intel position itself so that the attributes of the "Intel Inside" brand logo convey the meaning they desire to an end-user? Intel currently positions itself as follows:

> "At Intel, we constantly push the boundaries of innovation in order to make people's lives more exciting, more fulfilling, and easier to manage. Our unwavering commitment to moving technology forward has transformed the world by leaps and bounds. We're a

> company that's always in motion, fueling an industry that never rests. We inspire our partners to develop innovative products and services, rally the industry to support new products, and drive industry standards. We do this so that we can collectively deliver better solutions with greater benefits more quickly." (source: Intel public website)

You can see that Intel positions itself quite differently from the other examples, pivoting on innovation and moving technology forward as key corporate attributes. They put a more emotional and personal approach to the corporate positioning, i.e., making people's lives more exciting and fulfilling. They "inspire" partners, and they not only participate in their industry, they "fuel" it. These are the positioning points Intel would like their brand associated with. In fact, the tagline currently in use at the corporate level is "Intel: Leap ahead," which summarizes and directly maps back to the concept of innovating and moving technology forward.

From these few examples it is clear that there are numerous potential attributes and approaches a company might take to position the overall firm. Innovation, leadership, partners, expertise, resources, and product line breadth are all reflected above as disparate examples of the potential attributes one might pursue to position a business.

The range of potential attributes to position a product is no less diverse. Let's look at using product positioning to assist in a successful product launch and cut through the clutter of positioning attributes to get the correct attributes for your product.

Product Positioning Relative to Customer Needs and Competition

So how does one cut through the clutter? How do you know which are the correct positioning attributes to choose for your product?

The most important first step is to realize that when positioning a product both customer needs and the competition must be considered and included as the beginning reference points. Customer needs and competition form the basis for successful product positioning, and, through careful evaluation, can provide the answers and input necessary to discover the correct positioning attributes and successfully position your product for both the launch and post-launch time frame.

Figure 4-2 illustrates this point. The first example involves toothpaste, a

FIGURE 4-2: Product Positioning Relative to Segment Needs and Competition

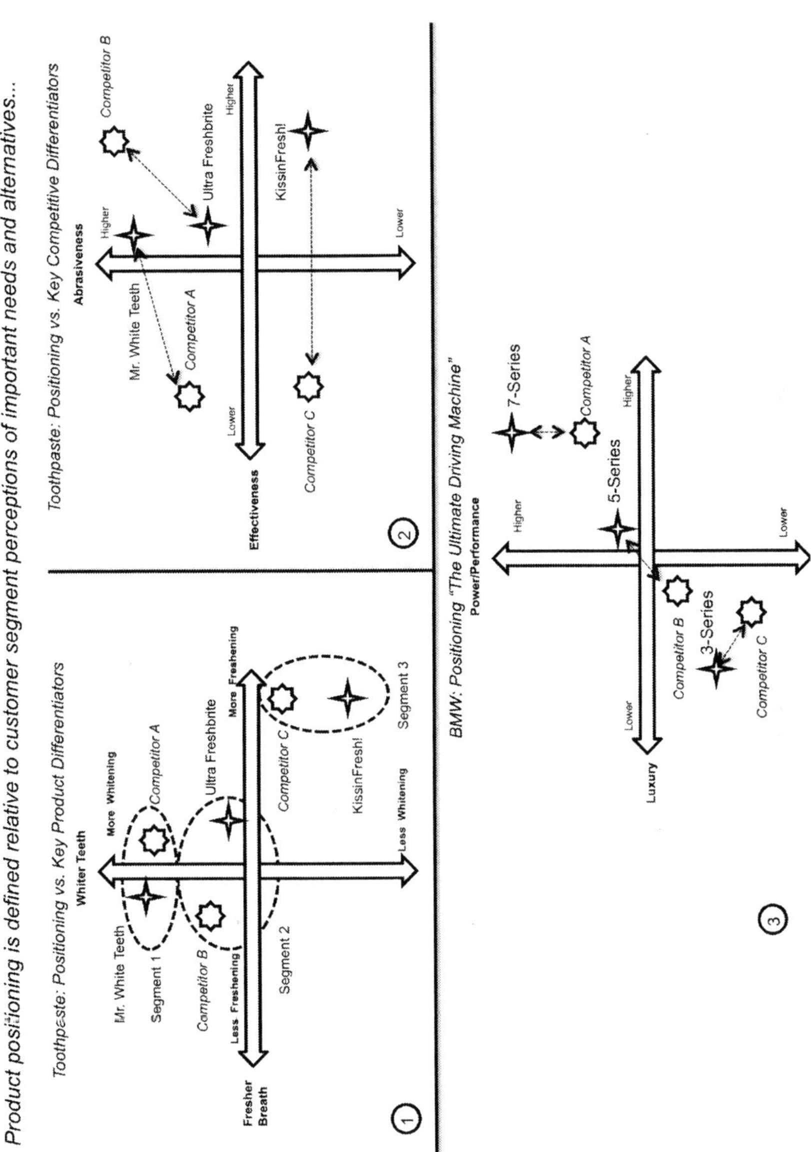

product most people are familiar with. The figure shows what are referred to as perceptual maps. These maps indicate various different product offerings or SKUs from one toothpaste manufacturer and positions these products relative to certain key attributes that market values in toothpaste, and also relative to the competition. In Area 1 the attributes are how fresh the toothpaste makes your breath ("Fresher Breath" on the X-axis) and how white the toothpaste makes your teeth ("Whiter Teeth" on the Y-axis). It is important to note that these attributes were not simply made up by the company developing this perceptual map. These attributes were discovered via customer research, testing, and validation as being important to consumers and that could differentiate the individual products from themselves and potentially from the competition.

There are three toothpaste products (not real products) on this perceptual map: Mr. WhiteTeeth, Ultra Freshbrite, and KissinFresh! The perceptual map indicates that research had identified three customer segments—those that primarily valued whiter teeth as their most important need (Segment 1), those that felt that fresh breath and whiter teeth were of equal importance (Segment 2), and those that only really valued fresher breath as most important to them in a toothpaste (Segment 3). Each of the products is positioned relative to, or against, the key attributes indicated as important for those customer segments—thus Mr. WhiteTeeth is both named for and positioned to Customer Segment 1 that values white teeth the most. Ultra Freshbrite goes after the combination white teeth and fresh breath crowd in Segment 2, and KissinFresh! goes after the fresh breath only crowd in Segment 3. It is also important to note that the attributes of fresher breath and whiter teeth are attributes that the customer indicated would clearly differentiate a product from another, or a SKU from another. However, this does not mean that these are the most appropriate attributes to position against from a competitive perspective.

To illustrate that point, note that competitors A, B, and C are also indicated on the Area 1 graphic in Figure 4-2. Each of these competitive products lines up against one of the toothpaste SKUs. In fact, you can see on the perceptual map that Competitor A is perceived as having the same level of whitening power as Mr. WhiteTeeth. Competitor B has slightly more whitening power than Ultra Freshbrite but is perceived to have a bit less freshening power. Competitor C has about the same amount of freshening power as KissinFresh! but is perceived to be more whitening.

In each case trying to use these attributes to position and differentiate from the competition would not be logical: there is not enough perceived differentiation between the toothpaste SKUs and their competition around freshening and whitening power. These would then be considered the basic attributes required by customers simply to be considered by the particular customer segment.

To provide clearly differentiating positioning, one would need to look at other important attributes that customers indicated are important when purchasing toothpaste. Area 2 of Figure 4-2 indicates two additional important attributes: abrasiveness and effectiveness. Creating a perceptual map around these attributes paints a different story—although Mr. WhiteTeeth is perceived as being more abrasive, it is also perceived as much more effective at whitening teeth. On the other hand, while Ultra Freshbrite isn't perceived as being quite as effective as its competition, it is perceived as being much less abrasive. Finally, KissinFresh! and its competition are both perceived as about the same in abrasiveness, but KissinFresh! is off the charts in terms of freshening effectiveness compared to the competition.

With this knowledge, truly differentiating positioning can be created. Taking the above examples, one could conceivably create positioning for each toothpaste SKU:

- Mr. WhiteTeeth: "The most effective super-whitening toothpaste"
- Ultra Freshbrite: "The optimal mix of whitening and freshening power, with the least abrasive damage to your teeth"
- KissinFresh!: "The most effective, super breath freshening toothpaste"

Note that these are potential positioning points, not necessarily marketing or sales copy. These positioning statements would then need to be converted into the appropriate verbiage for use in various marketing communications.

In an optimal situation, you would have this perceptual map created before developing a product, and actually design the products specifically for the segments to deliver against the value the customer desires. In a more likely and common scenario, these segment differences are generally discovered and become apparent after a product has been in market for awhile and the level of customer knowledge accumulates. It is possible to develop a product specific to a segment key value proposition, and to take a single product and reposition it against multiple segments as long as the product delivers the stated value. In this example, one could imagine there is truly only one product here—a generic tube of pasty toothpaste—that actually does both freshen your breath and whiten your teeth. A company could take this product, create three SKUs with different names, package them differently, and position these three SKUs along the lines of our example perceptual map.

The final example in Figure 4-2 is that of a real world corporation, BMW Group. At one point, the company positioned itself as producing the "Ultimate Driving Machine," a pretty lofty positioning to stake out. I've provided a quick overview of the BMW product series positioning in Area 3. In general, BMW chooses to position and differentiate along the attributes of power/performance and luxury. Each of its product lines fall into some variant of these attributes. All of the series, 3, 5, and 7, are positioned as luxury vehicles, which differentiates them from non-luxury vehicles to begin with. Within the luxury vehicle market, BMW differentiates their products against the power/performance attributes. So while the competition for each of their product lines may be in the ballpark of the BMW products when it comes to perceived luxury (some are near the same, some slightly more, some slightly less), BMW always stakes out the high ground around the power/performance attribute as a way to differentiate from the competition. They support this claim using German engineering excellence and road test data as proof points. It is clear that the positioning taken by BMW drives product development and the various product features.

Regardless of the approach taken (positioning drives product development, or product features/benefits drive positioning), the key point is that the product or SKU must be positioned against the important and differentiated customer needs for a particular customer segment. Also, be aware that positioning is a promise to the product consumers—the product actually needs to deliver on the promise with product features, benefits, and value. Positioning a product in a manner that the product value does not deliver on is a sure way to quickly kill product sales. If BMW positioned their products as higher power/performing vehicles and they drove like slugs, sales would plummet.

Perception Is Reality

It is important to note that Figure 4-2 indicates the *perception* customers have about these products relative to one another and relative to the key positioning attributes. It is very possible that the *reality* of the product features may not 100% accurately map to the perception. For example, while Mr. WhiteTeeth is perceived as having a bit more whitening power than Competitor A, the reality may be that Competitor A actually has more whitening power from a scientifically tested functionality perspective, but they have not been effective in positioning and communicating this fact to the target customer segment. This hits on a universal truth that permeates many aspects of our lives: Perception is Reality. Creating the desired perception for your target audience is a key outcome of good positioning work and creates the reality you desire as perceived by the target customers.

So how do you know when your positioning is good enough to create the desired perceptions, and how do you create this positioning? The positioning methodology used at Microsoft provides a good example for approaching product positioning and laying out some key positioning criteria that can be applied to ensure you have achieved good positioning.

POSITIONING THE MICROSOFT WAY

To understand how product positioning is done at Microsoft, it is important to understand the core tenets for developing positioning and to review a tool called a "Positioning Framework," which provides a structured format for product positioning development.

Core Tenets for Positioning

There are several tests, or checks, for proper positioning you should always have in mind. I state these in the form of questions below; you should ask them during your positioning development process until the answers are all "Yes." Then you'll have the basis for solid product positioning to take forward.

- **Accuracy:** Are your positioning points accurate as they relate to the product? Are they accurate as they relate to customer needs?
- **Credibility:** Are your positioning points credible to your customers? Partners? Press and analysts?
- **Defensibility:** Can you justify what you are saying with clear evidence?
- **Sustainability:** Can your positioning points hold up reasonably well over time even as the product, market, and competition evolve?
- **Flexibility:** Are they flexible enough to be refined over time, but strong enough to remain solid at the core? Can you use the positioning points in various forms for different target audiences as necessary?
- **Consistency and Repeatability:** Can your key positioning points be delivered consistently though a broad variety of delivery mechanisms?

Do you have a small enough set of core positioning points that you can repeat ad nauseam to pound them into your customers' minds in a consistent fashion?

- **Differentiability:** Does the product positioning clearly convey the key differences, advantages, and uniqueness of your product value propositions vs. competitive offerings?
- **"Needability":** Yes, I made this word up to connote the following questions: Are your positioning points designed explicitly for the target audience and based upon real customer needs? Does your positioning tell the customer why they should care about your product and how what you're saying relates to, or solves, a business problem or need that they have?

Some of these checks are clearly subjective in nature, and some can be quantitatively tested. Whether it's qualitative or quantitative, getting positioning feedback from your customers using these checkpoints as input guidelines is strongly recommended. This feedback will provide key insights into the underlying true needs of your target customer segments that can be leveraged in your positioning development work.

Customers Are People, Not Segment Clusters

In Chapter 2, customer segments were discussed from a somewhat academic perspective. However, that is only part of the complete perspective required to understand your customers and leverage this understanding via product positioning.

Many product marketers make the mistake of establishing a mental barrier between themselves and customers, in effect losing touch with the customer reality. One reason is that many product marketers spend a lot of their time reading research reports, looking at web content, preparing presentations, and doing planning work, and not talking directly with customers. Lack of regular customer contact and interaction, or over-reliance on research, can lead to myopic thinking of customer segments as paper descriptions of customers instead of the real, live people who are truly your customers.

This can be a problem in many ways, but it's a big problem when positioning is being developed. Why? Because an arm's-length academic approach to knowing and understanding your customer blinds the product manager to the underlying customer "Need Drivers." Need drivers are the base reasons that motivate a customer to be sympathetic to your positioning points and relate them to specific needs they have (in "marketingese," mapping their needs to your product value propositions). Need drivers are also the foundation upon which you develop your positioning framework. Product positioning should always be developed from the customer perspective and based on customer need drivers.

Customer need drivers come in two flavors: personal and business. Many (if not all) purchasing motivations at some point get down to the personal need driver, although it is usually not the explicit purchase motivation.

Here are some examples of what I mean by personal and business need drivers:

- Personal Need Drivers:
    - I want to be successful in my job.
    - I want to make more money.
    - I want to look good to my boss.
    - My job is in jeopardy and I want to keep it.
    - I need to keep within budget or I'm fired.
    - I need to meet my job performance objectives and metrics.
- Business Need Drivers:
    - I need to reduce costs.
    - I need to stay within budget.
    - My department needs to be more efficient and productive.
    - I need to communicate better.
    - I need my customer support department to be more responsive.
    - I need to network my computers together.

You can typically uncover the business need drivers through customer research or customer interviews, sales force feedback, partner input, or other mechanisms. The key point is that these business need drivers are always riding on top of a personal need driver. In other words, when a customer makes a purchase decision for your product, the explicit business need driver may be to "reduce costs in my organization," but the underlying implicit personal need driver may really be "If my departmental costs keep rising, I won't meet my objectives and I'll get the boot." By meeting the explicit business needs for the customer you are meeting their underlying personal needs. You need to dig deep to understand the personal need drivers to maximize the efficacy of your positioning and messaging.

Personal need drivers hit on another important aspect of positioning—the emotional aspect. This adds positioning complexity, but also opportunity, beyond the functional product value of features and benefits and the economic business value of cost savings or cost of ownership. When a customer makes a decision to purchase a product, they are personally putting themselves on the line in a variety of ways, especially if the purchase was particularly visible, expensive, or strategic. "Did I purchase the correct product and will this make me look good to my peers? Will I be proud and happy about my decision? Will my co-workers feel this was the right call? Can this product help me advance my career?" These are emotionally significant issues that become real during the purchase process. They relate to how the customer "feels" about their purchase and what impact the purchase will have on their personal need drivers, such as being successful in their job and looking good to their colleagues and superiors.

If you can discover what the key personal needs are for your target customer segments, decision makers, and influencers, and leverage any emotional attachments around these personal needs, you can be more effective in conveying the product value propositions and creating the desired perceptions you want to communicate through your positioning.

A good example for understanding the link between personal and business need drivers in the real world uses IT Professionals—the computer guys who run the datacenter, rollout software and hardware products, and support your department's desktop computer needs. In many cases, the success of an IT Professional is tied to the customer satisfaction of their internal customers—the people in the other business units that they support. IT Professionals get rewarded if their customers deliver a high satisfaction rating for them, and low/no reward if they receive low satisfaction ratings.

If you hadn't noticed, most non-technical people in an organization don't give IT a second thought unless there is a computer problem. This puts the IT Professional in a difficult position—their customers are only happy when they don't have computer problems, and when problems occur they are expected to be solved immediately (at the expense of everything else the IT department is working on). So if there are no problems, no one thinks about or interacts with IT and thus can't really provide a high satisfaction rating for them. When problems occur, it is always IT's fault; thus, they are screwing up and doing a bad job and deserve a low satisfaction rating. In this example, one business need driver for IT Pros is to "minimize or eliminate system down-time." The personal need driver is "If the system goes down, my internal customers are going to rate me low, and I'm not getting a good raise." Understanding this link can help elevate "minimizing down-time" as a priority value proposition and benefit that you convey to your customer via your positioning.

Discovering Optimal Positioning Attributes and Communicating Via the Positioning Framework

The core tool used at Microsoft to define positioning points is the "Positioning Framework." The positioning framework is a key document you must produce to organize, state, and defend your product positioning and value propositions. What you write in this document should make its way into PR activities/releases/interviews, your collateral, presentations, strategy, web content, demos, and just about any other place where you are communicating to internal and external audiences the key messages you want them to hear and internalize (and hopefully act upon). It provides a focal-point document to assist in organizing the information and to use across groups in your company to provide input, corrections, additions, and deletions and to bring everyone onto the same page on how the product will be positioned and messaged to external audiences.

The end goal of the positioning framework is to bring the optimal positioning attributes for your product to the forefront and present them in a consumable manner. Optimal positioning attributes can be viewed as the intersection of the most important unmet customer needs and your product's differentiating attributes and strengths. These optimal positioning attributes also explicitly remove any non-differentiating product attributes or strengths from your positioning as irrelevant to your communications. When attempting to divine your optimal positioning attributes, keep these questions in mind when assessing an attribute from a customer's perspective (usually done via a structured research mechanism like qualitative or quantitative research):

- Is the positioning attribute an unmet customer need?
- Is the positioning attribute important to the customer relative to other attributes?
- Is the positioning attribute viewed as differentiating from other product attributes, or from competitive product attributes?

Given that a discovery process has been executed to evaluate your product and its attributes against the above questions, the output can be presented in a format similar to that indicated in the Figure 4-3 Venn Diagram.

In Figure 4-3 I've created the end result of research around customer needs and product attributes for a fictional company called Global Teleportation, Inc., which is developing launch product positioning for TelSoft v2.0, their newest product. TelSoft v2.0 is a server software platform that enables teleportation (transmitting a physical object from one location to another).

FIGURE 4-3: Optimal Positioning Attributes

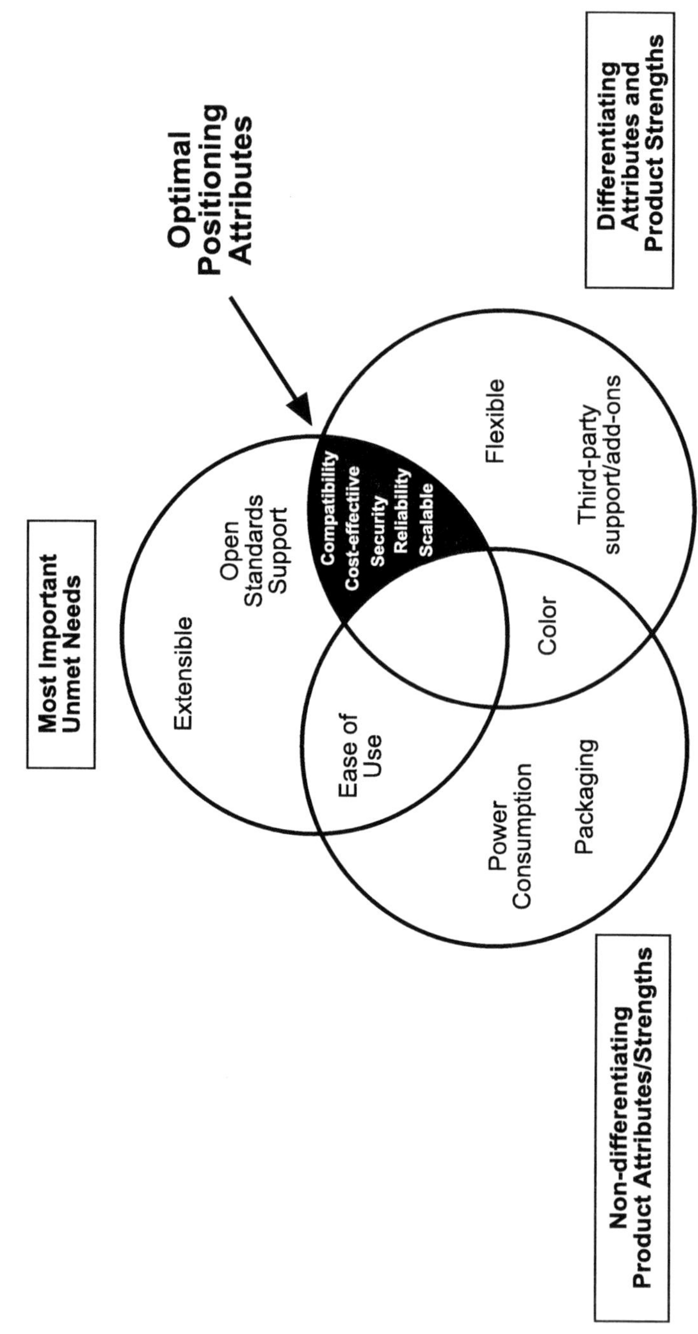

During the positioning research process, Global Teleportation discovered some of the most important unmet needs of the target customer segment(s) for such software were extensibility, ease of use, and open standards support. However, it was also determined that these were not differentiating attributes of the product for the customers or relative to competition. One might have a very easy-to-use product and customers may consider ease-of-use as an important feature or attribute; however, it is also a non-differentiating attribute and thus is not a candidate attribute for effectively positioning your product. Perhaps all the other competitive products in the category are also fairly easy to use, and this is why the attribute is non-differentiating. Similarly for power consumption—your product may be excellent at keeping power consumption low, but based on the research this feature is considered neither important nor differentiating from the customer perspective and, again, would not be a candidate attribute for positioning.

However, compatibility, security, scalability, cost-effectiveness, and reliability were all considered both important unmet needs and as differentiating attributes from the customer perspective and relative to competition for the TelSoft v2.0 software. These attributes are those indicated in the darkened area in Figure 4-3 and could be considered the optimal positioning attributes to focus on for your positioning framework development.

Obviously, your positioning research design needs to be built and structured to provide this type of output, but given that you have done so, the question then becomes "How does one use this knowledge to create a positioning framework?"

Describing the Positioning Framework

Figure 4-4 is an example of the first part of a positioning framework document created for Global Teleportation, Inc., directed at positioning TelSoft v2.0. The positioning framework document is the end result of the preparation work needed to produce, structure, and communicate good positioning and is driven by the research with customers around important unmet needs and differentiating product attributes. In this fictional example, it's obvious that this technology does not exist, but your technology and product does, or will. So, as we discuss the example positioning framework, think about how you could apply the positioning framework concepts and model to your product.

The positioning framework is an important output to the process you undertake to understand important customer pain points, needs,

FIGURE 4-4: Illustrative Positioning Framework and Value Propositions

Structuring your value propositions and benefits using the positioning framework…

Global Teleportation Inc: Teleportation Server Software (TelSoft v2.0) – Positioning and Messaging Framework

TARGET AUDIENCE	Primary: Technology Decision Maker at Teleport Hubs Secondary: Technology Implementer at Teleport Hubs Tertiary: Military Technology and Planning Decision Makers		
KEY CUSTOMER NEEDS	Scalability, Integration, Dependability, Cost-Effective, Manageable after Deployed, High Transmission Success Rates		
POSITIONING TAGLINE (CUSTOMER PROMISE)	Most cost-effective, secure, and reliable teleportation software delivering the highest teleportation scalability		
KEY VALUE PROPOSITION	**Multi-Platform Compatibility and Security**	**Highly Scalable**	**Most Cost-Effective and Dependable Platform**
HIGH-LEVEL VALUE MESSAGES	**Integrates with and securely deploys on all existing certified teleportation platforms and add-on extensions**	**Provides the capability to teleport only one person or a division of combat marines in a highly linear, scalable manner with minimal CPU drain**	**Delivers the highest number, and most desirable, features for the lowest price while maintaining the highest industry "Successful Transmission" ratios**
PRODUCT BENEFITS	**Interoperable and Compatible** • Installs on all certified teleportation hardware platforms • Interoperates with heterogeneous hardware platforms and teleportation add-on software extensions **Leverages Your Existing Assets: Backward Compatible** • 10-year backward compatibility for supported Trintium processor • Supports all existing multithreading versions of Tel-IX operating system software **Open Standards Support** • Native support for W3C Teleportation Standards and TelPort mark-up language (TPML) **Designed for Maximum Security** • Incorporates the latest and most advanced hardware and software teleportation cryptography • No security intrusion attempts have ever been successful- 100% secure • Protected from LAN intrusion by non-standard application attacks	**Simple for One Person Teleportations** • Permits easy teleportation of yourself or another person with a few basic commands **Supports Division-Level Scale Teleportations** • Basic configuration allows simultaneous teleportation of up to 500 combatants • MilGrade Upgrade configuration scales up to 10,000 simultaneous teleportations, without over-taxing the CPU • Minimal CPU drain/tax in any scale configuration **Remote Management/Operation Capabilities** • Perform software installation, maintenance, and operation from a remote location • Secure military-grade data links enable battle-field management of troop teleportation from Headquarters or remote field-based communication positions **Scales Up and Out** • Simply add more processors to your certified teleportation hardware platform to scale-up and keep management costs-down • Easily add more servers to scale-out for large deployments and to provide redundancy	**Fast Transmission Time** • Delivers your teleport objects with world-class throughput from origin to source quickly and efficiently • Maximizes operator productivity and allows maximum object transports per day **Lowers operating costs** • TelSoft v2.0 enables you to comprehensively monitor your teleportation SW processes without human intervention, and provides real-time auto-notifications so you can react to problems before they affect your bottom line. **Highly Affordable** • For current customers, upgrade pricing from TelSoft v1.0 makes the move to v2.0 affordable • New customers pay the lowest cost per teleportation unit in the industry **Most Dependable** • Built-in redundancy, back-up and replication functionality keeps your system up and running, maximizing your transmission time and minimizing your down-time cost (both dollars and lost productivity) • 99.999% up-time guaranteed

and product attributes, and summarizes your product positioning. The framework communicates the key positioning value propositions you develop, maps the relevant product or customer benefits that support each key value proposition, and supports the value propositions with credible and defensible evidence. If you do all this right, and the positioning you end up with will pass the core tenets tests previously indicated, you'll have a highly effective and defensible set of positioning statements that can be rolled into your customer communications.

There are a number of elements represented in the example TelSoft v2.0 positioning framework:

- **Target Audience:** A quick summary of the key target audiences for the product.
- **Key Customer Needs:** A summary of the top-level needs you have identified for the specific target audiences from your research, competitive analysis, customer discussions, partner input, or other sources.
- **Positioning Tagline:** The one-liner that quickly conveys the key value propositions of the product.
- **Key Value Propositions:** Summary statements that roll-up and top-line all of the related needs that are important to the customer.
- **High-Level Value Messages:** One-line descriptions of the key value propositions.
- **Product Benefits:** The primary benefits that support a key value proposition.
- **Supporting Evidence:** Data that can justify what you are saying regarding the benefits of your product as they relate to meeting the customer core needs as expressed through the value propositions.

One of the three value propositions for the TelSoft v2.0 software is stated as the "most cost-effective and dependable platform." This was driven by the positioning research that identified keeping costs down and reliability up for products in this category as both important and differentiating. This is also one of the perceptions that Global Teleportation, Inc., wanted to create for the product. To effectively create this value proposition as a credible perception there must be an association of the claim to the product, which is provided in the form of product benefits that directly align to and support the claim of being the most cost-effective and dependable. These are represented in the framework directly below the value proposition. Global has chosen to focus on transmission time, operating costs, affordability, and dependability benefits to enhance and support the credibility of the claimed value proposition.

The same structure is provided in the framework for the other two important positioning value propositions for the product—compatibility/ security and scalability. These elements build the story to be told to the market and communicated via marketing campaigns, collateral, and tools.

However, Global needs to go one step further. It is not enough to assume a customer will buy into a value proposition simply based on claimed product benefits. More evidence is required, and it is provided in the second part of the positioning framework as indicated in Figure 4-5.

This part of the framework provides concrete evidence to convince a customer that the value propositions and product benefits being claimed are credible. There are two types of customer evidence indicated in the framework—feature evidence and third-party evidence.

Feature evidence is used to support the benefit claims being made in the first part of the framework. For each product benefit there is associated product feature information that supports and validates the benefit claim. For example, supporting the fastest transmission time benefit are features like support for high-speed EtherGigaPort cables and wireless terabyte satellite connectivity. The lower operating cost benefit is supported by the product features of auto monitoring console and the out-bound notification wizard. The same format and logic applies to the other benefits.

While good and necessary to provide, feature evidence usually only takes a customer so far. To really support your positioning claims, the best practice is to use third-party evidence, e.g., analysts, industry publications, or other customers. Third-party evidence is perceived as more credible and less biased.

To continue the example, TelSoft v2.0 was tested and received the highest score vs. competition from a third-party product rating firm's research tests, and also won an award from a respected industry publication for being the most cost-effective platform. Other examples of third-party evidence include customer case studies and positive testimonials, respected industry analyst endorsements, and awards.

Developing this type of evidence is critical to providing support for the core tenets tests previously discussed. Not all these types of evidence will be available as you go through the launch process, but ensuring that you have a plan to create and develop these evidence pieces is important. For example, the analyst evidence support will derive from the hard work you do in your PR activities (Chapter 6). Customer case studies and testimonials will be

FIGURE 4-5: Customer Evidence Supports Value Propositions

Supporting the value propositions and benefits with evidence…

SUPPORTING EVIDENCE: PRODUCT FEATURES, RESEARCH, AWARDS, THIRD-PARTY DATA, CUSTOMER	Multi-Platform Compatibility and Security	Highly Scalable	Most Cost-Effective and Dependable Platform
	Product Feature Evidence: **Highly Compatible** • Installs on all certified teleportation hardware platforms • Full tested to mil-grade specifications (Milspec A324.V2 compliant and certified) **Backward Compatible** • 10-year backward compatibility for supported Trintium processor • Supports all existing multithreading versions of Tel-IX operating system software **Open Standards Support** • Native support for TW3C Teleportation Standards and TelPort mark-up language (TPML) **Security:** • Employs TeleCrypt 8000a cryptography algorithms, proven as unbreakable in all studies and in practice • Mil-Spec 2100.3.b hardware dongle required to enable system access and operation • Isolation firewall routines ensures protection against malicious or rogue viruses on the network	***Product Feature Evidence:*** **Simple** • TelepMe Wizard walks you step-by-step through the process of teleporting yourself or another person • Two-button operation **Supports Division-Level Scale Teleportations** • Built-in automatic buffering and RAM allocations assures adequate capacity for all scales without memory overflow • MilGrade Upgrade console allows easy management of multiple simultaneous transmissions • CPU co-processing modules assure low-CPU usage and low heat accumulation across multiple CPUs as scale requirements dictate **Remote Management/Operation Capabilities** • TelSoft Management Console installs on desktop or mobile device for remote management capability • Tracking and data logging and reporting capabilities for all remote management activities • Secure military-grade data links enable battlefield management of troop teleportation from Headquarters or remote field-based communication positions **Scales Up <u>and</u> Out** • ProcMon module enables quick and easy addition of additional processors for scale-up • ServMon module automatically integrates and configures additional servers and load-balancing for scale-out	***Product Feature Evidence:*** **Fastest Transmission Time** • Supports high-speed EtherGigaPort transmission cables • Wireless Terabyte satellite connectivity • Hyperpipeline enables huge bandwidth for highly compressed data streams **Lowers Operating Costs** • Auto Monitoring console • Out-bound Notification Wizard **Highly Affordable** • $500,000 per processor: 50% lower closest competitor cost • Unlimited free product support • License arrangements allow time-based payment options **Most Dependable** • Full system load-balancing and clustering redundancy features minimize downtime • Back-up power systems negate power system problems • Parallel data transmission offers full duplication/replication of transported bits
	Industry/3rd party/Customer Evidence/Awards: • Security: US government rated AAAA+ for security. Only platform with rating this high • Compatible: 75% of customers run 3 or more unique hardware and software platforms that integrate into their TelSoft installation. Testimonials available from ABC Co., SendEmFast Inc., and others • Third-party analyst firm (TeleAnalyst Consulting) places TeleSoft as having the most installations at Class 1 (most secure) facilities	***Industry/3rd party/Customer Evidence/Awards:*** • Customer/Scale: GiantCo installation largest deployment of teleportation systems in existence: 100,000 processors that transport 10 million users/month • Customer/Simple: MaxiPort Inc. CEO Brad Bucks: "Operating TelSOft 2.0 is so simple a usually incompetent executive like myself can use this system - it rocks!"	***Industry/3rd party/Customer Evidence/Awards:*** • Speed: Highest Score on TransBits/Sec Benchmarked Industry Standard: 10 trillion GB/Sec • Cost: Ranked "Most Cost-Effective System" by Teleportation Times editorial staff • Affordable/Dependable: "Best of Show" award at TeleDex trade show in Affordability and Dependability categories

an output of your pre-launch customer programs like the Early Adopter Program (Chapter 7).

Obviously, all of the examples I used for TelSoft v2.0 (value propositions, benefits, features, and third-party evidence) are not real, but were designed to be as illustrative and real world as possible to make it easy to see how you can visualize a similar framework for a real-world product. Given the context of what a positioning framework is and the elements comprising such a tool, the next step is to understand how to build such a tool for the product you plan to launch.

Creating a Positioning Framework Step-By-Step

Creating and developing a positioning framework is part art, part science, and part intuition. There are various methods to go about collecting the required data to develop positioning. Formal customer research can discover the important customer needs for positioning input and produce a Venn Diagram similar to the example in Figure 4-3. You can also use formal primary research to test your positioning framework and its content. However, it can sometimes be quite expensive, so you may need to get creative.

The following seven steps outline one process you can use to develop the positioning framework for your product.

Step 1: Create a Master List of Likely Customer Needs and Pain Points. To create your list of customer needs and pains you must gather and go through any existing information sources. As you review the materials, you will be looking for any content, sentences, and quotes that directly or indirectly indicate a need or pain point. You will identify, capture, and collect these and build a master list. There are a number of information sources to help you build your list:

- **Competitive or Similar Product Data:** Even though you haven't launched your product yet, there may be competitive or substitute products already on the market that are sold to the same target audience and that deliver a similar value proposition to what you expect your product to deliver, or that meet similar customer needs (e.g., reducing costs). There might also be generically similar products, for example, server software for email, databases, and e-commerce. Although they are functionally different, at a higher level they comprise a class of "server" software sold to IT Professionals that are deployed in the datacenter.

You need to identify these other products and get their product information from presentations, websites, and marketing material. A really great source is from competitive case studies that actually profile a competitor's product at a company and where the customer extols the virtues of their solution. Go through this information and identify all the benefit statements and key customer needs.

Doing so may provide some insights into what your target customers might want and highlight some proven messages directed at meeting customer needs. In addition, you must fully understand what the potential competition is saying so you can create effective counterpoints to their messages as appropriate in sales tools. Why not kill two birds with one stone? Put the culled-out benefit statements into your list.

- **Customer Needs Research:** This could be primary qualitative focus group or one-on-one interviews or quantitative research that you have performed. If you haven't done any research, you may need to spend some time and money doing the research to provide input for the positioning framework. Focus groups or one-on-one interviews are great ways to have deep discussions with the target customers and drill into their needs and pain points. Also, go to the industry research from analysts. Most products or classes of products have some type of analyst firm covering them. If you can get this data, use it. Again, you want to identify any research information that points to needs or key pain points customers have in regard to your type of product. Put these in your list.
- **Industry Trade Articles That Discuss Your Type of Product:** Search either through web sources or databases of trade journal articles. Microsoft subscribes to almost every imaginable business database and Internet resources, giving them access to thousands of journals and articles. However, many of these same databases are accessible at no charge through the public library system. Pull out any benefit statements or value propositions you find. Additionally, when business authors create articles, they typically want to talk to some customers as they research and will include customer quotes. Sometimes these quotes involve why the customer needed a particular product, what it does for them in terms of benefits and business value, and any problems or issues they've had. So you may get lucky and find the customer directly telling you the needs and pains. Put this information into your list.

- **Your Own and Colleagues' Thoughts:** What do you think are the key benefits of your product? What are the key customer needs that will be met by your product from your perspective? What are the unmet needs as you see them based on your experience? How is your product different based on your competitive research? Email your list of ideas to all relevant internal parties and ask them to add their own ideas about key product benefits, customer needs, and pains, then add all the comments to the master list.

Step 2: Consolidate and Cluster. Take a look at your master list of customer needs. Identify needs and value propositions that seem similar, or that could support each other if combined into a higher level message. Cluster them together. The goal is to come out of the clustering process with at most three or four clusters. Figure 4-6 illustrates this for the TelSoft v2.0 software.

You can see that I've taken a long list of customer needs derived from various sources and clumped them into what I thought were generally related groups. Then I thought about the clusters and came up with one or two words or concepts that best summed up what all the statements in each cluster seemed to be trying to convey. This clustering process can also be done using formal quantitative market research techniques like cluster analysis or factor analysis; however, these can be relatively expensive to implement. If you can't afford the quantitative analysis or just don't want to implement this type of research, you can get pretty good results using the manual clustering technique.

Step 3: Validate-Test and Stack Rank Your Clusters With Your Target Customers. You may end up with many more clusters than I have in this example. It's critical that you validate and prioritize these need clusters with customers. Never assume your feelings on priorities are correct. Ask the customers directly. As you may have done previously to populate your list of customer needs, you can validate via a focus group or other qualitative research such as one-on-one interviews.

This validation is an important step and is the de rigueur process at Microsoft. Discuss your clusters (cost, security, flexibility, etc.) with the customers; ask them if these are real needs, how important they are relative to one another, and if there are other needs you haven't discussed with them. Discover how your product strengths map to these important attributes and where they might be weak. Understand how these attributes are perceived relative to existing or potential competitive products. If you can't do formal research for some reason, at least call or visit and have

FIGURE 4-6: One Method to Identify Key Value Propositions

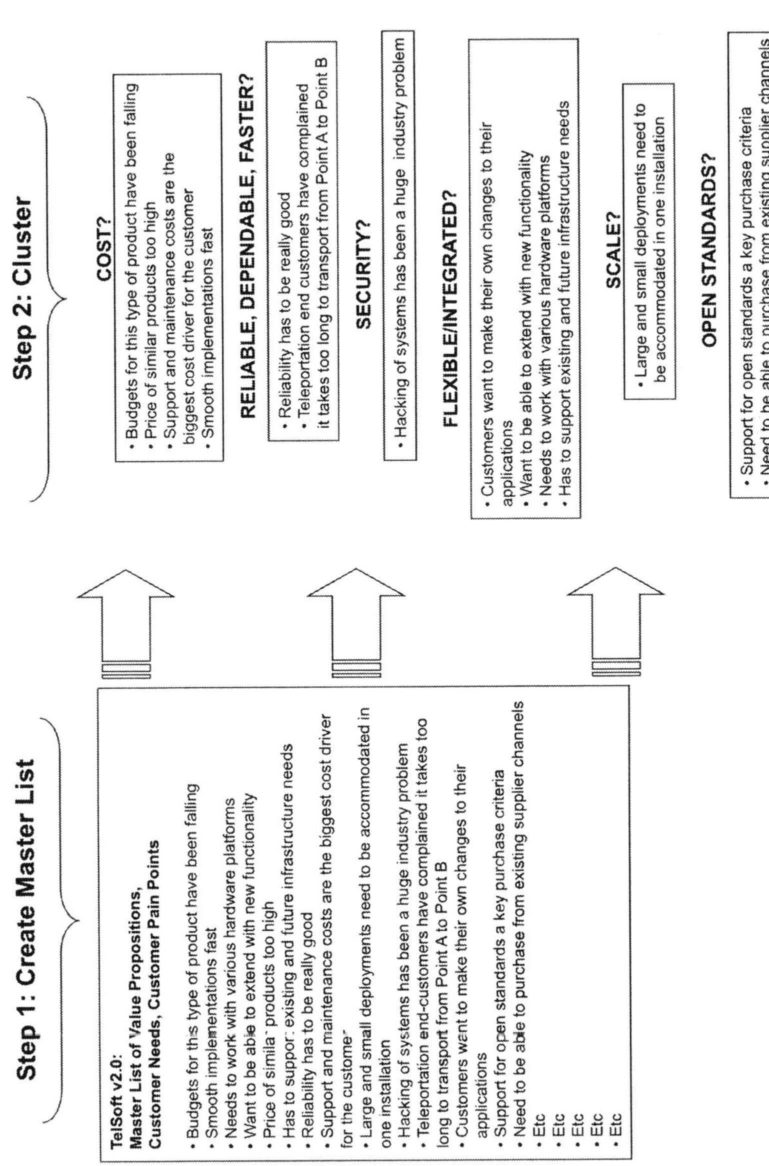

a one-on-one discussion with a small number of potential customers to get some sense of the need cluster relative priorities. Also get input from potential channel partners and the internal sales force to understand their perspective on relative cluster priorities and any potential key needs or pains that may have been missed.

Finally, if possible, perform another sanity check to confidentially bounce these off of an industry analyst that you respect and trust. The analyst should be able to provide input on how the value propositions you are deriving will stack up against competition and a perspective on which are the most important and should be used to position your product.

Coming out of this validation phase, you should have a very solid idea of your customer's top needs and pain points as they relate to your product and their business. This then forms the basis to create the needs and attributes Venn Diagram (Figure 4-3) for your product.

Step 4: Create Your Value Proposition Buckets. Now that you have your customer-validated needs and optimal positioning clusters, you need to prune and consolidate. For your framework, you must summarize however many clusters you have into three or, at the most, four buckets. Most of the consolidation will be based on the need clusters that are aligned to the optimal positioning attributes as indicated in your Venn Diagram. I've done this for TelSoft v2.0, taking cost, security, reliable/dependable/faster, flexible/integrated, scale, and open standards and summarized these clusters to create three top-level value proposition buckets (or optimal positioning attributes) for the product:

- Multi-Platform Compatibility and Security
- Highly Scalable
- Most Cost-Effective and Dependable

These are now the major positioning points that Global Teleportation, Inc., will relay to customers through all communications about TelSoft v2.0. These are based on real customer needs, and are the top needs the customers said are most important to them (and which are differentiating needs) when making a teleportation server software investment.

Step 5: Define the Benefits of Your Product That Support Each Top-Level Value Proposition. Next create benefit statements that address the customer needs for that particular value proposition bucket. The "Most Cost-Effective and Dependable Platform" value proposition bucket in our example TelSoft v2.0 framework in Figure 4-4 lists benefits that include Fast

Transmission Time, Lowers Operating Costs, Highly Affordable, and Most Dependable. These product benefits map directly to the final customer value proposition bucket. You must define your own product benefits based on how your product features will meet your customer's needs as expressed in your own product's top-level positioning value propositions.

Step 6: Provide Supporting Evidence for Your Benefit Statements. To be credible with your claims, you must provide evidence. This can come in the form of product features you have implemented, industry or analyst statements, customer examples, research results, product performance testing results, and awards. The more specific you can be, the more credible your evidence will be perceived. For feature evidence, work with the engineering team to fully understand the product features, then map them to your benefit statements as appropriate. Gather all the other non-feature evidence and perform the same mapping to benefits. I've shown how this might look in the example framework for TelSoft v2.0. Make sure that, as I've done in the example, you lay out your evidence to map directly to the key benefit statements that you claim in your framework. It's cleaner, more understandable, and will make it easier to use the framework when creating marketing material. Finally, if you can also provide specific "result" statements your messaging will be even stronger. A result statement would be something like "Deploying our product provided 80% of customers with an average $4 Million operating cost reduction."

Step 7: Back to the Core Tenets. Now think through the questions from earlier in this chapter as they relate to the three top value propositions and benefits being proposed. Here's my take as I think through these questions based on the example TelSoft v2.0 framework:

- Accurate: yes (this is a judgment call)
- Credible: yes (validated via research in Step 3)
- Defensible: yes (using feature and other evidence)
- Sustainable and Flexible: likely (again, judgment call. If your top value props are broad enough you should be okay)
- Consistent and Repeatable: yes (that's why I only have three value buckets)
- Differentiable: yes (e.g., TelSoft v2.0 is the "*Most*" cost-effective)
- "Needable": absolutely (totally based on customer needs research and analysis)

If the answer to any of the above is "no" or "not sure" or "unlikely," that is unacceptable. Work on it until they are all "Yes" answers.

USING THE POSITIONING FRAMEWORK

Once your positioning framework is complete, it is time to put it into use. The basic positioning, value propositions, benefits, and evidence points should be appropriately incorporated into the various marketing communication tools used for the launch. Incorporating the framework content will ensure alignment and consistency of messages across the marketing mix, and reinforce your positioning through multiple partner and customer touch points. In addition, your positioning should be used to drive the creation of the product name or brand you intend to take to market.

Driving Positioning Across Marketing Elements

Figure 4-7 provides a high-level illustration of where you will get the biggest bang for your positioning buck and highlights four key integration points the framework content should flow into:

- Agency or vendor creative briefs
- Any to-customer marketing materials
- Any through-partner marketing materials
- Your partner positioning framework

You may work with or manage a number of vendors that assist in driving your marketing launch activities. Website vendors, marketing collateral vendors, marketing campaign execution vendors, event vendors, creative and branding agencies, and public relations agencies are some of the outside vendors you will likely work with during your launch. None of these vendors has the same level of knowledge about the product or the target customer market as does the product marketing team. Therefore, effective knowledge transfer is an important function of working successfully with these vendors during the launch process. Typically, you will develop a creative brief to outline the scope of the work, especially for projects that will include content and messages to be viewed by customers. Advertisements, direct mail, web content, presentations, email marketing, and signage at events are all examples of such content.

To ensure that the messages are correct and accurately reflect your desired positioning when created, having the positioning framework

FIGURE 4-7: Positioning Framework Content Drives Consistent Communications

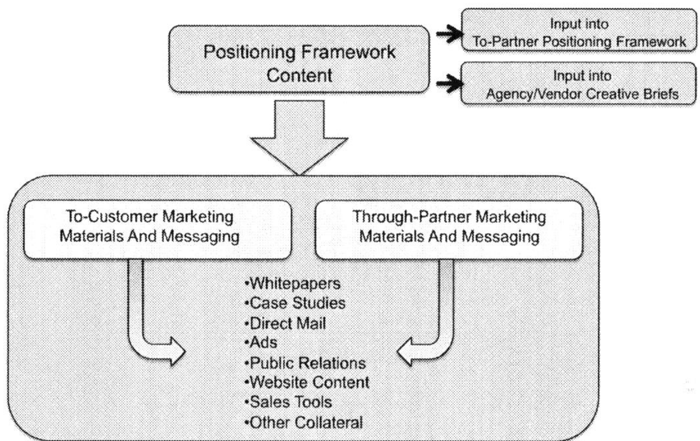

available and providing it to your vendors is key to correctly getting the messages done and transferring the positioning knowledge you have developed. The content from the positioning framework should flow into the vendor creative brief to guide the proper messaging, regardless of the communication distribution mechanism. If you create your own marketing materials like datasheets, case studies, direct mail pieces, or your own web content, the framework should guide the content and messages delivered via those mechanisms.

If the launch process and your product require that sales tools be created for your reseller or channel partners, the positioning framework should guide the creation of these materials as well. This is especially true if you will be providing materials that the reseller then passes on to the target end-customers. The positioning and messaging from your partners should be absolutely in synch with the positioning and messaging your company is directly sending to end-customers. This alignment is critical to ensure messaging consistency and to reinforce the positioning ground you are staking out for your product.

Chapter 7 discusses the need to create a "Partner Positioning Framework," essentially comprising the positioning points and messages that will be used to position your channel partner program. Elements of the customer positioning framework should also feed into the partner positioning framework to ensure alignment and consistency.

FIGURE 4-8: Windows Server 2003 Positioning

Dependable: Windows Server 2003 is the fastest, most reliable, most secure Windows server operating system ever offered by Microsoft. Windows Server 2003 delivers dependability by:

Providing an IT infrastructure that delivers fundamental value: improved reliability, better availability, and increased scalability.

- Including an application platform with built-in traditional application server functionality on top of extensive operating system capabilities.
- Integrating an information worker infrastructure that helps keep business information secure and accessible.

Productive: Windows Server 2003 provides the tools that simplify deployment, management, and administration and maximize productivity.

Windows Server 2003 does this by:

- Providing flexible tools that help match your design and deployment to your organizational and network needs.
- Helping you manage your network proactively by enforcing policy, automating tasks, and simplifying updates.
- Helping you lower support overhead by letting users do more on their own.

Connected: Windows Server 2003 provides an extensible application platform for quickly building solutions that keep employees, partners, systems, and customers connected.

Windows Server 2003 does this by:

- Providing an integrated Web server and streaming media server that helps you quickly, easily, and securely create dynamic intranet and Internet Web sites.
- Providing built-in services that help you easily develop, deploy, and manage XML Web services.
- Providing the tools that enable you to connect XML Web services to internal applications, suppliers, and partners.

Best Economics: When combined with products and services from the many Microsoft hardware, software, and channel partners, Windows Server 2003 provides the choices that help you get the greatest return on your infrastructure investments.

Windows Server 2003 does this by:

- Providing ease-of-use and prescriptive guidance for complete solutions that enable you to quickly put technology to work.
- Helping you consolidate servers by taking advantage of the latest hardware, software, and methodologies to optimize your server deployments.
- Lowering your total cost of ownership (TCO) to realize a fast return on investment.

source: Microsoft public website.

Microsoft Web Content Illustrates Framework Usage

TelSoft is a fictional company, and, while illustrative, it is not a real-world example. Therefore, it might be valuable to take a look at two examples of real-world Microsoft usage of top-level value propositions to show ways that positioning frameworks are put into use.

Figure 4-8 contains a Windows Server 2003 operating system content blurb taken directly from the public Microsoft website that provides the high-level product overview and introduces the product to the user. In this example, it appears that Microsoft has chosen to publish a summary of the Windows Server 2003 positioning framework on their external website. This is not the most optimal usage of positioning framework content being put into action.

However, Figure 4-8 is useful to show a real-world positioning framework to augment the TelSoft v2.0 example. In the Windows Server 2003 example, "Dependable," "Productive," "Connected," and "Best Economics" were clearly determined to be the optimal positioning attributes and key value propositions for the product, as evidenced in the copy. These would be the major columns forming the positioning framework document. For each value proposition, the copy provides a benefit description that provides more clarity, summarized as follows:

- **Dependable:** "the fastest, most reliable, most secure"
- **Productive:** "simplify deployment, management, administration"
- **Connected:** "extensible platform ... for quickly building solutions ... to keep employees, partners, systems, and customers connected"
- **Best Economics:** "get the greatest return on your infrastructure investments"

Each of these benefit claims is then supported in the copy by product feature evidence ("integrated web server built-in services, flexible tools"), illustrating support for the top-level positioning attribute/value propositions and the corresponding key benefits.

Another example shows a positioning communication presentation that is a bit more refined than the somewhat raw Windows Server 2003 example. Again, I pulled content from the public Microsoft.com website, this time from the Microsoft Office desktop application world, specifically highlighting Microsoft Office Excel 2007 spreadsheet software:

> "Microsoft Office Excel 2007 is a powerful tool you can use to create and format spreadsheets, and analyze and share information to make more informed decisions. With the new Microsoft Office Fluent user interface, rich data visualization, and PivotTable views, professional-looking charts are easier to create and use. Office Excel 2007, combined with Excel Services, a new technology that will ship with Microsoft Office SharePoint Server 2007, provides significant improvements for sharing data with greater security. You can share sensitive business information more broadly with enhanced security with your coworkers, customers, and business partners. By sharing a spreadsheet using Office Excel 2007 and Excel Services, you can navigate, sort, filter, input parameters, and interact with PivotTable views directly on the Web browser."

Looking through the content for clues and words that indicate what the core message being communicated is, we can infer and summarize that the short product tagline might be "Excel 2007 is a powerful tool to create … analyze … and share information."

Reading between the lines, we can pull out the product key benefits that are being communicated:

- "create and format spreadsheets … charts are easier to create and use"
- "analyze and share information to make more informed decisions"
- "share sensitive business information more broadly with enhanced security"

We can infer that the real Excel 2007 positioning framework may have something similar to the following top-level value proposition buckets:

- **Authoring Ease of Use:** "create and format spreadsheets … charts are easier to create and use"
- **Enhanced Productivity and Communication:** "analyze and share information to make more informed decisions"
- **Security and Peace of Mind:** "share sensitive business information more broadly with enhanced security"

You see again how the key benefit statements are mapped to the top-level value propositions.

This is a reasonable example of positioning framework content being incorporated into marketing verbiage and, in this case, being delivered in content on the Microsoft website. In both the Excel and Windows Server case you can be assured that those top-level value propositions were thoroughly tested with customers to validate them against the most important target customer needs that the product is designed to address.

The two real world Microsoft examples indicate how Global Teleportation, Inc., might place the top-level value propositions (Multi-Platform Compatibility and Security, Highly Scalable, Most Cost-Effective and Dependable) for TelSoft v2.0 into action on their own website and into other communication vehicles. To make the TelSoft v2.0 tagline, we take the top-level value propositions from the positioning framework and turn them into a sentence. In our fictional example, the product tagline becomes "The most cost-effective, secure, and reliable teleportation software delivering the highest teleportation scalability."

To come up with a web content blurb similar to the Excel 2007 example, Global Teleportation could leverage the positioning framework to create the following content:

> "TelSoft v2.0 is the most cost-effective, integrated, and reliable teleportation software delivering the highest teleportation scalability. Providing an extensive array of high-end features at an affordable cost, TelSoft v2.0 works with all industry-standard teleportation hardware and provides a dependable platform to enable teleportation functionality from single individuals to divisions of marines."

Given a well-designed positioning framework, the marketing materials produced by your firm or by vendors can easily and accurately be designed to incorporate the correct positioning for your product.

The positioning framework has another important use as well—helping to shape and define your to-be-launched product name and brand.

PRODUCT NAMING AND BRANDING RELATIVE TO POSITIONING

Naming your product for launch or developing a brand look and feel are two other fun launch exercises. Doing these well requires creativity, collaboration, and testing via research. Although product names and brands are very specific to a particular product, market, and company guidelines or precedents, I can offer some general considerations to help guide your product naming or branding process.

A good name or brand can help create competitive advantage and differentiation in the market in conjunction with your desired product positioning. The name or brand you choose for the product being launched should be reflective, supportive, and positively associated with the product positioning, or at a minimum not conflict with it. A name or brand is a communication element in the marketing mix just as direct mail, advertising, websites, and all the other mix elements are. Names and brands should add to the consistency of the positioning and messaging delivered throughout the marketing mix, not detract from it.

The typical process you go through to name a product includes:

- Review of product positioning, both against customer needs and competition
- Creative brainstorming of names and analysis of various naming type options based on the product positioning
- Trademark assessment
- Research-based testing of the best names from the brainstorm
- Name finalization

As the process moves from step to step, there are various factors that will begin to shape the naming decision. One key factor to determining the product name or brand will likely be driven by the business model of the firm. There are two general types of models that come into play for naming and branding purposes: a "Branded House" and a "House of Brands."

A branded house describes a company where the name of the company itself is the brand, and the product names generally do not take primary precedence. Much of the positioning equity is delivered by the company name and the company brand equity. Many technology, manufacturing, and services companies follow a branded house model. For example, McKinsey & Company in services, Oracle or Intel in technology, and Caterpillar in manufacturing all follow a branded house model.

A house of brands reflects firms where the company name does not take the lead, but the products themselves are the main focal point. Proctor & Gamble is an example of a branded house—you rarely see the P&G name except in small print on the product. Here the product names are being promoted, positioned, and branded. Many consumer product firms (detergent, dishwashing soap, hand soap, barbeque sauce, etc.) follow the house of brands model.

For the most part, Microsoft falls under the branded house model. However, in recent years it has become more of a mix of branded house and house of brands by adding more consumer-like branded products, such as Xbox, and continuing to invest in and promote large brands like the Windows operating system and Office.

Another factor that will impact the naming process involves the type, or genre, of name to choose. There are a number of genre options to consider, including functionally descriptive, created, experiential, and suggestive names.

Functionally descriptive names are generally a safe choice and can be used by a branded house oriented firm. These types of names are designed to literally convey the product in a manner that describes the core functionality of the product. Microsoft offers numerous examples of names in this genre, such as Microsoft SQL Server, Microsoft Speech Server, and Microsoft Management Console. These names are quite clear as to what the product is and its intended functionality. If I were to have pursued a functional descriptive name for the hypothetical TelSoft v2.0 software product, I could have named it "Global Teleportation, Inc., Teleportation Software Server v2.0," something plain, straightforward, and functionally oriented.

Created names are those that literally are made up, either based on Latin or Greek roots or combinations of existing words to create a new word. Some real world examples of such name types are car names like Prius, Elantra, and Boxster, and food names like Oreo. The product name "TelSoft v2.0" was created combining "Teleportation + Software," and is an example of a created name. Created names can be very unique and interesting; however, the monetary cost to connect the intended positioning attributes to the name in the customer's mind can be quite high. These names involve a lot of customer education and time to achieve the intended goal of accurately mapping to and conveying the product positioning.

Experiential names are those that try to convey a more emotional, experience-based association with a product. Using the TelSoft v2.0 example again, an experiential name for the product might be "TravelQuick" or "Jump" to convey the experience offered by the product—getting from one place to another very quickly.

Suggestively named products attempt to draw out a direct association with a positioning attribute. If TelSoft v2.0 had been named suggestively, it might carry a moniker, like "The Integrator v2.0," to convey the product positioning point of easily integrating into a customer's existing infrastructure, or "Assurance v2.0," to convey the positioning point of dependability.

Finally, regardless of the naming path you choose, when deciding between product name options, there are a number of general considerations that should be included in the naming process. Some of these considerations are as follows:

Multiple Audiences: The name needs to accommodate and span multiple target audiences. It is unlikely that your product is solely focused on one narrow customer segment. If you're selling to IT Professionals, developers, and consumers, the product name needs to work for all of these audiences. You can always make the trade-off to optimize the name around the most important segment, or the largest segment, but this should be considered a last resort. Try to make the name applicable to all your customers.

Naming Conflicts: The name should not conflict or compete with other products at your firm. The name needs to be distinct enough from other product names you have so as not to cause confusion between other products or product positioning between products.

Future-Proofing: Although the product to be named is being launched with whatever features and benefits it will have at launch, the product will likely continue to evolve and grow over time. You must consider product evolution when naming the product today. The name must be flexible enough to accommodate future product changes and still be a solid name to reflect its expanded feature/functionality and possibly future modifications to the product positioning.

Trademarks: You may need to trademark your name. This involves a legal search to determine if it is possible to trademark your proposed name in the product category you are launching into. The more generic the name, the less likely you are to have a need to trademark it. Descriptive functional names are examples of product names that probably don't require a trademark. The more specific or unique the name is the higher the probability that you should trademark, or that you may be prevented from trademarking as a competitive name may stand in your way. Experiential names will generally be common across many industries and will likely be difficult to trademark.

Globalization: If you are planning to sell your product into non-English-speaking countries, you may wish to consider a linguistic check on its spelling and meaning in the relevant languages of those countries. It would be unfortunate if, too late, you discovered that the Chinese meaning of your breath mint product name meant "stinky monkey breath," or that the written symbolic representation of the name in Chinese also had a derogatory interpretation.

Product Name Attributes: As you evaluate the possible product names, you should consider the consequences of various attributes of the name such as:

- *Visual Appeal:* Will the name lend itself to a visually appealing graphic?
- *Differentiation:* Is the name differentiated and unique from competitive names?
- *Positioning Relevance:* Does the name support the product positioning?
- *Verbalization:* Does the name easily roll off the tongue, or is it a tongue twister?
- *Written Appeal:* Can the name be easily written, or are there some oddities that might cause problems? An example of this from Microsoft naming involves a customer retention program called Small Business Plus. The actual graphic representation of the name was "Small Business **+**", and caused problems for internet searching, URLs, and the constant question of consistency—is it "plus" or "+" in written copy. If using "+" will customers understand if that symbol is part of the name in the text or a typo? Will customers pronounce the name correctly upon seeing the "+"?
- *URL:* Can you get an Internet URL or domain name with the chosen product name?
- *Believable:* Is the name believable to customers, or does it evoke incredulity?
- *Likeable:* Your target customers should like the name. If potentially negative images or associations are discovered around any particular name candidate during testing, it's best to drop that name to avoid the potential negative consequences.
- *Acronym Issues:* Watch out for multiword names or taglines that might be shortened into an unflattering acronym. The "Best Universal Translation Tool" has the unfortunate acronym of "BUTT," which might not convey the intended positioning accurately or could be used by the competition to negatively impact your naming and brand.

5

Ahead of the Curve: Business Development

To successfully launch your product, your firm may need to establish significant and deep business relationships with other companies. In a normal product launch cycle, a company may need to develop highly strategic relationships with a small number of close partners whose products, services, or technologies can fill gaps in the go-to-market strategy that your company cannot or will not fill.

The relationships formed with these types of companies are market-making relationships, meaning they can make or break the success of the product launch and post-launch activities. Market-making relationships are those that could:

- Provide critical technology you need for your product
- Enable key services to be delivered with your product
- Open important distribution channels for you
- Deliver applications or complementary products that work with your product
- Provide access to significant or hard-to-find expertise or knowledge, either technical or market/customer expertise
- Secure key go-to-market sales and marketing partners
- Provide market credibility and validation if your firm is new to the market

Given their broad scope, depth, and potential complexity, strategic relationships like these may take a fair amount of time to put into place, and their formation may need to be initiated and activated years before your product actually hits the market. With relationships at this level, a formal written agreement is typically required to define and codify in some detail each party's responsibilities in the relationship and any monetary commitments. As the rollout plan is being developed (Chapter 3), the specific needs for market-making partner relationships and the time frame to put these partnerships into place should be considered.

At Microsoft, these market-making relationships and partnerships are typically developed under the "Business Development" moniker. The folks in business development roles are responsible for strategizing, evaluating, selecting, and closing deals with market-making partners.

Market-making partnerships are different from typical relationships with other channel or market partners—the hundreds of smaller, more numerous industry partners that may have a role to play in your partner ecosystem, but are not fundamental to the launch success. Figure 5-1 indicates the high-level relationship between the market-making partners and the broad-breadth partner group. Business development resources should be targeted at acquiring the market-making partnerships. The broad-breadth partners are best acquired and managed via a more programmatic, arm's-length channel partner program (see Chapter 7).

FIGURE 5-1: Market-Making Partners

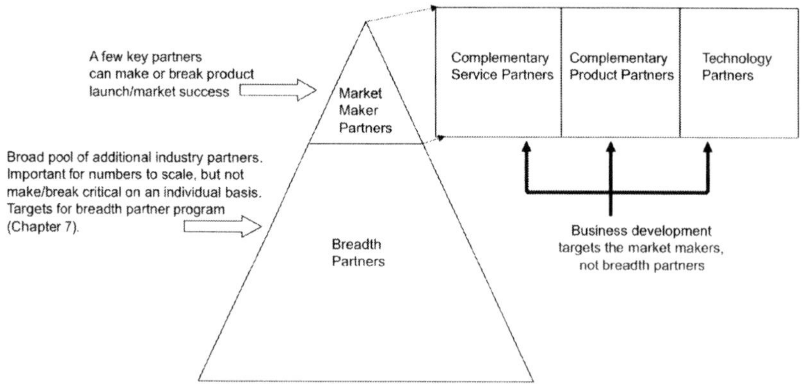

KEY FOCUS FOR PRODUCT LAUNCH-RELATED BUSINESS DEVELOPMENT

Without these relationships in place to fill any launch gaps, you may not have a successful launch. To successfully pursue the market-making relationships, your business development efforts should be focused on a few well-defined activities to maximize the effectiveness of these resources and their chance for success. From a product launch perspective, these activities should be:

- Define and identify the few critical long-lead strategic partners required to take the product to launch and make the product successful once in market. Don't waste time and energy on non-key partners.
- Engage these partners with a win/win relationship scenario. If there is no viable win/win scenario, get out—don't do a bad deal.
- Codify and negotiate the win/win scenario with the partners. Make sure you cover all the bases in a written agreement.
- Maintain involvement and management of the relationships after deals are signed and the product is launched. Deals go bad if they are simply "handed off." Consistency and continuity around a single point of contact is important to a positive ongoing relationship.

In a nutshell, that's the role for business development activities related to product launches. As indicated in Figure 5-1, the focus of business development is not on the large pool of small partners, but on the few key large or strategic partners that will enable market success via service, product, or technology offerings around your product. Of course, the devil is in the details to adequately execute on these focus areas, so let's take a look at them.

DEFINING MARKET-MAKING PARTNERS

The partners you are looking for are a small number of market-making companies that will enable the success of your product launch. Market-making in this context refers to companies that can offer you a value proposition or competency that:

- Your firm does not currently possess
- Your firm does not intend to invest in or have the ability to develop internally

- Is not a core competency or key differentiator for your company
- Is required to launch the product and for product success in market

Microsoft Project, the project management software from Microsoft, offers a simple example of a partnership that met the above market-making criteria. When Project 95 was being developed there was a significant amount of customer data from large enterprises that indicated a required feature was robust reporting tools with the ability to consolidate and aggregate reports from multiple projects across the customer's enterprise. Without this ability, it was nearly impossible to get large-scale enterprise sales wins for Microsoft Project, thus relegating the product to the somewhat less lucrative small- and mid-market customer segments.

The product did not have aggregation functionality, and reporting was limited to mostly simple canned reports. It was determined that although the feature was significantly important to drive product adoption, reporting and aggregation were not a core competency of Microsoft related to Project 95, and they didn't want to invest in this at the expense of other features. However, the feature/functionality was critical to launching the product successfully into the enterprise market.

To get this functionality, Microsoft partnered with another company that provided the enterprise-scale reporting and aggregation technology as an add-on solution and also offered integration and deployment services on the joint solution. The joint solution offered the ease-of-use attributes that customers enjoyed with Project, combined with the partner solution to scale-up on aggregation and reporting. This partner relationship was one important step to opening up the large-scale enterprise market for Project 95.

There are four primary reasons your company might choose to pursue long-lead business development activities with market-makers. Figure 5-2 illustrates the major value propositions that are typically sought after in such key partnerships and include:

- Access to significant third-party technology for inclusion into your product to fill feature gaps
- Expanding market reach via access to new channels of distribution that your company currently doesn't have and that might be too costly, too difficult, or too time intensive to develop independently
- Immediate and direct access to the target customer base
- Development of products and services that are complementary to your own product

FIGURE 5-2: Market-Maker Partner Value Propositions

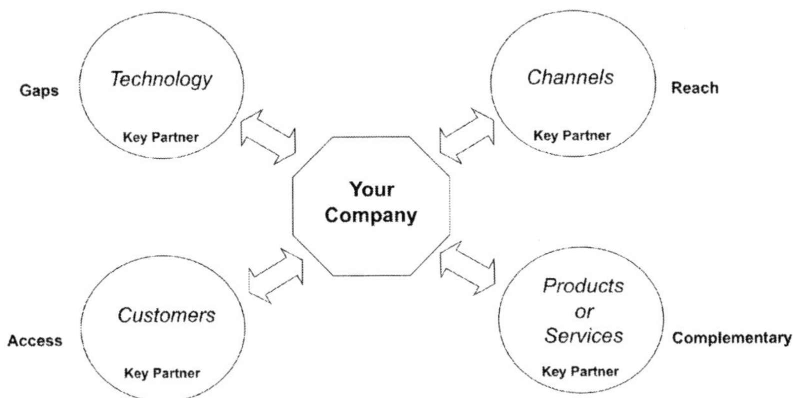

The Project 95 example demonstrated a partnership relationship regarding the development of a product (and service in this case) that was both complementary to Microsoft Project and met the market-maker criteria previously outlined.

A more recent, and larger, Microsoft example is that of Microsoft Speech Server (now part of Microsoft Office Communications Server). Speech Server is a Microsoft server product enabling the development and deployment of enterprise-scale speech-enabled applications like those used in customer service centers. For example, you could call your automobile insurance company and, by talking over the telephone to the automated speech system powered by Speech Server, you could retrieve account information, billing status, and claims information via speech recognition technology. The technology and effort required to produce such a server is formidable.

During the development of Speech Server, it was determined that the development of an enterprise-grade Text-to-Speech (TTS) engine (the part of a speech system that enables the automated voice you hear speaking back to you over the telephone) was not a core competency for Microsoft. They did not have such an engine and did not want to develop it on their own, but the functionality was required to launch the product and to enable success in the marketplace. In addition, Microsoft had invested a decade of research and development in the technology before Speech Server shipped, and in fact had shipped a number of other speech recognition products that were desktop-based, but had not previously shipped an enterprise-scale server speech product.

The target customers for desktop-based speech recognition and enterprise-grade server technology are quite different. Desktop-based systems are targeted at Information Workers, while server technology is targeted primarily at IT Professionals. Finally, not only were the target customers new, but both the method of access to these customers (the channel) and the necessary product deployment services were different.

Nearly three years before launching the product, Microsoft began business development relationships with a company then called SpeechWorks (since acquired by ScanSoft, which then acquired a firm called Nuance, with the combined entity named Nuance). SpeechWorks had good TTS technology, had a service team that could build solutions using Speech Server, and was already selling to the decision makers involved with purchasing large-scale speech recognition systems. They also had the technology, services, and channel to the market that Microsoft desired. So Microsoft partnered with SpeechWorks and began a two-year cycle of technology and marketing collaboration to incorporate the SpeechWorks TTS technology into the Microsoft Speech Server, and to resell the joint technology offering to enterprise customers. This relationship enabled Microsoft to focus on developing speech technology considered to be the core competency within the organization, to provide access to the target customer base, and to enable complementary service offerings to the Speech Server product. The deal's pre-launch lead time was significant and indicative of the lead times you might expect as you determine and engage your market-maker partnerships.

IDENTIFYING POTENTIAL MARKET-MAKER PARTNERSHIPS

The foundation for pursuing the right partnerships starts with a solid understanding of the holes and gaps in your product launch plans that may require one or more significant partnerships to plug. The first step in this process requires a clear understanding of the go-to-market value chain from both internal product and corporate competency, and competitive and industry perspectives. This understanding and insight will help direct your thinking around which gaps must be filled from a competency perspective and which gaps from a competitive perspective via partnerships.

FIGURE 5-3: Market-Maker Identification

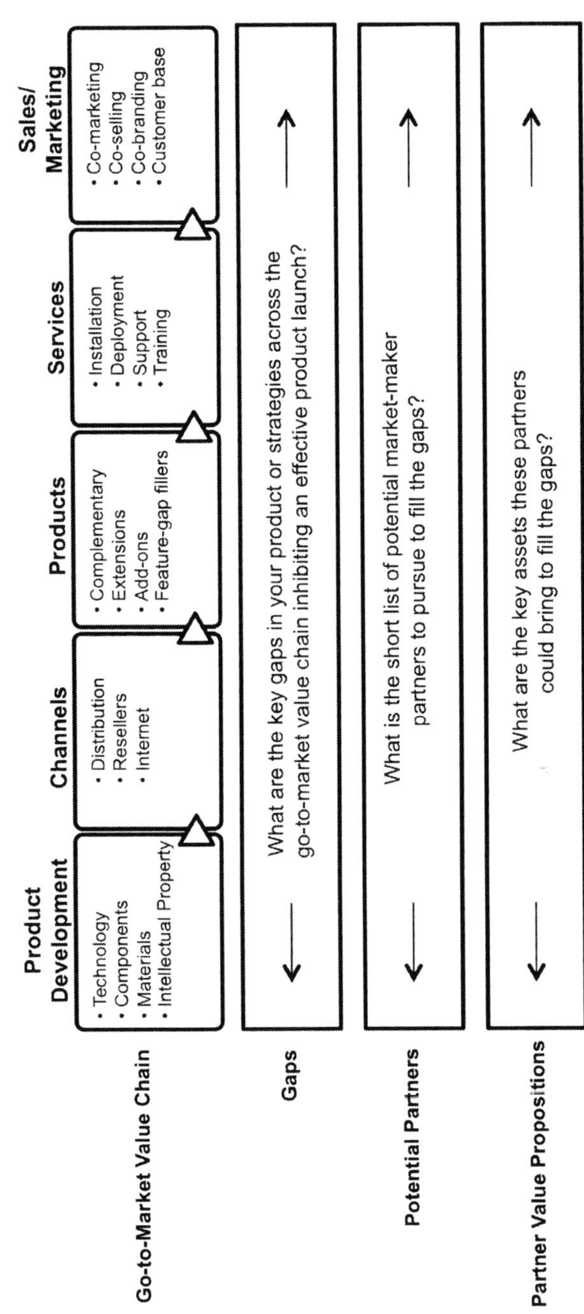

From either perspective, Figure 5-3 identifies five important elements of the value chain to consider:

- **Product Development:** Product technology required, components needed, materials required, or intellectual property that could be needed to plug a gap in the product itself.
- **Channels:** Go-to-market access via distribution channels, resellers, or Internet-based outlets that might need to be developed through partnership relationships to get the product to the target customer segment.
- **Products:** Important partnerships that could make your product more competitive via complementary products, product extensions, or add-ons. In addition, if engineering resources or time-to-market are constrained, your resources may not be able to build-out the features required for market success. Partnerships with feature-gap-filling partners should then be considered.
- **Services:** Installation, deployment, support, or training services needed for your product that your firm will not or cannot provide directly.
- **Sales and Marketing:** Partnerships that extend or complement your own marketing and sales efforts, that bring some brand equity to the table, or that provide additional access to your target customer base.

Some of these may be more critical to the product launch success than others; this will depend on the market needs and competitive landscape. For example, you may have well established distribution channels, but if your product does not reach the market with a few key complementary products, you may be put at a competitive disadvantage. Or the market may demand locally available service centers as a key purchase driver, and thus partnering with a services firm with national reach into local geographies and the associated facilities could provide a competitive leg up when you launch.

A more basic partnership need may involve the product itself. The Speech Server example illustrated a product feature gap requiring a partnership to enable the product launch. If you intend to sell in a broad geographic area, you may need to extend your sales and marketing reach with a few key partnerships that will take your product to market with you via their sales and marketing resources.

The important activity to pursue is to clearly identify where you have gaps in the go-to-market value chain, identify a short list of market-making partners that could help fill these gaps, and thoroughly understand how the assets of these potential partners will complement your firm's assets and fill the gaps for launch via a successful partnership.

Once the short list of partners is identified, the next step is to determine the most important companies with which to pursue a partnership relationship.

PRIORITIZING MARKET-MAKER PARTNERSHIPS

A number of elements will feed into determining which potential partners will be the most valuable and are the most critical for your launch. Because developing these partnerships takes a significant amount of time and effort, you should focus on those top two or three in a given need area that will provide you the biggest bang for your launch and post-launch in-market activities. Some factors important to making such a prioritization include evaluating the potential partnership around the following parameters:

- Natural alignment of interests
- Clearly complementary assets
- Non-competitive products or services
- Similar outlook on market opportunity
- Culture fit
- Financial stability
- Market position (market share)
- Reputation as a partner and in the market
- Solid track record of success in market
- Prior successful partnerships similar to the type you are contemplating
- Prior successful or unsuccessful partnerships with your company

Once you've evaluated each of the potential partners on the short list, you can prioritize them as in Figure 5-4 for each go-to-market gap type that requires a market-making partnership (e.g., technology, customer base and channels, and complementary products or services). The potential partners are identified as to their criticality to your launch and bucketed as a Priority 1, 2, or 3 partnership target, where the Priority 1 partners would be considered the best choice to fill the gap and the most desirable partner.

To prioritize the potential partners, you must establish some basis for how critical each partner is to the launch. For example, Figure 5-4 indicates that

FIGURE 5-4: Market-Maker Prioritization

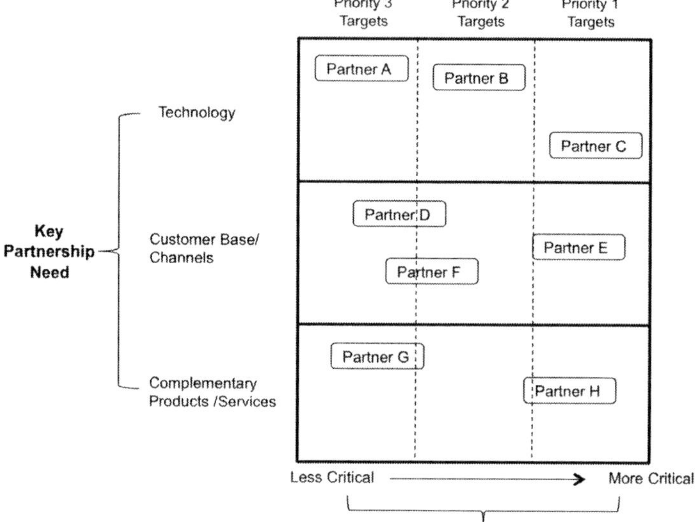

for key technology partnerships there are three prospects, with Partner C being the Priority 1, or most critical partner to sign up. It could be the case that criticality is defined here for potential technology partners as the best technology, or the technology most easily integrated to achieve the launch time frame, or some other measure. Here Partner C leads the prospects and is the preferred company. Similarly, regarding the need for complementary products and services, criticality may be defined as breadth of geographic services coverage which is required for local customer service. In this case, Partner H is identified as the top prospect having the broadest services coverage and thus is the most critical for a successful launch. Obviously, this is not the only way to prioritize potential partners, but simply underscores the point that prioritization needs to occur.

After identifying your partnership priorities and mapping them against your key needs, the next step is to begin developing the foundation to approach the top priority partners with the details of the proposed partnership. Before approaching any particular company, the details of the specific relationship must be thought through and evaluated in a highly customized manner to prepare an adequate win/win scenario for both the partner and your firm.

DEFINING A WIN/WIN PARTNERSHIP SCENARIO

The Project 95 and Speech Server examples illustrated high-level summaries of valuable partnerships. However, such partnerships require that both companies believe they will derive significant value from the relationship to create a win/win scenario. There are some characteristics you would look for to create a win/win scenario and set up the foundation for a good deal. Figure 5-5 lists some typical deal attributes or assets that companies may base a mutually beneficial win/win relationship upon, such as availability of cash, existing customer-installed base, and marketing prowess and power.

A key focus for generating a win/win scenario is to successfully identify and match your and the potential partner company's mutually complementary assets and needs. Figure 5-5 shows that Company X, in the process of launching a product, has identified the need for a market-maker partner and has identified Company Y as having a good potential for a deal. Company X has determined that for launch and market success they need expanded distribution channels, some additional technology, and a partner to deliver service offerings around their product. Company X identified Company Y and believes this possible partner has the distribution channels, technology, and service offerings they need. However, this is a hypothesis,

FIGURE 5-5: Mapping Complementary Potential Deal Attributes

Company X (instigator)			Typical Deal Attributes	Company Y (potential partner)		
Flexibility	*Has*	*Needs*		*Has*	*Needs*	*Flexibility*
High	√		Brand Recognition		○	
		○	Distribution Channels	√		High
			Sales Force			
			Existing Customer Installed Base			
		○	Key Technology/Patents/IP	√		Medium
		○	Complementary Products/Services	√		High
Medium	√		Cash/Co-investment Potential		○	
			Unique Expertise			
Irrelevant	√		Market Share		○	
			Buzz			
			Competitive Removal/Neutralization			
			Marketing Power			
Medium	√		Existing Partner/Reseller Base		○	
			Access to New Customer Segments			

since the companies have not yet actually spoken. You'll notice there is an exact match between what X needs and what Y has as well as the reverse—what Y needs and what X has. This is a dream scenario for illustration only; it would be rare to find such an exact match. More typically you'll find that the companies are able to offer a subset of each other's complete set of needs.

Another key aspect to finding a win/win scenario is understanding the *negotiation flexibility* each company has regarding the deal attributes. One company could be extremely flexible with one attribute, but constrained on another. For example, X has a lot of flexibility when it comes to offering the partner the ability to leverage their brand recognition (e.g., co-branded collateral, co-branded seminars, sharing event booth space, and logo usage rights). However, even though they have cash to spend on the deal, when it comes to parting with it, they have less flexibility. This could stem from specific company policies, investment criteria, and other cash commitments in the pipeline.

In summary, the basis of generating a win/win deal involves:

- Understanding your company's assets and needs
- Identifying potential partners with complementary assets and needs
- Developing an in-depth understanding of the partner's assets and needs
- Knowing your negotiation flexibility around each of your assets, and developing a sense of the same for the potential partners

Returning to the SpeechWorks example, recall that Microsoft got technology, services capabilities, and a channel-to-market from SpeechWorks. In return, SpeechWorks got cash via licensing their TTS technology, the potential to open up a new market in the mid-size customer segments that they were not previously able to reach, and the ability to leverage and associate with the Microsoft brand, among other things. At the time the deal was inked, this was set up to be a win/win scenario for both companies, with a good fit on complementary mutual assets and needs.

DEFINING RELATIONSHIP TERMS WITH GIVES AND GETS

After the background preparation work is completed and the win/win scenario is defined, it's important to get into the details for a specific

FIGURE 5-6: Partner Relationship "Gives" and "Gets"

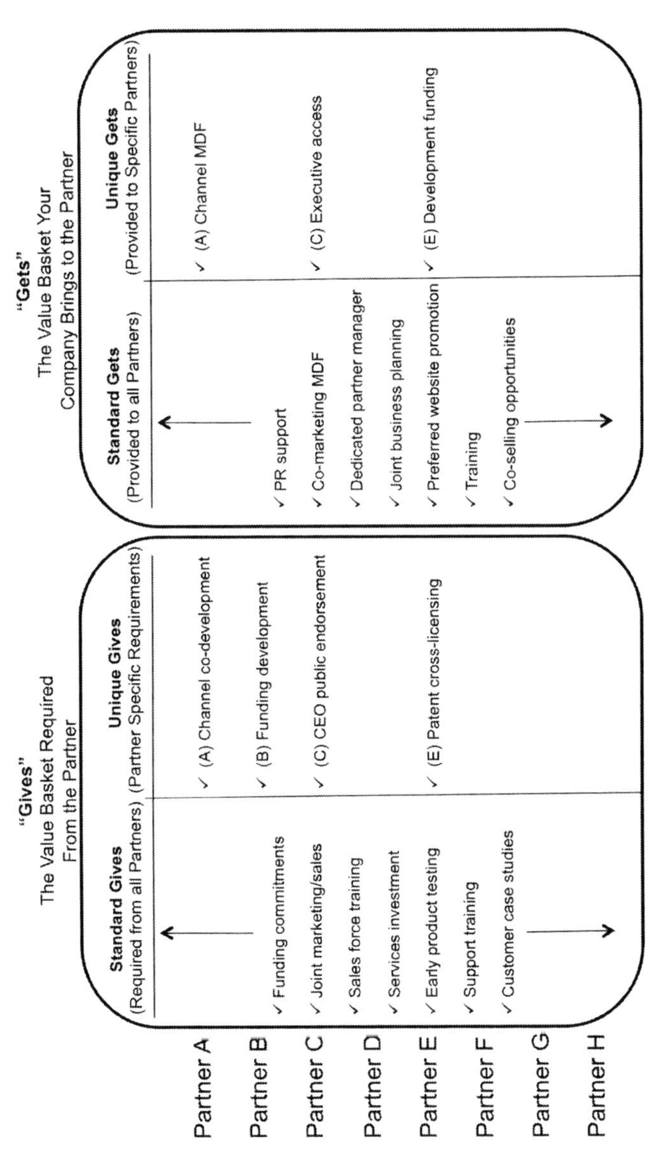

partnership proposal. These details are termed the relationship "Gives" and "Gets"—what specifically you are bringing to the table (your firm's "Value Basket"), and what specifically you want from the partner (the partner's "Value Basket"). Figure 5-6 illustrates how you might structure or think through defining the gives and gets for the various priority partners you wish to pursue.

Think about the gives and gets as falling into two major buckets where there are gives and gets provided to all the partners (the base, or standard, value basket), and incremental and unique gives and gets provided to specific partners. The standard value basket is essentially the core of the gives and gets. For example, there may be a required standard list of "gives" that all partners must be willing to provide, such as joint marketing and sales activities, training, investment or funding of services, and development of co-branded marketing collateral. Given this investment, your firm may be willing to offer all partners PR support, joint business planning, a dedicated partner manager resource, market development funding (MDF), and so forth.

Given the nature of the specific partner and the specific gap trying to be filled in your go-to-market strategy, you may need to customize some deals. For example, if you are doing a deal that attempts to provide distribution channels for your company, you may want to require a specific partner to co-develop the channel with you. Or if the partner has a highly recognized CEO, and your firm could use the awareness, perhaps a public endorsement of the deal by the CEO would be a required give. Again—this works in both directions—your firm may be willing to provide funding for development activities or special access to your own executives as a partner get. In any case, these customized offerings are specific to the particular relationship and the specific gap to be filled.

In most cases, it is best to stick to the standard gives and gets. This provides consistency across the various relationships, eases the relationship management and negotiations, and prevents ill feelings if one company discovers that another is getting more out of the relationship. You should expect that, regardless of any privacy agreements, the partners will talk with one another about their relationship with your firm.

PREPPING FOR NEGOTIATION

Getting to a point in the business development process where you can begin to engage partners involves a lot of work, a solid understanding of the partner and market landscape, industry dynamics, the ability to sell the possibilities of a deal internally before going outside to partners, and good intuition regarding the potential to complete the deal. To prepare yourself to meet the above challenges, the minimal background information you should understand about any key market-maker partner you identify and plan to begin serious discussions with should include:

- Revenues and breakdowns by product and channel
- Operating costs and cash flow; net income over past few years
- Key financial investments and commitments
- Identified top customers generating a significant portion of their revenue
- Current distribution channel strategy
- Vertical markets coverage
- Product portfolio, market share, and product quality
- Current reseller partner base: number of partners and their top partners reselling a significant amount of product
- Current strategic partnerships/alliances: how well have these progressed?
- Significant obligations (financial, contractual)
- Competitors: who do they view as their competition and why?
- What do they believe is their significant competitive advantage? Technology? Services? Flexibility? Price/performance? Unique product features?
- Service offerings and number of employees on professional services staff
- Number of engineering staff
- Marketing spend

You can get this kind of information from a variety of sources (and you will need them), such as industry and financial analyst reports, public financial statements, Dun & Bradstreet reports, competitive intelligence from your existing customers and partners, news and trade publications, and press releases. With this information you will be armed and ready to begin discussions.

To effectively negotiate a win/win deal, you will likely need to work with a number of internal stakeholders in your company such as:

- Senior business management, to approve the deal structure and terms and ensure commitment
- Engineering staff and management, to ensure technical feasibility and schedules
- Marketing staff, to ensure and deliver on marketing obligations
- Finance staff, to approve significant financial obligations and terms
- Legal staff, to ensure the contract is legally sound and there is minimal legal risk
- Services staff (e.g., Microsoft Consulting Services) to ensure they can fulfill any commitments on their behalf
- Sales force, to deliver on contractual sales obligations

As you work on proposals and plans in anticipation of the negotiations, make sure you are getting timely input, feedback, and buy-in from these stakeholders.

NEGOTIATING THE WIN/WIN SCENARIO

Entire books have been written on successful negotiation techniques. However, none I'm aware of have focused specifically on negotiations via business development activities around a product launch. Given that, I can offer the following negotiation advice and best practices as they relate to the business development aspects of launching a new product:

Approach More Than One Company: It's important to not let your efforts be held hostage by one company. While it is true that in some cases there is no alternative but to engage only one potential partner (e.g., unique technology is involved, or a specific patent is required, or a particular person with unique expertise is necessary), in the vast majority of cases you will have clear and viable alternatives. You will gain experience from your interactions with multiple potential partners that you can leverage in other conversations. If you are creative about it you can use the fact that you are engaging with multiple potential partners as negotiating leverage with your partner targets.

Create Clear Expectations on Both Sides to Avoid Misunderstandings: You don't want to get into any negotiation under false pretenses or without you and your potential partner being on the same page regarding the intent of the negotiations. Setting clear expectations and assumptions up front will help avoid negative interactions in the future.

Leverage FUD: Yes, instilling fear, uncertainty, and doubt can be used subtly during the negotiation process, but not in a negative or threatening way. For example, making it clear to a partner that this is the sole opportunity to engage on this product launch for the foreseeable future could cause them anxiety and instill urgency to take action if they feel they only have one shot and can't risk missing out. Another example might be that your product launch and entry into the market will create competitors for them that could eat into their revenue streams: isn't it better to get on board now than to risk that potential scenario? Finally, if your company has the muscle, clearly indicating the extent of your company's investment into your product and the money you are spending on building the market could create some doubt about the viability of other relationships your target partner might have: will they be around in a few years after your product starts taking market share?

Set and Hold to Clear Deadlines: Setting clear deadlines for yourself and your potential partner during the negotiation, and holding to them, sends a clear message that you are serious. It also allows you to monitor the partner's responsiveness to deadlines—very responsive is a good sign, not very responsive and missing deadlines indicates they are either incompetent or they aren't taking the opportunity very seriously.

Make Sure You Are Negotiating With the Power/Decision Makers: Don't waste your time negotiating with those that aren't the decision makers. Intermediaries will simply slow down the process and create confusion. Identify the person or persons that can authorize the deal, are the owners of the budget, and are senior enough to be taken credibly.

Get a Clear Picture of the Business Situation of the Partner: There is a lot of prep work and data you must collect before entering into negotiations to give you a clear indication of the potential partner's business situation. Not having this prep work will lower the chances of a successful deal. Once you begin discussions you should also immediately begin to validate the information you developed in your preparations and fine-tune your understanding of the business situation. This allows you to be more effective in the deal-making process, and enables you to make the right decisions and trade-offs when necessary.

Identify Areas of Potential Misalignment Quickly: If you have a clear understanding of the partner's business situation, you will be able to identify misalignments quickly. The earlier you can identify these issues the easier your deal process will be. For example, finding out late in the game that the partner actually has a different strategic intent than had been previously identified and that doesn't map to your company's strategic direction can be a showstopper. Then you've just wasted time and energy for nothing. If you do identify misalignments, you must quickly address them.

Have a Plan B: You always need a fall-back plan. You can't bet your product launch success on a successful negotiation with one potential partner. Have multiple partner options if possible, and make sure you can meet your needs in another way even if that is not the optimal choice. For example, if you need technology and can't get it from a partner, you must develop it in-house. Prep the engineering staff for this and at least have a high-level plan to achieve it if a deal can't be done. Or you may need applications developed by partners that will run on your product. If you can't sign up the right partners to develop the critical applications, you may need to develop them internally or acquire a company that already has them. Having a high-level back-up plan for these eventualities will cover your needs and increase the odds of a timely and successful product launch.

Maintain Good Project Management and Communication Skills: Responding quickly signals your partner that you take this seriously. Maintaining written documentation of your interactions enables clarity, avoids potential misunderstandings, and covers you legally. Finally, respecting your time and the partner's time is common courtesy and will help build a trust relationship. Good project management skills will make you more effective, which will maximize both the efficacy of your time and the partner's during the negotiation.

Ensure You Have Reasonable Knowledge on the Technology and Business Aspects of the Deal: This is one of the worst mistakes that can be made during the deal-creation process. If you don't know what the heck you are talking about regarding the technology at a high level, you can't make the right decisions about what to put into the agreement because you don't understand the implications. Plus it makes you less credible.

Protect Your IP: Use non-disclosure agreements (NDAs) before starting any discussions. I've mentioned this more than once, but it's so important

I'm mentioning it again! Without an NDA, you open yourself up to legal attack and potential loss of your company's intellectual property asset rights. Don't talk about or share any sensitive or confidential information or documents, especially technical information, before you have a binding NDA in place.

Maintain Sincerity and a Positive Mindset: Being positive fosters a cooperative relationship, which can make the deal construction process easier. It will also help create a trust relationship, making the deal process go that much easier.

These suggestions are good negotiation practices for any company. There is also a time and place for drawing the line on a negotiating point. Where that line is, and when you draw it, is where some of the art of doing a deal comes into play. The important thing is to recognize this and draw the line when required.

METHODS TO PARTNERING

Depending on the nature of the deal, there are a number of ways it could actually take form. Never do a significant deal on a handshake or based solely on a personal relationship. You must codify the deal in writing: verbal agreements will only lead to pain and suffering in one way or another!

Two of the most common methods to codify a written deal are Memorandums of Understanding (MOUs) and contracts. Both will likely be involved in codifying the results of your negotiations and the terms of the relationship. Always sign an NDA before talking seriously with any third-party company where potentially confidential non-public technical information will be exchanged. Your legal staff should provide a standard form for your company's NDAs. Be aware of any feedback clause in another firm's NDA. Unsolicited feedback can be freely used by the other company.

MOUs are typically used to codify a relationship in a non-legally binding manner. They are typically short (1-2 pages, but could be longer) and outline each partner's general agreements, actions, and responsibilities. MOUs are generally used when two companies are ready to commit to a relationship, but not yet ready to commit to a more formal contractual relationship. This situation occurs frequently when there is no established history between the two companies, where there is wariness or lack of complete trust, or where one company wants to keep other options open. It's a "more than tire-kicking but less than married" tool to codify the relationship.

An MOU should contain at least the following elements:

- Statement that the two companies desire to work together
- Why they want to work together
- Definitions of any key terms for clarity
- Statement that MOU is not legally binding unless terms are specifically called out as binding
- Explicit identification of the activities each party is agreeing to undertake
- Explicit identification of any legally binding terms
- Term of the agreement
- Signatures of both parties

Figure 5-7 is a simple example MOU. Your legal team should review any MOU and assist in providing specific language, especially for the binding terms.

Contracts differ from an MOU. Contracts are typically used when two companies are ready to make a serious commitment to a mutual effort. They can be very lengthy, and since they are legally binding, generally contain a substantial amount of legalese regarding warranties, intellectual property protection, termination clauses, breach of contract terms, and limited liability statements in addition to the more general terms, activities to be undertaken, and obligations of the parties involved. Your legal staff should be intimately involved in any contract development process.

Although the specifics of contract development are beyond the scope of this book and are best left to the legal staff, here are some considerations to address in a contract or MOU when you are codifying general obligations and activities you and your partner are pursuing:

- Product-related considerations
    - Development of prototypes, beta versions
    - Product release criteria
    - Reporting requirements
    - Testing results and criteria
    - Bug fix requirements
    - Product support requirements
    - Resource requirements, like lab space, tools, hardware, software
    - Requirements for trial or evaluation versions of the product

FIGURE 5-7: Sample MOU

Giant Technology Company Inc. Memorandum of Understanding

Giant Technology Company Inc. ("**Giant**") and *name the partner company* ("**Company**") desire to work together, as set forth in this Memorandum of Understanding ("**MOU**"), in the *name/ describe the project or activity this MOU relates to* ("**Project**") in order to *state the purpose(s) of the relationship*. As used in this MOU:

"**Product**" means the Zapper product being developed

"Services" means the services that Giant Technology company will be delivering

Except for the obligations set forth in Section 3, this MOU is not a legally binding agreement. Instead, it describes the actions that Company and Giant should take in order to achieve mutual success for the Company and Giant and for the Company's participation in the Project to be successful. Giant and Company are referred to individually as a "**Party**" and collectively as the "**Parties.**"

1. GIANT UNDERTAKINGS: Giant will use commercially reasonable efforts to undertake and/ or fulfill the following actions to assist Company with its participation in the Program:

1. Develop a marketing campaign to promote the joint solution
2. Introduce the Zapper product into Giant's top distributor (DistCo Inc.)
3. Deliver technical training to Company's engineering team

2. COMPANY UNDERTAKINGS. Company will use commercially reasonable efforts to undertake and/or fulfill the following actions as part of its participation in the Project:

1. Deliver 500 leads for use in Giant's marketing campaign
2. Start developing solutions for the Zapper product after training
3. Lower the price of Zapper for distribution into DistCo Inc.

3. BINDING PROVISIONS

1. Giant retains all rights to its products and services. No license is granted to any of its technologies.
2. The Parties agree to keep these MOU terms and any Confidential Information disclosed by the Parties confidential in accordance with the NDA.
3. MOU term is 5 years.
4. Either company can remove themselves from participation in this Project at any time.

If this MOU is consistent with Company's understanding, please sign a copy of this MOU in the place provided below and return it to the undersigned.

Acknowledged on behalf of both parties:

Giant Technology Company Inc.	**Partner Company**
By: ____________________	By: ____________________
Name: ____________________	Name: ____________________
Title: ____________________	Title: ____________________
Date: ____________________	Date: ____________________

- Service considerations
  - Requirements for training on each other's technologies
  - Any consulting services and associated fees required
- Marketing and sales considerations
  - Requirements for customer feedback on the joint effort/product
  - Public relations activities like press releases and case studies
  - Event participation requirements
  - Sales collateral (whitepapers, case studies, presentations, or joint development of these items) or demo requirements
  - In-person presentation requirements
  - Access to customer lists (names, addresses, phone numbers)
  - Access to or development of joint market research
  - Requirements for analyst or press engagements
  - Minimum/maximum promotional dollars to be spent by both parties
  - Any other co-marketing activities contemplated (seminars, videos, road shows)
  - Website activities (cross linking, posting content, email newsletters)
  - Logo usage rights and restrictions
  - Branding and co-branding scenarios/rights
  - Access to the party's partner channel, sales force, or customer base
- Relationship considerations
  - Minimal staffing requirements
  - Communications processes and methods to be used between the companies while managing the relationship
  - Identified executive sponsors for the relationship

Anything you put into the contract should be defined very explicitly and include a time frame, milestones, and dates for any specific deliverable.

RED FLAGS OF POTENTIALLY BAD DEALS

You never want to do a bad deal, and you can't do good deals with bad partners. Unfortunately, this happens more often than one would like. Surprisingly, it even happens to Microsoft!

Take for example the partnership with Sendo Holdings PLC. A partnership was formed between Microsoft and Sendo around smart phone initiatives, basically Sendo using a Windows-based operating system for its Z100 Smartphone. Unfortunately, in December 2002 Sendo filed suit, claiming Microsoft wanted "to plunder its proprietary information, technical expertise, market knowledge, customers, and prospective customers," in essence claiming Microsoft conspired to steal Sendo's trade secrets because they felt some of their technology was showing up in HTC Orange SPV Smartphone (Orange was a competitor to Sendo).

Or take the dot com boom in 1999. According to McKinsey & Company, there were more than three partnerships being formed every day during that time. Many of these partnerships were inked solely to drive up the stock price in the short term. Most failed.

Be aware. The following red flags could indicate that the deal you are in the process of doing, or have already signed, may be headed for trouble:

- Delaying tactics or complexity
  - Partner unnecessarily drags out negotiations over minutiae
  - Partner unnecessarily complicates the deal terms
- Competency issues
  - You know their business better than they appear to know it
  - Discovering during negotiations or after signing that your partner does not have the competency or assets they claimed to have
  - Low quality of engineering deliverables
  - Partner key company strategy changes during negotiation or after signing
- Communication issues
  - Missed dates on deliverables with or without communication to you about this
  - Lack of significant communication or engagement after the deal is signed
  - Every conversation becomes a debate, or requires constant reinforcement of term definitions
  - Frequent disagreements over what was "really meant" by a term or what the "real expectation or assumption" was behind it
  - You start talking more to their lawyers than the business or technical folks
  - Any hint of the word "breach" as it relates to the relationship or the contract

- Changes to the agreement
  - Attempting to change terms after the deal is signed
  - Persistent renegotiation of already agreed-to terms during the negotiation process
- Ethical or poor behavioral issues
  - Other partnership announcements along similar lines when the deal was considered exclusive
  - Post-signing complaints either directly or "through the grapevine" of how they got the short end of the stick in the deal
  - Unworkable requests by the partner on terms like pricing, sales volumes, and minimum commitments
  - Any feedback or hints that confidential information from your negotiation discussions is showing up elsewhere
- Process issues
  - Commitment by your company to begin activities before the deal is signed
  - Frequent escalation to senior executive sponsors of normal disagreements or issues during the course of executing the contract
  - Exchanging confidential information before a MOU or contract is signed
  - A significant or frequent change of executive sponsorship: different person(s), less senior person in the organizational structure, or a new sponsor every month
  - Late, delayed, or missed monetary payments to your company based on contractual milestones
- Lack of executive sponsorship
  - Executive engagement is never seen
  - Lower-level employees block access to higher-level management

If you become aware of any of the above red flags you need to take immediate, proactive steps, understand the implications, and implement the appropriate course of action. Because it's always possible for a deal to "go south," you must maintain regular engagement and excellent communications with the partner both during negotiations and after the deal is signed. Frequent meetings, quality meeting notes, email follow-up (always good for documenting interactions), and regular face-to-face meetings are all best practices for getting the deal done and keeping on top of it once it is signed. When problems or issues come up, it's your job to manage and resolve these issues in a timely and efficient manner. Staying closely in touch even after the deal is done will help you do this and ensure that you are cognizant of potential red flags.

MAINTAINING AN EFFECTIVE PARTNERSHIP

Once you've taken your market-making partner deals to completion and inked a deal, it's a big mistake to think the end has been reached. On the contrary, at this point the real relationships are just beginning. The business development person that has driven a specific deal must stay engaged with the partner for some time to ensure continuity and that the specifics of the agreement are fulfilled. In addition, a good partnership is one where both parties are happy and satisfied with the value of the deal and how they are receiving it. This is a critical point—what they are getting is often perceived as positive or negative by their perception of how they are being treated and how satisfied they are with the relationship itself.

To maintain an effective business-to-business partnership, the relationship satisfaction levels must be constantly monitored and maintained. Maintaining the relationship satisfaction levels is also a key post-deal activity for business development personnel. Remember, these are key partners that can make or break the product launch and/or its success in the market post-launch: you need to pay special attention to these types of partnerships to make them work and mitigate any downside risk.

You should focus and monitor four major areas to maintain a positive satisfaction level in the partnership:

- Factors specific to the relationship
- Process factors
- The nature of joint projects
- Deliverables required from the relationship

While there are numerous aspects of a business-to-business relationship that can go sour, it is possible to make sure that the relationship has the best chance to succeed by simply paying attention to a few key details in each of these areas as indicated in Figure 5-8. For example, ensure that both your company and the partner company are not understaffed and have assigned the appropriately experienced personnel. The ability to be

FIGURE 5-8: Relationship Satisfaction

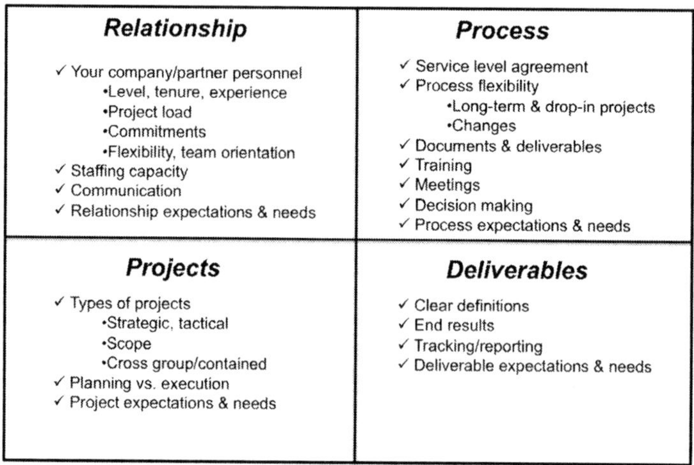

flexible and take on a team orientation, even though it is another company, is important. Imagine the damage that would be done to the relationship satisfaction if the work you've jointly agreed to do is being done with too few resources that are way too junior and rigid and exclusionary by nature. The relationship will only be headed one way—down. You can avoid this situation with good planning, good communication, and by clearly setting and holding to each party's expectations and needs.

The process by which the relationship is executed also has a strong effect on the satisfaction of both parties. Service Level Agreements (SLAs) are a simple, yet important, concept that will drive up the satisfaction of the relationship if put into place. An SLA basically codifies the expectation for each party to deliver on what they are supposed to deliver. For example, each party may be required to provide documentation reviews and provide feedback upon receipt of the content within a certain time frame. Whatever the nature of the "service" to be provided, creating and adhering to a clear SLA will define and provide clarity around expectations. Process issues can also be mitigated with clear communication mechanisms such as regular meetings (e.g., quarterly business reviews, monthly joint updates, weekly and bi-weekly phone calls), clearly defined decision makers, and ensuring that each party maintains flexibility to accommodate unanticipated issues.

For the actual work happening it's important to ensure that the nature of the work is well understood up front. For example, if projects were positioned as strategic in nature, but turn out to be tactical implementation projects, this will negatively impact the relationship satisfaction. The nature of the work also must be understood by both parties as it relates to the scope—is the work a very contained, departmental project, or is it a broad project that spans across organizational boundaries? Again, if the presumption going in does not match the reality once the work gets started, the relationship satisfaction could take a hit.

Finally, work to be done is usually driven by specifically agreed to deliverables. Given this, clearly defining the specific deliverables, ensuring that the end results of the work and the deliverables map to expectations, and ensuring that adequate tracking and reporting capabilities are put into place will enable the relationship to continue on a positive note.

6

Gettin' Slimy, Baby: Launch PR

Public relations (PR) is an often misunderstood element of product marketing, whether in a launch or sustaining marketing phase. The title of this chapter purposely underscores the false perception that PR activities are "spin," lies, and unsupportable, slimy marketing speak. These perceptions are generally held by those who think that PR is all about writing a press release, filling it with half-truths, releasing it on the wire, and voila, you're done! This couldn't be further from the truth. In reality, PR encompasses a broad range of specific, focused activities that involve multiple target audiences and deliver on specific goals to support all marketing mix activities required for a successful product launch. For a product launch, there are a number of key outcomes that your PR activities can help accomplish:

- Assist in creating broad positive awareness and education about the product, your messages, and your strategies to the target customer base. Awareness and education is the first step to incent trial and purchase of your product. PR is one element of the marketing mix that can assist in this regard.

- Help establish the product's credibility to the target audience and how it can help solve their business needs. Having solid positive press and analyst support can help place your product into the customer's purchase consideration set.

- Accurately position your company and your product. If you are not actively conveying the positioning points you want to claim, then someone else, like a competitor, will position you in the manner they choose.

- Assist in positioning the competition *from* your perspective, and re-position the competition *to* your perspective. You must position your company and product and actively convey the positioning perception you wish to create around the competition. If the competition occupies a positioning space that places you at a competitive disadvantage, then you need a strategy, talking points, and evidence to re-position that competitor.
- Help build excitement in the marketplace. A well-planned PR strategy can create anticipation in the market, which could translate into revenue post-launch.
- Build and enhance key partnerships and show a critical mass of support for your product. Not only will PR activities around your key partners provide evidence and credibility to the press, but working together on PR-related activities can strengthen the partner relationship and further publicly tie you together, creating a compelling incentive for win-win scenarios in your partnership activities.
- Create and show momentum and progress around your launch and the product's market acceptance. As you build to your launch crescendo, you want to show accelerating progress around key success drivers for your product—more partners signed up, more customers are interested, and large well-known customers adopting your product, among others. The pace of your PR activities and your strategy to release information will help convey the momentum and traction you are gaining in the marketplace, providing further evidence for press and analysts, which could lead to positive write-ups.
- Create fear, uncertainty, and doubt (FUD) in the marketplace. As a competitive tool, PR can help change thinking and create desired competitive responses. Just as in military communications, misinformation or misdirection can be a powerful competitive tool to shift a competitor's focus and capital or other resource investments to your advantage and to blunt the competitive threat you may face when your product gets to market.

Depending on your particular situation you may choose to optimize around a few or all of these outcomes.

To successfully meet launch goals and metrics, PR is obviously not the only element of the marketing mix to use, but it is important because of the leverage and breadth of reach that can be achieved. For example, a number of print publications also have Internet sites, and a print article about your product will likely also appear on the web. Some publishers also have multiple differently branded publications living under one corporate entity. One article can flow through and be distributed throughout these multiple publications. These are examples of PR leverage—one article, multiple messaging distribution channels. Multiply this by a large number of potential publications and the leverage upside can be enormous. As an example, one interview I did with the Associated Press was put out on the newswire and picked up by over 50 newspapers, including *The Wall Street Journal*.

Breadth of reach is also a PR benefit because you can reach a broad number of customers in a highly cost-effective and credible manner. Take the example of a publication that targets IT Professionals. If it's a well-regarded trade magazine, and has a broad readership base, a one-page advertisement could easily cost $25k-$50k or more to get your message out to the publication's circulation base of 100,000 readers. Contrast that with an hour of your time effectively spent with an editor from that magazine discussing your product, plans, or strategy. If a positive published article results from that conversation, not only did it cost you a lot less (your time and your PR firm's time and fees) to accrue awareness, but the article is more credible to the readership, as it derives from a trusted, third-party source vs. your for-fee and self-promoting advertisement. A credible message from a trusted source to your 100,000 potential customers—that is breadth of reach.

The real focus of your PR efforts is *how* to achieve that leverage and breadth of reach to gain the awareness, credibility, and other previously indicated PR outcomes for your product, messages, and strategy. That is where all the hard work lies. For example, you don't just willy-nilly call up an editor, have a quick discussion, and expect a great and positive article to result. A huge amount of both up-front and ongoing work is required to get the desired end results.

This chapter will illustrate how to think about PR in the context of your launch and help frame your planning process. To set the context, we'll explore the target press and analyst communities you must approach and how these professionals think.

UNDERSTANDING EDITORS AND ANALYSTS

In many industries, editors from trade and business publications and industry analysts are primary target audiences for PR focus. Before drilling-down into PR tactics directed at these audiences, I'll provide some perspective and background on editors and analysts to help shape your PR efforts. Figure 6-1 provides a visual overview of the PR landscape and summarizes the playing field at a high level. In a nutshell, your goal is to Influence, Convince, and Educate (ICE) editors and analysts.

At the bottom of Figure 6-1, I have indicated an important point: your customer targets, the folks you want to purchase your product when it launches, are the same folks that are the editors' readership and the analysts' clients. You are all talking to the same set of people. The idea is to get the editors and analysts writing about and saying the same things you are communicating to your potential customers. I don't mean you need to trick them or be untruthful in any way to accomplish your goal. Educating these folks, then providing a logical and defensible argument to overcome their objections, will influence these professionals toward your end goal. If the acronym worked, I'd probably write it as ECI: Educate, Convince, and Influence—because this is the order you need to follow for a successful PR strategy. This will help create positive PR outcomes. However, to accomplish this, you must first understand the mindset of editors and analysts. Then we'll explore defining and executing PR strategies and tactics.

FIGURE 6-1: PR Landscape Overview

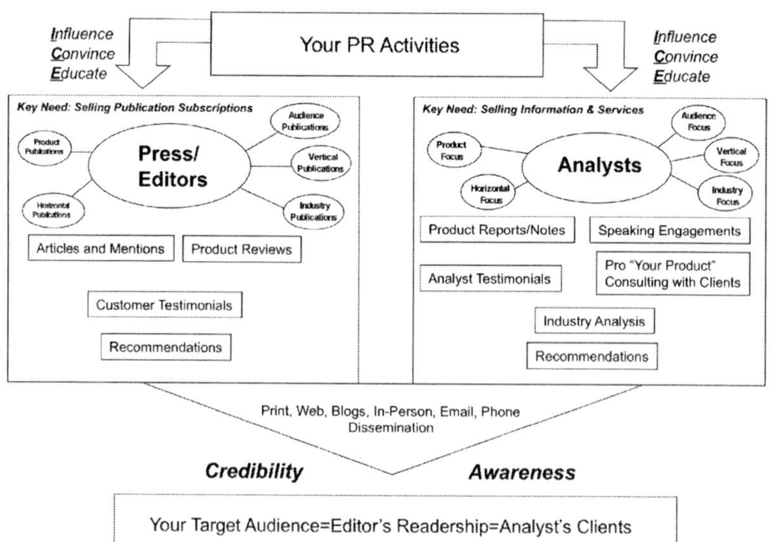

The Editorial Mindset

The Way They Want You to Think They Are. Editors will approach you in the classic journalistic manner. Skepticism will be their primary mindset to start. They assume a position of guarding their readership from false and inaccurate claims and information. Their content is not an advertisement, after all. They represent bastions of truth and hold the quality and accuracy of their content of utmost importance. They are the gatekeepers of information and strive to provide their readership with information that is accurate and relevant as it relates to their readership's needs. They want to establish a relationship of trust between themselves and their readers, albeit at arm's length through the publication. They will verify and validate what you are saying through their industry contacts, readership, analysts, and their own experience. They are the guardians and disseminators of knowledge.

The Way It Really Is. What I've said above is a generally accurate portrayal of the journalistic mindset. However, one overriding consideration must also be understood: they are employed by the content publisher and management to achieve one end goal—to sell more of the publication. Like any business, if they don't sell the publication, there is no money to pay them, and they are out of a job. So there is a balancing act going on here: they need the content and information you can help them provide to their readership so they can build a salable content product. They also operate within various constraints that limit the amount, type, and quality of content that can be produced. These constraints can include how frequently the content is published, its format, its technical depth, its organizational structure, the needs of their readers, the amount of content they have, and the quality and productivity of their writers. Let's add context to this by understanding what underlies some of my statements above.

"Skepticism Will Be Their Primary Mindset to Start." Of course this is the case if you do not have an established relationship with the editors. They have no basis to trust anything you are saying. They speak daily with a lot of people who tell them a great many things. Some of what they are told is true, but some is false. They don't want to be perceived as a dupe or mouthpiece that simply regurgitates information (especially false information) that is fed to them. If this occurs, they lose credibility with their journalistically minded peers and their readers. Healthy skepticism is the rule.

"They Assume a Position of Guarding Their Readership From False and Inaccurate Claims and Information....They Represent Bastions of Truth and Hold the Quality and Accuracy of Their Content of Utmost Importance....They Are the Guardians and Disseminators of Knowledge." Yeah, okay, right. Some folks have a pretty lofty perspective about their jobs, but in this case it's true. This is the perspective that journalists get fed when they go to college and take courses in journalism, or when they work at the newspaper, or another content publication provider, whether print or online. Cut to the core and understand that, from a business perspective, if they are putting out inaccurate or low-quality content, they will not be able to sell it, they won't look good personally, and the publisher will suffer financial issues that may cost them their jobs. Most editors start out with this holier-than-thou value-based perspective, but it gets tempered over time as the reality of the business world tightens its choke hold, as it inevitably does.

"They Will Verify and Validate What You Are Saying Through Their Industry Contacts, Readership, Analysts, and Their Own Experience." By now you should be thinking under the hood and understanding that it is not because of some immaculate personal value set that editors will pursue due diligence to validate what you are saying. They are making sure the information provided is accurate and that they understand what you are saying if they really don't understand it to begin with. They don't want to appear ignorant when you tell them something they don't understand, but many times will not admit it. So they'll turn to a trusted source, perhaps a relationship in which they feel more comfortable admitting ignorance, and rely on that validation before committing to writing. Editorial misunderstanding is a leading cause of factually inaccurate articles. Working to build a relationship of trust with the editor can help overcome this problem. Repeated conversations over time can also help. The editor's due diligence also plays another role. By talking to others about your information they can provide a broader perspective in their content and provide other examples, like real world customers, to make the article more interesting. Better and more relevant content means more publication sales.

The Analyst Mindset

Analysts are a different breed than editors, as they come from a completely different perspective. Whereas editors want to sell publications with their content, analysts use content they produce as evidence points of their expertise to sell more consulting services.

The Way They Want You to Think They Are: Analysts approach interactions assuming that they likely know more about the subject at hand than you do. They are industry or product experts and are important influencers in their clients' decision-making processes. Assuming a probing and skeptical approach is their generally accepted modus operandi. They interact with industry participants and customers to ensure they are on top of market and industry trends to enable the best, most insightful advice to their clients. Their firm's brand name is well-known and carries significant weight throughout the industry. Analysts are unbiased and neutral, and provide significant value-added insights and analysis to the products, technologies, and industries they write about. Editors use analysts as a trusted resource to validate an industry supplier's statements. Analysts are the trusted source that customers seek out to cut through the industry vendors' half-truths and lies to get the "real" story upon which to base their purchase decisions.

The Way It Really Is: There is some truth to what I've said above. Customers do engage with analysts to help them make decisions. Customers do read analyst reports and notes. Some firm's opinions do carry more weight than others. Analysts generally probe and stay in touch with many industry suppliers to understand what is happening. Finally, they provide insight, analysis, and perspective in their written and oral commentary. Bottom line: analysts are important. However, it's important to note that many end-customers do not rely on one analyst for their decisions. In fact, analysts are simply one of many purchase input factors used in a purchase decision. They are important, but just one of many inputs.

The unspoken truth is that analysts need you to provide them with the very insight and perspective they base their writing on. This is especially true if you are a market leader like Microsoft. Imagine an analyst writing a report on a particular technology and not including a perspective or analysis of a market share leader like Microsoft. What perception would that create in an existing or potential client's mind? What level of credibility would the analyst have? Likely it would create a negative perception, as the analyst would be supplying an incomplete view of the situation, and their credibility would be undermined.

How do you think industry analysts get information regarding market share, unit shipments, product information, and revenues for the companies they follow? Many industry analysts produce reports that provide this information for a particular product, like shoe shipments by size, or the number of mahogany tables shipped by vendor in a given year. In the technology world, computer industry analysts report on microprocessor shipments, server software shipments, and application revenue. They also provide in-depth product or vendor business analysis. Most of this information is supplied to the analyst by the vendors themselves, as are the capabilities, features, benefits, and deployment information for the vendors' respective technology or product.

Without good communication flow between analysts and vendors, the analysts would have little or no primary source material to create their reports besides customer or partner inputs. That means they couldn't produce solid written evidence of their industry expertise with a comprehensive perspective to win new clients and satisfy existing ones. Clients are the source of their consulting revenue stream. No new consulting revenue means good-bye to their job as well; thus the link between ongoing vendor communications and their job success. This is another example of a personal need driver masquerading as a business need driver.

KEY LAUNCH PR ACTIVITIES

Now that we are on the same page regarding the motivations of the press and analysts, let's recap the situation for a product marketer during the launch cycle. First, early on, the product is in the beginning development phases and is undergoing architectural definition and feature definition. This is a hazy time from the product perspective. It's likely still unclear what the definitive value propositions are for the product, plus the needs of the target audience (if the target customer has actually been clearly defined) are still being understood. There is really no product to market at this point, just the idea of a product (Chapter 1).

This is the time to get the basic PR infrastructure in place, including relationships with press and analysts, but primarily analysts. The overall goal at this point is to start the education process about your plans and strategy. This will create awareness of your efforts and plant the seed for the future—to play in the desired marketplace you need to get on the map now. It might seem early in the product cycle to start working with press and analysts, but believe me, it takes a long time to establish the relationships and discussions and to make sure the story that is being communicated externally is the right one and is correctly understood.

Also keep in mind that press and analysts are focused heavily on what is shipping in the market now, not what might be there in a year or two, so don't expect any significant early coverage about your product-to-be. Instead, focus on establishing mindshare and relationships with press and analysts early in the launch cycle. Later in the launch you can expect to see increasing placements and buzz as your product and marketing milestones, and creative PR activities, are executed and you begin to ramp up your efforts toward launch.

So what should you do from the PR perspective to prepare for launch? Focus on the following primary PR activities:

- Getting your PR firm in the loop and up to speed
- Establishing product marketing as PR owner/driver
- Identifying and training internal spokespersons
- Identifying and understanding the key editors and analysts
- Defining and creating your key messages and communication tactics
- Establishing communication with analysts and press
- Building PR relationships with your partners
- Defining your launch PR strategy, philosophy, and tactical plan
- Executing your launch PR strategy and tactics
- Creating your post-launch and sustaining PR plans

Let's take a look at each of these items in more detail.

Getting Your PR Firm in the Loop

I'm assuming you are already working with a PR firm: selection criteria for choosing a PR firm are beyond the scope of this book. If you don't have a PR firm, get one. Loop your PR firm into your launch planning at the beginning. The worst thing you can do is wait until you are part way through the launch execution, or nearing your product launch date, to pull in a new PR firm and expect them to perform wonders for you. That won't work. You must work in partnership with your PR folks from the start. Your business may have an internal PR department, or a combination of internal/external. If you have only internal, I'd recommend hiring an external firm that has experience in your market, since they will likely have already established relationships with some editors and analysts. Internal PR departments generally are more focused on facilitating the relationship between your company and the PR firm(s) themselves and handling corporate news.

Microsoft has both internal corporate PR and external PR. Internal PR focuses on assisting with relationship management of Microsoft's external PR firm (historically that has been Waggener Edstrom, although there are others). They also focus on executive PR (Bill Gates, Steve Ballmer, other senior VPs), and helping position Microsoft overall (corporate brand positioning, community affairs, government relationships, diversity, technology and innovation leadership, and legal issues). Waggener Edstrom assists internal PR with these corporate-level activities.

However, PR activities specific to Microsoft products are driven out of the Microsoft product and business groups and generally engage Waggener Edstrom as the key external PR resource. This includes PR for product launches.

Your external PR folks should be a key part of your launch team and be involved in, and definitely informed of, key business planning, strategy, changes, and eventualities. Help your PR contacts understand the product that is being developed and the key target audiences. Explain the business plan and strategy so you are all on the same page. The better informed and more involved your PR vendor is, the better their advice, planning, and execution will be.

Establishing Product Marketing as PR Owner/Driver

To have an effective PR strategy and execute it well you need to have a single point of ownership for PR activities. Product marketing as a function should own this, and a team member should specifically be on point to drive and execute the strategy with the PR firm. You don't want multiple contacts dealing with the PR firm. You must funnel and manage the activities and messaging from a single source to minimize confusion and maximize effectiveness and clarity.

Identifying and Training Internal Spokespersons

Even at Microsoft, clearly identifying and training internal spokespersons does not always happen. Doing so must be part of the launch PR process. Start with specifically identifying who will be tapped to interact with press and analysts. It's important to get this right, as these folks will be the face of your company to the outside community. They must adhere to the general rules and guidelines I specify later in this chapter, or significant PR disasters can occur.

Once identified, these folks must be trained. Many senior managers will balk at getting PR training, but I would make it a rule that whoever plans to interact with the press/analyst community must get trained. How you make that happen is up to you, but do it. Another piece of advice—make it clear inside your organization that non-spokespersons are *not* to interact with the press or analyst community, make statements about your product or strategy, or represent the official position your company is taking on anything. The rule to the organization should be: "If you (employee) find yourself interacting with press or analysts (e.g., at a trade show), point them to your primary internal or external PR contact ASAP. Don't express your opinion on anything. Don't provide any information. Don't answer any questions."

Identifying Key Editors and Analysts

Your PR firm must assist you in identifying the key influentials in the space you are entering. You must define the PR playing field early on in the launch cycle, which means knowing who is out there that you need to be concerned with and what their hot buttons are.

The PR firm should compile information that contains at least the following:

- For Analysts:
    - What are the key analyst firms in the space that are influential?
    - Who are the key analysts in these firms? What is their position on the industry? What is their key area of focus or expertise?
    - Profiles of the analysts' backgrounds, key publications they have written, positions they have taken, perspective on their current take on your company (like, don't like, aren't aware of you at all), companies they like/don't like.
    - Their perspective on your competitor's business strategy and products.
    - Vertical or horizontal market focus, if any.
- For Press and Editors:
    - What are the key publications in the space that are influential, both broad business press (e.g., *The Wall Street Journal*) and trade/

product specific publications (e.g., *CRM Today*), or audience specific publications (e.g., *Computerworld* for IT Pros, or *Visual Studio Magazine* for developers)?
    - Who are the key editors at these publications? What is their position on the industry? What is their key focus or expertise?
    - Profiles of the editors' backgrounds, key articles written and positions taken, perspective on their current take on your company (like, don't like, aren't aware of you at all), companies they like/don't like.
    - Their perspective on your competitor's business strategy and products.
    - Vertical or horizontal market focus, if any.
- For the Competition:
    - What coverage levels are competitors getting?
    - What products are being covered? What kind of coverage are they getting—positive or negative? What are the PR firm's opinions on why this is the case?
    - Where is coverage occurring—which publications, which analysts?

This information will be a key input into your tactical PR launch strategy and how it will be executed; it should be regularly updated. You should work with your PR firm to stack rank and prioritize the list of editors and analysts.

Message Creation and Communication Vehicles

The messages you plan to communicate publicly are the backbone of your PR efforts. If these are not on-point and well thought through, your PR efforts will be in vain. All your ongoing PR efforts will focus on getting the right messages to the right audiences.

Message creation and communication via PR is a large part of the public presence of your company and, specifically, for your launch. Because it is public, I strongly recommend you have adequate buy-in and consensus from all the key stakeholders around your specific messaging points. Creating this buy-in will cover you from the negative consequences of making a public mistake and rally the organization to continuously address and face the implications of the strategy being implemented, and, if necessary, to question, refine, and redirect it.

To formulate effective PR communications, there are three important activities to pursue:

- Determine your desired customer perceptions and address any gaps between desired and existing perceptions about your product or company.
- Define the key messages around your company and your overall business and product strategy.
- Identify specific news items to be communicated throughout the launch and the important messages to be conveyed around these news items.

Once these activities are accomplished, there are numerous PR vehicles available to get the word out.

CREATING DESIRED PERCEPTIONS AND MESSAGE ALIGNMENT

Before embarking on creating your business and product strategy messages, or your specific news item messages, first examine existing press, analyst, and customer perceptions of your company or your firm's other products. Evaluate any differences between these existing perceptions and the perceptions you wish to create. The delta between existing perceptions and desired perceptions is your perception gap. Closing that perception gap by creating compelling and convincing PR messages is a key goal for your PR activities.

Figure 6-2 indicates this with a few simple examples. If the existing perception of your company or other product lines is that your products are too expensive, and you want to move the perception to the great ROI value that your products deliver, you need to implement the right set of messages, with the right evidence, to close this gap. This concept is relatively straightforward and seems obvious, but it is commonly overlooked when contemplating PR plans.

Having a planning session to help frame your desired perceptions is a fun exercise. For example, if, after a discussion with the press, you opened up the newspaper, a website, or a magazine with the article or mention resulting from your interview, what would the perfect headline be? Thinking about this and brainstorming headlines in advance will help you refine and focus the desired perception to create in your target customers' minds via your press or analyst interactions.

Once you have figured out your desired perceptions and know where you stand regarding existing perceptions, you can begin to create the key PR themes that will help close any existing perception gap. To do this effectively, keep the Figure 6-3 framework in mind. The concept is to align

FIGURE 6-2: The Perception Gap

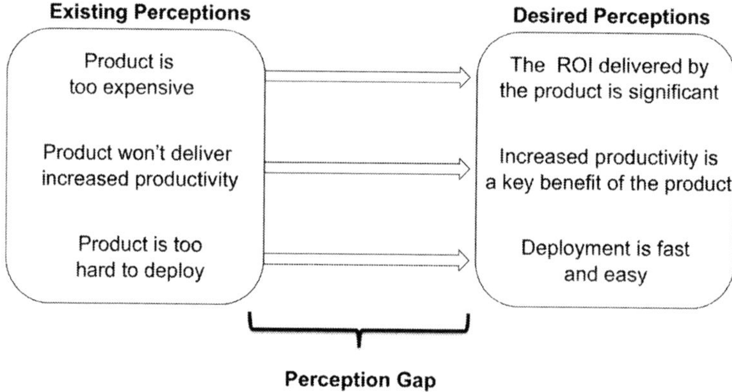

your key PR themes, or messages, to map to and support the core value proposition pillars you have created, with the end result being to drive the desired perception. I've used the TelSoft v2.0 example positioning pillars discussed in Chapter 4 for the example in Figure 6-3.

One of the desired perceptions I'd like to create is that the product I am launching will accommodate customer needs as their business grows. Thus I am focused on creating the desired perception "This product will meet my growing business needs now and into the future." This desired perception maps directly back to one of my value proposition pillars from the Teleportation Server Software positioning framework: a highly scalable product. To create the desired perception that aligns with this value proposition, I've created a key PR theme, or hook, centered on "Solution grows with your business," and I can build supporting messages and evidence around it. I can then pitch this theme as the angle for top stories to editors. The other examples in Figure 6-3 are developed following this same logic.

Ensuring alignment between the theme, positioning value propositions, and desired perception will enable consistency and focus throughout your communications, and move you toward leveraging PR successfully in your launch. You should continually review and assess the effectiveness and relevancy of your key themes and refine them over time to maximize your PR effectiveness.

FIGURE 6-3: Aligning Hook, Positioning, and Desired Perceptions

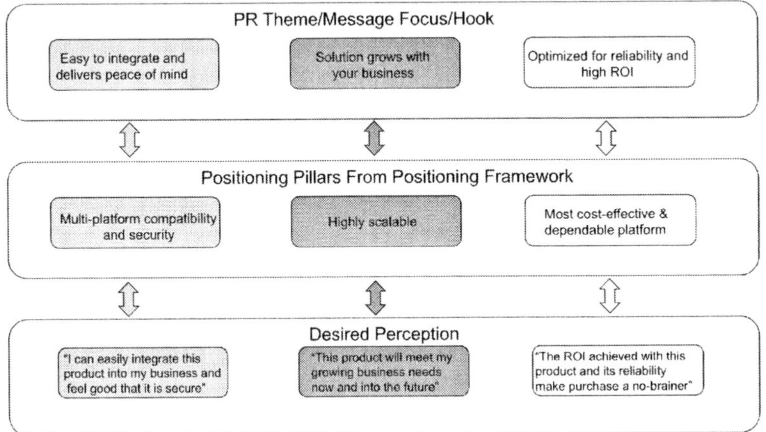

OVERALL BUSINESS AND PRODUCT STRATEGY MESSAGING

After focusing on your key themes and hooks and getting your alignment in order, the second messaging activity to tackle is around your business and product strategy. Because Microsoft is fairly well established, they can avoid much of the precursor and basic get-to-know you questions that you and your firm may face. Often the focus with Microsoft and the editorial/analyst community on a new product seems to be "Great—here comes Microsoft again to take over another market," so Microsoft product managers need to deal with all the baggage that comes with that mindset. Unless your company is a monopoly with gigantic cash reserves, you likely won't have that particular problem.

However, for firms that are less well established, are start-ups, have not done a lot of PR previously, are moderate- or large-sized companies with limited brand recognition, or are closely held private firms, you will need to answer some basic questions when first engaging and building relationships with the editorial and analyst community. When you are developing your top-level company and strategy messaging, you should be prepared to have solid answers to questions such as:

- Who are the key management representatives at your company? What are their credentials?

- Why is your company entering this market and not another? What's the big deal about your plans—why should anyone care?
- What is your vision for this product and market?
- What are the key elements of your strategy to enable your vision? Why do you think this strategy will be successful?
- How are you funding this effort: debt, equity, private placement, venture capital, internal cash flow?
- How will your entry affect the market?
- What are your key goals for the product? The market?
- Who are your key competitors? Why? Why not other companies?
- Who are your target customers? Why? Why not other customer segments?
- What is the value proposition of your company, strategy, and planned product offerings? How is this different from your competition?
- What are your key risks? Why?
- What defines success for you? Key success metrics?

You must also prepare to handle the negative objections you'll likely face, especially when you first go out. Be prepared to handle statements like:

- This is a dead market category, or it's already too crowded.
- Competitors are too entrenched: you'll never succeed.
- Sounds like a me-too strategy.
- Too late to market.
- Too early to market.
- Your company is too small, too big, not nimble enough, not focused enough, has failed in the past so why should your efforts succeed now, doesn't have enough cash flow to sustain entry.
- Your product won't technically be good enough.
- The technology isn't ready for market, it's unproven, it doesn't work.

I'm sure you can think of other possible objections. You should plan to identify likely objections in advance, and prepare your responses in writing before any editorial or press engagements.

MESSAGING AROUND SPECIFIC NEWS ITEMS

The third messaging activity involves message creation around your specific news items, such as product milestones, customer or partner programs, or strategic partner relationships. Whatever the specific news item to be communicated, you'll need to establish relevant messaging points to be communicated. Messages around specific news items should be consistent with and reinforce your overall messages and not contradict the higher-level messages. They should also be truly newsworthy.

Consistency

Being consistent and non-contradictory is essential. Most smart journalists or analysts will quickly catch on to a claim you are making that contradicts what you have said before. If this situation occurs during an interview or briefing it can quickly lead to a downward spiral in communications and result in a negative PR outcome and damage your credibility. Regardless of what your specific news item messages are, they must be consistent with what you've said previously. This reinforces the solidity of your business strategy and product plans and your path's momentum (and maintains your credibility).

Newsworthiness

Newsworthiness is a facet of PR that is occasionally (and sometimes more than occasionally) overlooked or ignored. I have interacted with many folks who do not understand what PR is (or even what marketing is) and feel that anything that can be said about what they are doing is worth "doing PR around." It can be difficult to explain that what they want to say does not map to the PR strategy, goals, and metrics that have been put into place, or that what they want to communicate is not truly newsworthy. The following list may help provide framing criteria around what is newsworthy. While certainly not comprehensive, these are significant PR hooks and claims that can help filter your proposed communication desires and determine newsworthiness.

New: If something is new, whether a feature, program, or initiative, it is likely of interest to the press or analysts that follow your product category and market.

First Ever: If you can make the claim that what you are doing is the first time it's ever been done, or the first product or event of its type, or some other "first," you can probably consider it newsworthy.

Large Numbers: Everyone is interested in large numbers; it's just human nature. Who doesn't want to know who is on the list of billionaires this year and how many billions they have? If you can make a large number claim, folks will be interested. For example, it is of interest if you can say your company plans to spend $X million or hundreds of millions on your product launch, or you've spent $X million or hundreds of millions on R&D. For the speech recognition product I helped launch at Microsoft, the amount of customer utterance data acquired and fed into the "corpus," or database of utterances, can drive the statistical accuracy of a speech recognition engine. Claiming more utterances than anyone else, and claiming a large number of billions of utterances captured, certainly helped create interesting news. The database market uses hooks like how many terabytes (trillions of bytes) of data a specific database can effectively hold, or how many millions or billions of transactions can be accomplished in a given time. Or how about "Over two billion copies of the Windows Vista preview edition downloaded!" Large numbers are a curiosity, grab interest, and are newsworthy.

High Rate of Change: Rate of change is a key element in creating the perception of increasing momentum, and is a key perception to create during a product launch. Showing a high rate of change is evidence to support momentum around your product. Has there been a significant rate of increase in the number of customers adopting your product, e.g., "We've gone from 100 to 10,000 customers in our pre-launch trial program in only one month," or a significant growth in the number of channel partners signing up to support your product? Has there been a significant and rapid rate of decrease of errors, or problems, in your pre-launch product development? High rate of change is interesting as it shows rapid progress to meeting goals, solving problems, or gaining adoption and market traction.

Uniqueness: An obvious but tricky news claim. There are very few unique things in the world. If you happen to have one of them it is definitely newsworthy. Perhaps you have a unique luminary at your company (only person to win three Nobel prizes in different categories), or a patented product feature that preserves its uniqueness and defers competition, or a unique solution to a problem (the only method to effectively mine lumber that exists underwater, or the only process to create rainbow-colored artificial diamonds). Whatever it is, if it is unique, you should make news around it.

Unusual: This is a step down from unique, but still newsworthy. If something is uncommon it is of interest. Perhaps you have an unusual type of customer that is adopting your product, or your solution can be applied to unusual situations, or your product is being used in unusual ways. Here again, the rareness of the claim and the curiosity it elicits is what makes it interesting and newsworthy.

Best in Class/Breed: This is a common claim and typically depends on the definition of "class" and the quality of the supporting evidence. For example, if a product review process from *Big Time* magazine did a competitive review and rated your product "Best in Class," it's pretty straightforward to make news around this claim via your PR activities, and you have supporting evidence. In the absence of a "gimme" like that, some firms rely on funded (mainly self-funded) comparative studies to create the claim. Sometimes how you slice and dice the market can make this easier. For example, a particular study may show that although your product places in the middle of the pack to solving most customers' problems, it was best at solving problems in the real estate vertical market. Voila! You are "Best in Class" for the real estate industry and can use this claim to help create the perception that perhaps plants the seed that your product is best in class elsewhere, too.

Free: Pretty much a no-brainer here. If it's free, and it has intrinsic value, odds are it is newsworthy.

Surprising or Unexpected: Perhaps you just won a big contract against a larger, more entrenched competitor that everyone expected would take the business. Or a large marquee brand customer switched from a competitor's product to yours. Or you've signed a distribution deal with a partner that has never carried a product like yours. Surprising or unexpected occurrences are newsworthy, as they sometimes call into question accepted norms or assumptions, which then becomes news itself.

Creating Controversy: Making a controversial claim can be newsworthy. For example, "We expect to take 90% market share one year after we launch," or "We'll have twice the performance at half the price as competitor X." The press thrives on controversy and playing one company off another. Expect a juicy controversial claim to be newsworthy and garner coverage, although you need to be careful—feeding the beast while not getting bit is a subtle art!

Compelling Business Value Metrics: Kind of plain vanilla, but standard fare for news items. Quantifying the high ROI, large revenue impact potential, significant cost reduction potential, or customer satisfaction increase can be newsworthy, especially if compared to other products or solutions.

Other items that barely make the list here include anniversary dates and awards. Sometimes you can use historical date points and make them a newsworthy item, e.g., "It's the One Year Anniversary of Our Social Giving Drive," or something more product related. Awards and commendations are also sometimes newsworthy: if you win a product review, or get a commendation or positive mention from a recognized analyst firm, that is likely a newsworthy item to use in PR activities and communications.

INCREASING YOUR MESSAGES' IMPACT BY LIMITING THEIR NUMBER

To communicate effectively with press and analysts, you will need to focus and distill your key messages into a very limited number of messages per interaction with any given press or analyst contact. This is important because:

- You likely won't have too much time with any given editor or analyst; this limits how much you can communicate effectively.
- To provide some depth and context around your key messages, you must discuss evidence points to support your claims and handle back-and-forth discussions. This takes time, so the fewer key messages the better.
- You have less chance to get randomized and misstate a point. Fewer points will keep you on track and focused. Trying to remember to communicate too many messages can reduce clarity and confuse you and the editor or analyst.
- Your messages will have a greater impact if they're presented in limited quantities and in digestible chunks. If you present three key messages, they can all be regarded as important. If you try to cram in 10 messages, it's a stretch to convince someone that they are all super-critical, and you risk getting coverage focus on the less important messages instead of the important ones.
- Fewer key messages have a greater chance of being properly understood and internalized by the editor or analyst. These folks can encounter a

broad range of topics and people daily. The less they need to note and remember the greater the odds that they will recall and reiterate your messages correctly in any resulting coverage.

My experience is that three key messages is a good number, and five is the most you want to attempt. You may think differently, but I'm sticking to my numbers based on a lot of PR experience.

PUTTING MESSAGES INTO CONTEXT FOR THE SPECIFIC AUDIENCE

As you formulate and communicate your specific PR messages you must put them into a context relevant to the media target audiences, presenting the key messages appropriately for different customer groups. Doing so is typically known as "spin" in the PR world.

For example, assume you have three different end-customer audiences you are trying to address: developers, business decision makers, and channel reseller partners. Assume you have two key business messages and claims you want to go out with:

- Your new product will enable a new class of solutions.
- Your company will dramatically drive down prices to enable wider adoption of this type of product or solution.

For each customer audience you must think through questions like:

- Why should they care?
- How do these messages relate to the needs of the specific audience being addressed?
- What's the specific benefit to them as a developer, business decision maker, or channel reseller partner?

The answers will most likely be different for each customer type. For a developer, enabling a new class of solutions may translate into an opportunity to develop a new type of product, extend an existing product into a new space with enhancements your product will enable, or make for easier and faster programming. You would focus on these points when communicating the message about a new class of solutions to developers.

For a business decision maker this same message may need to focus more on the business value to the enterprise that the new class of solutions offers, such as lowering costs and raising productivity. These are more compelling points to make for business decision makers and differ from the points directed at the developer audience.

For a channel reseller, you may need to focus more on what the market opportunity is for them around these new classes of solutions. So, while it is the same key message (enabling a new class of solutions), the approach and presentation of the message will differ for each audience.

The same goes for the second message around driving down prices. While this will likely be positively viewed by developers and business decision makers, as it will make the solution more cost-effective for them to obtain and leverage, channel partners may have a problem, as it could reduce the resale revenues or profits they accrue at today's higher price points. Communicating a price decrease message to resellers will require a different message presentation and talking points than that used for developers and business decision makers. Think through the potential ramifications of your messages and adjust the presentation for each audience before making your claims public.

For the tough, contentious, or potentially controversial claims (like the possible backlash from channel partners with your price reduction message), one would typically prepare what is known as a Rude Q&A document; it lists the possible issues and questions by audience and provides the answer if such a question should arise. Typically this will not be a public document and would be used only by your PR firm and your spokespersons. Having this document in place before going public will force you to think through the hard questions and issues, and to be prepared.

Of course, in the early stages of a launch, there are some questions that you might not want to answer at all—either for competitive reasons or because the plans are not yet definitively formulated. For example, you may want to defer all questions about distribution and channel strategy, pricing, unannounced partnerships, licensing and SKUs, revenue and unit projections, and detailed product features and functionality. Many of these topics will be your news items and discussion points for press and analysts later in the launch cycle, so you want to reserve these until they are nailed down and final, and can be disseminated for maximum coverage impact. You need to identify these topics and include them in your disclosure road map and strategy plans.

PR MESSAGE DISTRIBUTION MECHANISMS

Given that you have newsworthy items to take to the editorial and analyst communities, and your themes/hooks, messaging, and evidence are in place, you must determine the best approach or combination of approaches to get the news out. Your PR firm should shine in explaining and providing you with the best options for this process. Some of your option choices will be driven by their appropriateness for your situation and their effectiveness against your PR strategies and metrics. In other cases, the reality of your PR budget constraints will dictate choices—your budget may be unable to accommodate all possible options for every news item you develop.

Some of the major PR distribution mechanisms are illustrated below. You can use this list to shape discussions around the optimal mechanisms.

Press Releases: Pretty much the standard fare for getting news out, and the most familiar mechanism. A well-written press release can generate media pickup and buzz for those you have not directly briefed and provide primary source content for those you have briefed. What does a well-written press release consist of? I've summarized my take on structuring a solid press release in Figure 6-4. Typically, make sure you have a strong attention-grabbing headline that summarizes the most compelling news point you are relating in the release. Support the headline with a subtitle that provides strong supporting messages for the lead news nugget. You don't want to make a press release too long—a few pages at most. I suggest breaking the content into three primary sections: the "Overview Block," up to three "Drill-Down Blocks," and the "Summary Block."

The Overview Block will summarize up front your high-level news items and any claims you are making around them. You should clearly identify the newsworthiness of your claims and any business benefits. It's important to get this information out up front as this is the meat of your release. You also need to support your claims with your company executive quotes and third-party analyst quotes to show commitment and credibility around your claims and to provide references to any other key evidential support like awards, reviews, and customer or partner wins. If editors read no more of your release, they should have the gist of the news after reading the Overview Block.

You can then drill-down into more detail around the top three messages you are conveying, and provide specific back-up evidence. Again, I say three messages as, to be effective, you need to limit the communication to the most important elements and messages you are trying to communicate.

Finally, the Summary Block should summarize the key messaging points in the release and provide a specific call-to-action for both the press (e.g., your PR representative's contact information) and for the end-customer target market (e.g., a link to a desired website landing page for more information).

FIGURE 6-4: Press Release Elements

Typical press release structure…

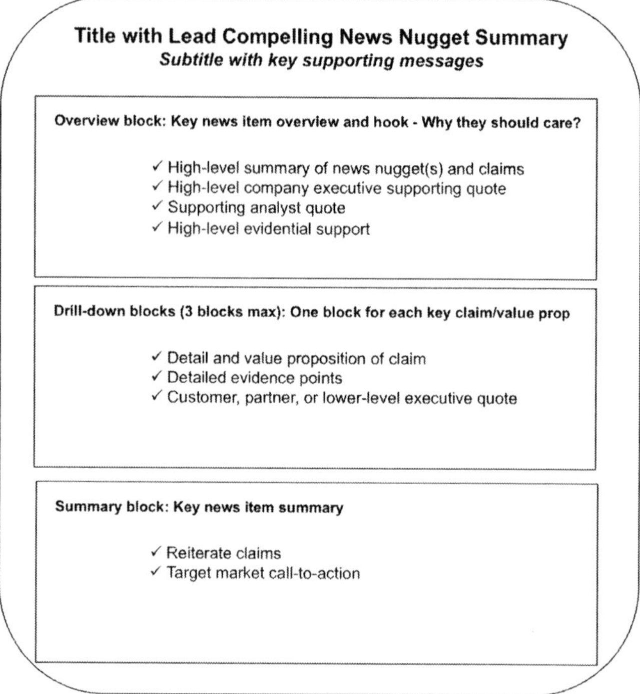

Umbrella Press Releases: This mechanism is actually multiple press releases tied together by one overview (umbrella) press release. You can use an umbrella press release if you have multiple news items from different products or groups that are related and support each other. This single high-level press release summarizes the news items of all the products or solutions, tying them together and putting things into context with overall messaging. The umbrella press release then provides links or pointers to the press releases that contain the product or solution-specific news items.

For example, say Microsoft is announcing its entry into a new market. The umbrella press release would discuss the corporate level intentions, key products, or solutions and why they're entering the market. As the umbrella release goes out, the groups developing the related key products and solutions release their specific releases that are "under the umbrella" of the overall release, and drill into the specific value and messages for those products.

If you get really ambitious, you can try to time any partner releases with the umbrella release. Opportunities to take this approach are generally limited and require a lot of coordination, pre-planning, and time. However, this mechanism can provide a giant PR push and, if well coordinated (and with newsworthy messages), can provide a large PR spike in impressions and placements.

Radio News Releases: These are short radio spot advertisements that convey your messaging via a creative audio approach and provide filler material when radio stations have unsold advertising space (it's not good for radios to have dead air time, thus the potential for your spots). These are hit-and-miss opportunities, but are relatively inexpensive to produce and distribute.

In-Person Interviews: In-person interviews are perhaps the best mechanism to convey your news, but require the most training to execute effectively. When you are conducting a one-on-one interview, regardless of the mechanism (phone, in-person meeting, radio, TV), you can emphasize and explain your messages, respond to and overcome objections, and control the conversational flow to meet your end goals. In-person interviews also enable you to establish a personal relationship with an editor or analyst and let your friendly, sparkling, and likable personality shine through! The more one-on-one interviews you can get, the greater your chance for positive coverage. They hinge on the spokesperson's ability to be effective in one-on-one communications and employ the PR training techniques they have acquired—so yet again I say make sure your spokespersons have adequate PR training.

One-to-Many Internet Webcasts: You can now easily hold news briefing meetings over the Internet. Microsoft Office Live Meeting is one product that can provide the necessary platform technology to do this. It allows you to present a PowerPoint presentation while the audience listens on the Internet using Voice Over IP (VOIP) technology or via a regular telephone dial-in conference call. Holding a one-to-many press update or news disclosure session on the Internet works great for regular updates, when you want to communicate the same news without customization to a broad press or analyst audience. You can also record your live session and press or analysts can view it later on an on-demand basis. One-to-many briefings are a good method to educate and bring new editors or analysts into the fold.

Email Updates: Email is another effective broad reach mechanism to communicate information and news. Email allows you to include appropriate follow-on web links and attach documents, like press releases, to support your communication messages. Your PR agency will maintain a list of analyst and editorial email addresses and can send the email updates on your behalf. They should be a component of your quarterly media update communication process.

Short- or Long-Lead Press and Analyst Tours: These tours are business trips you take across the country (or the world) to meet in person with press and analysts. Long-lead trips happen earlier in the product development cycle, and short-lead trips occur closer to the final launch. In-person meetings are the best way to communicate and establish personal relationships, so you should strongly consider these types of tours. Flying out to meet a member of the press or an analyst at their place of business indicates the importance you place on the relationship with them and can pay dividends as you continue to release your launch news items.

Analyst Summits: These briefings are events you generally would hold at your place of business, and the analysts fly in to meet with you and your colleagues. Topics run from getting feedback on your business strategies and activities to news updates and progress reports you want to communicate in person. You'll typically need to schedule these far in advance so the representatives from the key analyst firms you are targeting are available. You should also plan on paying travel and lodging costs for each analyst, so it can get pricey. However, this engagement has the same benefits as other in-person meeting options. Typically, you will either hold an analyst summit early in the product cycle for strategy feedback and input, or later in the cycle as a pre-briefing mechanism for significant news and updates for the final phases of the product launch.

Press Summits: Similar to analyst summits, you host an event at your place of business that brings in press from around the country or the world for daylong (or multi-day) briefings. Typically you would structure such a day with a PR firm representative acting as a handler or host for each press member, putting each editor into their own conference room, and scheduling half-hour to one-hour meetings with other representatives from your company. This is especially effective for update briefings if your company has a lot of products and the publications represented are broad enough to cover the range of your product set. In such a scenario it is more cost-effective to pay for bringing the press to your location than to fly 100 product managers all over the country to do briefings. For both press and analyst summits, it is sometimes possible to hold these in conjunction with large key industry events that you can be sure both press and analysts will attend.

After engaging the press or analyst community via one of the above mechanisms you'll see your efforts reflected in different publications, including blogs, print magazine articles, website articles and content, analyst publications and newsletters, radio or TV shows, and podcasts.

Outreach Considerations

Whatever your choice of outreach mechanisms, there are other considerations to keep in mind. For example, you may consider reserving some of your juicier and potentially big news as exclusive offerings for key publications. It's also important to protect the timing for releasing your information to ensure the resulting press mentions coincide with other planned marketing activities. For such considerations, you'll want to evaluate embargos and pre-briefings, exclusives, and non-disclosure agreements as part of your planning.

Embargos and Pre-Briefings: An embargo is an agreement you and your PR firm have with an analyst or media representative to withhold publication of news that you will be briefing them on until a certain date or time. This prevents disclosure before it is intended to be made public. For example, if you have a major announcement coming, and you are using a press release timed to hit the first day of an industry event, you don't want to have the news coming out before that day. However, you also want to ensure that your media and analysts are informed in advance, so you must brief them in advance. The pre-briefing helps build the relationship with your media buddies and keeps them in the loop before the general public hears your news. This is appreciated by analysts and media and helps them appear knowledgeable and on top of industry happenings. Pre-briefs also give the analyst and press enough time to write their coverage to have it ready to hit about the same time the news comes out. This is obviously what you want. The embargo agreement is attached to the pre-briefing so no news gets out early. It's possible, though unlikely, that some media or analysts will not abide by the embargo and will leak your news. In this case you'll need to decide whether to pre-brief with this particular person again.

The fear of being shut out of future briefings will generally make most analysts and media members adhere to the embargo agreement.

Exclusives: To get a large well-known publication to write a headline story, it is sometimes necessary to provide the news item (or items) on an exclusive basis. Exclusivity is a good hook and incentive to get the story actually written given the hyper-competitive news environment, where the first to publish with the story generally gets most of the audience views. The potential downsides include limiting your impression reach to that specific publication's audience and making other publications unhappy at being scooped. However, an exclusive in-depth article published by *The Wall Street Journal,* for example, provides many other PR benefits for re-use, evidence, and credibility that may well outweigh the potential risks of using exclusives. Your job with the PR firm is to weigh the risks vs. the benefits and proceed accordingly.

Non-Disclosure Agreements (NDAs): In some cases, before communicating sensitive information, you should consider having the editor or analyst sign a non-disclosure agreement. This protects you against the untimely release of sensitive information and can be used when you are not looking for immediate or near-term coverage, but are disclosing confidential and sensitive information that can enhance your relationship with the press and analyst community. Using an NDA to convey confidential information and plans can enable feedback for your product development and launch strategies that would otherwise not be possible to acquire. This can enhance your credibility and remove objections, concerns, and incorrect statements that may have pestered you in articles and mentions because the media was not fully informed.

Timing Your Communications and Some Pitfalls to Avoid

You must decide the appropriate timing for your news releases. A number of considerations can drive timing. Sometimes it will be driven by an external trigger, such as an industry event. Your company may be attending a big industry event, perhaps with speaking sessions and presentations, and you want to coordinate the news release with it because you will have spokespersons present to discuss or announce the news. Or the timing may be driven by your product development schedule or partnership agreements in place contractually requiring a news release or PR activity at a given time. If there are external triggers, you must accommodate these and plan appropriately.

Another consideration is news-hogging events: other events occurring in your area, the country, or even in the world that can affect your news release. These could include planned events (presidential speeches or major corporate acquisitions) to unexpected ones (big competitor announcements, significant legal issues at your firm, industry upheaval, and natural disasters). These aren't good times to release news, as your potential pickup and coverage will likely be drowned out. Wait until the noise dies down and the news traffic is lighter to maximize your chances of news pickup.

Outside of these issues you should try to pick an optimal time during the week of your news release, whether or not there is an external trigger driving it. If you plan a press release, pick a day that has the best chance of maximizing pickup. Holidays and weekends are bad times to release news. Mondays are generally the busiest news day, so unless you are announcing a globally significant news item avoid them. Thursdays are media deadlines, so they are slow news days. This leaves Tuesday and Wednesday as your top choices, with Friday at third place.

Another external trigger that can drive a news release is when an unexpected competitive activity occurs. For example, perhaps out of the blue the competition announces publicly that they are developing a similar product but they are getting to market much earlier. This unexpected information catches you and your PR firm by surprise and forces you into a reactive PR mode vs. the preferred proactive mode. When unanticipated situations like this arise, you must have reactive processes in place with your PR firm. These include the ability to respond rapidly to the incoming news bombshells, create a messaging response, and handle any incoming press inquiries. This may also trigger a subsequent news release from your firm with your own product announcement to counter the competitive news item.

While it may seem obvious, it's always better to be ahead than behind and not get caught in a reactive situation. Avoid being caught by surprise and having to react and scramble. Pay attention to the eyes and ears you may have on the street to highlight potential issues ahead of time so you can prepare. Your PR firm, customers, analysts, partners, and field sales are all potential early warning conduits; the better relationship you have with them, the more likely they are to drop a hint or inform you of something coming, so you have time to prepare a response or to get your news out ahead of the competition.

When you are unsure of what the competition is doing, or when they might announce something big, you may want to consider a pre-announce. A pre-announce is going out earlier than intended with your news given the potential, or likelihood, for the competition to release news earlier and thereby take a perceived leadership position. Pre-announcing allows you to assume the high ground over the competition and garner the first-mover advantage. It also allows you to blunt any competitor's follow-on response, positioning them in the "me-too" category, making their news less newsworthy because your firm has already announced similar information.

Establishing Press and Analyst Communications

Once you know who you need to work with in the press and analyst community, your messages are created, and you have defined your planned outreach mechanisms, you need to start the engagement process. The analyst and editor mindsets I discussed earlier now come into play.

GENERAL RULES FOR EFFECTIVELY ENGAGING EDITORS AND ANALYSTS

There are some high-level guidelines or best practices to effectively deal with editors and analysts. They should apply to all your interactions while you implement specific PR activities to influence, educate, and convince these parties. The guidelines form the basis upon which I and other marketers have achieved successful PR outcomes around various products and initiatives at Microsoft.

Create a Win-Win Value Proposition: Be clear about why their clients or readers will care about what you are saying. If you can convince the analyst or media representative that writing about your news is good for their audience and for them, you can create a win-win scenario that will increase your chances of positive coverage.

Be Honest: The last thing you want to do is lie. There is likely a 100% chance that your lie will be exposed at some point, upon which you will have lost all credibility with that media representative and any chance of ever getting coverage again. It's not worth the risk, so don't do it.

Communicate Regularly and Maintain Context and Continuity: Having a discussion about some news and then not talking to that person again for six months can cause problems, including no coverage resulting from an "out of sight, out of mind" situation. Unless you keep the relationship going, it's possible that every time you reengage, you will waste time having to re-educate and cover old ground to get them up to speed. The idea is to continuously build on prior conversations and news to maintain continuity and context with the media representative, keeping top of mind, and thus enabling richer and deeper news coverage. This is not possible or likely with sporadic and intermittent interactions.

Establish a Personal Relationship: Meet in person when possible, and put a face to your name. People are more open and accepting of one another if they are personally acquainted. Anonymous interactions over the telephone are fine, but you can't fully exploit the relationship's potential without also establishing an in-person one.

Acknowledge Their Expertise and Valuable Perspective: Many analysts and media representatives do have significant knowledge of the market, competitors, customers, and products in your space. Genuinely acknowledging their expertise and insights is polite and will build rapport that will help you in the long run. Who knows, you may actually learn something from them!

Don't Be Argumentative or Negative: This is a terrible way to engage with your media audience. Being argumentative or negative only leads to a poor relationship and potentially no or negative coverage. Even if you are being baited, it's always best to take the high road, stay on point with your messages, and don't get into the muck.

Focus on Your Product or Strategy Positives, Not Trashing the Competition: It's one thing to attempt to reposition your competition and their products appropriately; it's another to talk trash about them. This is unprofessional conduct and does not add to the positive image you wish to create about yourself as a spokesperson. Again, staying on messaging points around your product or strategy, and appropriately messaging around your competition, is the way to go.

Take a Long-Term Perspective: You can't expect to get immediate coverage from every member of the press or analyst community that you engage with. You need to build up the relationships over time. Keeping the longer-term perspective on results is a realistic way to frame your approach and to define your PR metrics.

Focus Your Messages to Your Audience: Map your messages and discussion points to the customer base of the specific editor or analyst. Wrap your messages in the correct context for your intended audience.

Provide Tangible Evidence: Back up your statements and claims with evidence to provide credibility. This evidence could be provided by customers, partners, test results, and awards. The more tangible you can be, the more credible you will be.

Anything You Say Can Be Quoted: Be careful—"off the record" can be interpreted differently from person to person. You should always assume that whatever interaction you have with the press or analyst community is fair game for publication. Unless you have a really tight personal trust relationship with your media colleague, it's better to stick to your messages and not get off point and say something that could end up hurting you when it appears in print.

Newsworthiness: Bring something new to the table in each interaction and make sure it is newsworthy. Don't waste anyone's time on discussions that are not valuable.

Don't Overload Them With Information: Limit thc number of messages in any given interaction and parcel out your news items in digestible chunks over time.

Be Prepared—Get Your Thoughts in Order: If it's a phone conversation, have notes and talking points in front of you. Think through the conversation before you actually make the call or meet with your media contact.

Control Interactions With Press or Analysts: To reiterate: do not let just anyone talk with the press or analysts if you want to maintain the consistency of your messaging and avoid having information show up in the media that is incorrect or should not have been made public.

Your PR Agency Is the First Stop: Reinforce the practice of sending press/analysts to your PR firm as their first stop to gain access to you. The PR firm is set up to handle inquiries, schedule meetings, and pre-screen the media contact to assess what information they are seeking. This gives you time to prepare for the interaction and gather the information and talking points properly. Fielding out-of-the-blue random phone calls from press or analysts is a recipe for disaster.

Get PR Training: I reiterate this because of its importance. If you don't have PR training, you need to get it. You need to refine your skills in oral communication in a media engagement. For example, bridging is a technique that teaches you how to move a conversation that has drifted back onto your messaging points politely and effectively. If you can't bridge effectively, you end up in a random conversation where your key messages are communicated improperly or not at all. In training you will often be videotaped in a role-playing scenario; it's enlightening to review the tape and see yourself in action. Most likely, you will be amazed at how much better you could do.

Before engaging with press or analysts, make sure you have a number of relevant go-to customers or partners that you have prepped in advance and trust to be positive about your product and strategy. This is a good method to provide tangible evidence to back up your claims. Since there is no doubt that your press or analyst contacts will want to talk with some existing or potential customers or partners to validate what you are telling them, this activity falls into the "must do" category. Having invested time in creating these trust relationships will pay off in dividends as your PR strategy unfolds.

With press contacts you'll also want to provide friendly analyst contacts that can speak positively about the news at hand as further evidence of your credibility. It's critical to get these analyst relationships in place, since the press will approach them to validate your claims. The press may also seek out analysts that are not positive about your news and incorporate those perspectives. Your insights into what these analysts may say, and any preparations to handle potential negative ramifications, should be considered in advance and incorporated into your reactive PR planning.

ANALYSTS FIRST

Given the importance of analysts, the first discussions you need to pursue are with these folks. Early in the launch, you'll likely have no "big news" per se, so talking to the press is going to be tightly focused around the general scenario that you are planning to enter the market and are developing a product, have an interesting business strategy, or perhaps about your company if it is new. The mere fact that you are launching a new product and have an interesting business strategy with potential market ramifications may be newsworthy. However, at this point it's mainly vaporware and talk—you have few if any proof points that would interest an editor. Thus, your biggest return on your PR effort will be to start with analysts. The general process I've outlined below using analyst engagements can also be leveraged and used when preparing and holding discussions with the press, with some minor tweaking.

The first step is to form a relationship with the analysts, educate them, understand their perspectives directly, and use the information from those conversations to further inform your strategy. If you have dealt with these analysts before, great, you have a relationship; however, this is new information that can extend your existing relationship to new areas or with new analysts at that firm. If you have no existing relationship with the analyst firm, you have a great opportunity to establish the relationship correctly the first time.

I'd recommend having your first few meetings with your Tier 2, or less influential, analysts. This will allow you to vet your messages and presentation and get a heads up on the type of questions you may be getting. The saying "You only get one chance to make a first impression" applies here; prepare for the Tier 1 analyst discussions and make the optimal first impression by warming up with Tier 2 analysts.

The following suggestions may assist in preparing for and running a productive analyst meeting.

Getting the Meeting Set Up: Your PR firm should set up these meetings. You want to communicate your strategy and educate the analysts. It's important to also establish that this is not a consulting gig for them (you should not pay for these interactions), but an opportunity for them to get in on the ground floor and gain early understanding of a significant event that will be occurring in the industry, market, or product space they track. Remember these are busy folks and you need a hook to gain their interest. If you can get an hour of their time, that's great. A half-hour would be the minimum. Phone discussions or conference calls are the best approach.

Document the Meeting: The PR firm should be present during the analyst discussion and take copious notes to document the tone of the interaction, questions asked, and answers you provide. The history of these interactions will be valuable over time to refresh your memory for your next interaction with the analyst and to ensure that you specifically address any key issues raised in earlier calls. You can also use these reports to track your progress over time to get the analysts to support your cause.

Send a PowerPoint Deck: I highly recommend that you create a PowerPoint slide deck that outlines the conversation and makes all the key points you are trying to convey and the questions you are posing. This will dramatically improve the flow and focus of the meeting, especially in a first interaction. Mail this to the analyst ahead of the meeting.

Confidentiality: If necessary, make sure your PR firm makes it clear to the analyst in advance that your discussion will be confidential: you must have a non-disclosure agreement in place with the analyst firm. In addition to the points I made previously about the benefits of NDAs, you also don't want your competitors knowing what you are up to, so you need to make sure that your discussion is confidential until you give permission to make it public.

Understand Your Audience: Before the actual meeting, make sure you understand who will be present on the analyst side and what their background and perspectives are. This info should be readily available from the background documents that your PR firm pulled together for you and provided you as briefing documents before the call. Read them. When you actually get on the call, make sure everyone is introduced and you know who is on the other end of the line. Your PR representative should act as moderator and host for the meeting and take care of any housekeeping activities.

Prepare Answers to Questions in Advance: To prepare for these meetings you should prepare a Q&A document. This is a brainstorm of all the potential questions the analysts might ask and your general answers. It will make sure that you answer questions consistently and that you've thought through the issues. It will also make sure you are internally clear on what you want to communicate to the analyst and what you want to reserve as confidential and not-to-be-disclosed at this time. The PR firm can drive getting this document created, but you will need to make sure the answers are what you want them to be.

Focusing the Discussion: You must pursue a number of non-promotional activities to initially engage with analysts. These generally fall under the education element of our ICE goals:

- Communicating the business and product strategy
- Understanding key objections and issues to inform product development and messaging

- Establishing and validating your early messages, strategy, and positioning framework
- Building the relationship for future leverage

The first thing you want to do is lay out the business and product strategy. If you can, try to preempt basic questions by answering them in your presentation before they are asked. This is likely the first time you are discussing this externally, except for the partnership discussions during your business development activities (Chapter 5). Since your first engagements with analysts should be early in the launch cycle, the primary focus should be on your business strategy: what you are doing and why you are doing it. You need to communicate how you see your company fitting into the market, what you bring to the table—in essence your company's value propositions as they relate to the market you are pursuing. Secondarily, you can focus on your product strategy at a high level: what the product is, where it fits in the marketplace, and what its rationale and core value propositions are.

During these discussions you will be getting feedback and objections from the analysts about your strategy, product, and positioning messaging. If you can effectively assuage any objections, it's a big win. However, the odds are that you will not be able to provide enough depth or evidence to overcome an analyst objection at this point. You are just not yet far enough into the cycle. You should note and document these interactions so you can create effective answers in the future (incorporating them into your Q&A document).

You are also looking for trends. Consolidating the notes you have from your many analyst meetings will paint the broader picture of what you face regarding the analyst community and their perspectives. Use these perspectives to inform your PR strategy and plans.

These initial conversations will lay the groundwork for your ongoing relationship with the analysts. It's important to remember the general guidelines: be honest, be credible, be prepared, take the high road, don't trash the competition, promote your strategy value proposition, listen and don't interrupt. Thank the analyst for taking the time and providing the valuable insights they have offered. Your PR firm should also send a recap email of the conversation to the analyst and again thank them. End the conversation ensuring that the analyst will get follow-up answers to any questions that could not be answered. Make sure this actually happens: it's bad for your credibility if you promise something and don't follow through.

As the launch progresses, your will have more of these sessions, but they will become update and briefing meetings as you convey breaking news, product development updates, and new and changed plans. These meetings need to be a regular part of your ongoing sustaining PR strategy and activities.

Building PR Relationships With Your Partners

The partner relationships you establish as you head toward launch can be an important arrow in your PR quiver. This is true whether the partner is a large strategic partner or a smaller reseller—the only difference is the type of PR activities you can execute together and the potential impact of these activities on your PR goals and metrics.

As with most business-to-business relationships, there must be a mutually beneficial context to a PR relationship. Both parties are seeking awareness and buzz through PR, so executing PR activities with a partner must fulfill both party's needs. The value that co-PR activities will bring to each partner can vary based on the relative situation between the partners.

One such situation involves the relative amount of "PR equity" that either your company or the partner brings to the table. One partner may have a significant amount of existing market awareness, credibility, and buzz—the PR equity—and so working with that partner and messaging together allows the partner with less PR equity to leverage the other's market awareness, credibility, and buzz. This is generally the case when Microsoft executes partner-related PR activities with smaller partners. Having a company like Microsoft or another large, well-known firm provide an implied endorsement via co-PR can provide both substantial awareness and buzz opportunities and enhanced credibility for a smaller, less well-known company.

A different situation exists when both partners each provide a significant amount of PR equity. For example, when Microsoft and Intel or Best Buy and Hewlett Packard join forces around PR, each company brings a lot to the table around the specific news items, brand awareness, and in access to key editors and analysts. The resulting co-PR effects and results are multiplied by working together beyond what each company individually might achieve.

Finally, it's highly likely that neither of the partners brings a large amount of PR equity to the table. Unless your firm is a well-known BigCo, it will fall into this category. Although both parties alone have little equity, by combining forces around PR they can produce a multiplicative effect that will gain more PR results than if they went at it alone.

Regardless, there are numerous activities to potentially leverage via a PR relationship with a select subset of your partners. Some of these activities are as follows:

Joint Press Releases: This scenario involves one press release sent out by both parties jointly. Both parties help write, review, and approve the content's language before it is released.

Supporting Press Releases: In this case, each party puts out their own press release, usually at the same time, and each release reinforces common messages. This is an especially effective technique when you have many partners, perhaps 20, all putting out releases on the same topic at the same time. The news pickup from such an action can be quite good given the volume of communication going out at once.

"Go-to" Partner List: You will most likely be asked to provide a partner reference to add color around your messages and provide supporting evidence to your claims or about your relationship. This is where advanced planning to create an established PR relationship can really pay off. If you properly set up your PR partnerships and make sure that each party is trained on your key messages you will have your go-to list of partners ready. This is generally not something you should be trying to pull off at the last minute, i.e., the press asks to speak with some partners, you have no one ready but commit to providing the reference, and then you scramble to get a few partners lined up. The risk here is that the partners will be ill-trained and unable to effectively convey your messages, or perhaps even say something damaging, resulting in negative PR. You need to select your PR partners carefully and make sure that they are well trained and you can rely on them to be positive about your firm.

Joint Calls or Briefings With Press and Analysts: In addition to being go-to references, your key PR partners can also participate in joint phone or in-person briefings with press and analysts. This is an effective technique, as it further reinforces the depth of collaboration between the partner companies and offers a PR opportunity to one of your partners that can help enhance the partnership.

Supporting Quotes in Press Releases: Again, having third-party quotes in your messaging can provide credibility for your company and product. Including a partner quote in one of your press releases is one way to provide this and is a generous PR opportunity for a partner. It is especially good for smaller partners that are being included in a release with a firm that has significant PR equity.

Mentions by Partners in Their PR Activities: As your partners are trained in your messages, it can be advantageous to agree to convey each other's messaging as appropriate during PR engagements where you are individually addressing the press or analysts and can slip in a plug for each other.

Keep in mind that we have been discussing joint PR opportunities *with* your partners. This is different from PR opportunities *about* your partners. For example, you will have the opportunity to generate PR about a newly signed partnership relationship, the new partner program you have created, the growth in the number of channel partners supporting your firm, or the great applications, services, or complementary products that your partners have created around your product. These are all potential opportunities to work with partners through PR, but do not necessarily require their active participation (just their permission to use their name and publicly disclose the particular news item). The potential incremental and positive effects of incorporating partners into your PR plans make it worth your time to consider doing so for your launch planning.

BUILDING YOUR LAUNCH PR PLAN

By now you can appreciate some of the high-level considerations you'll need to think through regarding your approach around launch PR. You'll need to pull it all together into a PR plan for launch. My approach to a PR plan is to address it like you would any other plan—identify and prioritize the key objectives and strategies, define your tactical execution activities relative to the objectives and strategies, and define the detail around the tactics, timing, key metrics, and any supporting evidence or data needed to effectively execute.

Garnering Share of Buzz

At the highest level, the results from your launch PR plan and strategy should be focused around the primary outcome of acquiring the largest share of buzz for your product and business. Figure 6-5 illustrates the results of an effective launch PR strategy: the overall amount of coverage for a particular product space or market space has increased (i.e., a bigger piece of coverage), and your company has taken an increasingly large "Share of Buzz" as the launch has proceeded. That means that your product or business is increasingly mentioned more than others in articles and mentions around products, companies, and competitors in your space and in market segments you are targeting. Thus you have taken "share" of the buzz being generated, similar to how one would take revenue or unit market share by effectively gaining traction through marketing and sales efforts.

Baseline your share of buzz in the beginning launch time frame and incorporate this metric into your ongoing tracking and reporting process. It's a good indicator of the absolute PR results, your PR velocity, and overall PR progress for your business and vs. the competition. Your PR firm can help with this via their research department and the various clipping services they use. If you want to do it yourself you can estimate and track share of buzz by leveraging a broad article database like Factiva, defining the relevant search terms for your product and market, and tracking the article counts.

Balancing Marketing Activity Driven vs. Sustaining PR Efforts

As you develop your PR plan, you should recognize there are two major categories of PR activities you will need to consider as you progress through your launch. The first is PR around activities primarily based on product milestones and marketing activities that are executed via your overall marketing plan. For example, you hit a product development milestone such as an interim release like a beta release. Or perhaps your company is attending or holding an industry event, or releasing product training courses, or executing a pre-launch marketing campaign with a special offer. All of these marketing activities offer the opportunity to create awareness for your product via PR activities. These activities will be discrete and occur at irregular points of time during the launch cycle. Thus, they will not be generating a regular, smooth run of articles and mentions about your company and your product. I call these "splash" opportunities because you have a chance to "Make a Splash" using PR around these happenings.

The second major category to consider is the sustaining PR activities. These are not necessarily based around a marketing activity, but are the nuts and bolts activities you must constantly and regularly do to create

FIGURE 6-5: Quantifying "Buzz"

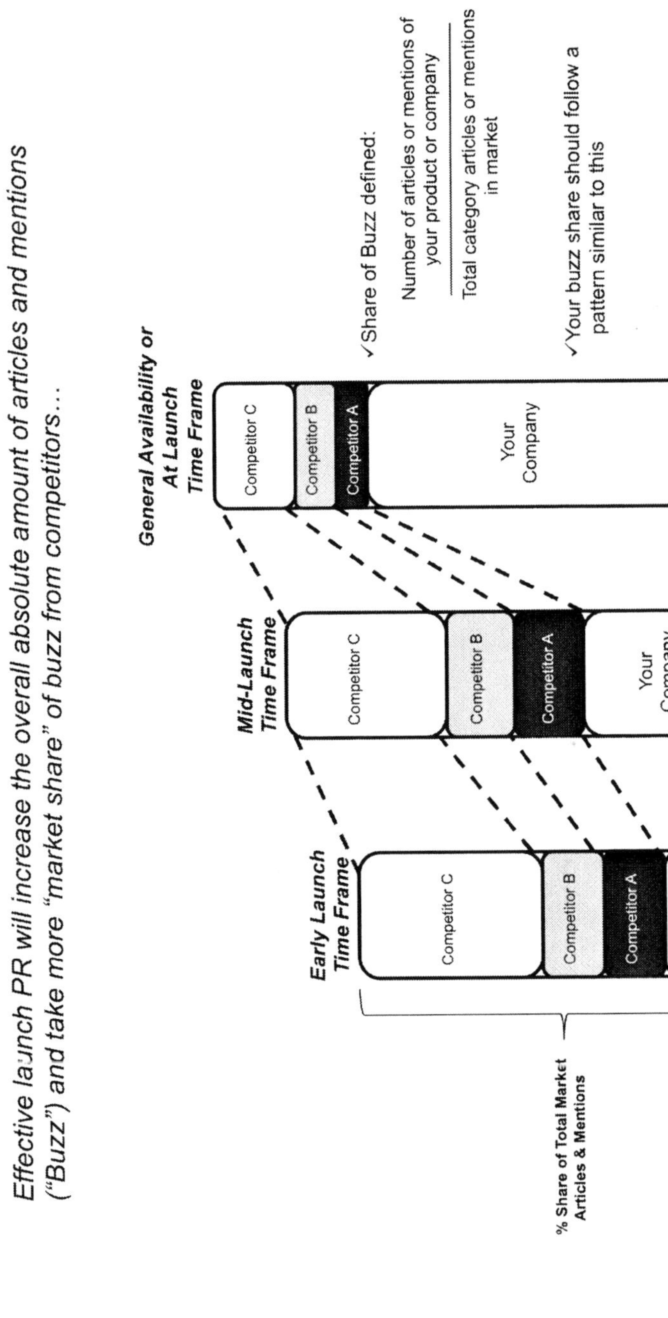

Effective launch PR will increase the overall absolute amount of articles and mentions ("Buzz") and take more "market share" of buzz from competitors…

Early Launch Time Frame: Competitor C | Competitor B | Competitor A | Your Company

Mid-Launch Time Frame: Competitor C | Competitor B | Competitor A | Your Company

General Availability or At Launch Time Frame: Competitor C | Competitor B | Competitor A | Your Company

% Share of Total Market Articles & Mentions

✓Share of Buzz defined:

$$\frac{\text{Number of articles or mentions of your product or company}}{\text{Total category articles or mentions in market}}$$

✓Your buzz share should follow a pattern similar to this

a regular stream of articles and mentions to fill the gaps between your splash activities. These are the "Beating the Drum" activities that create a constant drone of PR outcomes in the marketplace. Examples of sustaining PR activities include regularly scheduled (i.e., monthly, quarterly) press and analyst updates to the people you have existing relationships with, attracting and creating relationships with new press or analysts, and writing and getting articles placed in trade magazines or on content-appropriate websites. Sustaining activities could also include special one-time creative projects, like a stunt that can generate some buzz, or creating speaking opportunities, or meeting informally with the press at industry events to nurture the relationship and keep you and your product top of mind.

Figure 6-6 lays out these concepts visually and poses the key question: How should you split your PR budget around each primary category of PR activity? Many PR plans I've seen tend to put too much weight on the splash activities, primarily because these are obvious PR targets and are pretty plain vanilla to consider. However, this leads to very lumpy PR results, and misses out on the opportunity to amplify your results through ongoing sustaining activities. In addition, by not keeping and building relationships with your press and analyst contacts through sustaining efforts, you risk the chance that the write-up you do get around a splash activity may not be as lengthy, positive, or accurate as it could be if you had been more active during the non-splash times.

If you want to ramp-up and acquire your rightful share of buzz, a well-balanced portfolio of both splash and drum beating will go a long way toward getting you there.

Finding the Right Mix of PR Activities

In addition to viewing your PR planning as sustaining vs. marketing event driven, you should apply another lens to ensure that you have fully considered all factors in your plan. This lens looks at your PR activities via key areas of focus. During a launch, the key PR focus areas will be around to-customer, analyst relations, sustaining, partner, and specialty activities. To-customer PR activities are those that go directly to the end-target customer and that do not necessarily require a press or analyst intermediary to execute, e.g., creating articles that can be placed in print or online properties or radio news releases.

Analyst relations are exactly that—the core activities you need to do to build and sustain relationships with key analysts in your industry.

FIGURE 6-6: Sustaining vs. Marketing Driven PR

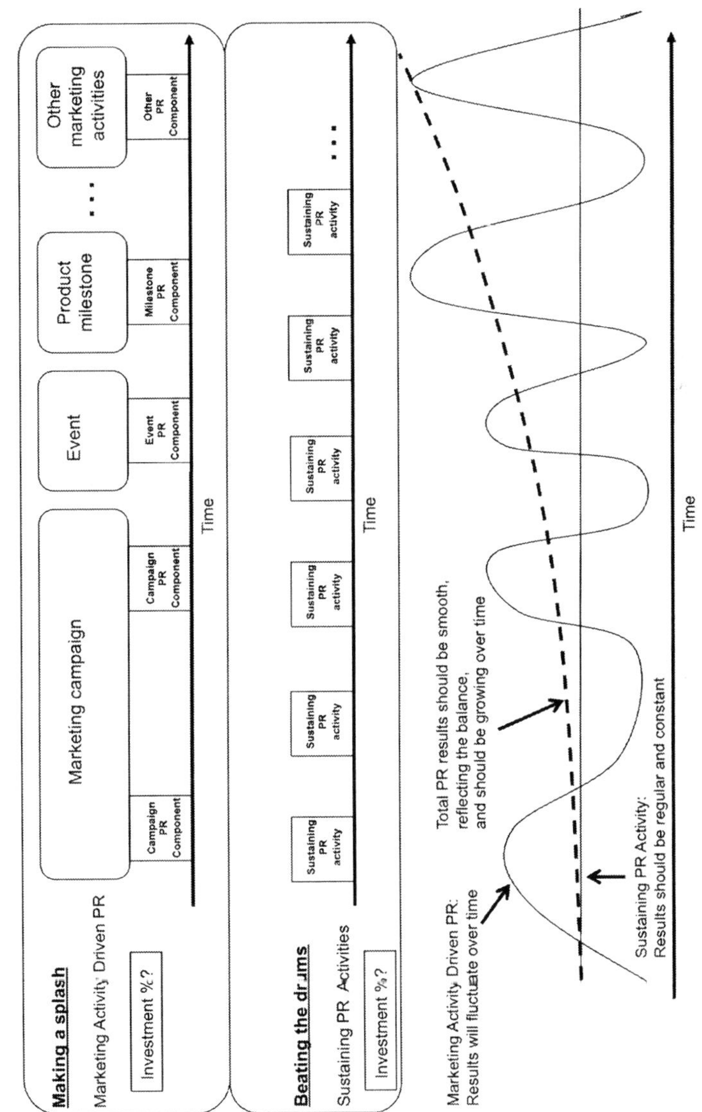

They include meetings, briefings, and analyst summit events. Sustaining activities are the standard interaction activities with the press, including the splash and beating the drum activities. Partner activities to attract partners to resell with you and co-PR activities with key partners are also important planning elements. Finally, specialty PR, like creative one-off splash ideas, vertical market PR, or local community relations activities fill up this bucket.

The key point is that you need to think through these buckets of activities and decide where to place your bets in terms of time and PR dollars to create the highest possible return on your PR investment. Figure 6-7 describes one possible view, or perspective, on looking at this holistically. You see that for each bucket of PR activity there is a decision to be made about what percentage of your PR budget you need to apply, how much of your time and your PR firm's time will need to be spent, and what the expected PR impact will be in terms of placements or impressions that drive your share of buzz.

In this example, I've placed 50% of my PR budget around sustaining activities, as I know that beating the drums is a critical element and is expected to drive a significant portion (65%) of my share of buzz. These activities should take up 30% of dedicated resources time (my time, the PR firm's time). At the same time I've chosen to invest 20% of my budget toward PR both to and with partners, which will take up a significant 25% of resource time investment and not deliver near the same number of results. Why would I do this? Because there are other factors that drive the need to invest in PR with partners, like relationship building, market perception creation, and showing commitment. These factors outweigh the needs around impressions and placements in this case.

The investment in analysts in this example is another one that may be perplexing. In this case, I've chosen to invest only 10% of my PR budget into analyst relations activities, but expect that these activities will require 30% of time investment, and only deliver 10% of my mentions and impressions. Seems like a lot of time to be spending for limited results. However, if you peel back the onion a bit, you see the logic.

Analyst relations investments are generally not too costly in dollars, as they are mostly executed via personal relationship building activities, phone calls, meetings, and briefings. Most of the analyst relations PR dollars should be spent on paid analyst feedback sessions, paid presentation appearances at events, or paying the travel, lodging, and fees to bring a group of analysts to your location for an analyst summit. However, analyst relations activities do cost a lot in terms of time spent on non-monetary activities. It simply

FIGURE 6-7: Allocating PR Investments

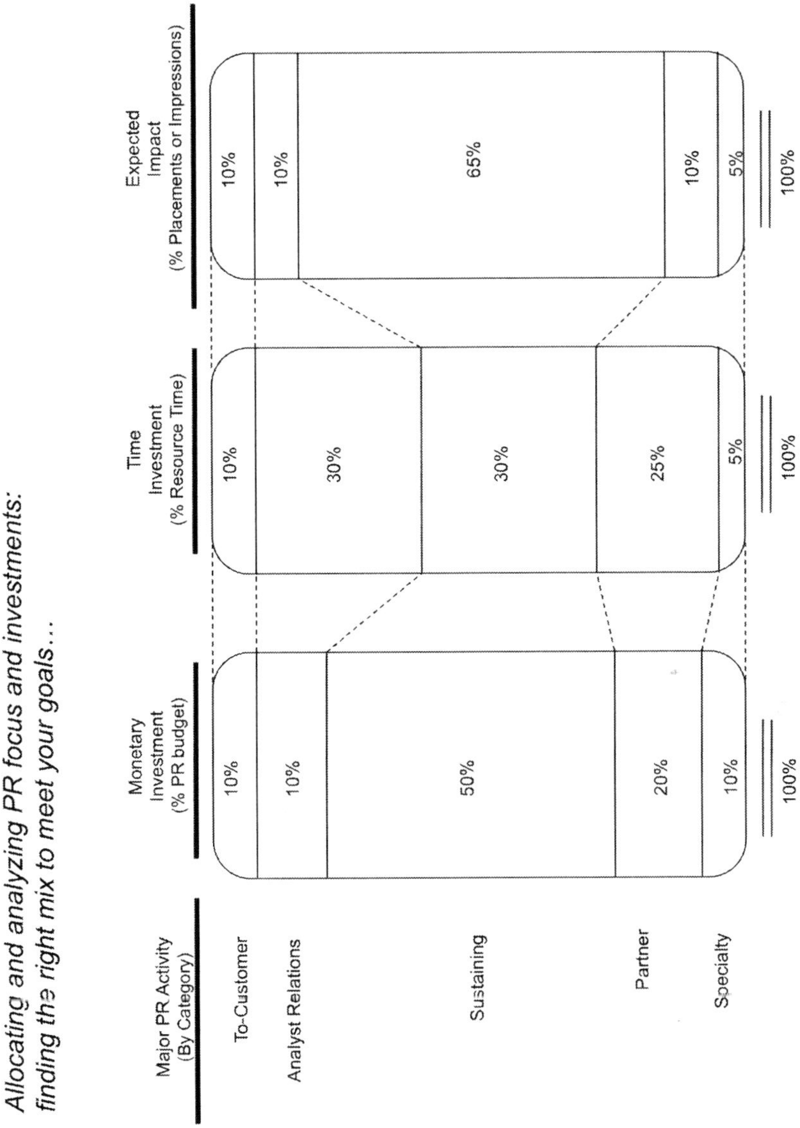

Allocating and analyzing PR focus and investments: finding the right mix to meet your goals...

Major PR Activity (By Category)	Monetary Investment (% PR budget)	Time Investment (% Resource Time)	Expected Impact (% Placements or Impressions)
To-Customer	10%	10%	10%
Analyst Relations	10%	30%	10%
Sustaining	50%	30%	65%
Partner	20%	25%	10%
Specialty	10%	5%	5%
	100%	100%	100%

takes time to continuously educate, re-educate, and build relationships and interest in the analyst community. These folks are very busy.

So you spend all this time with analysts, but only get 10% of your impressions and mentions from the fruits of your labor? Peeling one more layer of the onion here reveals that there is also an element of significance of impact—the impact of one type of mention or impression is not necessarily equal to another. Gaining the public and positive endorsement of a well-regarded analyst's firm is worth much more than a one-time article in a trade magazine and will go much further to move a potential customer to purchase your product over another. So, although you may have fewer quantitative results from your analyst relations efforts, the quality of those results will have a greater impact on your launch.

Structuring Your PR Launch Plan

Figure 6-8 outlines a conceptual structure for a launch PR plan where your high-level strategies and priorities are up front and driving your entire plan. Up front is where you would also detail your PR investment-mix thinking and rationale. By laying out your plan in this manner you should be able to ensure that your PR goals align and support your overall marketing goals, which, of course, are aligned to your overall business goals.

Supporting the overall goals and strategies are the various tactical pillars, structured and focused around the big-bet buckets that you have determined are the drivers for your PR launch success, and, when taken together, will deliver against your overall PR goals, and, thus, your marketing launch goals. Going deep in planning up front with a relatively long-term perspective is not a strength I've generally seen in many PR firms. It's up to you to help ensure you've got a thorough, consistent, and integrated plan. I'd also suggest including a detailed schedule for each main bucket to ensure that you have the appropriate workback time frames allowed for each activity.

That said, like any plan, it needs to be fluid and adaptable to changing conditions. I'd recommend planning out your PR strategy with the overall launch time frame as your base perspective, but managing and fine-tuning the plan on a quarterly basis. This allows time to modify as conditions require, yet still provides enough stability for quarterly execution so you are actually getting something done and not being randomized and inefficient.

FIGURE 6-8: Structuring a PR Plan

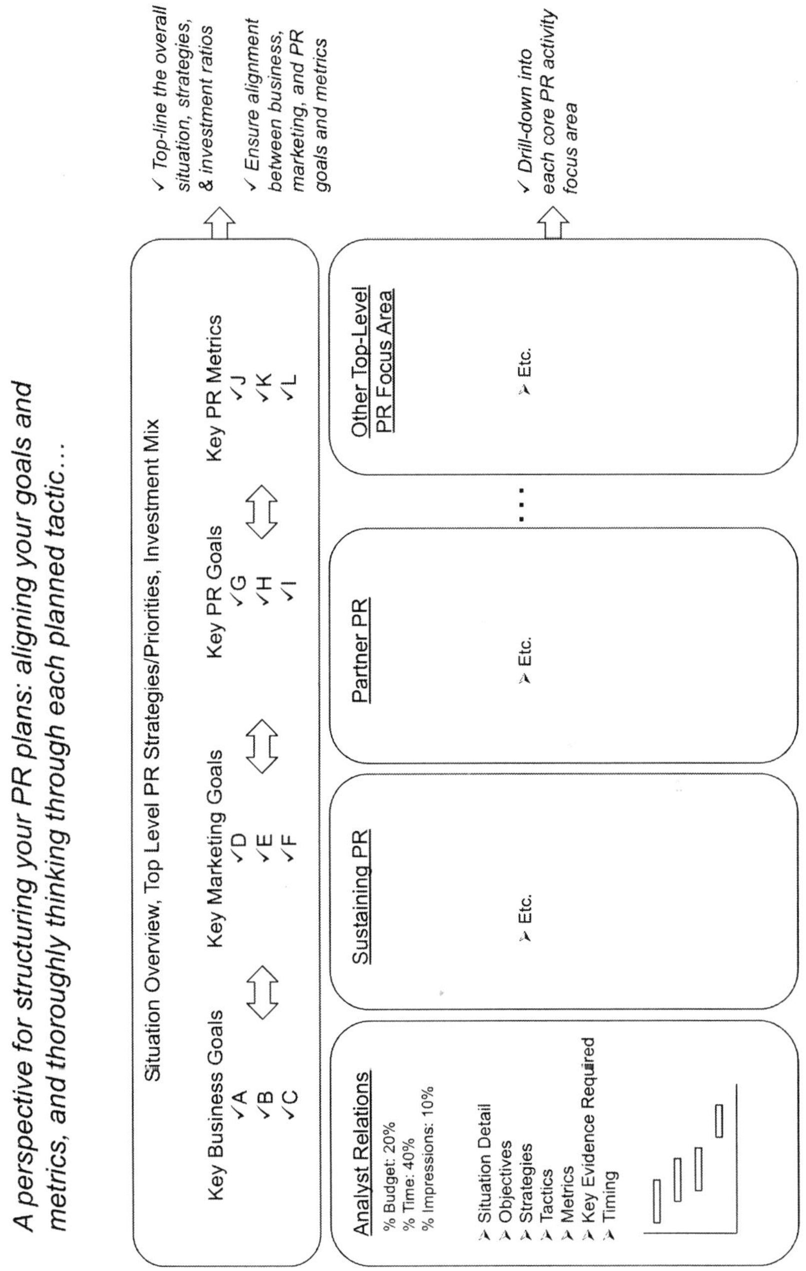

A perspective for structuring your PR plans: aligning your goals and metrics, and thoroughly thinking through each planned tactic…

Situation Overview, Top Level PR Strategies/Priorities, Investment Mix

Key Business Goals		Key Marketing Goals		Key PR Goals		Key PR Metrics
✓A	⟺	✓D	⟺	✓G	⟺	✓J
✓B		✓E		✓H		✓K
✓C		✓F		✓I		✓L

✓ *Top-line the overall situation, strategies, & investment ratios*

✓ *Ensure alignment between business, marketing, and PR goals and metrics*

Analyst Relations

% Budget: 20%
% Time: 40%
% Impressions: 10%

- Situation Detail
- Objectives
- Strategies
- Tactics
- Metrics
- Key Evidence Required
- Timing

Sustaining PR

- Etc.

Partner PR

- Etc.

…

Other Top-Level PR Focus Area

- Etc.

✓ *Drill-down into each core PR activity focus area*

Defining Your Key PR Metrics

Much of your plan will be tactical; however, these tactics need to deliver results that meet the overall metrics and goals put into place for launch. Some of the key metrics you should consider for your plan are:

Share of Buzz: Discussed earlier in this chapter, this is the overall metric for your share of articles and mentions in the marketplace. If you are not tracking this, you have no relative concept if your activities are making an impact. It's not enough to know you are generating more buzz if you don't know the relative amount of buzz you are creating vs. the competition. If you've increased your articles and impressions run rate by 10 more per month, but the competition has increased by 20 more per month, then relative to the competition you are falling behind and the competition is outdoing you on the PR front.

Number of Placements: You'll want to consider the absolute number of placements you are getting relative to prior years vs. plan. The number of placements is an important driver of the number of impressions you achieve, thus the awareness you create.

Message Pickup: You spent a lot of time defining and refining your key messages—how often are these messages being picked up in placements? How accurate is the message pickup? If the placements you are getting are not reflecting the messages you are conveying or are inaccurately reflecting them, you may need to re-think your communication strategy or better refine your methods. It could be you have the wrong spokespersons, or they are just not effective at PR. Whatever the case, you are wasting your PR dollars if your messaging is not being picked up or being picked up inaccurately.

Top-Tier Publication Coverage: Are you getting coverage in highly visible, respected, and well-read publications or web properties? Or are you getting covered only in *LittlePub Today* magazine? To effectively scale your PR and help create compelling buzz you need some coverage in top-tier publications for your industry. How many of these publications do you plan to claim as PR wins by getting coverage? How will you do this?

Tone of Coverage: This metric relates to the quality of the coverage. If you are getting coverage and your messages are being picked up but the tone of the coverage is highly negative, that's bad PR and something you do not want, obviously. Working through negative coverage is a process, but the first step is to understand the landscape. Setting goals for your PR coverage tone will help raise your game by giving you a target to shoot for and a manner to track when you might be failing. There are a variety of scales to set tone of coverage metrics. A good one is a five-point scale that buckets your coverage into five groups: Positive, Neutral-Positive, Neutral, Neutral-Negative, Negative. I would shoot for 95% of your coverage to be Neutral-Positive or Positive. Anything less and you need to course-correct your PR efforts.

Frequency of Coverage: An obvious metric but important one. How frequently are you getting coverage? This goes back to the points around making a splash and beating the drums. Effective PR will output a regular and steady amount of coverage and not simply spike time-in-point splash coverage. Just as in other elements of marketing, repetitive impressions over a period of time are what will place your product or business into a customer's awareness and consideration set.

Breadth of Coverage: This metric can be defined via a number of axes, including breadth and depth of publications, editors or analysts, or media types. Are your efforts expanding the set of PR targets being reached? For example, are you getting placements in new print magazines or websites to expand your reach pool, or are you attracting or engaging new editors or analysts for news briefings? Staying inbred and not increasing your breadth of coverage can lead to stagnation. You should set goals to attract and expand your circle of influence along these lines. Similarly, how broadly are you getting placements across various media types: print vs. websites vs. blogs? Are you too concentrated on getting placements in print publications and missing web-based opportunities? Again, setting metrics around increasing breadth of coverage across media types will help expand your potential placement opportunity set.

Depth of Coverage: Apply the lens of depth to your coverage wins—are you getting a lot of short little quotes in larger stories, or a paragraph or two in a story, or an entire article built around your product and strategy? What is your mix here? What do you want your mix to be? A lot of little mentions is great for your impressions and overall placement metrics, but may not be as effective as getting one cover story in a top-tier publication. So going for a balanced and realistic mix is something to consider. You can set metrics like 50% of placements are quotes or mentions, 40% multiparagraph placements, and 10% are depth or headline stories based on focused editorial pitch efforts and wins.

Number of Impressions: This is the absolute number of impressions you are getting via your placement wins. You can never be sure that every potential impression inherent in a particular placement will become an actual impression. It's just impossible to track. So the best proxy is simply tracking impressions overall and assuming that you are getting some percentage of readers. If you get placements in 10 publications, and each reaches 100,000 readers, your number of impressions is 1,000,000 if everyone sees your mention. As I said, 100% may not be the real number. If you have data to support a real number, then you can apply this—otherwise keep it simple and use the 100% number. Growing the number of impressions is key to growing your share of buzz.

Blogs and Newsletters: I call out a specific metric around blogs, as this is becoming more of a key reach mechanism for PR activities. Influencing blogs can be extremely beneficial from a PR perspective, as blogs have become an accepted, ingrained, and influential medium for many audience types. Similarly, opt-in newsletters are a highly targeted reach vehicle to get your message out, and working with the editors around incorporating your news into them can also pay dividends. You should have some metric in your PR plans around blog and newsletter penetration, placement, and impressions.

Review Wins: There are many sources a potential consumer or business customer can explore to assess whether they should purchase a particular product. Comparative reviews are an important source for such an assessment. Whether it's a magazine that rates products, a software testing laboratory assessment, a trade publication bake-off, a lab-testing effort, the Gartner magic quadrant, or editorial top picks from any number of publications or web properties, you should plan to proactively go after at least a couple of these review opportunities and make a strong showing. Because these efforts are so time-consuming you will likely need to limit the number of review opportunities you can support. However, having a couple of review wins under your belt can provide a significant amount of credibility for your product. It is completely reasonable to approach the review opportunity even if your product is not quite yet generally available. Once it has reached a point of stability and is pretty much ready for trial, get the product into an appropriate review opportunity. Typically, this will be mid-to-late launch time frame. And consider this—if you want to make a big splash at launch to drive momentum, having a solid review or two come out right around your launch date would be fantastic. To accomplish this you need to get your product into the review cycle pre-launch (3-4 months before launch date). Of course, if this is not possible pre-launch, it is still a crucial PR activity to pursue post-launch when you are into sustaining marketing activities, and it should be incorporated into those plans at the appropriate time.

Favorable Third-Party Quotes: When third-party evidence is available, such as positive and favorable analyst, customer, or partner support, you should always attempt to obtain a quote. Third-party quotes support your own messages and are often viewed as more credible by your target audience. If you can get 70% of your mentions to carry a third-party quote, you are doing a good job on this metric.

These are a few of the key high-level PR metrics you should consider putting into place and tracking on a regular basis. Use these metrics in your quarterly PR planning review cycle to course-correct and assess progress.

Defining Your Disclosure Strategy and Philosophy

Your information disclosure strategy essentially forms the approach and timing strategy you wish to take to disclose key news as your launch progresses. There are varying philosophies and perspectives about the best approach. The right approach to take highly depends on your key goals and your company's culture. Here are a few examples of disclosure approaches one might take for a disclosure strategy.

Dark Until Launch: In this approach, you do not announce anything or release any news about your product until it is ready or near ready to be released to market. This can be an approach for a highly competitive market to protect your plans and product functionality from duplication by key competitors. The risk here is of unintended news leaks to the press. It is difficult to completely control the flow of information outside your company, especially if you are at a large firm like Microsoft. Apple is a company that effectively uses this type of PR disclosure strategy—the iPhone is the latest example of Apple not announcing or even acknowledging the existence of the product until it was essentially ready to hit the market. Apple's culture and position in the market are oriented to make this type of disclosure strategy effective. Any pre-launch buzz you get from this type of strategy is speculation. This approach can also provide significant anticipation if you are at a firm that has the potential to really rock a market with a new product entry. If you don't care about generating pre-release buzz for some reason, this approach may work.

Incremental Throughout Launch: This is the typical bread and butter approach many firms take, where news is released following a product milestone completion, a new program creation, or around any other newsworthy item that occurs or is created during the launch. This approach allows you the potential to build and grow buzz around your product and strategy over time as the launch progresses. News is portioned out to the level of creating interest, but not necessarily giving away key information to competitors at the wrong time. Obviously, this is not an approach to take if you are in stealth mode.

Intentional Leaks: This is a hybrid approach between being totally dark and proactively and publicly releasing information incrementally through launch. Here one intentionally regularly leaks information throughout the launch via third parties to create speculation and anticipation, and, thus, buzz.

Bi-Polar: I refer to this approach as bi-polar as you release a good amount of information in the early portion of the launch to create awareness, go totally dark for most of the mid-stage launch, and finally re-engage the media at the end of the launch near product release. This is a technique that can be used to create FUD: fear, uncertainty, and doubt. The competition knows you are entering the space with your product—you've planted that seed—but then there is no news. What are you doing? What are you up to? When will the product come to market? These questions will resonate throughout your competitors; in the absence of concrete information they will potentially, and perhaps incorrectly, take steps to counter your efforts and spend time and resources doing so.

The optimal approach for your launch could center on one of the above strategies, or you could combine the strategies. For example, you may combine the bi-polar approach with intentional leaks during the dark period to further confuse the competition. Whatever your direction, you need to decide on the disclosure philosophy up front when you are building your launch PR plans and make sure that you and your PR firm are in synch.

Outreach Focus

As you refine your disclosure strategy, you'll also need to consider the type of media you will approach. There are a number of considerations to address and think through such as:

Targeted or Broad Outreach: Are you looking for coverage in a select few targeted publications or trying to reach out as broadly as possible to many publications? For your intended audience, there may be only a few key media outlets you need to go after to meet your PR goals. Or, to be effective, you may need to have broad coverage in as many different types of publications as possible. Your approach depends upon the nature of your product, the customer segments, and the available media outlets.

Local or National: Some media is national in coverage and scale like *The Wall Street Journal*, and some is local like *The Seattle Times*. If your target market and customers are geographically focused, then pumping up the local PR efforts to have coverage in those areas is an approach you should incorporate into your planning process. Or, if you have specific marketing campaigns that are geographically focused, this also begs for a local PR component to your planning.

Business or Trade: Do you need to achieve coverage in more business-oriented media, or should the focus be more heavily weighted around trade- and industry-specific media? Generally, one would pursue an approach that involves both these types of media; however, you may wish to optimize and invest more heavily in one or the other depending on your specific situation.

Online vs. Offline: This has become a key issue for both time and money investments. How much focus should you place around online web-based media vs. offline print media? Again, this will depend on the specific context of your product and the target customers. For example, software developers spend a lot of time online and are highly accessible via the web. A PR strategy more heavily weighted toward online media makes a lot of sense for this audience. However, CEO business decision makers in large corporations do not spend as much time online as do developers; thus a strategy weighted more toward print might make sense for this target audience.

As is the case with most marketing activities, you'll likely pursue a mix of outreach focus activities. Just be sure you don't end up in a middle of the road situation where you have spread your focus and investments too thinly across the various options and thus are not generating the bang-for-your-buck that you could achieve with a more focused and concentrated approach around a more limited set of outreach mechanisms.

AWARENESS AND BUZZ: SPECIFIC PRE-LAUNCH PROMOTIONAL OPPORTUNITIES

At the time you are ready to begin disclosing information more publicly there are a number of PR activities that can be accomplished during the ramp-up to launch to create early buzz and excitement. The goal early on is to create initial awareness and establish your credibility as a viable potential player in the market you will be addressing. These early activities will also define the foundation upon which you will proceed to generate momentum with follow-on PR activities in later launch phases.

I reiterate an earlier point to underscore its importance—before you communicate with press and analysts to seek coverage, make sure what you are going to communicate is *newsworthy* (unless you are engaging with an analyst for feedback or advice). I emphasize newsworthy because you need to have some meat behind your engagements with press and analysts. If it's not big enough news, or interesting enough, or won't appeal to their readership, or doesn't fall into some of the newsworthiness criteria I outlined, don't waste your time doing any kind of outreach. Consolidate the little pieces of news and information into a weightier larger group, then go after the press and analysts with the consolidated larger story.

Figure 6-9 gives some examples of newsworthy pre-launch PR activities that would be addressed via PR at Microsoft. Some of these may also be applicable to your product and industry, so please leverage these ideas once you are ready to start talking publicly, and, of course, have your story straight with the correct messaging.

Some of the examples in Figure 6-9 are self-explanatory, such as creating PR around product development milestones, naming contests, and sponsorships or contests. Others, such as Joint Development or TAP programs, Early Adopter Programs, and Customer or Partner Councils, are explained in more detail in Chapter 7. The following ideas are explored here in more detail.

Industry Figurehead Speaker or Technical Expert: If your company happens to be lucky enough to employ a highly visible industry participant, either from the business or technical side of the house, you can leverage

FIGURE 6-9: Illustrative Newsworthy PR Focus Areas

LAUNCH PHASE	Product	Customer	Programs	Partners	Creating News
Early	Intention to build, launch, enter market Development milestone reached Product Preview release Industry standards support		Joint development programs or TAP programs (Chapter 7)	Key strategic partner-ships formed	Thought leadership articles, whitepapers Executive or luminary speeches Key influential hires
Mid to Late	Product name or branding strategy Hitting product development milestones Key positive test results around critical market-making product attributes (e.g., performance, safety) Limited feature disclosure/leaks Pre-release product awards	Brand-name participants in customer programs Customer council creation or progress (Chapter 7) Celebrity or influential third-party appearances, testimonials, or endorsements Customer training and education programs/ efforts Vertical market efforts Association memberships or key activities	Early adopter or customer programs (Chapter 7) Beta or broad preview programs Broad partner channel program establish-ment Channel training programs availability Pre-release marketing and sales offers and incentives Certification programs	Partner Council creation or progress (Chapter 7) New partner support, offerings, or relevant service/ product news New partner-ships established	Key customer or partner research findings Momentum data around customer or partner interest, adoption rates Create an expert or rock star Pitch a headline story Evangelize positive analyst reports Key industry event sponsorships Business value news releases: ROI, productivity, cost reduction, satisfaction Partner or supporter recognitions Contest creation or sponsorship Community service awards Major analyst endorsement wins
At General Availability	Product launch release—complete feature/ functionality	Key customer adoptions and case studies New customer wins	Post-release marketing and sales offers and incentives Company initiatives	Partner programs and co-launch press releases Partner offers and incentives	

this person in your PR activities. For example, if your notable employee is keynoting or presenting at a conference or event, and will be speaking about or referring to information regarding your launch or market strategy, it's worth giving a heads up to your hot list of editors and analysts. They may just happen to be going to the event already, or it may be in their area and they can swing by to catch the keynote. And, of course, using this person as a conduit to talk about your news is the optimal situation.

Your Entry Into the Market: Whether it is small, mid-size, or large, your firm's entry into the market could be newsworthy. Whether it is news depends on such factors as the potential impact of your entry, product technology, and track record of your firm's management. Perhaps you have a goal or objective that is radically different than existing industry competitors. This could be interesting to potential customers, and therefore to press and analysts. Making some noise about your entry into the space may spark some coverage.

Industry Standards and Organizations: In the technology industry, nothing seems to spark religious fervor like standards discussions. Standards are the agreed-upon industry definitions and specifications of the detail and underpinnings of a particular technology. Common technologies such as HTML and XML are two simple examples. Companies come together through various organizations such as the World Wide Web Consortium (W3C) or the International Standards Organization (ISO) and discuss, debate, and agree on specifications that describe the technology and its implementation parameters. Every company has their own agenda for participating and influencing the specification in one direction or another to gain advantage for their products. These can be contentious discussions and take a long time to achieve resolution and agreement. Open vs. proprietary, this standards body vs. another, complete adherence to the standard or adding proprietary extensions, is it a standard or a specification—these are a small subset on the list of potentially debatable issues around standards that are endlessly discussed at these meetings. And there are a lot of standards out there.

However, understanding and engaging in the standards discussion can be leveraged to your benefit, especially when you are in the pre-launch vaporware phase. Some press and analysts are well-tuned into the standards arena. You can create some buzz if you announce that you are supporting a particular standard or joining a particular standards body. Sometimes your firm may choose to create a new standard and start a competitive situation with an existing standard—that's always fun to do (and newsworthy). Joining a standards body or efforts also gets you awareness and potential PR opportunities via that consortium's efforts to market the standard to the industry.

Creating an Expert/Rock Star: If you don't employ a well-known industry participant, you can create one and generate news. You'll need to pick the right someone carefully for this type of effort. For example, at one point when Microsoft developed the .NET Framework and the underlying technology, one of the marketing strategies to create awareness and adoption of the technology was appealing to the developer audience to start incorporating the .NET Framework into their development. One component of the effort was to take the lead software architect at Microsoft who was essentially the brains behind the technology and turn him into a rock star/guru to the developer audience, which, by nature, would be attracted to and would want to engage with the .NET architect. So promoting this person, offering speaking gigs and contests to meet him, and building up his external persona created a mystique around him and helped to generate significant awareness for the .NET technology. Can you do the same with someone at your company?

Writing Articles for Trade Publications: Many smaller or specialized-industry publications, whether print or online, are always at a content deficit—they need content to fill up their publications. In most cases, they will be willing to print an article that you or someone at your firm writes pretty much intact as you have written it. The primary filters that will determine publication are that the article can't be an advertisement for your company and it needs to be on a topic of interest to the publication subscribers. It's okay to plug your company in the article, but generally it should be done via a low-key approach. Of course, the mere fact that your company is writing the article and identified as such is promotion in its own right. This approach is also an opportunity to put your firm in a thought leadership position during your launch process.

Evangelizing Research Data: Research data and results will generally be of interest for pickup by the press, especially if it provides new insights, or contradicts existing industry assumptions, or is just simply fascinating information. By publishing parts of the research and creating a press release talking about some of the juicy findings, you may garner media pickup and placements. Your company can sponsor and pay for the research, or you can team up with others to fund it.

Of course, in parallel to the more product-centric PR efforts, there are also company-level PR opportunities to create mindshare that may or may not be directly related to your product. For example:

- Financial news like new investments or investors, equity and debt transactions, earnings releases, dividend announcements
- Corporate strategy changes (product line discontinuation, focus change), key personnel changes (hiring, firing, retirement), mergers and acquisitions
- Feel-good programs: environmental, community, social, philanthropic programs, efforts, or collaborations

If at all possible, you should leverage these broader PR opportunities to include plugs and positioning for your product that are supportive of and consistent with the broader corporate news. As you move into your post-launch sustaining marketing activities, further PR opportunities will be available, but those are out of scope for this book. However, you can likely re-purpose some of the activities in Figure 6-9 to use in your sustaining activities.

LAUNCH PR TIMING

It's always a good idea to lay out the elements of your PR plan in a timeline. This is a great way to overview, manage, and communicate your planned and ongoing PR activities. In Figure 6-10 I've laid out a generic but generally correct timeline for some of the more common launch activities. The time frames before launch for some of these activities are not set in stone, but are in the general ball park. You can adapt this perspective and customize it for your own PR launch plans.

PR is a multifaceted endeavor that covers a lot of ground and that can provide significant awareness opportunities for your product throughout, and after, the launch. That PR is slimy half-truths and press releases should no longer be your perception, if it ever was. Using PR as a tool is an important arrow in your launch quiver, but gaining the rewards takes a significant amount of work and planning. Internalizing the content of this chapter will help you get the most out of this element of your launch planning and execution.

FIGURE 6-10: Illustrative PR Launch Timeline

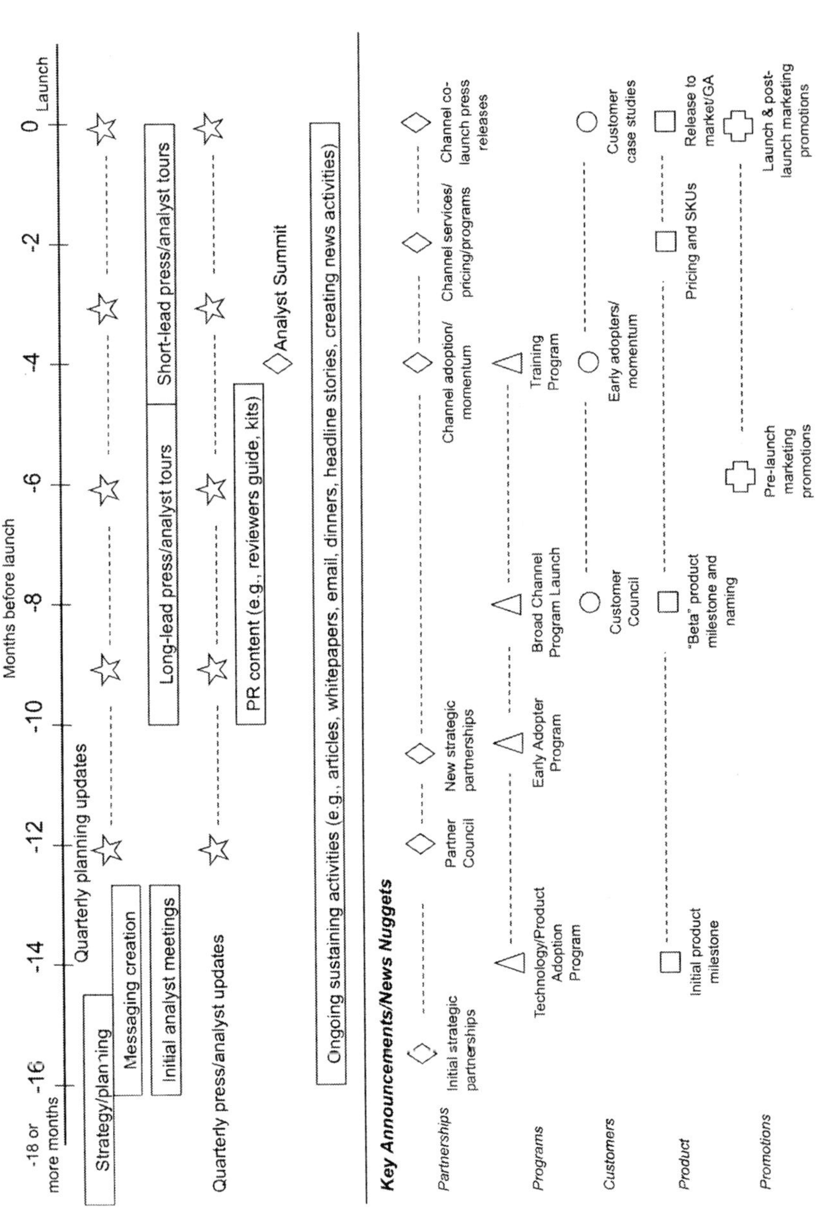

7

Core Pre-Launch Customer and Channel Partner Programs

At the point in the launch cycle when the pre-launch programs and marketing infrastructure need attention and focus, it should be safe to assume that the rollout plan is in place, market-making partners have been signed up, positioning and messaging frameworks have been solidified, and early PR efforts have been instigated. The focus should now be on defining and building out pre-launch customer and partner programs and getting the core marketing program infrastructure activities executed. These programs and activities were alluded to in the high-level rollout plan, but at some point you must go to the next level to define and implement the specifics. This chapter focuses on the pre-launch customer and channel partner programs, defined as follows:

- **Pre-Launch Customer Programs:** Programs generally intended to generate pre-launch feedback, early awareness, and trial of the product in the target market.
- **Pre-Launch Partner Programs:** Programs intended to create, train, and sustain a broad partner and channel ecosystem before launch.

This chapter will expose, explain, and provide insights into some of the major elements that comprise the important programs within the above categories. I'm focusing on the "Big Rocks," those programs or activities that will account for the bulk of the time and that will generate the most impact for the launch and into the post-launch sustaining environment.

All of these programs and activities should be well-planned and structured programs. As with any structured program, whether a development project or an out-bound marketing campaign, these pre-launch programs should be resourced and funded appropriately if they are to be successful.

GAINING FEEDBACK AND AWARENESS VIA PRE-LAUNCH CUSTOMER PROGRAMS

Pre-launch customer programs are specifically designed to address and include the intended target customers. A number of important customer programs must be in place to maximize the effectiveness of a launch. The most important are those that:

- Provide early product usage and feature feedback, such as a "Technology/Product Adoption Program" or an "Early Adopter Program," to garner initial marquee customer wins.
- Establish a one-to-few mechanism for in-depth customer feedback on a variety of product- and business-related topics. These programs are sometimes called "Customer Councils."
- Initiate broad public trial and awareness creation, such as a "Marketing Beta" program in the software industry.

Clearly, each of these customer-facing efforts fulfills a specific role at different times during the launch process. The earliest of these customer programs to rollout are generally the Technology/Product Adoption Program and the Early Adopter Program.

Technology/Product Adoption Program: Working Out the Product Development Issues

The first quasi-public program that should be in place is what Microsoft refers to as a Technology Adoption Program, or TAP. These programs were previously called Joint Development Programs (JDP) and Technical Preview Programs. They occur early in the product release life cycle and are usually based around the alpha release (or first limited public release in software terminology) of the product. This release is typically the first time a company would allow a small number of outside companies, or customers, to actually have the product under development.

This type of early technical program is generally, but not exclusively, synonymous with technology products, whether hardware, software, or a combination. However, other products and industries can benefit from these programs, so I have used a similar naming process, extending and generalizing the program name to include the word "Product." Examples of non-software products along these lines include consumer products (feedback on ease of use), machinery (feedback on production ease, integration in customer environment, assembly/maintenance), and furniture manufacturing (ergonomic feedback, fit, and finish).

The primary goal of a Technology/Product Adoption Program is to gain early and detailed technical, feature, and usage feedback on the product from partners and customers. Secondary goals include early partner and customer engagement, relationship building, and the potential to generate early buzz and momentum. Participants may well be among your key strategic "poster child" partners and customers when you get the product to general availability.

Typically, a partner or customer is brought into the program to co-develop a product or service that will complement the host product being launched. Simple examples in the Microsoft world include program participants working early on in a release cycle developing applications that run on top of a server product like Windows Server or SQL Server. In many cases, this program turns into a co-development effort, where the products of the participants and those of the program hosting firm are defined and developed so that all the products work together or complement each other, increasing the potential market for all. The market-making partners (Chapter 5) are usually heavily involved in a program of this type, primarily if they fall into the Technology or Complementary Products/Services partner category.

The level of effort and involvement in this type of program is both long-term and intense, starting in the early stages of the launch and product development process and continuing through to the actual launch, and perhaps beyond. This work requires significant and long-term commitments for all parties. The expectation is that the partners and customers will work in tandem with your firm as the launch progresses to the broader customer preview and early adopter programs later in the product launch cycle. Both the company developing the product and the program participants must have a mutually beneficial and committed relationship for the program to succeed: the benefits of involvement must flow both to your company and to the participants.

Participants may benefit by:

- **First-Mover Advantage:** Being involved early in the product development cycle, thus having the opportunity to influence the product feature set to their liking. It is also important to many companies to get a time-to-market advantage over their competition, and these programs offer this opportunity.

- **Relationships**: Establishing close working relationships with your internal engineers. In the Microsoft case, many companies strongly desire the opportunity to work directly with the software engineers that are developing the products. These developers are not generally accessible to outside companies, so this is a significant benefit to the participants, especially to the more technical parties.
- **Public Relations:** Garnering PR exposure provided via program participation and activities.
- **Incentives:** Receiving free product or monetary incentives. Getting partners and customers to commit serious business and technical resources early on for a new product can be difficult. Being willing to provide each participant, whether partner or customer, with a certain amount of your final product or subsidizing development funding can help.

For the company rolling out the product and hosting the program, benefits can include:

- **Product Feedback:** Early product development and feature feedback that can drive the right features with the correct implementation.
- **Relationships:** Development of market-making partner relationships.
- **Customer Evidence:** Creation of both early partner and customer wins that can be leveraged later in the launch.
- **Problem Identification:** Identification and exposure of significant product flaws or issues.
- **Support Needs:** Identification of support requirements, processes, and infrastructure for both pre- and post-launch time frames.
- **Documentation:** Product documentation requirements necessary to fulfill partner and end-customer needs.
- **Public Relations:** PR and analyst exposure and opportunities with the program participants to generate buzz, excitement, and momentum.

With a program of this intensity, limiting the number of participants is a wise idea from cost, resource, and manageability perspectives. A minimum number of participants will likely be required to address all required product feedback and testing requirements. Determining this minimum number will depend on the product type, complexity, industry, and availability of partners and customers willing to participate. Too many program participants will make it unwieldy and difficult to execute. Ten partners and customers in a Technology/Product Adoption Program is generally a sustainable number for an average product. Obviously, if the product is a giant product on a Microsoft Windows or Office scale, more will be required. The exact number will depend on the scope and complexity of the product and its development and testing needs.

Early Adopter Program: Developing Marquee Launch Customers

An Early Adopter Program (EAP) is a somewhat less restrictive program than a Technology/Product Adoption Program. A significant difference between the two programs is that the EAP generally focuses on getting the marquee (or well-known brand) customers signed up, running, and using the pre-launch product—with an end goal targeting production deployment of the product post-launch. Therefore, for this program, the primary focus is not feedback on the product and features but on ensuring that a reasonable number of marquee customers will be available as the "poster child" customers at launch.

A key benefit for the company hosting and running the EAP is the acquisition of real-world customer evidence for the product. The participating customers should be some of the initial go-to resources for customer referrals in the sales process, case studies, testimonials, press and analyst references, and other forms of customer evidence. These are the folks to have on stage with you at your launch event to talk up your product and show off how they have used it for their business.

Although the customer's time and resource investment for EAP involvement is not quite as onerous as the Technology/Product Adoption Program, it is still not a light investment. Again, both the company hosting and the participants must feel there are mutually beneficial gains for involvement.

To maximize the benefits to your firm and the usable output from an EAP, you should include some key participant marketing commitments when developing the participation agreement (a MOU is useful here). These include:

- **Real-World Product Usage:** Commitment to publicly deploy or make the product externally available within a certain time after it is formally released to market. At Microsoft, this is typically at launch or within 60-90 days after launch.

- **Willingness to Commit to Public Relations Activities:** This could include signing up to act as a sales reference to other customers considering your product, jointly developing a case study for publication, and being a reference customer for press and analysts to interview and quote. Preferably, you should get a commitment to all of the above.
- **Launch Event:** Participating in your launch event, and publicly appearing on stage with you to present and sing the praises of your product, company, and their solution developed with, or on, your product.
- **Developing a Demo of the Customer Usage of the Product:** This is a deliverable that your sales force or partners can use as a sales tool. In the software world, a good demo is a strong selling tool, especially if it is based on real world customer usage. If your product is not a software product, a Flash demo or video of the product being used by the customer can be a reasonable substitute. The key point is to leverage some kind of demonstration as evidence to support new customer sales.

For the EAP participants, the primary benefits are similar to the Technology/Product Adoption Program benefits—the ability to use or take the product to market first to gain competitive advantage, publicity benefits through PR, and, of course, the product or monetary incentives that accompany program participation.

Customer Program Participant Recruitment

With the level of effort involved, the unknowns at this point of the product development, and the mutual effort required between the program hosting company and the participants to maintain effective relationships, you can expect that about 50% of your partners and customers will drop out. Thus, if you have a goal to sustain a mix of 10 partners and customers through to final launch in your Technology/Product Adoption Program or EAP, you need to over-recruit for the program and start with 20. This will require more recruiting effort up front and more initial resources (people and money) to manage a larger number of participants. You must make a trade-off between supplying these additional resources or recruiting fewer participants and accepting a smaller number than originally desired.

With the potential for drop-off in mind, it's critical to recruit a mix of partners and customers that will represent the key product or market scenarios identified in the rollout plan and that planned marketing demand generation campaigns will address. If the intent is to take the product to large companies in the healthcare vertical market, it probably does not make a lot of sense to recruit small financial services companies as program participants. The point is to try to match the makeup of your intended target market to the makeup of the participants. You will thus be getting the appropriate feedback, and the resulting marketing collateral, demos, sales tools, case studies, and referrals will reflect your specific target market. After launch, if a prospective new customer emerges that is a large healthcare company, showing them the customer evidence generated by a similar healthcare company will be more help in closing a sale than if the evidence came from a small financial services firm.

If you can recruit well-known brand-name companies, all the better. It simply adds credibility to your customer evidence pieces. In addition, snagging program participants that are market share leaders in your particular target customer segments also can help in the post-launch time frame from a FUD factor perspective. Potential customers who are not the market share leaders may feel that a competitor's adoption of your product puts them at a competitive disadvantage, further increasing their propensity to purchase. The same holds true for partner recruiting—brand-name and market share leading partners lend cachet and credibility, incenting smaller partners to get onboard.

It is extremely beneficial from a recruiting perspective to offer some level of exclusivity. Since a first mover advantage is an important benefit to the participants, recruiting their competitors into the program will not be an incentive to signing them up. If possible, offer exclusivity to the participants in some form or another, whether by vertical market (e.g., only one banking industry participant), by application type (e.g., only one ERP firm), or by type of partner (e.g., only one hosting services company).

Most recruiting for these programs will likely be done on a one-on-one basis—these are not broadscale demand generation efforts. Leveraging potential customer or partner nominations from the direct field sales force or from participating partners is a good recruiting method. Business development folks in the organization may also be a good resource for potential participant leads and for actively recruiting these companies.

Your company needs to *sell* the partners and customers to gain their participation. The level of commitment and potential asks of these prospective participants are not lightweight. Building a "pitch" deck, or presentation, that outlines the program goals, benefits, requirements and commitments, and timeline is important and should be a basic tool used during the one-on-one recruiting process. It may take a number of calls or in-person visits and meetings to secure each participant, so ensuring enough lead time (a minimum of 4-6 months) to recruit before the program actually kicks off is important.

In summary, to achieve the appropriate coverage for launch needs from both customer and partner participant recruiting, keep the following checklist in mind:

- Do they fit the correct target customer and partner profiles?
- Are the product usage scenarios a good fit for launch needs?
- Is there appropriate vertical and horizontal market coverage?
- Is there a sense of commitment and motivation for participation?
- Is there appropriate PR value to be derived from the participant? How strong is their brand influence? Are they market leaders in their segments?
- Does the participant have the necessary technical expertise and resources to deliver on program commitments, with high quality, in the necessary time frame?
- Are they willing to sign an MOU?
- Are they willing to be included in public marketing materials and as customer references?
- Can you offer exclusivity in a category and still make your recruitment numbers?
- Is the value proposition for the program strong enough to incent prospective participants to join up and collaborate?

Customer Program Operational Tips

Once the right customers and partners are enrolled, the work is only beginning. A number of unfortunate circumstances could drive these programs in the wrong direction. To ensure smooth progress in the right direction and to mitigate potential issues, you may want to incorporate the following tips into the participant MOU or some other written agreement:

- Communications
    - Have in place mutually agreed to and defined expectations on communication processes and turnaround time to respond to various communications.

  - Gain commitment to report product issues back to your company in a timely fashion.
  - Identify a "buddy" from your company for each program participant. This person will act as the primary interface for the participant to handle communication, escalations, and project management and to be the one-stop entry point into your company. This person also serves to put a face to your organization and personalize the program. For an EAP program, you can generally get away with one point of contact for multiple organizations, since the product will then be more mature, and the program is more standardized and programmatic. For a Technology/Product Adoption Program having one buddy for each partner or customer is important, since the level of co-development intensity is high, rapid and urgent changes will be occurring, and each participant will have more customized needs than those in the EAP program.
- Resources
  - Gain a firm commitment from the participants to provide a certain minimum level of dedicated people resources to support the major program execution needs and technical product and business co-development activities, weekly synch meetings, and quarterly executive status briefings. In fact, both weekly working meetings and quarterly executive meetings are important to have in place to ensure all stay on the same page and that the intent, spirit, and commitments of the relationship stay on track.
  - Name a senior level executive sponsor from each company that will act as the escalation path to keep things on track or to resolve disagreements. Preferably, this would be someone in the participant's company that has a personal vested interest in the program's success. Of course, your company should also have an appropriate level executive sponsor.
- Support and Training
  - Offer or take any necessary training to enable customer and partner success. If your participants need training up front, it's critical to get this into place.
  - Get your support and customer service organization involved from the beginning, as you need to begin the knowledge transfer process from the product development group into the customer service and support organization. This will pay dividends over

time because you may need to provide a high level of technical and product support for the program participants. You should plan to have dedicated support staff from your customer support organization participate in these programs to answer questions, create the beginning of a support information or knowledge database for your product, write technical content for product installation, manage workarounds and problem fixes, and author papers on important concepts related to the product or its supporting technology.

- Process
  - Have a clearly defined and written plan from participants around their use of and development around your product or technology. Make sure there is agreement for a written test plan. Clear timing expectations are also important. It does you no good to provide great benefits to the participants, expecting they will have a complementary product or customer evidence piece available at launch, if it is not in their planned schedule.
  - Have an efficient infrastructure set up for reporting product problems and available fixes, accessible by all participants. Typically, this means a password-protected website where participants can post problems, issues, and technical questions. It's an important best practice to limit and partition access to the website so each participant can only see their own information and your specific responses. If you do not partition, you run the risk of participants believing their company's confidential information may be leaking out. If you are having significant problems with a particular participant (e.g., a major technical problem or disagreement) leaking could negatively affect the other participants. Keeping things partitioned will mitigate these potential issues.
  - Ensure there is a defined plan to convert customer and partner participation in the program into usable and effective customer evidence pieces. Again, these pieces are key output deliverables for these programs, and if there is not a plan and process in place to get the customer evidence pieces created as the launch progresses, the risk is that there will be nothing available at launch—or, worse, sloppy work hastily thrown together at the last minute.

Finally, while it is tempting to let the world know as soon as possible that you have this amazing program going with your amazing soon-to-be-launched product, be careful about what information is disclosed right away. While it is probably okay to let the world know you are running these programs (for momentum purposes), don't publicly announce the Technology/Product Adoption or EAP program participants right away. Some participants will drop off, and you don't want negative PR like the potential headline: "EAP Program Falls Apart: Key Participants Bailing from Program." It's also important to let the rhythm of the relationships evolve and settle before announcing the participants. When you do announce them for the PR value, you'll want to make sure you announce when these companies are happy and when they have seen some progress and value in the program. If you wait you'll have a greater chance the participants will speak positively about their experience and about the product you are rolling out.

One special note on partners and customers speaking externally about their experiences—make sure they are up to speed on the key messages you spent so much time creating. My experience has been that, from the close relationships built in such programs, participants are generally perfectly willing to "toe the party line" and incorporate your speaking points into their communications with external parties, such as press, analysts, or prospective post-launch customers. You just need to get them trained and comfortable with your positioning and messaging points.

Customer Council: An Open Dialogue for Feedback

There is a gap between the product development focus of a Technology/ Product Adoption Program and the customer evidence creation focus of an EAP program. These programs are hands-on, specifically directed programs where the agenda and focus are fixed on a well-defined specific end goal and purpose. Given that, there is a need and opportunity for a less structured and more open dialogue between your company and the target customers that can help discover and avoid potential go-to-market mistakes or misses. A customer council can fill this gap and provide an open forum for discussion.

In essence, a customer council is a select group of representative target market customers that serve in an advisory capacity to your company on a broad variety of possible topics related to the product launch. The council members should be seen as an important purveyor of the "Voice of the Customer." As such, the intent of this forum is to provide your company with open, honest, and direct input on key business or product issues or questions faced in the pre- and post-product launch environment. Typically 10-15 customers form the council membership. Keeping the group size down to a manageable number is important, as these forums are for *discussion* and for your company to *listen*, not talk.

Well-run and managed customer council meetings can provide a wealth of benefits through the honest examination and discussion of topics that impact important business and product decisions. Examples of possible topics are:

- Brainstorming features or product usage scenarios
- Providing feedback on product usage and associated issues in the customer environment
- Evaluating new product concepts or service offerings
- Discussing possible business models or model changes
- Evaluating positioning and messaging, or marketing concepts and materials
- Indicating preferences or impact of new sales or marketing offers being considered
- Addressing satisfaction issues and problems
- Understanding support requirements and needs
- Gaining insight on SKU strategy, pricing, and licensing/sales terms
- Understanding purchasing requirements, budgets, and preferred purchase channels

While it seems obvious that your firm could gain significant benefits from council input, what would drive and motivate someone to spend precious time participating and providing your company with this free advice? Some typical reasons are:

- **Shape the Product:** The opportunity to provide direct input into the product development process and shape future product direction. Many times a customer has a vested interest in your product: they want it to work best for them in their business environment. What better way to optimize the product to meet their needs than to provide their input directly to the company making it? A nice bonus is gaining early access to product prototypes.
- **Access:** Involvement in an environment providing a forum to air and address unmet needs or vent frustrations. Whether from a business or product perspective, a direct pipeline into the decision makers of a major product supplier can provide significant access to address issues.

- **Insight:** The ability to gain early insights into private, non-public future business and product strategies. Early information allows customers to inform their specific business plans with higher quality information.
- **Networking:** Relationship building and networking with peers in such a venue can provide new business or collaboration opportunities.
- **Goodies:** Desired access to hard-to-reach senior executives in your firm, prizes and executive-level giveaways, and potentially special business deals or arrangements structured exclusively for the council members. In some cases, your firm may pay for travel and/or lodging for council members.

You should be clear on the benefits of participation and develop a solid customer council recruiting pitch presentation similar to the EAP recruiting presentation that incorporates these benefits.

CUSTOMER COUNCIL PROGRAM OPERATIONAL TIPS

Running a customer council can be a fun, informative, and rewarding experience. The following suggestions and tips can help shape a successful council.

Frequency of Meetings: While the level of activity can vary depending on the interest and willingness of the council members and your firm's needs, you should expect to have at least quarterly meetings. Meeting in-person is optimal but not always practical. It is reasonable to have two face-to-face in-person meetings and two phone conference or video teleconference meetings per year; however, the mix can vary depending on your needs and the flexibility and interest of the council members. If you have the facilities, it's reasonable to host the meeting at your place of business; otherwise, a private off-site meeting room facility will suffice.

Set a Clear Agenda: Generally these meetings are set up to run a day and a half, with the agenda structured around the key business issues to be discussed, meal and rest breaks, and a fun group activity or event in the evening. The intent is to listen, not talk. The daily sessions should be 20% presentation and 80% discussion. Hiring a moderator or facilitator for these meetings is a useful process tip. A skilled third-party moderator can sometimes more easily mediate issues and keep the meeting moving smoothly.

Take the Long-Term View: Don't view such a council as a short-term project that encompasses a couple of meetings. Optimally, the customer council is an ongoing process and engagement that does not end at the product launch, but continues as the next product to be launched enters the product cycle. Think of this council as part of the ongoing element of your company's business infrastructure and a platform for testing ideas and hypotheses.

Reflect the Target Market: The council members should reflect the intended target market. As with EAP customers, acquiring well-known brand customers as marquee representatives is optimal. Obviously, if the product hasn't yet shipped there will be no product customers to recruit. Approaching customers from other parts of the business or from other internal product lines which also focus on the same target customer profile is a potentially low-hanging opportunity to acquire council members. Be open to including customers that are neutral or negative toward your firm—one can sometimes learn more from the negative customers than the positive ones. Also, be sure to have the right organizational level representatives for your needs, e.g., if the participants are CxO level, they probably would not be interested in discussing the positioning and messaging value propositions or reviewing marketing collateral. If you are looking for feedback from technologists, don't involve the CxO's; get the developers or IT Professionals, or the appropriate functional department manager from accounting, manufacturing, customer service, or whatever department the target market customer is in. Council representatives should be knowledgeable about your company, the product, and the market you are launching into to get the best possible feedback.

Realize the Limitations: Like focus group research, the input received from the council is informative and directional but not statistically significant research. Consolidate this input with other market intelligence to help paint the big picture and for decision-making. Use the knowledge gained with the council to better understand the customers and to refine and impact customer knowledge tools such as Persona definitions, usage scenarios (Chapter 2), and positioning frameworks (Chapter 4).

Gain PR Commitment: If you can get PR commitment and support, all the better. This should be a strong and firm ask from your company.

NDAs: Have the council members sign non-disclosure agreements. The information and plans being shared are likely private and sensitive.

Communicate Effectively: Follow-up on action items and take responsibility for maintaining effective communications. For example, sending summaries of meeting notes, upcoming agendas, and regular status emails to council members helps create a more cohesive, informed, and engaged group.

Set Expectations: Set clear expectations on council responsibilities for what your company and the customer will commit to. Get agreement from members to respond in a timely fashion to ad hoc email or phone queries.

Set Minimum Participation Time Frames: Get a minimum participation time frame commitment from each council member, e.g., one-year minimum commitment. It is not reasonable to spend a lot of time recruiting and prepping for council members who are going to attend one meeting and drop out. Consistency and immersion of the council members around your business and needs is crucial to getting the best input. However, be willing to swap in new council members for those that are not contributing.

Initial Pre-Launch Public Trial and Awareness Programs: Marketing Betas or Customer Preview Programs

An excellent way to gain awareness and usage of your product in the early stages is to provide a large-scale mechanism for product trial before product release. Essentially, a pre-launch release program around your product (a marketing beta or Customer Preview Program, in software industry parlance) is a structured, well-managed process to get the product to your intended target customers before broad general availability, and often before the product is fully (but usually nearly) baked.

Many companies in various industries pursue this type of pre-release before general availability. Consumer food firms may trial a new packaged food product in a limited number of cities to assess demand. For example, Frito-Lay ran an interesting and creative pre-release program. In essence, the company released a product mysteriously packaged as "X-13D" that indicated it was clearly a Doritos-like product; however, the packaging was not a "release" version of packaging, was clearly different from the standard Doritos packaging, and had the mysterious X-13D name to it. The X-13D product was made available in certain markets. Frito-Lay created a program and a contest where customers were given the opportunity to try the product (you had to buy it) then guess the "secret" ingredient that made X-13D different from other Doritos (it turned out to be cheeseburger flavor). Whoever guessed correctly would win a prize and help create the actual product name. Presumably, Frito-Lay also received a tremendous amount of product feedback that helped inform the final ingredient mix and flavor for the product. A Windows Live Search on X-13D returns 24,600 results, one indication this initiative was successful.

Software firms generally have a well-established practice of providing pre-release versions of their products to the public. Hardware or consumer product companies sometimes follow a similar path, especially if the item's Cost of Goods Sold (COGS) is fairly low (e.g., a flash memory drive or dishwashing detergent).

Unlike Technology/Product Adoption or EAP programs that are designed for a small number of customers, pre-launch awareness programs like customer preview programs should be designed to scale and reach hundreds, thousands, or even larger numbers of potential customers. Some of the benefits to providing a structured product preview to the intended target audience include:

Lead Generation: A structured pre-launch trial and awareness program can help build an early pipeline of interested customers for use by demand generation or sales programs post-launch. It is a *very important, if not the most important*, goal for a pre-launch awareness program to help build the initial sales prospect pipeline. Once the product is launched, the awareness program participants should be among the first to send to your channel partners or direct sales force to gain initial sales revenue. It is extremely important to capture the customer contact information of the program participants for later follow-up. If you wait until the product launches to start building a prospect pipeline, revenue will be delayed, perhaps unacceptably so. Get out of the gate running with a healthy list of leads at launch generated through your pre-launch awareness program.

PR: An opportunity to create some buzz around the first public availability of the product. In addition, a chance to get some broader editorial and analyst feedback beyond the initial, more focused influential community.

Testimonials: A pre-launch program like a marketing beta is an avenue to build an early base of customer testimonials, case studies, or other customer evidence like customer references for early PR usage or website content.

Assessing Demand: Pre-launch customer awareness programs can help fine-tune projections and provide early indicators of demand for the product.

General Market Feedback: Feedback from a significant number of early product users regarding likes/dislikes can help point to gaps in preparation pre-launch and give an early warning to potential stumbling blocks or difficulties during the post-launch phase.

Broader Messaging Feedback: The positioning points and messages communicated about the pre-release product should be what are intended to be used in materials, marketing tools, and demand generation programs post-launch. You will get some early indicators on message and value proposition effectiveness through the pre-launch trial and awareness program.

A pre-launch awareness program should not provide specific, detailed technical or feature-level feedback to drive product feature changes before launch. This level of feedback should have been provided in earlier technical betas or other technical assessment and testing programs, like the Technology/Product Adoption Program or Early Adopter Program.

When formulating a broad pre-launch trial and awareness program there are a number of questions to ask to solidify the plan, including:

- What are the customer coverage goals needed in the program, i.e., how many customers per sales district, region, vertical, or customer segment?
- How will the program be marketed? By what mechanisms and at what cost?
- How many customer participants will be included? What are the specific customer criteria or requirements to enter the program?
- How will the participants be supported or get questions answered?
- Will partners be allowed to participate? If so, what are the criteria for their involvement and how many will be included?
- How will customer feedback be collected, analyzed, and acted upon?
- How will the product be delivered to the customer?
- Will there be any cost to a customer for participating? For example, if the product involves a physical good with manufacturing and shipping

costs, it might be reasonable to require that these minimal costs be covered, generally not an issue for software-only products.

- Are there any special training requirements needed?
- What content and collateral need to be created for the program: website, marketing collateral, feedback mechanisms, documentation? A good tip is to use the program as the mechanism to create the early versions of your key go-to-market collateral, trying to get these as buttoned up as possible so they are ready with minimal revision after the product is released for general availability.
- Does the product need to be returned to your firm after the program, or can the customer simply keep it? (For software products there is typically additional special software included in the product that will disable the product functionality at some point after the program ends.)
- What is the sales and marketing follow-up process to convert these customers to paying customers once the final product ships?
- What licensing, legal, or usage restrictions need to be in place?
- Are there any significant opportunity costs associated with allocating scarce launch resources and dollars for the trial and awareness program?

Thinking through these and other questions that may arise can help shape a solid pre-launch trial and awareness program that will pay dividends in awareness and sales once the product is available in final form.

As is typically the case, successful programs need strong leadership to drive them and a champion to see the implementation to completion. Identifying a single internal resource as the primary lead and decision maker for each pre-launch customer program will help achieve success.

Have Some Fun

Don't forget to have some fun with the partners and customers in these programs, especially for the Technology/Product Adoption Program, the EAP, and the customer council participants. Take them to dinner, show them a good time, plan a fun event. The relationship side of the business is just as important as any other. If you create a positive, trusting, and fun engagement with your participants the programs will be more enjoyable and probably more successful.

While these pre-launch customer programs are critical for a successful launch, they form only half the story regarding the types of programs needed in the pre-launch time frame. The other half involves the other key constituents for launch—the channels and partners that will be reselling the product.

DRIVING REVENUE WITH PARTNERS: BUILDING AND LEVERAGING A CHANNEL PARTNER PROGRAM

To maximize the potential market success of your product, a good bet is to go to market with a sufficient number of trained, skilled partners that will resell your product and provide additional value-added products or services. One way to do so is to build a program designed to recruit and manage a large number of channel partners that will extend the reach of your product into the market and create incremental revenue opportunities for your company.

As I indicated in Chapter 5, there are many types of market-making partners that you could or should bring into the launch. Other partners may also be necessary to ensure market success. Distributors, online resellers, technology partners, retailers, VARs, and many other potential partners could populate a channel partner program. These partners differ from the market-making partners in that they are not *absolutely* required to successfully get the product to market. However, they can be crucial to cost-effectively scaling out your business and driving large amounts of incremental revenue if partnering is a viable model for your product and market. These partners can also provide a foundation to drive further innovation around your product.

This section assumes that you don't have a channel partner program in place, so the concepts are foundational. However, there are plenty of perspectives here that can be applied toward enhancing an existing partner program as a go-forward strategy for the product launch.

Partnering as a Strategy

While many companies maintain a direct sales force, large direct sales forces accrue large fixed overhead costs that can drive up the cost of sales. Going solely direct can put your company into a competitive situation with every other firm in your industry, and at a competitive disadvantage by limiting broad end-customer reach and touch opportunities.

One solution to these limitations is to focus the direct sales force only on the limited number of key large customer accounts that require a one-on-one management presence, and rely on a broad channel partner program, programmatically managed, to scale the end-customer reach of your product. The Windows operating system business model is a classic example. There is no way Microsoft could sell as many copies of Windows, or have anywhere close to the thousands of applications built on Windows, if the product was only sold direct by Microsoft, or if Windows applications were solely developed by Microsoft. Broad customer reach is achieved through a large number of channel partners that distribute and sell Windows itself, as well as products and applications built on the Microsoft operating system.

To acquire this scalable reach into the end-customer market, you need to develop and deploy a channel partner program that enables the right partners to distribute, deliver, sell, install, service, and support your product, and possibly build solutions that include it. This is true for technology and non-technology products alike. For example, to broadly resell a lower-tech product like ballpoint pens you need distributors and resellers like office supply companies (e.g., Office Depot), retailers (e.g., Wal-Mart, Target), and possibly specialty retailers (e.g., travel supply outlets, pharmacies like Rite Aid). For software products, you need distributors like TechData, and possibly ISVs to build solutions using your product or VARs to resell it.

When discussing business development activities in Chapter 5, the focus was entirely on strategic partners. However, the one-to-one or one-to-few model of business development is not a scalable model to generate a large number of partners and sustain a broad partner ecosystem. You can't effectively recruit and manage hundreds of partners on a one-to-one basis. What is required to achieve partner ecosystem scale is a "breadth partner program": a programmatic, scalable, arm's-length approach to engaging and retaining small to mid-size (and perhaps some large) partners. A breadth partner program is all about creating and managing these relationships in an efficient, scalable and profitable manner. It cost-effectively enables product revenue generation from a larger number of customers without the need to rely on a large direct sales force.

Key Objectives for a Broad Channel Partner Program

Figure 7-1 illustrates a number of key objectives to focus on when planning, building, and maintaining a partner program. The primary objectives are:

FIGURE 7-1: Partner Program Requirements

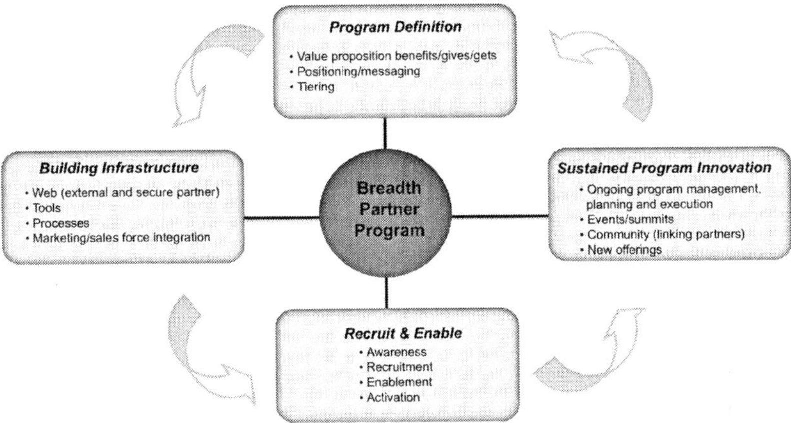

- Designing the right program: the right incentives, value propositions, and benefits for partners that entice them to join with you
- Building the right program infrastructure to launch and maintain the program and its processes
- Driving revenue by providing sufficient partner enablement and activation resources, allowing them to effectively resell and deliver solutions and services around your product
- Sustaining partner program innovation so partners continue their commitment to your product and continue to find value in the program

Designing the Right Program

To attract partners to support, resell, extend, or provide services for your product, there must be compelling value propositions created as incentives to engage. The partner program itself should be designed with features and benefits that provide the basis for these compelling value propositions. Think about the program as "the product" and your potential partners as "the customers"—if you don't design your product to meet your customers' needs, they aren't going to buy. If the partner program does not contain features and benefits of interest to your potential partners, they won't join, participate, or truly engage.

To create an effective channel partner program you'll need to do the following:

- Understand and target the correct set of partners required for your product, and identify what their key needs are relative to the product.
- Develop clear and compelling program value propositions for the partners, and clearly define the commensurate gives from you and gets from the partners.
- Create compelling program positioning and messaging that spells out the value propositions, program features and benefits, with any supporting evidence.
- Define the appropriate program structure: whether a one-size-fits-all program or a tiered program with various levels and benefits per tier.

The Correct Set of Partners

Getting the correct set of partners into your program is important, as it will enable the smooth end-to-end delivery of your product and any associated solutions to the targeted end-customer. The right partners will also effectively drive incremental revenue for your firm. On the other hand, including the wrong partners in your program will cause problems and inefficiencies in the delivery process and generally be a source of anguish and pain. They will not help meet the product revenue and unit sales goals. The specific type of product you are developing and the partner business model the product enables are key drivers to defining both the type of partners you need and the number of partners required to achieve your business goals.

Using a Microsoft software industry example, Figure 7-2 provides examples of pure platform products like Microsoft BizTalk Server or Microsoft Speech Server (a product now embedded in Microsoft Office Communications Server). These products provide a great platform infrastructure for building solutions but deliver little or no out-of-the-box functionality, and require the value-add of a broad range of partners to actually build and deliver complete solutions to end-customers.

Semi-platforms, like Exchange, Windows, and even Office, provide some out-of-the-box functionality, making them immediately usable upon installation (e.g., Outlook for email, OS functionality for your PC, and packaged applications like Word or Excel). These products are also architected to be extensible platforms for partners to create enhanced and

FIGURE 7-2: Product Type Drives Partner Profiles

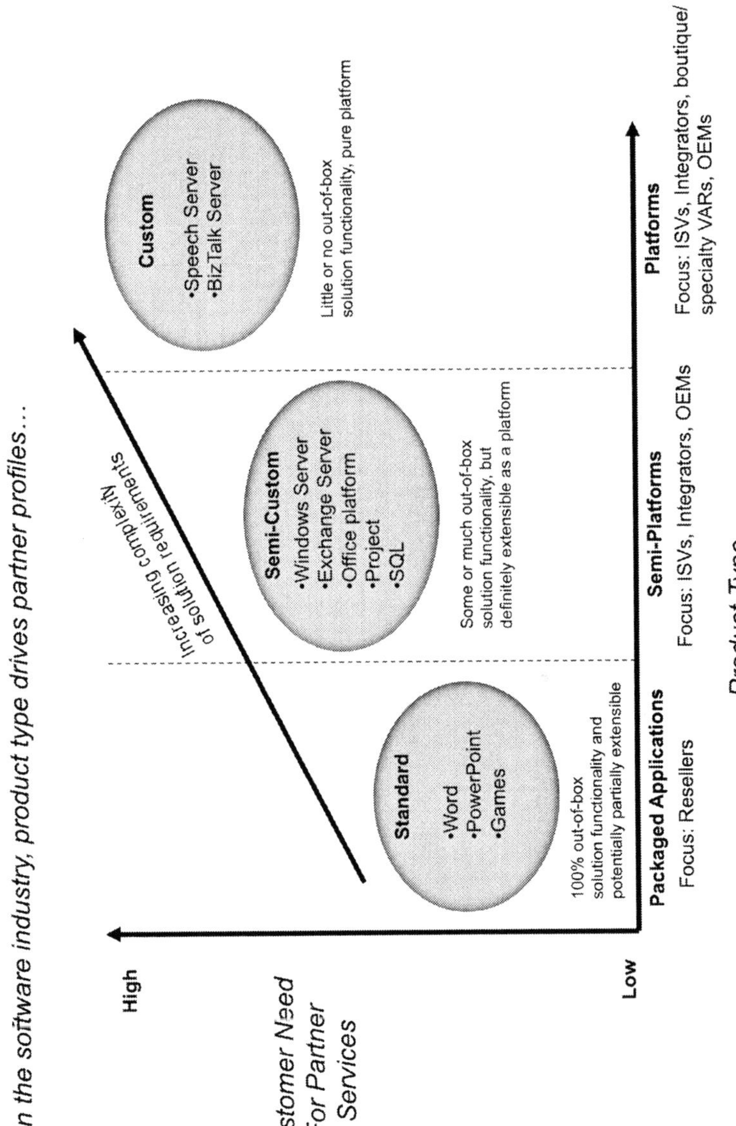

innovative applications upon, e.g., creating macros, or building applications that reside on top of the base product to provide incremental functionality.

Finally, packaged applications like Microsoft Office pretty much give you all the functionality upon install and really don't require partner enhancements for customers to take advantage of and use the product. However, simply because these products have significant out-of-the-box functionality doesn't mean reseller partners are not required.

The point is that you need to figure out, given the kind of product you have and business model you wish to pursue, what is the correct set of target partners. How do you determine this?

One approach is to consider the value delivery chain from your company through to the end-customer. Consider the stages from product production through to product delivery and addition of incremental value-add along the way. At each stage of this process, there could be a possibility that you will need a partner, regardless of how vertically integrated your company happens to be. Figure 7-3 provides one framework for thinking through this, positioning the stages in the product value delivery chain against the specific partner selection criteria to determine the types of partners you may need at various stages. Partner selection criteria includes the following:

FIGURE 7-3: Selecting Partners

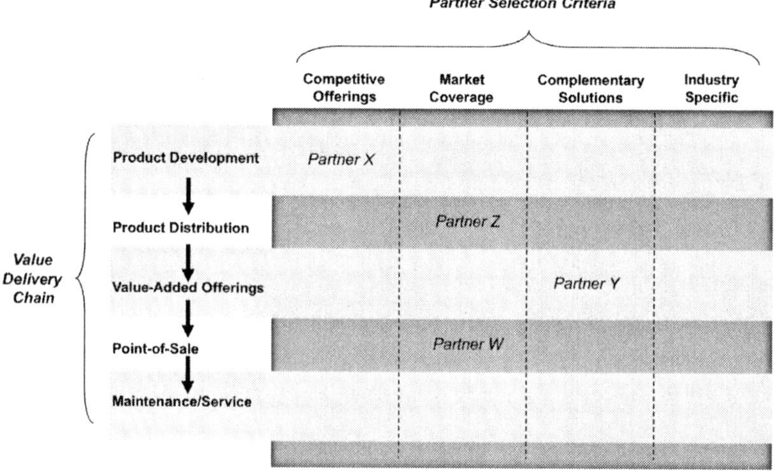

Competitive Offerings: Partners that offer products that are competitive or substitutes for your product are potential allies. This is clearly the case in the software industry, where companies produce solutions on top of Windows, Linux, and UNIX. They do not limit their products to only one operating system. In other lower-tech industries, such as the chemical, pump manufacturing, and uninterruptible power supply industries, there are manufacturers' representative companies (i.e., sales companies) that represent and sell multiple manufacturers' product lines, even though these are competitive lines. Potential partners that are involved with your competitors are already knowledgeable and involved with your target market. Through a partner program with the right incentives and business arrangements, these companies could also help drive your product's sales.

Market Coverage: Partner selection may also depend on market coverage requirements, and what defines market coverage may vary depending on the product and the target customers. For example, market coverage could constitute a geographic perspective if you need to focus on getting partners within particular geographies around the country or the world. A vertical perspective could apply as well, ensuring that you have partners that serve the various vertical markets you are pursuing. A horizontal approach might also be applicable—perhaps you need partners that have specific departmental expertise, such as manufacturing, marketing, or customer service and support. Or, market coverage could be defined by company size, like small businesses or the Fortune 500.

Complementary Solutions: It's great if you can attract partners who provide their own solutions to augment your product's value. In the software industry, application developers or independent software developers that produce applications running on Windows or other Microsoft platform products like Exchange, SQL, and BizTalk are examples of partners with complementary solutions. However, the concept extends well beyond the software industry. Simple technology examples would be skins for iPods or mobile phones—if you are building and selling these skins, partnering up with resellers of iPods and mobile phones probably makes sense. Whether your market is high- or low-tech, try to find and attract partners that can extend your product's value. They can add additional functionality (e.g., customized document templates or new macros in Microsoft Word or Excel), bundle your product with other complementary products (e.g., toothpaste with a toothbrush), or incorporate your product into theirs as a core component (e.g., Intel microprocessors into personal computers).

Doing so can create product pull-through sales opportunities for your product.

Industry Specific: There is always something about any particular industry that will be unique and will require specialized partners that cater to its nuances. One example comes from the speech recognition industry and companies having specific expertise in the human factors design of user interfaces for voice-only applications. These are the folks that design the way you interact with those sometimes annoying self-service phone applications (i.e., "Please say or enter your social security number now"). Companies creating and selling products in the speech recognition and Interactive Voice Response industries may need partners with this industry-specific skill set. Potential partners are out there to help meet the unique needs of your industry as well.

Together, the value delivery chain and partner selection criteria can help determine what type of partners you may need.

Defining Partner Program Value Propositions

Viewing your partner program as a "product" adds perspective to building and communicating the value propositions of the program from a feature and benefit standpoint. Like a product sale to an end-customer, you are trying to build and sell the features and benefits of your program to the partner audience. You need to clearly state the case for *why* a partner should care and *what* is in it for them. You need to communicate how the program offerings will help meet the target partner's core needs, in effect answering this question for the partner: "Will this program help my business gain incremental benefit and value?"

A number of potential program value propositions will provide a positive answer to this question. "Yes" will be the answer if your partner program can:

- Help partners increase revenues or profitability.
- Reduce their time to market (sales, marketing, or product development).
- Decrease their dependency on another product line (preferably a competitive product).
- Reduce their operating costs (support, collateral, selling, and training).
- Open up new market opportunities (e.g., acquire new customers, up-sell existing customers with the new product opportunity, address

a new vertical market, access an emerging growth business, enter a horizontal market, or develop a new market niche).

- Maintain or extend the core skill set of the partner company's employees.
- Fill a gap in the partner company's business needs (e.g., ability to generate qualified leads, close more deals).
- Build a closer relationship with your company (e.g., access to your company's marketing team, sales team, engineering team, executives, or enable regular communication channels to and from the partner).
- Expand the partner's networking base and business opportunities with other companies.
- Enable access to key resources that would otherwise be unavailable or difficult to create (e.g., sales tools, valuable logos or certifications, and co-branded literature).
- Offer assistance from your company in marketing, selling, or product development (e.g., having a dedicated partner account manager from your firm, making available business investment funds to prime deals, or providing marketing offers your company develops).

There may also be industry-specific value propositions that apply in your case, which you can add to this list.

Developing Partner Program Features and Benefits

You may choose to build a partner program that incorporates some or all of these potential value propositions, with the right program feature and benefit offerings in place to support them. Approach the development of these offerings as you would approach product development. What are the partner needs? What are their pain points? What are their business goals? What benefits can you provide for all partners? Which benefits serve unique needs for special types of partners? Competitive partner programs can also provide ideas for program offerings. Analyze competitor partner programs in your industry. What benefits do competitors offer partners? How do they position the value propositions of their programs relative to yours? How can you differentiate your program vs. the others?

Planned program offerings must be defined to meet the needs of the specific partner types being targeted, just as a SKU is defined relative to the target customer segment needs. Figure 7-4 provides an illustrative planning framework for mapping various program benefits relative to

FIGURE 7-4: Illustrative Framework for Planning Program Benefits

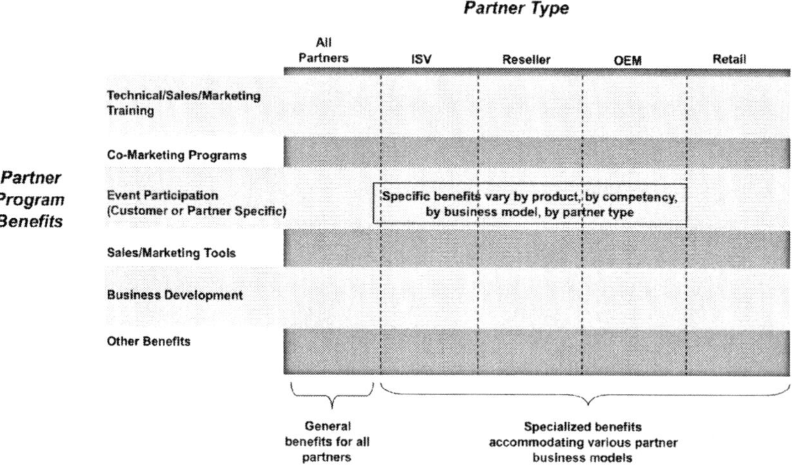

specific partner types, and can be used to ensure that the program offerings are being defined relative to the target partner needs.

There are a number of different conceptual perspectives to help structure program feature and benefit development. Figure 7-5 illustrates three possible perspectives. The first maps benefits against partner functional business activities. Generally, all businesses will need to plan, market, and support customers. The specific business model of the partner, product type, and industry will drive unique business functions in addition to these general functional areas (e.g., application development in the software industry). Defining program benefits to help partners across functional business activities is one approach to program feature definition and development.

A second perspective maps program features and benefits to core partner needs. Skill development and training, opportunity and lead generation, and closing deals are important partner needs. How can the partner program assist a partner in these areas? Defining the program offerings, features, and benefits around core partner needs is a good approach.

Finally, a partner program could be structured with different levels, or tiers. This third perspective would focus on designing program features and benefits specific to each tier of the program. Companies taking this approach sub-segment their partners into these tiers. Typically, there is a quid pro quo involved in such segmentation where the partner receives

FIGURE 7-5: Program Benefit Views

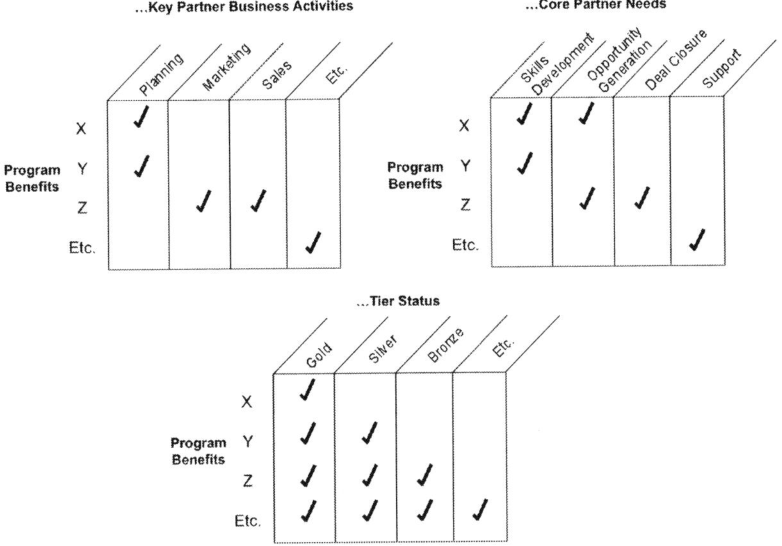

increasing levels of benefits for increased commitment to your company. The most active partners that sell the most are in the highest tier level and get the most benefits.

Sometimes you'll see the tier nomenclature as something like "Gold, Silver, or Bronze" levels. The Microsoft Partner Program (MSPP) provides three levels of sub-segmentation: Gold Certified is the highest level, Certified is mid-level, and Registered is the base level. These are illustrated in Figure 7-6. The Gold partners generally get the most one-on-one attention, are the most committed, and drive large amounts of revenue for Microsoft. They also tend to be larger partners and have a significant level of market presence themselves. There are not a lot of companies that fit this category.

The Certified partners receive a good amount of attention and benefits, but less than the Gold. The Registered partners receive the fewest benefits.

Tiering a partner program has both pros and cons, and it can be difficult to decide whether tiering is the right approach. After reviewing various partner programs, and knowing the Microsoft program, I suggest that the decision to tier or not to tier depends on a variety of factors. Figure 7-7 overviews a few partner and market characteristics that might help influence the tiering decision.

FIGURE 7-6: Microsoft Partner Program Tiers

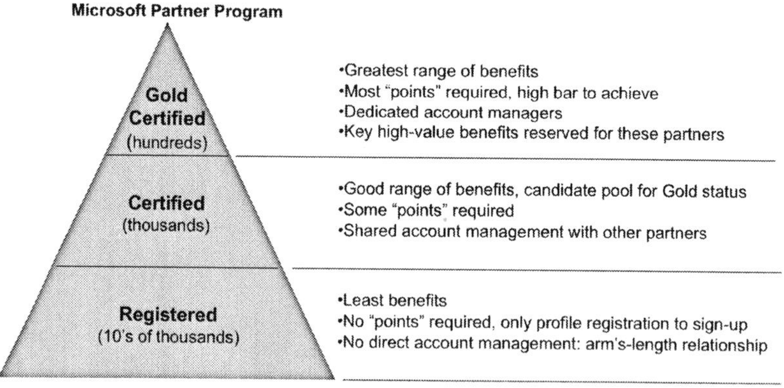

FIGURE 7-7: Program Tiering Decision Influencers

Some Characteristics Supporting a Tiered Program Model	Some Characteristics Supporting a Non-Tiered Program Model
The market is mature and large.	A new or emerging market which is smaller in size.
A large supply of potential partners exists.	New types of products or technologies.
You have the budget and resources to manage a tiered model.	A small supply of potential partners exists.
You can set public, objective, and quantitative criteria for the different tiers (if not you risk being viewed as playing favorites, and potential legal issues).	Your budget is small and you don't have the resources to manage a tiered program.
Partners are for the most part generalists in their skill sets and solution delivery capabilities.	The partner pool is composed of specialists.
Competitive programs set a precedent for tiering as a basic program requirement.	There is no competitive advantage to be gained by tiering the partners.

Developing Partner Program Positioning and Messaging

Once they are defined, you must effectively communicate the program value propositions. Similar to developing the to-customer messaging framework for your product (Chapter 4), you should develop a *to-partner* positioning framework, or something similar, to help frame the key program value propositions and postioning points. Clearly defined, these important communication points can be used throughout marketing collateral and activities to help attract new partners to join your program, increase your share of business with existing partners, and switch competitive partners to your product line. Make sure you are able to support your value proposition claims with program features, benefits, and any available third-party information as evidence (e.g., analyst or press information, ROI assessments, positive channel program comparisons, and awards).

Test and validate your positioning points and value propositions with a select set of partners before you finalize your positioning framework. This sanity check will not only be fruitful in learning what you didn't think of, but will also save you time and money in reworking everything later on. Your partner council (defined later in this chapter) is a good venue for testing your positioning points and messages. So are informal discussions with partners at events, meetings, and on phone calls. Structured market research is always a wise choice to use to ask hard questions about the value of your program, potential shortcomings, and possible new program feature additions—while maintaining the anonymity of your company if necessary or desired.

Implementing the Partner Program Via Web Infrastructure

Once the core program is defined and structured, the infrastructure to put the program into effect must be built. This infrastructure must accommodate all aspects of running the program, including recruiting partners, sustaining ongoing communications, delivering content and sales tools, executing co-marketing programs, and connecting partners to customers and to other partners.

A breadth partner program must be designed to accommodate an arm's-length relationship with many partners while enabling program scalability and self-service. The web is a key implementation mechanism, with the central hub for such a program being a partner program website. Typically, this is a secure website, requiring recruited partners to sign-in with some sort of login ID and password to gain access to the program deliverables and benefits. There should also be a public, open element to the site. This area is a prime location to evangelize the value and benefits of the program for recruiting and acquiring new partners. The site makes a pitch to join the program and makes a registration process available to those that may choose to do so.

The website infrastructure also needs to accommodate ongoing communications with the partner community. Email newsletters, announcements and notifications, and in-person event opportunities can be delivered via the web infrastructure. Feedback and communications from the partners back to your firm is another feature the partner website hub should accommodate. The site should also enable partners to locate and contact the relevant people inside your firm to get help, assistance, and support.

Content especially designed for the members of the partner program can be delivered through the secure portion of the website. Sales tools, marketing collateral, sales presentations, and other elements comprising through-partner marketing tools should be made available to partners.

Community building features are also excellent. Partners will sometimes need to contact other partners, perhaps to team up on a project where they have complementary skill sets, to seek real-world advice from a peer, or to market their services and products to other partners. Examples are partner blogs, newsgroups, and referral tools.

To maximize the site's effectiveness it is important to maintain an up-to-date and accurate database of partners. Incorrect partner contact or descriptive information about the partner business (e.g., their products, the services they provide, and their core competencies) will dilute the value of activities that depend on this information. For example, a key site element should be a "Partner Finder" tool, enabling end-customers to search for program partners to help them do whatever it is they need to do with your product—purchase it, deploy it, fix it, whatever. If the partner database is inaccurate (e.g., partner phone or email information is incorrect, they list the wrong competencies—or too many competencies, or the geographic location is wrong) the end-customer ability to find the right partner will be limited or simply not possible, hindering the connection of customer to partner, and limiting revenue generating opportunities.

When designing the partner web infrastructure, plan the website to accommodate the activities necessary to maintain an effective partner program: awareness creation, recruitment, partner enablement, and partner activation. This will mitigate the chance of missing important program infrastructure requirements.

Growing Your Revenues Through Partners: Awareness, Recruiting, Enabling, and Activating

After the program is defined and the infrastructure is in place, you will need to start program execution. One conceptual framework for partner program execution follows a process cycle that includes awareness activities for educating partners about the program, recruiting efforts to sign-up partners, enabling and arming partners to sell, and activating the partners through marketing programs.

Figure 7-8 illustrates this framework and organizes the primary activities for partner engagement into four major categories: Awareness, Recruitment, Enablement, and Activation. Develop detailed tactical plans for each stage of the cycle, and define specific success metrics. You can use the framework as a guide to developing partner program plans for each cycle stage.

PARTNER PROGRAM AWARENESS CREATION

Awareness activities focus on marketing the program and creating interest throughout the target partner audience. Primarily a communications exercise, you evangelize the core program value propositions to the partners of interest. If you have an existing channel partner program, these are the most obvious targets to approach on business opportunities with the upcoming product. You should communicate and evangelize the incremental revenue and profit opportunities to this audience. It's straightforward to use existing communication mechanisms like email, newsletters, and any existing partner events or partner account managers to reach out to this community.

If there is no existing partner program, communications to new prospective partners can involve a number of different outreach tactics and include advertising, direct marketing, events, and referrals from market-making partners. You should consider all mechanisms to reach the potential partner pool, given available resources, time, and money. These awareness creation activities are similar to other marketing programs you run to sell your product. However, in this case, you are not marketing a product, you're marketing the partner program to your potential partner pool. The call-to-action is for partners to sign-up and join the program.

The key communication points include being clear about what the business opportunities are, why the partner should care, and what they need to do to act and take advantage of the opportunities. Make sure that your messages are clear and presented in a compelling fashion to prospective partners. If you have clearly defined your program's core value propositions, its benefits, and the opportunity your product offers, and you have kept the barriers to joining at a reasonably low level, these communications should successfully generate awareness and interest in the partner community.

FIGURE 7-8: Partner Program Process Cycle

The partner program process cycle has four major components, each with different goals, tactics, and key issues…

	Partner Awareness →	Partner Recruitment →	Partner Enablement →	Partner Activation
Primary Goal	Creating interest and awareness about your partner program and key value propositions among potential partner candidates	Gaining demonstrable commitment from partners to join the program	Preparing partners to sell your product	Implementing co-marketing and sales programs with partners
Typical Tactics	• Print Advertising • Email • Newsletters • Direct mail • Web advertising • User groups • Industry events • 1-1 meetings • Partner referral	• Web-based sign-up • Events sign-up • 1-1 biz dev sign-up • Sales force sign-up	• Partner sales/marketing tools • Partner summit events • Online training • In-person training	• Program engagement infrastructure • Offers/rebates/incentives • Campaign specific tools • Lead generation • Community/networking • Communication mechanism (newsletter, councils, summits)
Key Issues	• Cost to reach • Messaging efficacy	• Program value proposition • Time frame to commitment • Barriers (program entry) hurdles • Process ease	• Partner motivation • Tools/training quality • Asset availability	• Partner motivation • Mapping to partner business model • Ease of engagement • Manageable communications flow • Sales force integration/PAM • Sales support model • Standard vs. custom

Once the product is launched, partner awareness activities are extended to include creating awareness about your partners to the end-customers. In addition to executing awareness programs for partner recruitment, it is equally important to spend time and money creating awareness within your end-user target market *about* the partners that you have. Do your customers even know that you have a partner program? Do they know the value that your partners can bring to them through their services and training? Do your customers understand how to contact and engage one of your partners?

Connecting your customers to your partners is an important and necessary activity. Doing so will help fuel your business pipeline by creating demand for partner services around your product, providing opportunities for increased product sales. It will also help create more satisfied end-customers, as they will be working with trained and knowledgeable partners to meet their needs. Partners will view these customer connection activities positively, and will value the fact that your firm is helping to create awareness and business opportunities.

RECRUITING PARTNERS

After becoming aware of the program, interested partners must actually join the program. Just as in an end-customer sales process, you must close the partners and overcome objections to taking the final step—making a firm commitment to the program. The easiest way to sign-up a partner is through the partner website portal. Creating a simple online form to capture the relevant partner information is straightforward. This helps keep barriers to recruitment low. However, make sure the information supplied on the form is comprehensive. The supplied data should feed into your partner database, the primary repository for partner information that will feed tools like the Partner Finder for customers.

Once the form is filled out and submitted, the partner has initiated the formal process for joining the program—they have been recruited. Any due diligence and follow-on partner communications, next steps, and congratulations should follow from your firm.

When planning the strategy and tactics to close the partners, you should consider:

- Nuances among the different types of partners being recruited: new partners, existing partners, and competitive partners
- The time it takes to recruit a partner

- Partner quality level
- Trading-off revenue goals vs. partner quality

New Partners: These companies have no existing relationship with your company and may be completely unaware that you even have a partner program. If so, your awareness marketing activities to evangelize the value of the program will become an important first step to attract them. Once aware, a typical issue is that they don't understand or believe your program value propositions. This is a significant recruitment barrier, but there are ways around it.

For example, you could engage the partner one-on-one to clarify and explain your program's value propositions, features, and benefits. This can be a time-consuming approach; however, if you leverage existing events, phone, or webcasts you can effectively and efficiently reach these partners. Another approach for partners who are skeptical of your program's value propositions is to use any existing partners to advocate on your behalf. If you have an existing program, there are likely many partners who are very satisfied with the benefits they've accrued. These, and market-making partners, can be highly effective advocates. Asking them to discuss their experiences and the value they have derived from your partner program via webcasts, email testimonials, case studies, or even meeting other partners with you or one-on-one will generally be acceptable. They are helping you and themselves by creating awareness of their businesses and growing their network with new business colleagues.

The important point is that just because the program value propositions have been communicated does not necessarily mean they are believed or internalized. Be aware of this and assume that follow-on activities will be required to close the partners.

Existing Partners: These are partners that are already engaged in an ongoing relationship with your company. This relationship may or may not be within the confines of your partner program (though engagement within the program structure is preferable). These partners should be the easiest ones to reach and recruit to sell your new product. The best bet is to approach existing partners having complementary businesses that will benefit the most from the incremental business opportunity. Barriers to recruitment with existing partners include any dissatisfaction issues within the partner community, unwillingness to commit to a larger share of their business with your company, and lack of resources or time to be trained on or sell a new product.

Competitive Partners: Recruiting competitive partners is the most difficult, time- and resource-consuming effort you may undertake. Depending on the level of your resources, you may choose to lower the priority of this effort and focus primarily on recruiting new and existing partners to support your product. However, if you choose to focus on competitive partners, you may want to consider an incremental approach. For example, you may choose to focus on larger competitive partners that are fewer in number yet broader in impact and that can be a reached via a one-on-one business development engagement process. This allows you to minimize marketing costs and focus your efforts to achieve the greatest return on your investment vs. spending large amounts of marketing dollars in broad out-bound competitive marketing campaigns that may be ineffective.

Recruitment Timing: It takes time to convert a partner into a signed-up program member that will take on the product. The time it takes from initial awareness to becoming a member will depend on such factors as the cost of entry into the program, the volume of the prospective partner's ongoing business activities, training requirements, and program costs. You should count on at least three months to take a partner from awareness to membership. Other entry barriers to your program, such as sales reporting requirements, ongoing program overhead, and ease of sign-up, will also add to the time required to fully incorporate a partner into your program.

Partner Quality: The quality of your partners and the work they do for the end-customer will directly reflect on your company and the product. There are various ways to ensure the quality of partners. For example, screening partner program applications for the length of time they have been in business, seeking positive customer referrals, and pulling Dun & Bradstreet credit reports are some initial quality screening activities.

You may also wish to implement an entry barrier to your program such as a training requirement. This could be technical or business training, or a combination. This provides a level of quality assurance, but it adds cost and overhead to your program, requiring you to develop and administer the training and track partner progress. However, you get peace of mind that the partners you are sending to the end-customers are adequately prepared to sell or implement solutions around your product.

Requiring a modest fee to join the program is another option to help ensure partner quality. Tire-kickers will generally not be willing to put up any cash to join the program, but serious and committed partners will do so.

Revenue vs. Quality Trade-off: To generate the level of product revenue desired, a certain number of partners will be required. The specific number of necessary partners will be driven by the sales capacity and velocity of the partners, in aggregate. To reach the revenue goal, a trade-off between maintaining high partner quality and getting the necessary number of partners to reach that goal may be required. Training programs and other quality checks are great for keeping partner quality high, but they also act as a barrier to recruitment. Many good prospective partners don't have the time, money, or inclination to go through any level of significant training or deal with quality checkpoints. Or they may feel like they are already adequately prepared. This presents a recruitment barrier, making it harder to recruit the necessary number of partners to get the sales capacity necessary to meet the revenue goal. This is where the trade-off comes in—are you willing to lower the program entry requirements and possibly lower the program's partner quality levels (and accept the risk of potential negative ramifications) to build the program capacity more quickly to reach the revenue goal? Give adequate thought and consideration to the answer, and understand any potential impacts.

ENABLEMENT AND ACTIVATION

After you've successfully recruited partners you will need to adequately prepare, or enable, them to sell your product. To enable a partner, it's important to provide an adequate supply of partner-ready sales and marketing tools—you need to arm the partner with the tools, information, and execution resources required to market, sell, and engage in business opportunities for your product. It is also important to provide technology and business training opportunities enabling an in-depth understanding of the product and *how* to sell and market it.

Partner Training: It is best to provide training for partners across all facets of the business. Figure 7-9 illustrates a framework for planning partner training needs, mapping partner type by training focus. Partner type means the various partner business models associated with the partners in your program. In this example, independent software vendors, value-added resellers, retailers, OEMs, and manufacturers' representatives are different partner types that may be in the program, each operating under different business models. Against this, one would map the types

FIGURE 7-9: Illustrative Framework for Planning Partner Training

Planning partner training relative to partner type . . .

Training & Enablement Focus

Target Partner Type	Services	Product	Business
	Planning, deploying, installing	Features, usage, technology	Business value, sales, marketing
ISV			
VAR			
Retailer			
OEM			
Mfg. Rep.			
Etc.			

Considerations:
- ✓ *Level of information depth and breadth (e.g., overview/top-level, deep)*
- ✓ *Technical depth*
- ✓ *Content delivery (e.g., video, web, whitepaper, brochure)*
- ✓ *Intended consumption/distribution model (e.g., web, kits, events)*
- ✓ *Self-paced or instructor-led*
- ✓ *Specific audience target (e.g., senior/junior technical or business decision maker role)*
- ✓ *Reusability? Can content be repurposed for to-customer or PR purposes?*

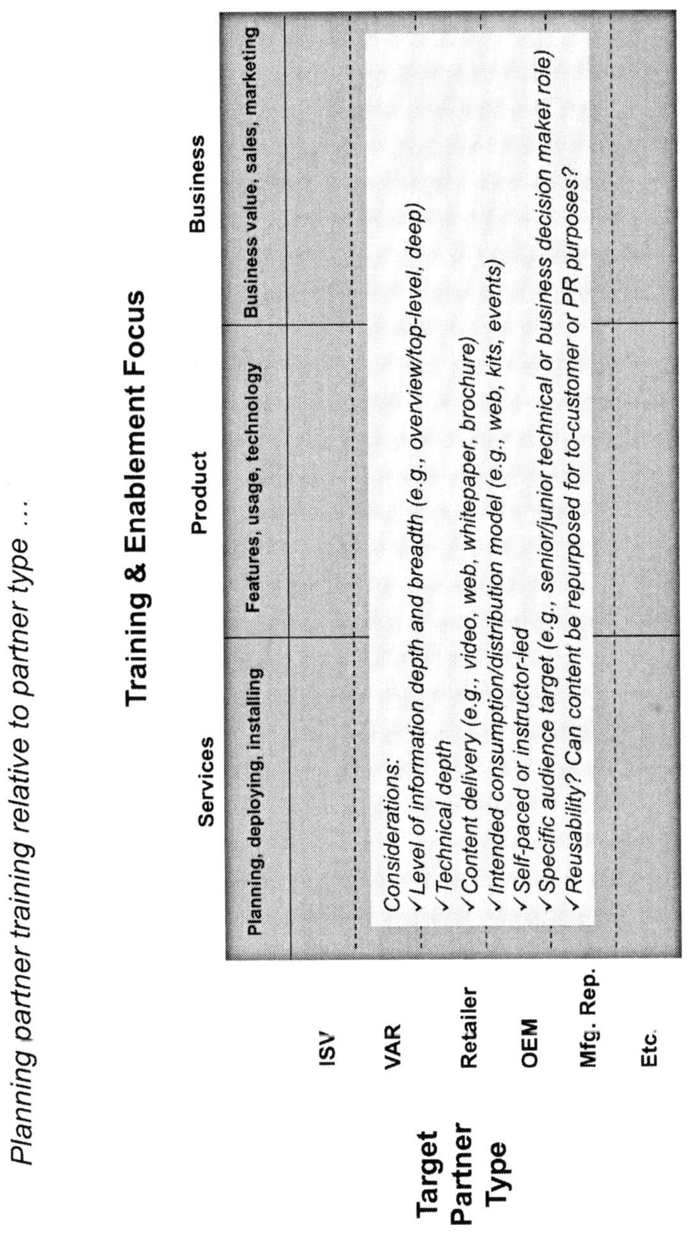

of training required for each partner type across services, product, and business needs.

There may be overlap and similarity between the training provided to each partner type. For example, product training focuses on the product itself, its features, benefits, usage, and underlying technology. Other than the training depth and detail, this won't vary much (or possibly at all) as the partner type varies. However, for services training, there could be significant differences in the type of training necessary. A value-added reseller that is deploying a solution on a customer premise using your product and their services would need different training than a retail partner who is simply selling your product to end-customers at a retail location. Consider the impact of different partner business models on training needs when building training offerings.

When planning training offerings, keep the following in mind:

- How technically deep does the training need to go? Should multiple offerings be available with various levels of depth?
- How should you package your training for delivery? Online? Instructor-led?
- Should your training content be reusable for other purposes, such as public relations, whitepapers, or events?

Partner Marketing Tools and Activation Offerings: You should listen to your partners and provide them the marketing tools and resources they say they need, and what you think they need. Microsoft has done a good job in this regard. The company business model depends on partners. They do an excellent job of listening to partners' feedback and incorporating it into their programs.

However, while providing the necessary training and marketing materials enables a partner to sell, it is not typically enough. To motivate and assist a partner to actively market and sell involves the activation phase of the cycle—you need to "activate" the partners. Figure 7-10 illustrates some examples of marketing tools and activation offerings that have proven valuable to Microsoft and offers suggestions for incorporation into your partner program.

I've divided Figure 7-10 into High, Medium, and Base Value examples. These groupings reflect how a partner would value these offerings. High Value program offerings including sales offers, leads, and investment dollars are extremely important and provide great motivation. These benefits generally directly affect and increase the likelihood of a sale for the partner

FIGURE 7-10: Core Partner Program Offers and Benefits

High Value	Medium Value	Base Value
Monetary incentives: product discounts, rebates, service subsidies, business investment funds Exclusivity for anything Support (pre/post sales) Lead generation/leads Free product for internal use Executive engagement Co-selling opportunities Dedicated go-to internal person/contact as a sales aid resource	Business value offers Event attendance/activities Networking opportunities/ community building Customized collateral Co-branded collateral In-person training opportunities Feedback opportunities on sales/ marketing, engineering, and products Free stuff (branded company hats/shirts, etc.) for relationship building Inclusion into customer case studies ROI tools	Sales/marketing tools and collateral Secure/private partner website Industry analysis/research information PowerPoint sales slide libraries Online training Competitive literature Communication/outreach tools (newsletters, kits with literature, etc.)

and so provide great value. Other high value benefits like exclusivity and executive engagement are great for showing partner love, support, and commitment from your company. Providing an environment and the resources from your company to enable co-selling opportunities also means a lot to a partner.

It's also smart to have a dedicated "go-to" person as a resource to help partners in both pre-sales and ongoing sales efforts. For example, in the Microsoft world there are partner account managers that are dedicated either to a single partner account or to multiple accounts. These Microsoft employees take on many roles for the partner, such as business planner, sales partner, information resource, and internal access point. A good partner account manager can really help a partner sell effectively and provide many opportunities for co-sales engagements.

Medium Value business value offers are a mainstay of any partner program. Offers like kits, Flash demos, whitepapers, or training material can provide valuable incentives for the partner in their to-customer demand generation activities. The trick is to know what types of offers will resonate with a customer, moving them to take the desired action. Your firm's investment in business value offer creation, and making these offers accessible to partners for their use, is hugely valuable to partners without the resources to invest in creating such offers. Including partners in customer case studies produced by your firm is another desirable offering. Partner solutions, products, and services are showcased alongside your product, providing free marketing and awareness for the partner as your firm uses these case studies for your own marketing activities.

Collateral that can be co-branded, allowing partners to place their logo alongside yours in the same marketing material, will be highly desired. Partners will benefit by leveraging your company's brand awareness and credibility to accrue a brand halo-effect for their firm. Where your company does not have a significant brand presence, allowing co-branded material to be delivered to end-customers from the partner also indicates your tight-knit relationship to the partner firm and to customers, and acknowledges the partners' expertise.

Customizable marketing collateral is another highly valued offering. In this case, marketing material your firm creates is partly customizable by the partner. For example, on a one-page datasheet, your firm may create the content for the top half of the page, perhaps conveying the product value propositions and other key messages. This content would not be changeable by the partner to ensure the consistency of your messages. However, the last half of the content would contain text, graphics, or messages created by the partner touting the partner's business, their services, or their complementary products along with their logo.

Don't overlook the benefits of enabling social interaction with partners and end-customers. For example, allowing partners to attend events, gain space in your booth, or locate their booths near yours displays partnership and showcases partner solutions and offerings associated with your company's product offerings. This also provides a great networking opportunity for the partners to interact, learn from each other, and form business relationships.

Base Value offerings are the minimum offerings your program should provide, e.g., having PowerPoint slide libraries that allow partners to mix and match slides to create their own custom sales presentations. Creating a program newsletter to keep partners informed is a good idea. Online training should be available to ease learning accessibility. Since many of your partners will also be selling competitive products, it's important to provide information allowing them to compare the features, benefits, and business value of your product and offerings to the other lines they sell and show why your product is the better choice. Basic sales and marketing tools like pre-created banner ads, direct mail pieces, print advertisements, and the like should be standard elements for program offerings.

PARTNER ACTIVATION VIA MONETARY INCENTIVES

As was indicated in Figure 7-10, monetary incentives are a highly valued element of a partner program. The downside is that they are just that—monetary incentives—which are direct costs to your business and can decrease profitability and impact cash flow. Monetary incentives are essentially investments to buy the desired partner behavior. Just as with any investment, the idea is to generate a positive ROI. While profitability may suffer somewhat, if the post-investment volume of sales increase is large enough, greater gross profit dollars may result (lower profit per deal, but larger number of deals equals larger gross profit). You should do a detailed financial analysis when planning any type of monetary incentive to partners and it should, within reasonable sensitivity parameters, ensure a positive ROI on any monetary partner incentive.

While Figure 7-10 listed various examples of different monetary incentives, some of these, such as business investment funds, are generally targeted to a small number of partners and don't broadly impact the partner ecosystem. On the other hand, rebates are one popular and effective form of monetary incentive that can be broadly applied to all channel partners in the partner program. Because monetary incentives are so valued, and rebate incentives can have a broad partner channel impact and reach, I'll focus on avoiding a serious mistake on rebate planning and implementation.

One big mistake that frequently occurs when executing rebates is a lack of alignment throughout the channel and with the end-customer. Essentially, the rebate strategy and implementation are not thought through from top to bottom, from the distributor, to the reseller, to the end-customer. All too often the rebate structure is misaligned among these various constituents, causing confusion and an ineffective channel rebate strategy. This can occur because of a siloed organization without good communication, no central rebate planning and optimization functional process in place, a lack of basic high-level planning, or even too many rebates occurring at the same time for different products.

Figure 7-11 illustrates both a poor, misaligned rebate strategy and a better, more aligned strategy using a hypothetical Microsoft product rebate. The figure shows a typical 2-tier distribution model with product flowing from the manufacturer (your company) through distributors or OEMs, then to resellers such as VARs or retailers, with product finally arriving at the end-customer.

At each level of the distribution tiers, Figure 7-11 maps an example of a misaligned rebate structure ("Misaligned and Doesn't Work") and an

FIGURE 7-11: Incentive Alignment

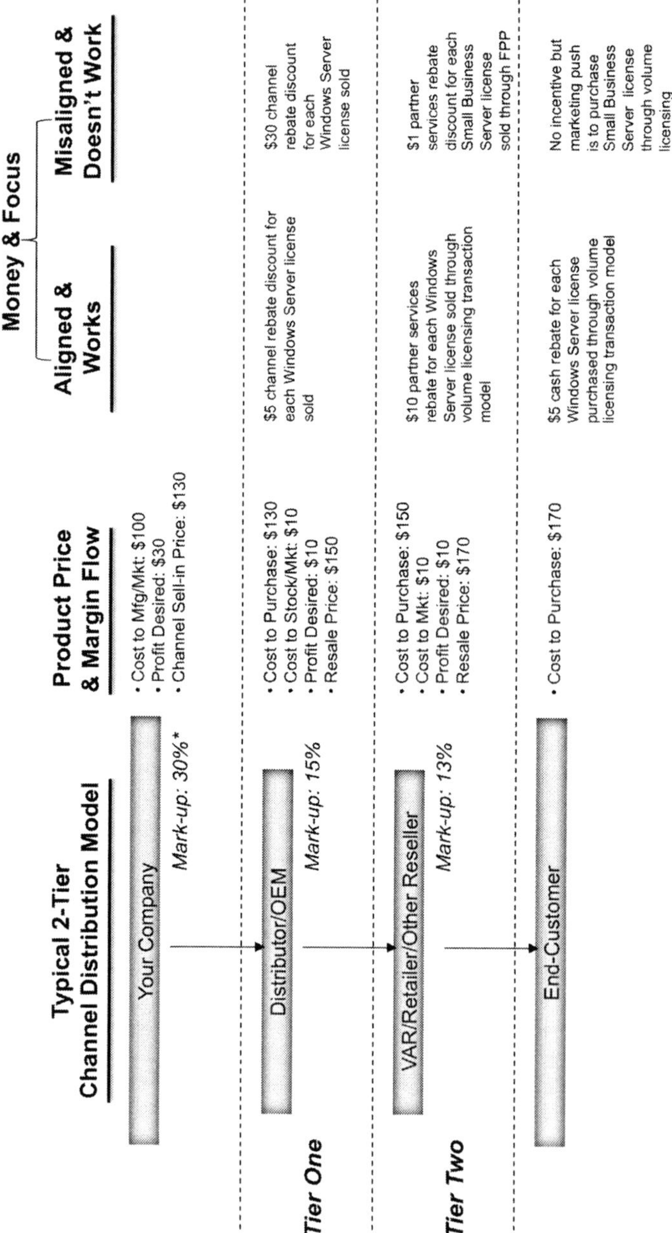

aligned rebate structure ("Aligned and Works"). The intent of the rebate provider is two-fold: get the channel focused on selling Windows Server, and shift the purchasing pattern to volume licensing contracts instead of buying a box of product at retail. In the aligned rebate example, distributors are offered a $5 rebate (a 50% increase in desired profit for firms in this tier) for each unit of Windows Server sold (dollar amounts are hypothetical for illustrative purposes—these are not real numbers used by Microsoft). To reinforce that rebate and ensure that all tiers are focused on pushing the same buttons, a complementary rebate is put into place for the next tier down—the resellers.

Implementing a rebate at this tier incents members of that tier to act and functions as a reinforcing demand generation tool for the distributors (Tier One) to drive demand for Windows Server from their customers, the resellers (Tier Two). The Tier Two rebate is a $10 partner services rebate (a 100% increase in desired profit for these firms) focused again on Windows Server (reinforcing the product focus and ensuring consistency), essentially increasing the profitability of the partner services required to deploy Windows Server. The twist is that the rebate only applies to deals where the product is sold via the volume licensing contract mechanism, thus reinforcing that element of the desired rebate intent.

To cap it all off, a $5 cash-back rebate is also offered to end-customers to create demand for Windows Server, and is the focus of any out-bound awareness and demand generation activities delivered to the end-customers during the rebate time period. It's not a huge deal for end-customers, but better than a sharp stick in the eye. Overall, the rebates add up to $20 total, leaving a $10 profit margin for the manufacturer. Given a $30 profit per unit desire from the manufacturer, there needs to be a 3X (3 times) increase in units sold to breakeven on overall gross profit dollars with the rebate in place. Presumably, the financial analysis and projections done up front indicate that the expected increase is higher than 3X, making this rebate a good bet to pursue. It is clear that in this example all of the rebates for each tier of channel delivery are aligned and reinforce each another from a product perspective and to meet desired rebate intent and goals.

In the misaligned example, it is now clear what mistakes are being made. The Tier One distributor/OEM rebate is $30, and while focusing on the right product, essentially immediately removes all profit from a unit sale. The Tier Two reseller rebate has numerous problems: the dollar amount is too small (only a 10% increase in desired partner profit goals), it is the wrong product (Small Business Server vs. Windows Server), and it focuses on the wrong purchase transaction model (Full Package Product vs. volume licensing). Finally, there is no end-customer rebate in place for Windows Server, and all the marketing demand generation activities happening in the rebate time frame are focused on selling Small Business Server. What are the odds that the desired rebate goals of profitably selling more Windows Server and increasing the volume licensing purchase transaction rate will be met? Pretty low.

Setting the wrong rebate amount is another problem. In these examples, a hypothetical rebate amount was used. To set the correct rebate amount in the real world, understand for each tier the true product price markups, purchase costs, profitability goals, and resale prices. Without a clear understanding of these numbers, it is difficult to know how much of a rebate would actually make a difference to the channel partners (or end-customer), and what percent impact these rebates could make to partner profitability. Rebates that are too small and do not make a reasonable impact on profitability are less likely to be adopted by the channel. Rebates that are too large create a scenario where your firm is giving away more money than necessary to generate incrementally higher profits for your firm. The right numbers must be calculated for each tier; knowing these key numbers is an important prerequisite to the rebate size calculation.

These types of rebate planning and execution problems are common. If your firm plans to deliver monetary incentives like rebates to the broad channel once the product gets out the door, all the planning for this takes place pre-launch. Optimally, the rebate planning and delivery as a partner activation tool will result in an aligned and profitable rebate strategy.

Revenue Growth Through Partners: Strategy Options

Clearly, the end goal for your firm's investment in building and running a partner program is to create revenue through the partner channel. Given the program is in place and operating, there are a couple of options, or levers, to apply that can focus investments in the partner program and its activities to acquire this revenue. The two primary levers are: deriving more revenue from your existing partners, and adding partners to grow channel capacity.

Figure 7-12 illustrates these levers, outlining the key options and indicating the corresponding key success factors (KSFs) required to effectively execute. For example, when attempting to grow revenues with existing partners, you are in essence trying to gain a larger share of their ongoing business activities and revenues, or "share shifting" their business

FIGURE 7-12: Strategic Options for Growth

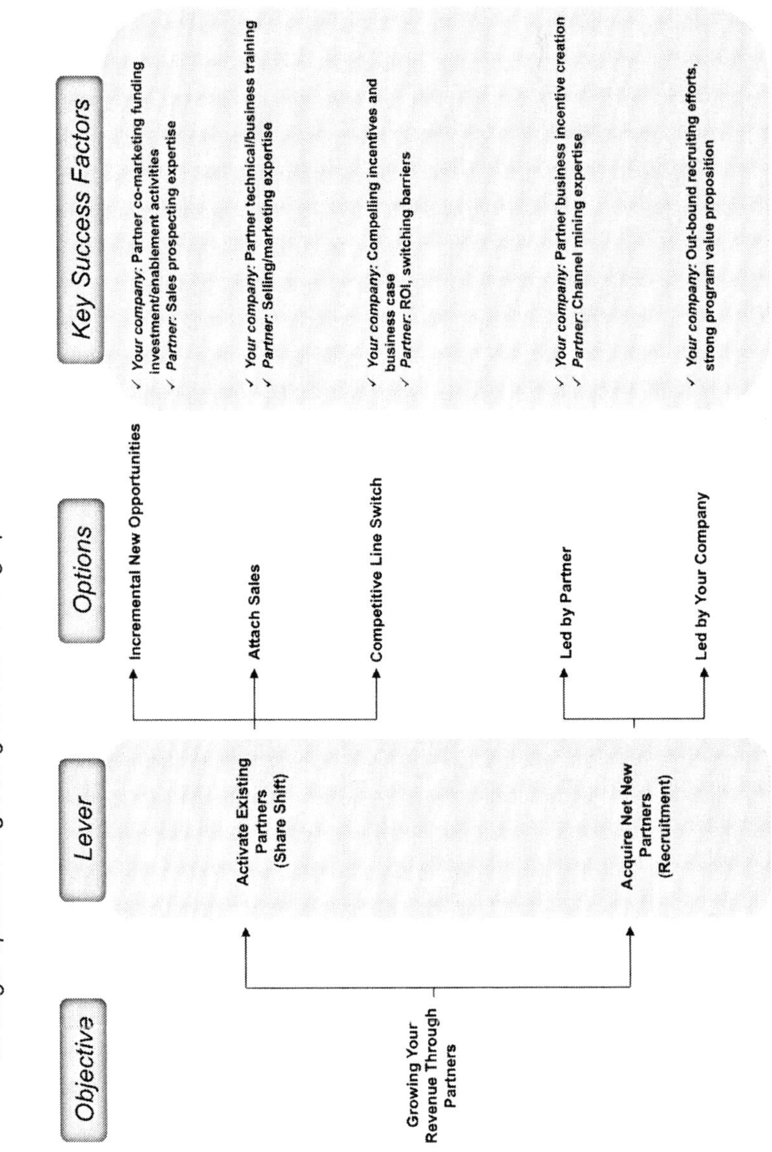

to your favor. If you move a partner to grow their sales around your products from 20% to 50% of their revenue, you have gained share of their business and shifted the situation dramatically to your favor. There are three ways to gain this share shift with partners:

- **Incremental New Opportunities:** This constitutes partners selling to net new customers and growing their customer database. Key success requirements include sufficient co-marketing funding from your company to help the partners acquire new customers, or investing in new customer lead generation activities for partner follow-up. Partner sales and marketing skills are key to new customer acquisition.
- **Attach Sales:** This option considers partners potentially selling multiple products from your company in each transaction (presuming that you have multiple products and that selling them together makes sense). The intent is to move from selling only one product per transaction and "attach" other products, driving up revenue per transaction. Success factors for this option include excellent technical and business partner training, and partner selling and marketing expertise to pitch and win a cross-sell or up-sell opportunity.
- **Competitive Line Switch:** This involves switching a partner's business away from selling a competitive product or product line to selling your product(s). Competitive switching is a more difficult option to succeed at and requires well-structured incentives to move the partner away from the competitive product to your product. A clear and compelling ROI and business case needs to be created to show the partner the value of taking this path.

New opportunities or attach sales could be initiated by your company, bringing a partner into the deal later in the process, or could be led by a partner that might or might not bring your firm into the deal. A competitive line switch clearly involves only efforts initiated by your firm.

The other primary lever to create increased revenues through partners is to acquire more partners. Obviously, there is a cost to recruit, train, and sustain the partners in the program, and the more partners, the higher the costs may go. Once again, a financial analysis on the ROI of these costs relative to the return from increased unit sales should be applied before recruiting large numbers of new partners.

One way to mitigate these costs is to incent the existing partner channel to handle the recruitment and sustaining activities for new partners. For example, distributors and OEMs typically manage large numbers of VARs in their own channel programs. Thinking creatively about how to incent these firms to sign-up new VARs focused on selling your products is one way to off-load partner program costs while retaining the benefit of incremental revenue. If the case can be made to a distributor or OEM that they would benefit from helping your firm sign-up partners, the cost to acquire a net-new partner can be dramatically decreased by leveraging the distributor/OEM partner communication infrastructure.

If growing revenue through partners seems straightforward, it actually is at this high level. The devil is in the details of doing the analysis, making the right investment trade-offs, and executing efficiently across one or more of these options to maximize the ROI for your business.

Given these options, Figure 7-13 takes things one step further and provides a framework for planning. The framework maps partner revenue growth strategic levers against the partner program process cycle. For each available lever, e.g., incremental new opportunity, the infrastructure, content, and marketing programs to support the execution must be developed. The tactical elements will likely vary between the different opportunities.

Once again, unless you have unlimited funding and resources, you'll need to make trade-offs that will optimize the ROI for your investments. For example, what is the relative importance to your business of pursuing incremental new opportunities vs. attach opportunities vs. competitive switching opportunities? Should you spread your money across all these levers, focus on only one, or take a phased approach that addresses each option over time, but in an incremental manner? Whatever approach you take, you'll also need to determine where to place your chips in the process cycle—for each lever you'll need something at each stage of the cycle, but for each lever each stage of the cycle may not have equal importance. These are questions you'll need to think through with the right analysis and evaluation process to make the right lever investment choice for your business.

Partner Council: Another Open Dialogue Opportunity

A partner council is similar to the customer council in purpose and structure, though with an engaged, select group of partners rather than customers. Composed of motivated and interested partners, a partner council offers another opportunity for an open dialogue that can discover and avoid potential go-to-market gaps or issues.

This group of partners will serve in an advisory capacity before and after product launch. The members constitute the "Voice of the Channel" and, like the customer council, can provide your company with direct input on key business or product issues occurring in the pre- and post-product

FIGURE 7-13: Planning Using Strategic Options and Levers

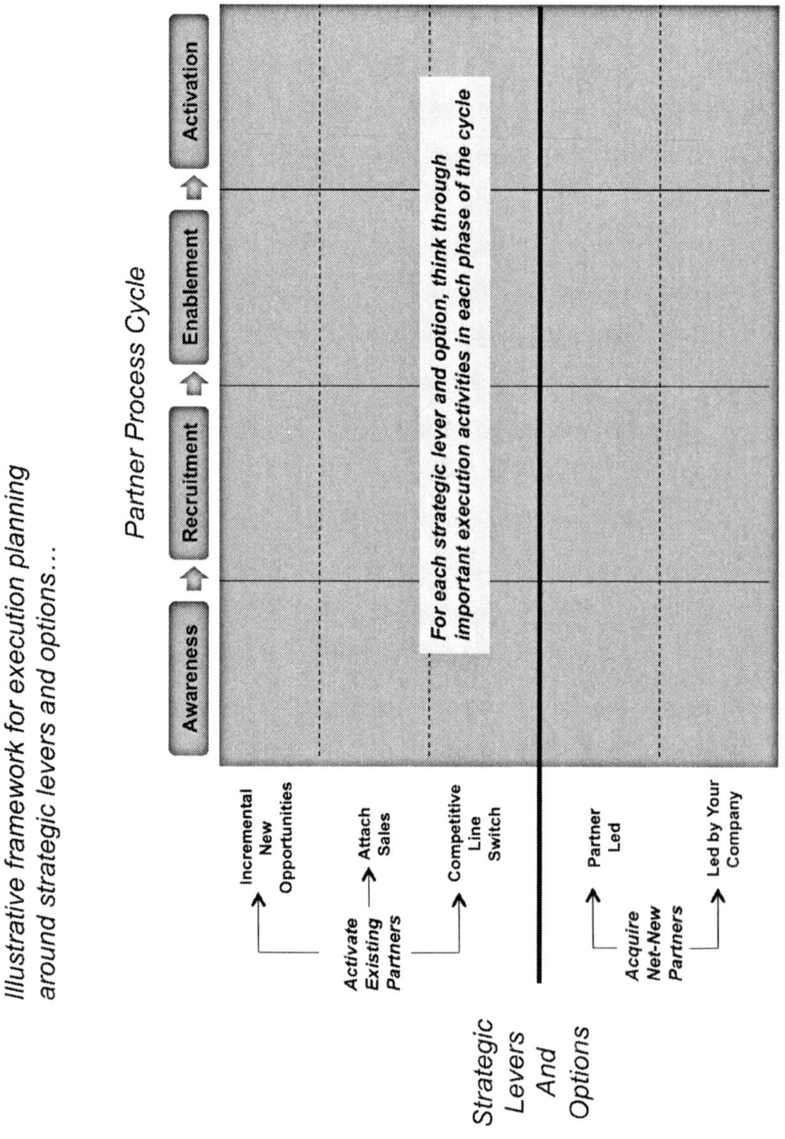

Illustrative framework for execution planning around strategic levers and options…

Partner Process Cycle

Awareness → Recruitment → Enablement → Activation

For each strategic lever and option, think through important execution activities in each phase of the cycle

Strategic Levers And Options

Activate Existing Partners
→ Incremental New Opportunities
→ Attach Sales
→ Competitive Line Switch

Acquire Net-New Partners
→ Partner Led
→ Led by Your Company

FIGURE 7-14: Timeline for Execution

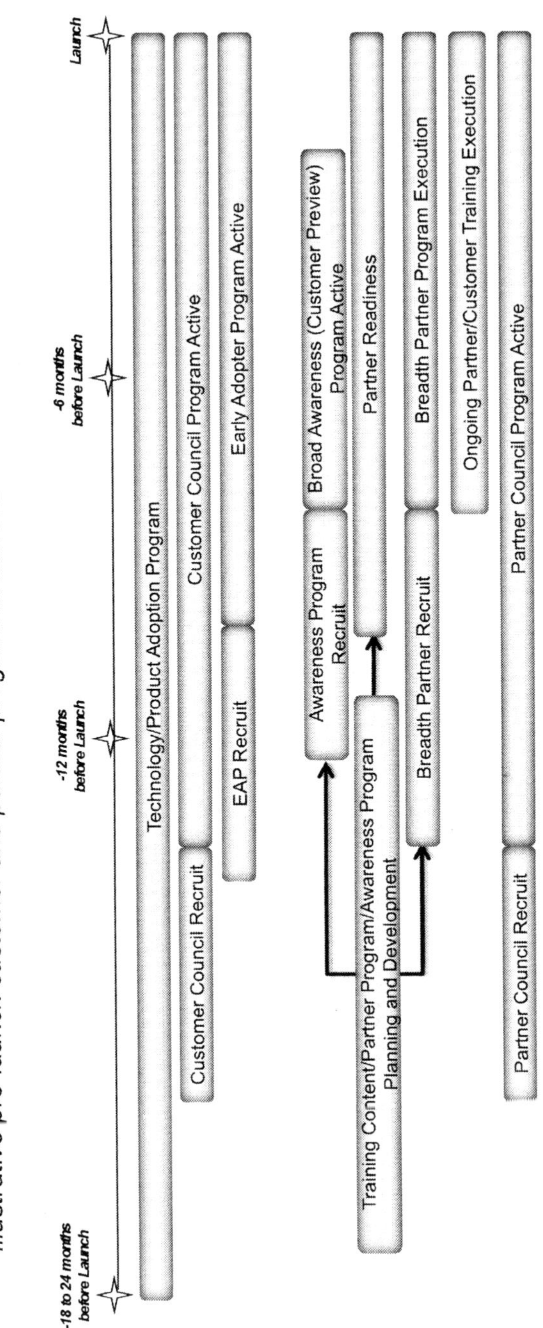

launch environment. The partner council should also be kept relatively small, with interactions focused on listening and understanding the council feedback to provide your company with additional data that may inform key launch decisions.

The topical areas of value provided by partner council feedback are similar to the list of topics for customer councils. Addressing these same issues with representative partners can provide a balanced perspective so decisions and directions are taken with both customer and partner input in mind. In addition, a partner council can also provide input on the partner program structure, benefits, and any perceived program gaps or blocking issues.

The motivations for a particular partner to commit to and participate are similar to the customer council motivations: the ability to shape the product direction to their benefit, access to company decision makers, early information that can be used to direct their business, and networking opportunities. The operational tips for effectively running a council, provided earlier for customer councils, apply here as well.

One potentially tricky element of a partner council is that the partners may well be competing with each other in the marketplace. This dynamic must be carefully managed to avoid situations where partners are unwilling to speak up and provide honest input during council meetings, fearing that they will be giving away secrets or competitive advantage. This isn't necessarily a major issue, as I have been involved with many partner councils where the partners are direct competitors and the dialogue has been open, with none really holding back. However, one way to mitigate this concern is to bring in council partners that are geographically separate and don't directly compete. Another is to find a mix of different partner types, i.e., the council could be composed of an OEM, distributor, ISV, VAR, retailer, and systems integrator, where the business models are different and not competitive. The downside is that you will not get a comprehensive or deep perspective of any one partner type.

Pre-Launch Customer and Partner Program Timing

Figure 7-14 indicates the general time frames for kicking off and executing the pre-launch customer and partner programs. The specific timing for any given activity can vary depending on industry, market, and product types, but these are reasonable timing proxies. Regardless of when you choose to implement these programs, the important thing is that you do implement as many as possible to help ensure a successful launch.

8

Pre-Launch Block and Tackle Marketing Activities

There are many basic block and tackle activities that need to be in place to support a product launch. These activities are the nose-to-the-grindstone, nitty-gritty launch activities that leverage the earlier pre-launch work. These include taking the positioning and messaging documents and building marketing collateral and sales tools around these messages, or building case studies leveraging the pre-launch customer programs, or getting the product SKUs defined in the rollout plan set up in the sales, marketing, and manufacturing databases to enable order processing.

The major activities comprising the block and tackle marketing activities include:

- Creating and producing marketing and sales tools
- Selling product into your distribution channels for launch availability
- Ensuring that a customer and partner product support infrastructure is in place
- Preparing for international sales and distribution as required
- Defining and managing pre-launch events
- Synchronizing and coordinating with the direct sales force
- Creating and launching the public website
- Finishing and rolling out training and readiness content and delivery mechanisms
- Planning and executing the big launch event

- Developing product packaging
- Marketing operations activities, such as setting up product SKUs in the manufacturing systems, finalizing the product price, and ensuring correct pricing in the price system
- Creating the post-launch sustaining marketing plan

Before diving into the specifics of these activities, I'll provide some context using a generic overall launch plan timeline. Figure 8-1 is a high-level illustrative timeline for many of the major pre-launch block and tackle activities and provides some perspective around rollout timing of these activities relative to pre-launch customer and partner programs.

Although many of the block and tackle launch activities and timing are indicated at a high level, each requires an underlying plan that includes more detailed and specific elements. Developing the specific plans and deliverables underlying these activities can vary tremendously because of different markets, product and service types, channel models, and customer segments. However, the underlying details affect critical needs and timing for these activities.

For example, the channel sell-in and development process timing can vary depending on the type of channel partner involved. Retail distribution, OEMs, and VARs all require different timelines and deliverables to effectively get product into these channels for resale. You may need a 12-month lead time to engage retailers like Best Buy or Target for product availability at launch. On the other hand, VARs are better engaged later in the launch cycle when the partner program is in place and running. Put in place detailed plans to support the higher-level activities; depending on the underlying details for your specific product and business, the high-level timelines in Figure 8-1 can shift to accommodate any specific dependencies.

Figure 8-1 also clearly shows that the pre-launch customer programs need to begin early in the launch cycle and continue to launch. As the launch progresses the volume of activities continues to grow, and the last 12 months are jam-packed with things that all must get done at the same time. The only way to remain sane in such an environment is to make sure that excellent forethought and planning have gone into the underlying plans well in advance of execution.

Many of these activities can be interrelated and may depend on each other, such as those noted with the stars in Figure 8-1. Interrelated activities may include training efforts, partner program activities, customer preview or awareness programs, and launch of the public website. Some of the interrelationships among these efforts are as follows:

FIGURE 8-1: Program and Activity Timeline

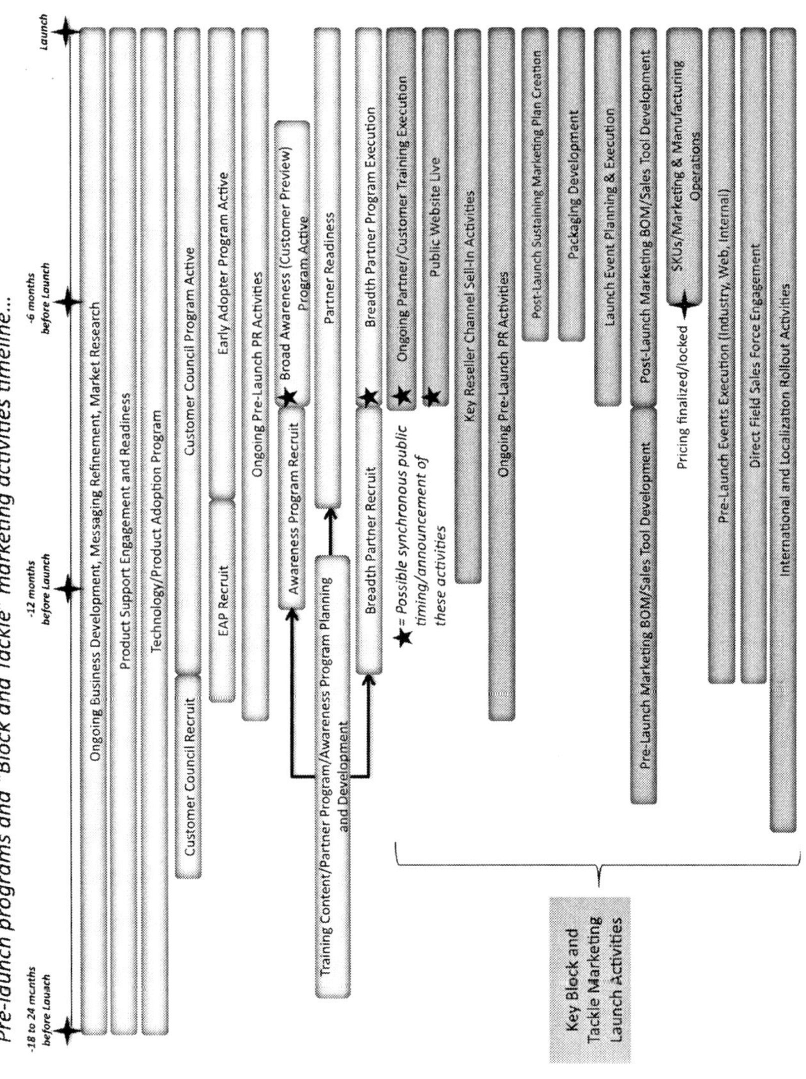

- Especially for complicated or technology products, training must be made available for partners and customers. To have partners support the customer awareness program and be ready to help customers, they must be trained in advance; training content needs to be developed and made available no later than when the first partners are being recruited into the partner program. Trained partners can be promoted to the customers during the awareness program rollout as helpful resources. If the product is sufficiently complicated that a partner is required, then trained partners are a prerequisite to the awareness program.
- To promote the awareness program, attract customers into it, and continue to enable more programmatic recruiting for the partner program, a public website must be available. This means that early content and collateral incorporating the appropriate positioning and messaging must be created and ready for the website to go live and drive program recruits. These content pieces can also be delivered at pre-launch events or through other activities to help promote the awareness program and drive end-customer participation.
- To attract partners into the program, some level of promise must be made about the number of end-customers that will be brought into the awareness program. Partners want leads and sales opportunities. To attract customers into the awareness program a key benefit might be that trained and ready partners are available to help them install, deploy, and test the product in their environment, and the public website must help to recruit the end-customers. The public website also needs partner recruitment content, leveraging the to-partner positioning framework, to assist in continuing to recruit partners into the breadth partner program.

The timing for going live with the partner program, training programs, customer awareness program, and public website needs to be synchronous; all these launch activities are interdependent and related. This also provides for a major big-bang PR momentum push when all these goodies are announced at the same time.

Figure 8-2 maps which of the key block and tackle marketing activities depend on or are interrelated with other activities. It's clear that, for better or worse, many of the key activities have a dependency or interrelationship.

FIGURE 8-2: Interrelated Launch Activities

Many launch activities are dependent on or interrelated with other launch activities…

	Sales Tools	Channel Sell-In	Support	International	Pre-Launch Events	Website	Marketing Operations	Training & Readiness	Packaging	Launch Event	Post-Launch Planning	Sales Force
Sales Tools		X	X	X	X	X			X	X	X	X
Channel Sell-In	X		X	X	X		X	X	X	X		X
Support	X			X	X	X		X			X	X
International	X	X	X		X	X	X	X	X	X	X	X
Pre-Launch Events	X		X	X		X		X				X
Website	X		X	X	X			X		X	X	X
Marketing Operations		X		X					X			
Training & Readiness		X	X	X	X	X					X	X
Packaging	X	X		X			X					
Launch Event	X	X		X		X		X				X
Post-Launch Planning			X	X		X		X				X
Sales Force	X	X	X	X	X	X		X		X	X	

X= inter-relationship or dependency

BUILDING THE BOM: MARKETING AND SALES TOOLS CREATION

To sell or market a product, you need collateral and tools. Which do you create? With a finite budget, trade-offs must be made to decide what is mandatory and what is nice to have. The marketing Bill-Of-Materials (BOM) is the set of marketing and sales pieces that must be created to support the launch and post-launch sustaining marketing activities. A standard set of marketing materials can be defined and created that will generally support most anticipated pre- and post-launch marketing activities. Doing this will help standardize the marketing materials, ensuring consistency across the elements, reducing costs, and minimizing random marketing material requests. Chapter 9 describes Microsoft "Customer Campaigns," the primary company-wide focused marketing campaigns. Each of these customer campaigns has an associated standard marketing BOM.

Three primary pivot points will help determine what BOM content elements to create: the marketing efforts and plans they will support (the marketing campaigns or sales efforts), the target consumer (to-customer, through-partner, to-partner), and the distribution mechanism (print, email, web, in-person).

Figure 8-3 illustrates one way to structure the BOM element planning and maps the major content focus areas against the type of content categories that commonly require BOM material. Thinking through the various intersections of content focus areas and categories can help define BOM content needs relative to the three primary pivots. For example, for the specific pre- and post-launch to-customer marketing campaigns being planned, what type of technical evidence content must be created, what sales and marketing awareness pieces must be developed, or what product specific content must be created to enable evaluation?

Given these needs, what is the most effective delivery format for the content or materials: electronic, print, or both? It's possible that BOM content does not need to be created for every possible intersection of content focus areas and categories, but thinking through the grid can help ensure nothing significant is missed. I've included a few examples, but clearly BOM content could be created for just about every spot on the chart.

Typically you might create two BOMs: a to-customer BOM and a through-partner or channel BOM. The to-customer materials are those that your firm will use for your own marketing campaigns. The through-partner BOM includes deliverables from your firm to make it easy for partners to execute their own to-customer campaigns. A few basic BOM elements can be created to support each of these scenarios. For the to-customer and through-partner BOMs, the marketing materials can be similar, except branding elements may be different and some of the content for the through-partner materials may be customized for the partner's usage.

So what types of BOM materials might be created for the Figure 8-3 grid? Because this is an endless list, I've identified and described some basic examples of standard BOM marketing elements in Figure 8-4.This is a subset of all possible BOM materials and represents a reasonable set of core materials to be created for a product launch.

You may also need specialty BOMs for specific or more customized purposes. Examples include a special marketing campaign (e.g., vertical market focus), or pre-launch customer programs (like the awareness and trial programs), channel specific BOM elements to support the retail channel (shelf talkers, end caps, point of purchase displays, and coupons) or other channel partners such as OEMs and VARs, special supporting materials for key events (e.g., the launch event), and to-partner materials for partner recruitment and training. These marketing activities all require a specialized set of marketing and sales materials beyond the basic BOM.

FIGURE 8-3: Planning the BOM

Illustrative framework for BOM planning...

BOM Content Categories

	Awareness	Evaluation	Proof/ Evidence	Competitive	Press/ Analysts	Partner/ Channel	Customer Segment
Product		*Datasheet*			*Reviewers Guide*		
Technical				*Competitive Feature Comparisons*		*Training Content*	
Business Value/ Sales/ Marketing	*Direct Mail Piece*		*Customer Case Studies*				*Segment Specific Pitch Deck*

Selected subset of content as examples-not comprehensive

BOM Content Focus Areas

FIGURE 8-4: Typical BOM Elements

BOM Category	Example BOM Elements	Description
Demand Generation	Direct mailer	Standard direct mail piece. Could be self-mailer, 8"x10" letter, postcard or other format. For through-partner branding content may be customizable.
	HTML email	Graphic and content placeholder template for sending emails. For through-partner branding content may be customizable.
	Web ads	Banner ads or other format ads to be used on third-party sites. Can be made available to partners as is or customizable.
	Reusable video snippets	Short video pieces for use in presentations or on website. Can be product based, tips and tricks, informational, training or other focus.
	Print advertising template	Template for print publication advertising in magazines, newspapers, etc.
	Stock photography	Library of photographs that can be used on website or in other marketing collateral pieces.
	Positioning-based reusable content blurbs	25, 50, and 100 word content blocks that can be used on web or in marketing collateral that essentially convey core positioning messages from positioning framework.
	Flash demonstrations	Flash-based product, training, or informational tool. Used on web or on CD/DVD.
	Webcasts	Live or on-demand web-based presentations on varying topics, e.g., product, training, readiness, or marketing campaigns.
Customer Evidence	Case studies	1-3 page web or printed content focusing on a customer and/ or partner usage of the product. Key element of focus is the business or economic value derived by customer through product usage.
	Business value/ ROI tools	Sales tools that assist partner or sales force to quantify the customer ROI through purchasing and using the product.
	Customer testimonial video vignettes	Short (1-3 minute) video pieces showcasing positive customer narrative about the product and its use in their business. Can augment case study. Focus on supporting positioning messages and business value/ROI.
	Customer testimonial content blurbs	Short positive statement by customer around product or business value derived from product, similar to customer video vignettes, but written. Can be used on web or in print collateral.
Marketing/ Sales PowerPoint Presentations	General customer or segment pitch deck	Base pitch deck for presentations about the product and product/business strategy, business value, key messages, etc. Can be used in live speaking engagements, etc. Can be customized for special purpose usage (vertical market, specific customer segment). Can be augmented with customer video testimonials. A version can also be supplied to partners for their use.
	Sales-oriented customer pitch deck	Variant of the pitch deck but more focused on sales, overcoming customer objections, pricing, and SKUs.

FIGURE 8-4: Typical BOM Elements (continued)

BOM Category	Example BOM Elements	Description
Marketing/ Sales PowerPoint Presentations	Reusable mix/ match slide libraries for customer decks	Library of stock PowerPoint slides that can be used by marketing, sales, or partners to create customized presentations. Can augment general pitch deck or sales decks.
Training	Training deck	PowerPoint slides specifically designed for training on product, sales/marketing, or technology.
	Audio or video training	Audio or video specifically designed for training on product, sales/marketing, or technology.
	Self-paced training guides	Written or electronic content (whitepaper, book, e-learning) specifically designed for training on product, sales/marketing, or technology focused on enabling an individual to learn on their own.
	Instructor-led training content	Courseware designed for training on product, sales/marketing, or technology focused on live delivery by an instructor.
Cheat Sheets	Battle cards	Core sales cheat sheet. In 1-3 pages summarizes key selling issues such as product description, key talking points and product benefits, customer objections and responses, customer needs and pain points, probing sales questions, and competition.
	Quick reference cards	Typically 1-page product summary with features and benefits.
	Feature comparison cards	Can be short feature comparison between SKUs, or competitive product comparisons.
Reference/ Guides	Whitepapers	Typically Word document format informational pieces. Could be product, business, or technically focused. 5-50 pages generally. Sometimes co-developed/branded with partners, analysts, or research firms.
	Datasheets	Usually 1-2 page overview of product and product specifications.
	Product usage guides	Detailed guide to setting-up and using the product.
	Product or company brochure	High-level brochure that overviews the product and/or the company. This is the standard generic glossy brochure.
PR/Analyst	Reviewers guide	Whitepaper guide that walks an analyst or editor through the product step-by-step, highlighting key features, emphasizing positioning points. Used to educate press and analysts about the product.
	Analyst evidence/press quotes deck	Consolidated library of press articles, positive analyst quotes, analyst reports that can be used with web content or in printed content to convey positive press and analyst support of the product, company, or strategy.
FAQs	Technical FAQ	Compilation of FAQ related to the technical aspects of the product.
	Business FAQ	Compilation of FAQ related to the business aspects of the product (pricing, licensing, features/benefits, and SKUs).
Other Sales Tools	Bid/quote tools	Electronic or written tools to assist sales force or partners to create bids and quotes during the sales process.

Some Tips for Creating Launch BOM Materials

Because building out a BOM can be a costly and time-consuming (but necessary) effort, and these are the core materials to sell and market the product, they must be created with care and forethought. The following can help maximize the investment in the BOM:

Build Content So It Can Be Repurposed: Build BOM material that can be used for more than a single purpose. For example, when developing customer evidence pieces like case studies, think about how the information can be used in print and online, and design the content up front to meet both needs. Leveraging and sharing content between the partner and customer BOM elements can save time and money. Transforming a to-customer direct mail piece for use as a through-partner direct mail piece usually requires minimal changes if the piece is intentionally designed for dual-purpose usage. Another tip here is to think about the various campaigns planned and to determine if BOM content from one campaign could be reused for other campaigns with few or no changes. For example, product datasheets or whitepapers can generally be used in any campaign without changes.

Don't Blow All the Budget on the Basic BOM: Identify the minimal subset of pre-launch BOM materials that must be created to start with—don't build everything that *could* be built from the beginning. As the launch progresses new information and knowledge will shape the need for updates or even different BOM elements. Save some money for these additional elements as the shifting launch landscape needs arise.

Get the Key Messages Into the Content: Make sure that the positioning and messaging points from the positioning framework flows into all the BOM collateral. A lot of time was likely spent on getting the positioning framework messages created and correct; using those messages throughout the BOM material is a good practice for both to-customer and through-partner BOM. This ensures consistency in the to-customer materials and that positioning messages are being communicated properly and consistently through the partner when delivering end-customer communications.

Use Expected Customer Benefits Pre-Launch: When you hit the launch date and the product is released for general availability, the only customer evidence collateral likely to be available are those based on the pre-launch customer program participants (e.g., EAP and customer preview program). Since these customers have limited experience with the product it is impossible to quantify many important evidence points like ROI, total cost of ownership, and revenue increase or cost decrease impacts. When developing these pieces pre-launch for your use post-launch, use *expected* customer benefits in the content. For example, it may be that a case study or customer testimonial can make the claim that the customer "*expects* to drive down costs by 50%" or "*expects* to see significant return on investment." After the launch, track these customers and update the evidence pieces with real world usage information that accurately quantifies the benefits.

Consolidate Content Into Kits: While highly useful on a stand-alone basis, many of the BOM content pieces can be more useful when delivered in conjunction with other content. Creating and assembling kits composed of multiple BOM content elements can be an effective sales tool or offer. For example, for awareness purposes or lead generation, a kit could be assembled with a product datasheet, customer case studies or video vignettes, positive articles reprinted from magazines or online sources, and a relevant whitepaper. Combining the BOM elements into a kit adds some heft and can increase the customers' perceived value of the content.

Minimize the Number of Vendors: Using one or a minimal set of vendors can reduce costs and minimize training and knowledge transfer requirements. Getting a particular marketing vendor up to speed on the target customers, marketing processes, product features and benefits, positioning and messaging, how you want marketing copy written, and nailing down efficient working processes and interactions can be time-consuming. You do not want to do this with a lot of vendors, as it takes up bandwidth better used on other launch activities. Minimizing the number of vendors saves time, creates a better chance for BOM content consistency and accuracy, and saves costs through discounts provided by giving a larger volume of work to the smaller set of vendors. Minimizing vendors can also help ensure branding and "look and feel" consistency throughout the BOM elements. All the BOM elements should carry a consistent creative look and feel that helps convey the brand perceptions and positioning and creates a unified and consistent presentation. Maintaining this consistency can also help reinforce customer awareness of multiple marketing touches.

CHANNEL SELL-IN AND ADOPTION

Selling-in is the process of engaging and activating the partner channel. At a high level, the goal for sell-in is to persuade the partners to adopt and resell your product once it is available. Different sell-in activities are required for different partner business types. For example, the sell-in process for a VAR requires different activities than selling in to a distributor, the retail channel, or the OEM channel.

By definition, VARs are the second tier in a two-tier distribution model, placing orders for products primarily from distributors to resell to end-customers. Chapter 7 discussed the primary sell-in activities for VARs, the development of a breadth partner program, and partner enablement and activation activities as some key pre-launch activities for the VAR sell-in process. The creation and deployment of partner training, the creation of incentives and offers, the development of a breadth through-partner marketing BOM, and the communication and awareness processes around these items to the VARs generally comprise the sell-in process to the VAR community. Since the VAR activities have been covered, the focus here is on selling into distributors, retailers, and OEMs.

As it relates to pre-launch sell-in, distributors, retailers, and OEMs have commonalities in their business models that enable a somewhat standardized conceptual approach to selling into these channels, including:

- They all generally stock and hold product inventory, which must be ordered, packaged, and shipped to these companies.
- They all resell to another level in the go-to-market chain. Distributors and OEMs generally sell to VARs and other resellers, but can go direct to end-customers as well. Retailers generally sell direct to the end-customer.
- They each generally maintain a direct sales force, a telesales call center sales force, an e-commerce website, and a catalog for reselling product. Sell-in and co-marketing plans must address each of these sales channels.
- They are all generally "coin-operated," meaning they won't market and sell your product for free—you must pay them to do just about anything, although sometimes these partners can provide funding to match or augment your marketing dollar investments.
- They all carry a large number of SKUs from many different companies and across many different product lines, so getting mindshare for your product is never easy.

- Their profit margins are generally small as a percentage of revenue, and high inventory turns are important. If a product is not moving, it has a higher chance of being dropped from inventory. Putting marketing programs into place to enable a high turn rate is a good idea.
- The ability to return product is an expectation and is part of their business models.
- Rebates and discounts are important incentives for these channels. These types of promotions should play a solid role in sell-in and co-marketing plans.
- Price protection from pricing decreases is a valued offering (and sometimes required) from manufacturers supplying product.
- There is an expectation that Marketing Development Funds (MDF) will be made available from the manufacturer to fund co-marketing and sales activities.

Retailers have some special nuances. For example, the retail channel generally does not offer service and support for products, leaving that to the manufacturers. And because retailers are selling directly to the end-customer in a physical store, marketing collateral and tools developed for a retail BOM for in-store use can be quite different from BOM tools developed for distributors and OEMs.

The commonalities lay the groundwork for the activities needed to sell into these channels. There are differences to approaching these different types of channels for the sell-in process, but these commonalities enable the development of a sell-in process and infrastructure that can be leveraged across each of the channel types to reduce cost, time, and sell-in resources required.

Figure 8-5 overviews the sell-in landscape related to OEMs, distributors, and retailers and indicates some of the key sell-in activities required from manufacturers. These channel partners need one-on-one engagement as part of the sell-in process. Adopting your product for resale will entail a potentially significant commitment from them, and a cogent business case must be made to encourage these businesses to take on your product.

Remember, these channel partners are looking for products that will sell, and they have many other companies approaching them. For each product that is taken up, the channel needs to SKU the product into their systems, create content around the SKU, train and educate their sales force, update ordering systems, update their websites, commit marketing resources, and perform a host of other activities to enable the product to flow through

FIGURE 8-5: Sell-In Landscape Overview

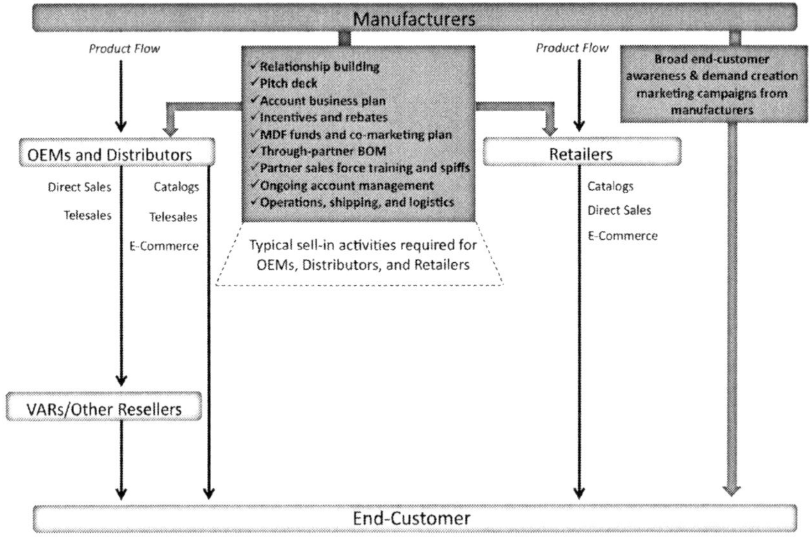

their businesses for successful resale. These activities obviously require resource time and money commitments, so picking up a SKU entails work and risk for the channel, and there must be a valid business case for them to do so.

Having already established relationships and products proven to sell, Microsoft and other large companies generally don't have to make a significant effort to pitch these channels to take up the products. In fact, it is practically a given that any Microsoft product that comes to market is essentially automatically adopted, assuming it is a relevant product to flow through a particular channel. This makes the sell-in process easier for Microsoft, but most companies will not have it that easy. Establishing good relationships with the channel buyers, creating a compelling pitch deck that builds the business case for channel, and persistence will set the stage to get the product into the channel. Building the business case for sell-in must include the obvious elements of product market size and revenue opportunity, target market, and product details as well as the following:

- Explaining synergies between the target market segment and customers the channel serves and the product's target market. There should be a solid match between the end-customer segments and targets.

- Drawing a connection between how the channel partner business goals and objectives will be aided by taking on the SKU. Understanding the partner's key business goals and objectives and mapping the impact your product can make to these goals and objectives for each channel partner approached is crucial to making a relevant, customized, and effective pitch.
- Clearly indicating and itemizing how your company will be investing in marketing the product and driving demand for the channel partner. Partners will expect some level of investment from your company to increase awareness to the target market and bring prospects to their doorstep. It can be helpful to define your planned demand generation campaigns, lead generation activities, rebate plans, and opportunities so the partner can plug into your firm's planned activities.
- Including MDF as part of the incentive to take on your product. The channel will want your firm to spend money on pull marketing and want money allocated and available for promoting the product through their own marketing and sales activities, e.g., website, catalogs, circulars, and newspaper ads. Understanding the available marketing resources from the channel partner and preparing an investment plan will assist in a successful sell-in process.
- Arming the channel partner with tools to make it easy to sell by creating a through-partner BOM also can facilitate the sell-in process. For example, knowing that the channel partner has a catalog and that your firm will plan to invest MDF funds to advertise in it, then creating pre-made content blurbs with key positioning and product photography makes it easy for the partner to include your product in the catalog. Creating business-value offers as part of the BOM that that partner can use in their own to-customer marketing activities is always an effective use of BOM funds.
- Presenting a clear plan for partner sales force training and launch readiness, whether for the call center telesales representative, floor sales people, or direct sales force, shows commitment and initiative on your firm's part and is a valued activity by the channel partner. Training can include in-person training activities or training tools like selling cheat sheets or interactive training materials that make it easy for the channel sales staff to understand the product features, benefits, and key selling points and value propositions. These channel partners often have specific processes, times, and activities for training their sales force on new products. It makes sense to understand this in

advance and present your plan to plug in. Don't overlook spiffs and sales contests. Getting and keeping mindshare from the channel sales staff who have potentially hundreds of products to sell is important; spiffs and contests can assist in getting and keeping the focus on your product.

- Allocating resources for ongoing account planning is another benefit that should be discussed as part of a pitch meeting. An account manager from your firm must be in place to manage the account, create business and marketing plans, and allocate the MDF. Indicating this commitment is valuable during the sell-in process.

There can be a significant lead time when working with OEMs, distributors, and retailers to gain product adoption and complete all the necessary sell-in activities. Figure 8-6 provides an example and realistic timeline for the sell-in process, which could involve a lead time of 10-12 months in advance of the actual product availability through the channel. This example is admittedly retail-biased, but is in the ballpark for distributors and OEMs. The example assumes the product launch date coincides with the holiday selling season, and overviews the major activities needed to get the marketing and sales promotions in place during the peak holiday season. The example timeline uses typical timing for software product sell-in, though other product categories may have different time frames for any given activity. Regardless of product type, the major activities required for execution will not vary significantly.

The first necessary activity is to build relationships with the key channel partners and successfully persuade them to take on your product. Assuming this is successful, the specific marketing campaigns your company will execute alone and with the channel partners (including MDF spending, rebates, in-store promotions, and awareness creation) must be defined. These plans will drive the definition and creation of the through-channel and to-customer marketing BOMs, and will need to incorporate the standard positioning points from the positioning framework or any partner-specific positioning points.

You should plan to get the marketing and sales materials to the channel partners in time for them to incorporate the materials into their holiday go-to-market processes and setup, and to meet deadlines for channel sales force training activities. The timing for these channel deadlines will in part drive the date by which product pricing must be finalized and which specific product SKUs will be included as part of the holiday promotion. About 6-8 weeks before product availability by the channel partner, the

FIGURE 8-6: Channel Sell-In Timeline

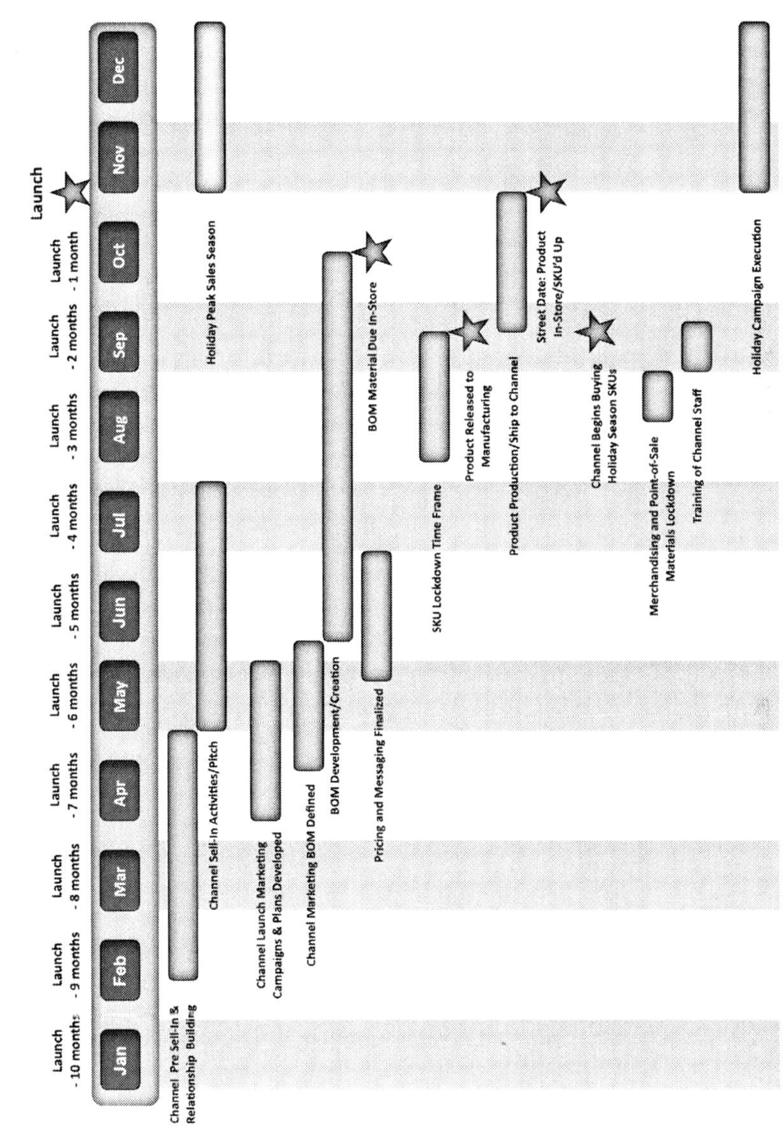

buyers will place orders for SKU quantities, initiating the manufacturing and shipping process to get product built and delivered to the channel, which can also take 6-8 weeks. After this, all that is left is to execute the campaigns and generate revenue.

CUSTOMER SERVICE AND SUPPORT INFRASTRUCTURE

It is extremely critical to develop an effective customer service and support infrastructure during the pre-launch time frame. While it may seem obvious, it constantly amazes me that support is usually one of the last things considered by a product development group, when it should be one of the first. Customer service and support resources are generally the unsung heroes during a product launch. Perhaps service and support is not the glitziest element to plan, but once the product is launched, customer service and support will become one of the primary customer interface and interaction points, and the support organization will be the face of your company to the end-customers.

These interactions can make or break the customer experience with your firm, help or hinder customer satisfaction with the product, and affect whether the current customer becomes a long-term customer with recurring revenue opportunities. If getting product support is difficult, or if the support organization is staffed with inefficient, untrained, or incompetent resources, there is a world of hurt coming your way once the product is launched.

To mitigate a worst-case scenario, it is important to build the product support process and to develop the proper support competencies into the launch process early in the launch cycle. The support staff, or representatives, should be included as part of the core launch team; the product should not be allowed to ship until the support organization signs off that the product quality is high enough and the necessary support infrastructure is in place to handle customer and partner issues.

You should first involve service and support resources when the Technology/Product Adoption Program is being planned and executed. Support staff involvement should then continue throughout the launch process. Involving support resources in key pre-launch programs enables the necessary product knowledge transfer from the product development team to the support organization. This knowledge transfer should start as early as possible in the launch cycle to maximize the support organization's readiness to deliver quality customer service to customers and partners post-launch. Typically, only a small number of support personnel will be involved in these early programs; as they are trained, they become the trainers to the rest of the support organization (a "Train the Trainer" strategy).

Integrating and Involving Support Resources in Key Pre-Launch Activities

Effectively leveraging support resources during launch activities is smart and necessary. As illustrated in Figure 8-7, a number of core infrastructure activities are intertwined with or dependent on support staff, especially for technology products.

For example, support resources should be heavily involved in the Early Adopter Program and the Customer Preview Program, helping to enable high-quality customer and partner experiences during these early programs while also learning themselves. During these programs support

FIGURE 8-7: Key Customer Support Activities

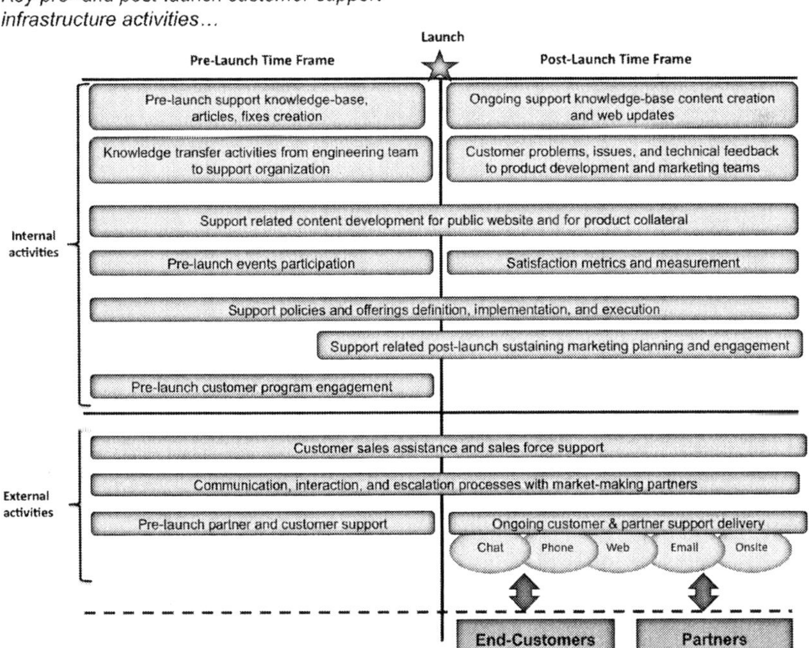

staff can learn about the product through hands-on experience and meet with the engineering teams for in-person knowledge transfer, review product documentation and provide feedback, and create any necessary written documents enabling broader knowledge transfer, i.e., whitepapers, technical guides, and problem/solution content.

This early content forms the basis for a "knowledge-base" of support-related information, a knowledge repository that should be maintained and augmented during the post-launch time frame. Customer service and support staff should also be involved in customer and partner councils, enabling additional learning opportunities about the target customers and partners. Insights acquired through participation can raise the effectiveness of post-launch support processes and infrastructure.

Support resources can play a critical role in enabling the sales force to effectively and credibly gain customer prospects during the pre-launch time frame, supporting the sales staff with their in-depth technical knowledge during sales presentations. The same is true for channel sell-in activities: presenting effective and competent support resources to the channel can help assure the channel partners that there is a resource to turn to for help and that potential product or service problems and issues are planned for and will be managed.

Pre-launch events are another area where support staff can be efficiently leveraged. Staffing booths at events, delivering training webcasts, or presenting at internal training events are key opportunities to extend the launch team with highly competent resources and deliver quality results from these activities.

Service and support also play a key role in the post-launch sustaining marketing environment. They should be engaged to provide input into these plans and to help define processes needed to ensure synchronization with out-bound marketing activities and service and support resources. In the post-launch environment, the service and support staff must be aware of important customer and partner communications, strategy changes, marketing or sales offers, product updates, and continued sales support requirements. The public website must be ready at launch with support information and regularly updated as customer support issues and fixes are discovered and solved. Pre-launch planning for these activities as elements of the post-launch sustaining plans is crucial to avoiding blunders after the product is out the door.

Leveraging Support Resources for Partner Activities

Assuming partners play a key role in the product launch and post-launch success, addressing partner support needs is another important pre-launch issue. The two primary partner categories of concern are the market-making and the breadth partners managed via the programmatic channel partner program.

In Chapter 5 I discussed the process of acquiring market-making partners. The support staff must be involved in defining and reviewing the support aspects of any partnership agreements with the market-making partners, especially those that are complementary product or technology partners. Support involvement with these deals is especially critical for the following reasons:

- With technology partners, your product includes third-party features or technology in the shipping product. Once the product is out the door and customers are calling about problems there must be a process for determining where the problem lies (within the product components your company developed or within third-party components), and also a process for communication, engagement, and escalation to the third-party company support staff to resolve issues.
- For complementary product partners, their support staff may be receiving calls from their customers about their own product. They need to determine if the problem is being caused by their product or your firm's product. What is the process to enable a seamless rapid closure to the problem from the end-customers' perspective? What are the communication and escalation paths in place to resolve issues? What level of training is required for your internal support staff around the third-party product? What training is required for the third-party support staff around your product to enable problem resolution? Not taking ownership of the issue and simply bouncing a customer from one company to another does not help solve the problem and can create significant negative customer satisfaction issues.

Handling customer issues across multiple market-making partners should include working agreements, setup pre-launch, with each partner company around the following areas:

- Defining the incident process flow and escalation criteria or triggers
- Providing at least basic product training of third-party products across the various support organizations

- Enabling third-party organizations to open trouble tickets or incidents at the partner company

Breadth partners will also need access to the support resources. As mentioned in Chapter 7, access to support resources is a highly desirable feature of a partner program. Various levels of support access can be created, with the types of support available varying by program tier, if tiering is part of the program structure. If the partner program is of any significant size, there should be plenty of options put into place to assist the partners, and these options should be highly scalable. For example, managed newsgroups can be set up where partners can post questions allowing other partners or company representatives from the support organization to post answers. Online chat or telephone interactions with a support representative can also be useful and scalable ways to provide partners with direct access to the support organization.

Newsgroups and website support databases are generally made available to the partners free-of-charge as a program benefit. Support via online chat and phone access is generally for-fee. However, it may make sense as a partner program recruiting tool and as a program benefit to provide a few free support incidents via phone or chat. It is perfectly reasonable to require that partners purchase a support-offering package from your firm in order to receive more extensive product support offerings.

Defining Support Offerings

Defining support offerings is an important pre-launch exercise and must consider both partner business needs and end-customer needs. Some support offering planning considerations to ponder during the pre-launch phase include:

- Response time service level agreement (SLA)
- Time and availability of services
- Number of included incidents
- Support delivery options (chat, email, web, phone, in-person)
- Price

Each of these considerations can be combined to form packages of support offerings for partners and customers. Figure 8-8 illustrates this with three conceptual support packages.

FIGURE 8-8: Defining Support Offerings

Illustrative framework for defining support offerings...

		Support Offering Packages		
		Basic Support	Extended Support	Super-Duper Ultimate Support
Support Offering Features	Response Time SLA	3 days	24 hours	Immediate
	Availability	Mon-Fri 8-5pm	Mon-Sat 7am-9pm	Mon-Sun 24 hours/day
	Delivery Options	✓Email ✓Newsgroup	✓Email ✓Newsgroup ✓Chat ✓Phone	✓Email ✓Newsgroup ✓Chat ✓Phone ✓Onsite
	Supported Incidents	2/month	20/month	Unlimited
	Price	$20/month	$200/month	$2000/month

If the product being launched has the potential to become a significant or mission-critical aspect of the end-customer business, it is probably a good idea to provide an immediate rapid-resolution path to the support organization for a problem causing critical damage to the customer's business. For example, if the end-customer business is an online, e-commerce reseller and your product is bringing down their servers, that company faces an immediate and significant potential to lose a lot of money. In such situations, making mission-critical support resources available goes a long way to ensuring customer satisfaction and peace of mind. You should also implement a service level agreement between your firm's support organization and the product development group so if significant issues arise an escalation path is defined and in place to address them.

Finally, as an important customer and partner interface, the support organization plays a key role in driving customer and partner satisfaction. Key support satisfaction metrics must be defined in the pre-launch time frame, put into effect, and measured regularly post-launch.

PRE-LAUNCH EVENTS

It's impossible to get through a launch process without having to host or participate in some events and related activities. Some needs and objectives for a successful launch simply cannot be effectively executed against from a distance—they need an in-person, face-to-face element. For example, it is difficult to enable your channel partners to effectively network without getting them into a room together so they can meet. You can also more effectively convey enthusiasm and purpose and instill confidence in potential customers in a face-to-face environment than through advertising and direct mail.

Event Objectives in the Pre-Launch Environment

For a launch, events are an important engagement mechanism that can serve this face-to-face requirement, addressing a number of objectives for different target audiences. Figure 8-9 lays out some of the more important and typical objectives for pre-launch events.

Each of these possible objectives will be more important at certain times during a launch than at others. Looking back at Figure 2-2, if the strategic intent puts you into the Brand New Ball Game scenario, meaning the launch is focusing on a new product in a new customer segment or market, then generating corporate awareness and engagement and showing thought leadership is critical in the early stages of a launch. This will help to ingratiate your firm with the industry and customer segments being addressed. Involvement in key industry events to make your presence known early in the launch cycle is a good first step toward meeting these goals.

Chapter 6 identified the need for press and analyst summits during the launch. These events are focused on overtly or subtly influencing these parties and changing their perceptions so they better align with your ideals and generate positive coverage. These events generally occur later in the launch process after press and analyst relationships have been firmly established.

Training and readiness events also form a core element of the launch process, playing a key role in the overall readiness efforts and providing the in-person element. These events may target both internal audiences like the field sales force and external audiences like the partner channel members, providing the necessary product, marketing, and sales knowledge to arm these audiences for launch at the appropriate point in the launch process.

FIGURE 8-9: Typical Pre-Launch Event Objectives

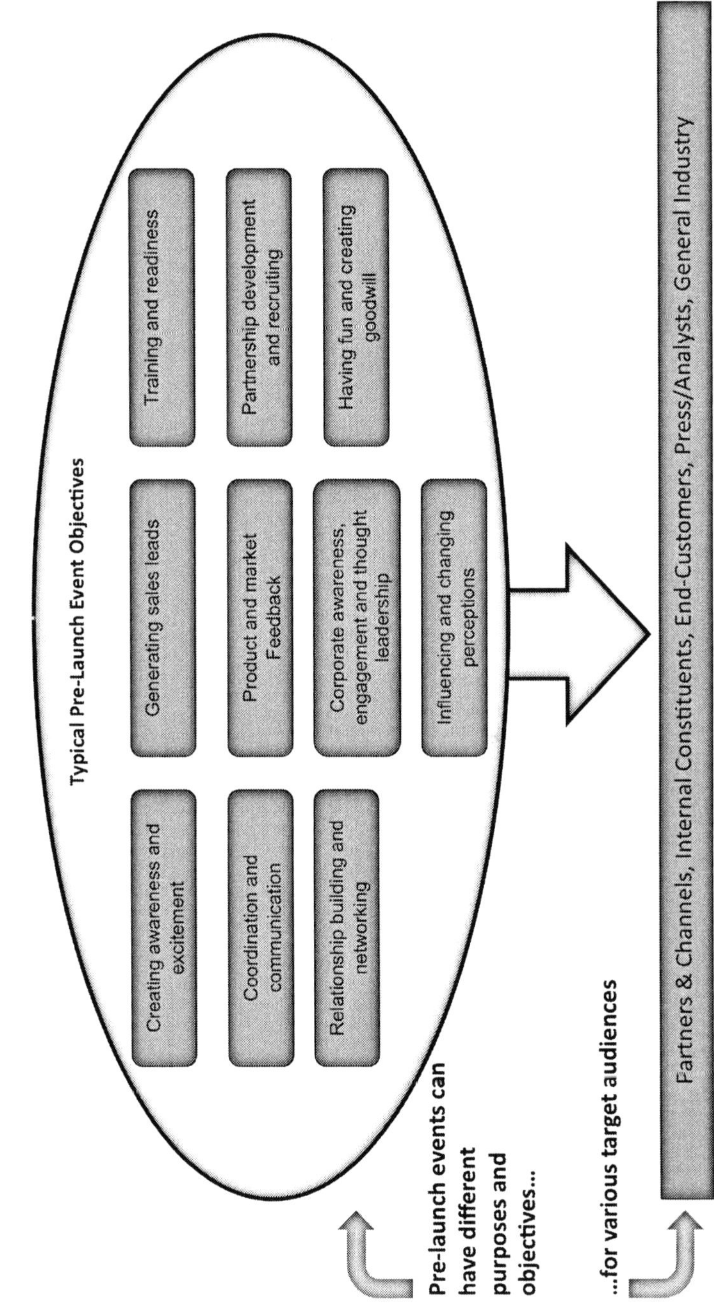

FIGURE 8-10: Important Pre-Launch Events

Target Audience	Event	Description	Primary Goals
Internal Constituents	Early Sales Force Training	Long-lead sales force training. Primarily targeted at more technical field sales force needing to understand product at a deep level. Also for engaging top-level sales management for awareness and long-lead planning purposes.	• Training & Readiness
	District Sales Office Tours	In-person events held in sales locations across the country. Intended for corporate product launch team representatives to meet with key sales personnel across various geographies and transfer important high-level product information, positioning, market and revenue opportunities pointers, and updates on launch activities and opportunities for engagement and further education. Sales goals/quota coordination can also be part of these events.	• Training & Readiness • Communication and Coordination • Awareness and Excitement
	Sales Force Launch Training	Intended to convey final details of launch plans, channel plans and programs, launch event, final sales and marketing tools and resources from To-Customer BOM, post-launch sustaining marketing plans, and air cover activities. A "lock and load" event.	• Training & Readiness • Communication and Coordination • Awareness and Excitement
Industry	Awareness & Engagement Industry Events	Attendance at industry events with the intent of inserting your firm and company into the industry ecosystem and becoming a player.	• Industry Awareness, Engagement, Thought Leadership • Relationship Building and Networking • Influencing and Changing Perceptions
	Partner Recruitment Industry Events	Events attended by target partner firms focused on the goal of recruiting partners into the Breadth Partner Program.	• Relationship Building and Networking • Partnership Development and Recruitment
	Customer Awareness & Program Recruitment Industry Events	Events attracting target market customers. Primary focus is to recruit for Early Adopter Program and Customer Preview Program.	• Relationship Building and Networking • EAP and Customer Preview Program Recruitment
	Customer Sales & Pipeline Creation Industry Events	Industry events attracting target market customers that occur later in the launch cycle. Primary focus is to generate sales leads and Marketing Qualified Prospects (see Chapter 9 for more on MQPs).	• Awareness & Excitement • Generating Sales Leads
Partners	Technology/ Product Adoption Program Training	Training event focused on ensuring partner business, process, and technical readiness to support program.	• Training & Readiness • Communication and Coordination
	Partner Council	Small partner panel events focused on business, market, product, and strategic feedback and input.	• Product & Market Feedback • Relationship Building and Networking • Having Fun & Creating Goodwill

FIGURE 8-10: Important Pre-Launch Events (continued)

Target Audience	Event	Description	Primary Goals
Partners	Partner Summit	Partner event for early members of the breadth Partner Program and market-making partners to understand Customer Preview Program plans and engagement processes, planned marketing and sales tools, launch progress and updates, and networking with other partners.	• Training & Readiness • Relationship Building and Networking • Having Fun & Creating Goodwill • Product & Market Feedback
	Partner Marketing/Launch Summit	The "lock and load" pre-launch partner event focused on educating partners about final launch plans, launch event opportunities, post-launch marketing programs, available sales/marketing tools from Channel BOM.	• Training & Readiness • Awareness & Excitement
Customers	Technology/ Product Adoption Program Training	Training event focused on ensuring customer business, process, and technical readiness to support program.	• Training & Readiness • Communication and Coordination
	Customer Council	Small customer panel events focused on business, market, product, and strategic feedback and input.	• Product & Market Feedback • Relationship Building and Networking • Having Fun & Creating Goodwill
	EAP Summit	Training event focused on ensuring both customer and partner business, process, and technical readiness to support program.	• Training & Readiness • Relationship Building and Networking • Having Fun & Creating Goodwill
	Road Shows & Seminars	Multiple geography 2-4 hour seminars intended to create in-person awareness of the product to the end-customer and generate sales leads. Typical attendance from 10-50 customers. Can include partners in these events.	• Awareness & Excitement • Generating Sales Leads
Press / Analysts	Press/Analyst Briefings & Reviewers Workshops	Press and analyst briefings to provide product and launch updates. Can be held at corporate office or leveraging industry events where these parties will be in attendance. In addition to regular email & phone updates. Reviewers workshop oriented to press members who will be reviewing the product for a product review type article or lab testing and results—leverages Reviewers Guide BOM element.	• Influencing and Changing Perceptions • Product & Market Feedback • Relationship Building and Networking • Awareness & Excitement
	Analyst Summit	Core event with purpose of influencing positive analyst coverage of the product and market strategies. These events are typically 1 to 1.5 days in duration and generally occur near the end of the launch cycle. Last chance pre-launch analyst input—can be used for final input on product features, SKUs, pricing, competitive comparisons, addressing analyst concerns, etc. May have to pay at least travel and lodging expenses for the analysts if not consulting fees.	• Relationship Building and Networking • Awareness & Excitement • Influencing and Changing Perceptions
Everyone	Launch Event	The big blowout event culminating the launch process.	• Awareness & Excitement

Other events, such as partner-related events designed for recruiting partners and facilitating networking among the partners, can be necessary and may occur at various times throughout the launch cycle.

Important Pre-Launch Events

Clearly, events are important elements of the pre-launch activity mix. The type of launch events that can be included may be custom to the industry, market, and product. However, there are some foundational core events that should be considered. They need to be aligned and connected with other important pre-launch activities: executing disconnected stand-alone events in the pre-launch time frame is a waste of time and money. Figure 8-10 outlines these core events.

These pre-launch events may not lead to a readily quantifiable ROI, although many of the event objectives can produce quantifiable results. For example, awareness and excitement is difficult to measure, but the number of attendees, or follow-on increases to website traffic, or event offer take-up rates can be measured. Press and analyst output post-events can be compared to prior output to determine if any positive position changes have occurred. However, it may not be possible to link these results directly to revenue creation, because the product has not yet launched, and is not generating revenue.

In general, it is difficult to link pre-launch event results to revenue occurring months or years down the road. This is due the nature of the results themselves. Using the press and analysts as an example, many customers rely on analyst recommendations to influence product purchase decisions, but directly linking particular customer sales driven by analyst coverage from a pre-launch event would be difficult if not impossible. The key point here is not to use ROI metrics for pre-launch events as a decision factor on whether to do the event.

Timing for Important Pre-Launch Events

Figure 8-11 provides a general timeline for when these important pre-launch events most likely would happen during the launch cycle and a timing template for launch planning. Again, the specifics of different markets, products, and customers, specific launch needs, and corporate policies and procedures can move these time frames, so the timing indicated here is general guidance.

FIGURE 8-11: Illustrative Timeline for Pre-Launch Events

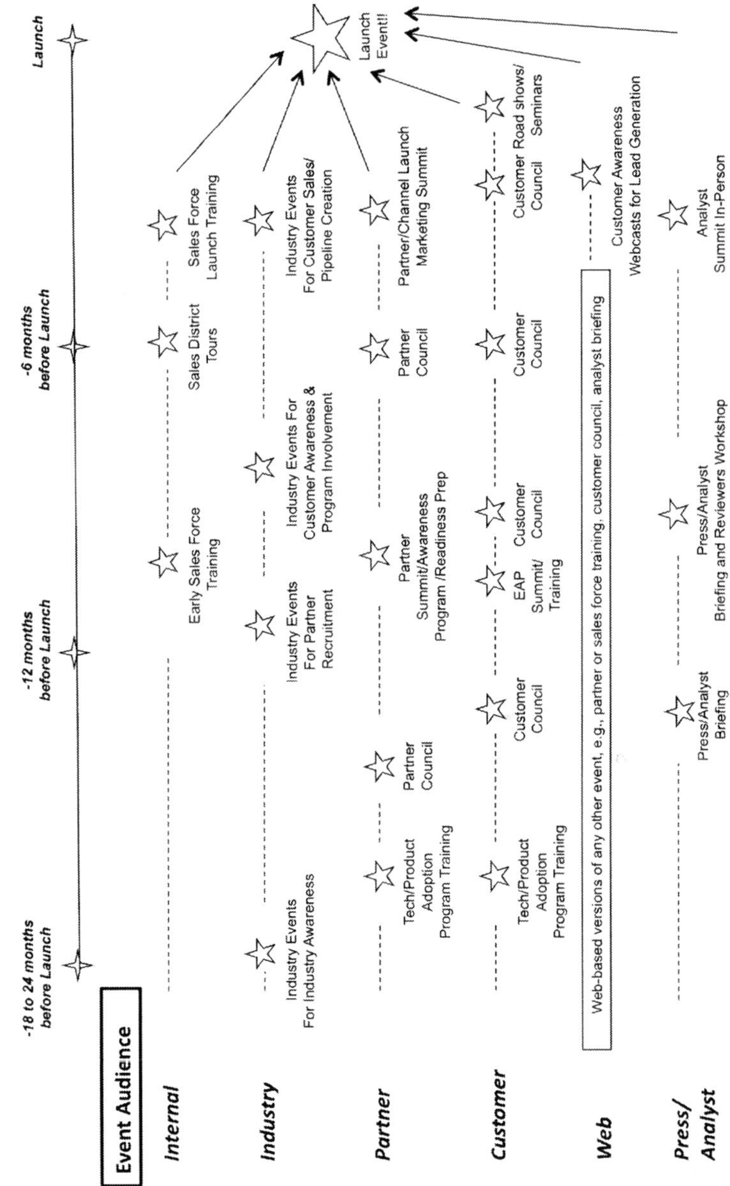

Minimizing Event Costs

It is possible that your firm has the resources to handle these and many more events. However, for most companies not the scale of Microsoft even the limited number of events mentioned here can appear overwhelming. Whether hosting or attending an event, the preparation time, resource commitment, attendance time, and costs can be prohibitive. To save time and money, it's important to manage and limit event involvement and to prioritize the events that are most critical to the launch goals.

Other than limiting the number of events, additional ways to minimize pre-launch event time and cost investments include:

- Combining different events to minimize cost and effort, e.g., combine partner and customer training events for the Technology/Product Adoption Program and make sure the content created works for both audiences.
- Expanding the goals for attendance at industry events to cover more than a few focused goals. Make the event work for you to achieve multiple launch goals.
- Executing events together so the launch team is not constantly doing event work and taking resources away from other important launch activities, e.g., schedule a customer seminar at the same time as you participate in a large industry event so the launch team resources and customers are already geographically available.
- Teaming with close partners, pooling resources, and sharing event costs.
- Leveraging and integrating into existing events.
- Creating and effectively selling for-fee event sponsorship opportunities to third parties like partners can help augment and offset event costs.

You can also use the Internet to conduct some of these events remotely without requiring elaborate event preparations and travel time. Web-based events are cheaper, more flexible, and can have broader reach, but do not create same sense of excitement, commitment, or sense of urgency as in-person events. While the face-to-face element of an event is important, limited resources require trade-offs. The Internet can both augment and replace some key events required in the pre-launch time frame. For example, Microsoft Office Live Meeting training and readiness webcasts can be implemented for channel partners, the internal sales force, and analyst and press briefings. Virtual road shows and seminars can be streamed over the web to end-customers. Decide which events are more beneficially delivered in-person, and which are better delivered over the web.

Creating the Event Plan

I am not covering the nitty-gritty details of event planning and execution. However, any pre-launch event must have a written plan. Without a plan the event will likely fail on multiple fronts. Planning, preparation, and execution time frames for an event will depend on such factors as the size of the event, scope of activities required, and resource availability. At a minimum, I've learned that planning and executing smaller events (e.g., a small seminar for 20 people) requires an eight-week lead time. For moderate or large events (e.g., large industry events), planning and execution might need to begin six months or more in advance.

Since I'm a stickler for detail, Figure 8-12 lays out some important high-level event checklist items and activities to think through and address while formulating the event plan (not all of these items will apply to every event).

PRE-LAUNCH PRODUCT WEBSITE CONSIDERATIONS

The public product website plays a central role in many launch activities. Among other roles, the public website may act as a:

- Customer engagement, education, awareness, and communication interaction point
- Delivery and interface mechanism for marketing campaigns and offers
- Sample and content provider
- Mechanism for delivering web-based events and presentations
- Customer loyalty program delivery mechanism (see Chapter 9)
- Customer community center
- Repository for product support information
- Partner program member hub for content, community, education, and communication
- Portal to communicate branding, positioning, and messaging
- Direct purchase channel or link to indirect purchase channels such as resellers
- Venue for PR-related announcements
- Directory for company contact information

FIGURE 8-12: Pre-Launch Event Planning Checklist

Before the Event	At The Event	After the Event
Obtain executive sponsorship and buy-off for the event plan	Badges for attendees and staff	Tear-down of booth, signage, collateral, staffing, stage, lighting
Registration requirements and process	Setup of booth, signage, collateral, staffing, stage, lighting	Post-event sales lead follow-up process
Content and collateral creative design, messaging reflecting positioning framework, print and production management	Internet access and audiovisual needs	Post-event content distribution to attendees
Speaker recruitment, training, and presentation creation	Executive handlers, process, and coordination	Session and speaker evaluation form assessments and event metrics/goals achievement analysis
Recruiting executive and partner participation	Entertainment and fun activities	
Partner participation and sponsorship opportunities, and partner participation fees	Promotions at the event	
Defining key event activity delivery options: presentations, roundtable discussions, panels, networking activities	Analyst or third-party subject matter expert presentations	
Defining the event "theme" and branding	Giveaways, gifts and tchotchkes, and swag	
Attendance fee and fee structure for attendees	PR for announcements at event, press and analyst meetings at event	
Dress codes for staff	Event facilitators such as speaker managers, master of ceremonies, etc.	
Defining key event messages, goals, objectives, metrics, Q&A documents, and pre-event staff training in these areas	Parties and networking sessions	
Internal event rollout process, communication, and regular coordination meetings	Customer or partner dinners with staff and executives	
Reserving event onsite meeting rooms for staff, partner and customer business meetings and room scheduling coordination	On-demand or real-time web video or audio	
Agenda and content track definition, content reviews for internal speakers and partners	At-event strategies to drive attendees to your firm's presentations (e.g., a handout of your firm's speaking times and locations)	
Non-partner third-party sponsorship and participation opportunities	Creative at-event awareness activities (sponsorships, room-drops, stunts)	
Budget and cost item identification	Product demonstration delivery	
PR for event awareness	Food and drinks, catering, etc.	
Keynote opportunities definition and inclusion	Pencils, pens, paper and pads for attendees	
Venue booking and reservations	Session evaluation and feedback forms	
Staff and guest hotel booking and travel reservations		
Registrant event attendance reminders shortly before event		
Assigning an event lead or point person		
Event website and content creation		
Attendee participation and registration incentives		
Specification and definition of the required booth, signage, collateral, staffing, stage, lighting		
Demand generation/attendee recruitment activities		
Product demonstration creation		

Clearly, the website content, information, and structure depend on many of the pre-launch marketing infrastructure activities and on the customer and partner programs. Figure 8-13 indicates and maps some of the key pre-launch activities to some of the possible public product website components. In the pre-launch phase, the site architecture needs to consider these activities and interdependencies when being defined, as each is a potentially functional component of the overall product website information architecture. It is best to think through the information architecture as serving both pre- and post-launch goals across all program and marketing infrastructure activities. This minimizes potentially expensive site architecture changes down the line and creates an effective, compelling, and integrated customer and partner experience.

If you have a one-product company, the company website may well be the product website. In larger corporations with many products, like Microsoft, the product website will likely be a sub-site, or mini-hub, within the overall company website. Each of these scenarios may drive different or additional requirements for the site information architecture. Whatever the scenario, the website needs to support all necessary pre-launch needs and anticipate and plan for post-launch activities and needs.

FIGURE 8-13: Pre-Launch Public Website Structure

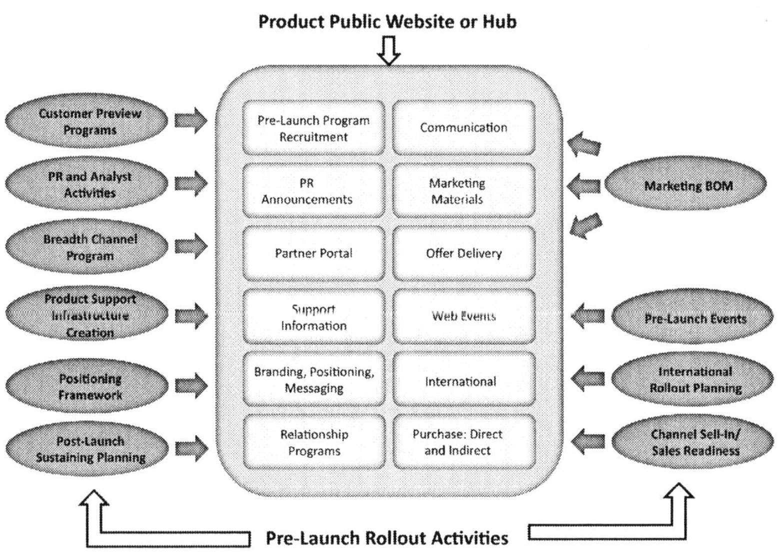

The public website should be launched in conjunction with the Customer Preview Program and the breadth partner program. This is the time when a critical mass of content will be ready and available for the channel and the product, and when significant out-bound awareness activities will kick in.

Once the site is live it must remain in synch from a content and messaging perspective with other pre-launch marketing and PR programs, messaging, and content requirements. For example, as part of the pre-launch awareness creation activities, there may be a period of time when certain segments are being targeted via PR and pre-launch marketing campaigns. BOM materials will have been created to support these efforts. The website needs to remain in tandem with these efforts and reflect the focus areas and priorities driven by marketing and PR needs, with content and messaging reflecting and supporting these requirements.

To effectively maintain synchronization, it is a good practice to institute a website content and editorial calendar process that schedules out the key marketing campaigns and message focus areas in advance (Figure 8-14). This will assist in providing the lead time necessary for web content creation, web design, and content propping and help ensure the continuous synchronization of what is being delivered to the customer via marketing and what is on the website.

PRODUCT PACKAGING

The need for product packaging is driven primarily by the distribution channels through which the product will flow and the product's physical properties. Some types of products, such as software delivered via an Internet service, an intangible product like intellectual property, electric power, or products like cars, bulldozers, and real estate do not require product packaging.

Generally, if a product is moderately sized and is available via Internet purchase, catalog, retail purchase, or another channel where the end-customer will shop for, evaluate, and receive a physical good, some type of packaging must be created. Packaging is most important for in-store retail channel distribution. It is through the in-store retail environment that potential customers have the opportunity to physically engage with the product, whether having actively sought it out or finding it when searching shelves.

Effective packaging is a key selling opportunity. At retail, the packaging functions to enable demand creation, awareness, evaluation, and sales. The

FIGURE 8-14: Aligning Web Content to Marketing Messages and Campaigns

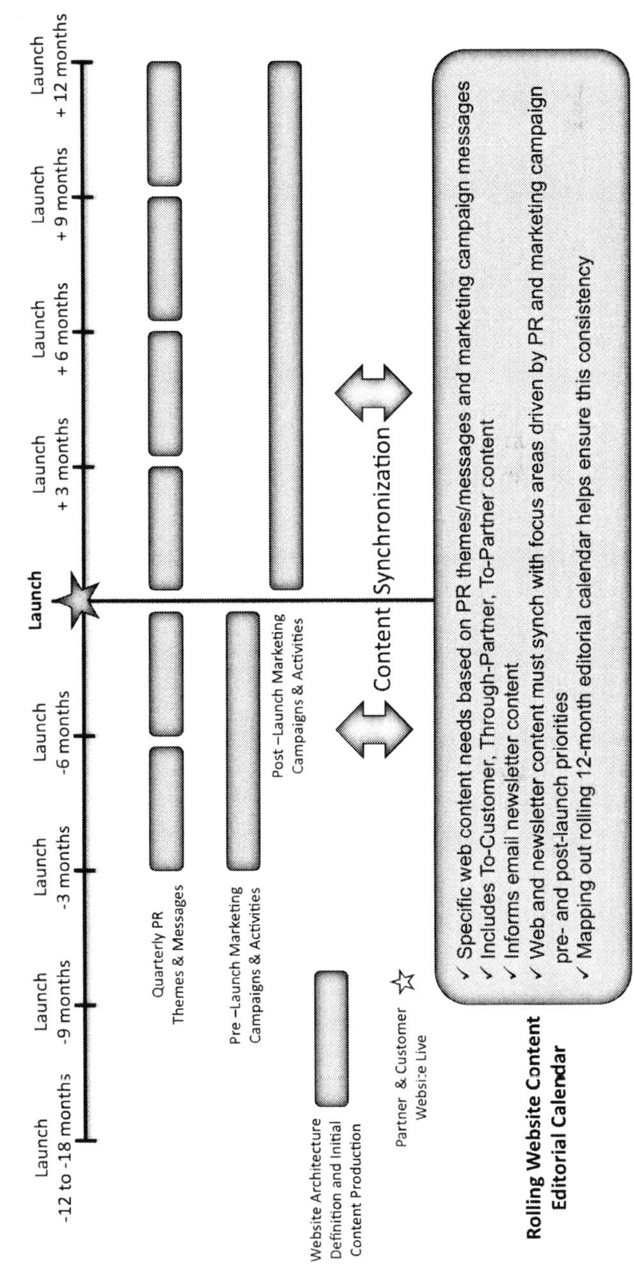

packaging style, written content, and visual graphics on the packaging must be created to incent a product sale assuming no other influences are available. It may be the first and last opportunity for a sale when the potential customer picks the box off the shelf. Don't count on the retail salesperson to be an expert on your product and help a sale: the packaging must act as a virtual salesperson to sell the product in that environment.

Microsoft's packaging for its various product lines has changed and evolved over time and now generally falls into line around the core brands. For example, this means that the Microsoft Office branded products generally all share a similar packaging style. Server and tools products share similar packaging designs across product lines, but with a different look and feel than the Office-branded product packaging. Pure consumer products such as the Zune and the Xbox each have their own packaging design and style, with no design commonalities between the two product lines, and each being wholly distinct from the Office and server product packaging.

Why is this the case? Why wouldn't Microsoft simply use a standard packaging design for all the products and brands in the company? The answer is that in many ways product packaging is similar to branding: both entail the creation and conveyance of product attributes and desired perceptions.

Thinking carefully through the desired product attributes and perceptions, and how they will be expressed to the customer, forms the core of the packaging development process. As indicated in Figure 8-15, the product packaging should align with and reinforce the key marketing assets, of product positioning and messaging, branding strategy, and product naming strategy. Ensuring this alignment will enable the packaging to effectively convey and express the desired product attributes and perceptions based on these marketing assests, reinforcing the brand and more effectively selling the product. If the packaging implementation does a poor job, damage to the product brand and lower sales are possible.

For Microsoft, the Office, server, and consumer products generally all have distinct value propositions that are conveyed via positioning and messaging, and via different product naming and branding strategies; these product lines are mostly targeted at different customer segments. Thus, each of these product types has different desired attributes and perceptions that must be conveyed to their specific target audience; this is why each of the packaging designs is different.

FIGURE 8-15: Aligning Marketing Assets for Product Packaging

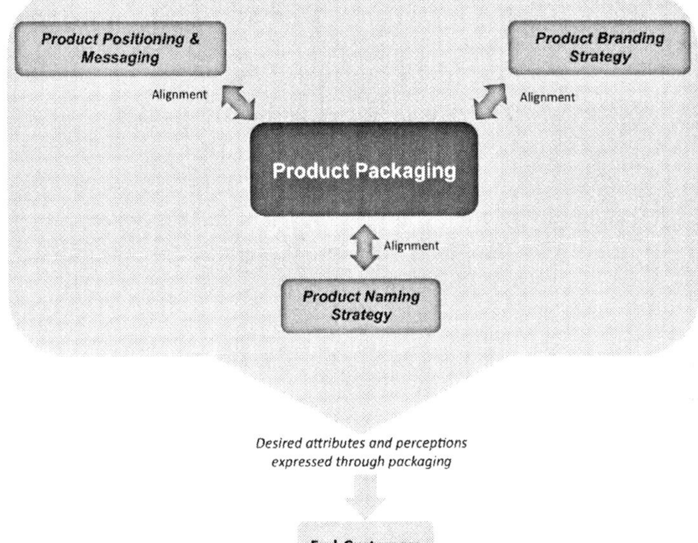

Given the wide variety of possible product types and the desired attributes and perceptions to be conveyed, there is no one best packaging strategy that can be applied to every product. However, there are some basic considerations for developing product packaging that can be applied regardless of the product category or the product physical makeup.

One key consideration is that a primary goal for packaging development should be focused on differentiation and contrast to competitive product packaging on the retail shelf. If your product sits side-by-side with the competition, yours needs to stand out and draw the customer to it like a moth to a flame. Once the customer has the product in hand, the packaging has a very limited amount of time to convey the sales pitch to incent purchasc.

To summarize, the goals that the product packaging must support are:

- Expressing desired product attributes and perceptions in alignment with positioning, branding, and naming
- Differentiating and contrasting with competitive product packaging
- Providing a cogent sales pitch to incent purchase in a short time

To deliver these goals each element of the packaging design considerations must individually and collectively support them. When thinking through product packaging, it might be worthwhile to map each of the following packaging considerations against these goals, as suggested in Figure 8-16.

How is each of the primary packaging considerations going to serve and support the key packaging goals? For example, what packaging form factor and materials best support the expression of the desired product attributes and perceptions? How will the packaging form factor and materials play their role in differentiating and contrasting from competitive product packaging? How can the form factor and materials assist in delivering a cogent sales pitch? Answering these questions across the various primary packaging considerations can help drive the creation of the strongest possible product packaging.

When designing the packaging, the various product SKUs also need to be considered. The packaging design must be flexible enough to accommodate the various flavors of the product being launched and differentiate the SKUs. The packaging differentiation needs to be clear enough to indicate different SKUs, but consistent enough across them to convey the fact that the SKUs all belong to the same product family.

FIGURE 8-16: Primary Product Packaging Considerations and Goals

Illustrative planning framework mapping packaging considerations against packaging goals…

Primary Packaging Considerations*

Package footprint/size
Branding Elements
Form Factor & Materials
Color
Visuals and Graphics
Messaging
Aesthetics

Expression of desired attributes and perceptions ← *How will each consideration support expressing desired attributes and perceptions?* →

Differentiation and contrast to competitive packaging ← *How will each consideration support differentiation and contrast to competition?* →

Delivery of cogent sales pitch in minimal time ← *How will each consideration support the sales pitch delivery?* →

Key Packaging Goals

*Don't forget any specific packaging requirements for product security or other channel specific requirements

Using differing colors and visual images is one way to achieve both consistency and differentiation for the packaging across SKUs yet still visually convey that these products are members of the same product family. Microsoft also tends to include product SKU comparison charts with the various SKU features and benefits as a standard item on each package to enable customers to choose the correct product for their needs.

The ability of packaging to sell does not end with the product purchase. Making effective use of the space inside the package to deliver content and collateral that can cross-sell and up-sell other products is a smart move. Of course, packaging costs must be considered in the process, including design costs and the ongoing unit costs of assembling and manufacturing the packaging and any ancillary in-package content or collateral. These costs will affect the per-unit COGs (cost of goods sold) and affect product profitability.

Packaging overkill and clutter should be avoided. Too much content and too many messages on the packaging can work at odds with the short amount of time available for the sales pitch. There is definitely both an art and science for effective packaging. You must strike the correct balance to deliver effectively against the key packaging goals. Check out the hilarious packaging parody video created by a Microsoft group that compares Microsoft product packaging to the Apple iPod packaging. This parody was for internal Microsoft use to create awareness of the importance of design in the product development and delivery process. The video can be found on the YouTube website.

INTERNATIONAL LAUNCH PLANNING

This section highlights some of the high-level considerations and thinking required to launch a product into international geographies. If your intent is to take the product into international markets, consider international requirements as the domestic rollout plan and tactical plans are being formulated.

There can be many reasons for taking a product beyond the domestic market and into international markets, including international revenue and profit opportunities. Why not leverage all the time and effort spent developing the product and make potentially incremental changes to open up a large international market? Going international also serves the needs of domestic customers that are multinational corporations with international operations. A prime purchase consideration for these potential customers may well be that your product must serve their needs domestically and globally.

Of course, the decision to go international brings with it a new set of issues beyond the domestic launch considerations that must be addressed, such as:

- Increased launch process complexity
- Higher initial launch investment costs in dollars and resources
- Higher ongoing sustaining and marketing costs
- Trade-offs between the ROI of resources applied internationally vs. domestic resources
- Opportunity costs of international opportunities vs. domestic opportunities
- Timing of international entry/expansion

There are three primary aspects to an international launch. First is the product itself and any localization or feature changes required to accommodate particular international geographies and customers. Second is potential incremental or modified launch execution activities taking place in parallel to product development. Third is the timing—it may be that from a strategy and timing perspective your firm is planning to co-launch domestically and internationally, or that the domestic product will ship first and the international versions will follow later.

Regardless of the timing or any product changes, if the intention is to launch the product internationally, it is a big mistake to wait too long in the launch process to begin international planning, because it cuts across almost every element of the launch process and activities. Incorporating this planning and execution in parallel with the domestic launch plans gains time and leverage.

Figure 8-17 provides some perspective on how international launch considerations impact nearly every element of the launch planning process. It is clear that a significant amount of thinking and re-thinking of each element of domestic launch planning must be done with an international lens applied. To have an effective international rollout plan and strategy, everything in this book must be reexamined with the international perspective in mind, and a complete international plan incorporating these perspectives must be created in parallel to the domestic launch plan.

Take target customers as an example. Chapter 2 discussed acquiring a clear understanding and in-depth knowledge of the customer. Applying that planning approach to an international audience requires determining

FIGURE 8-17: International Launch Requirements Span Launch Execution Activities

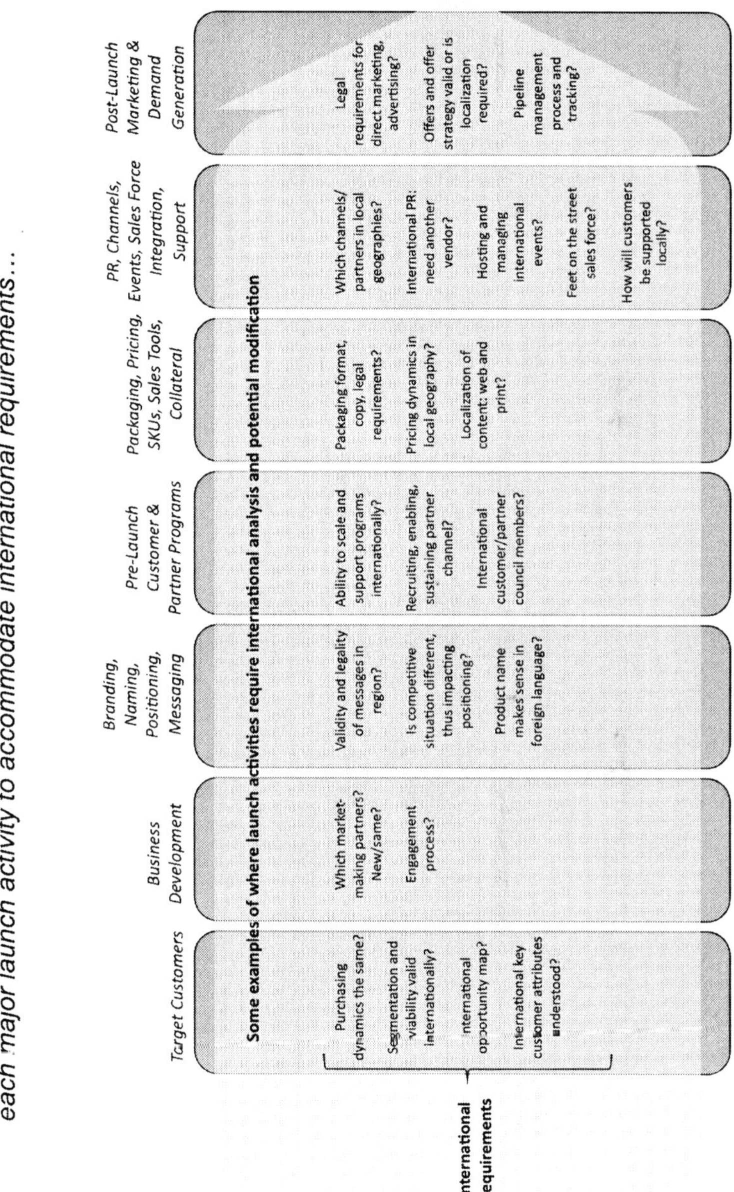

whether the domestic customer segmentation definition is valid in the geographies planned for entry. At the time the segmentation is being researched and defined, both domestic and international segmentation considerations should be built into the research and the process; assessing the viability of the international customer segments then takes place. Are the key customer attributes the same or different among the various geographies? Are the purchase channels the same? The information sources? The purchase influencers?

Chapter 5 covered the process of dealing with market-making partners. Who are these firms in the international geographies planned for entry? Should one of the selection criteria for these partners be the ability to serve your needs globally? Is there a separate business development processes that must be put into place to define, recruit, and maintain a sustaining relationship with additional partners in the international geographies?

Positioning, messaging, and naming were discussed in Chapter 4. How are these elements affected by the international needs? Will the messaging as defined domestically be as effective in the international geographies? Do they need to be modified and must positioning frameworks for individual geographies be created? Legal issues play a role in international messaging communications, and these must be understood. For example, in some European countries, it is illegal to advertise and sell based on price. If one of your messaging pillars is "The cheapest product," it might need to be re-thought for particular geographies. The international competitive environment may be different than the domestic situation, so your product's positioning points must take into account both customer needs and the local competitive products and their positioning.

What about the pre-launch customer and partner programs discussed in Chapter 7: the Technology/Product Adoption Program, EAP, Customer Preview Program, customer and partner councils, and the breadth partner program? Should they and can they be scaled internationally? If so, what is the plan to achieve this and at what resource and dollar cost?

Any required international pricing and packaging issues must also be considered, and the to-customer and through-partner marketing BOM may all require localization into the languages of the countries being approached. International website development, product support, distribution and retail sell-in activities, events, and branding must have the international lens applied.

Clearly, there is a lot of incremental work, thinking, and planning required to take a product international. This is especially true if multiple international geographies are being considered for simultaneous rollout.

One way to mitigate these complexities is to take an incremental approach. Target the easiest one first—countries with similar languages, markets, and customer and partner makeup with the highest revenue potential and the lowest cost of entry. First approaching one or a limited number of international geographies will allow the international infrastructure to be built up and put into place, providing time to learn what works; then you can leverage this knowledge to scale out to other countries at the appropriate time.

Another primary consideration for an international rollout is whether to create a physical presence in the international geographies being considered. Your firm may already have such a presence, and that makes it much easier to rollout a product in those regions. If your firm does not have such a presence, Figure 8-18 outlines some of the key high-level local resources and processes that must be considered when planning for a physical presence in an international geography.

OTHER PRE-LAUNCH BLOCK AND TACKLE ACTIVITIES

There are several additional block and tackle activities. One is actually getting the product through the manufacturing and operations process. The product SKUs must be entered into the company pricing and ordering systems. Product packaging and packaging collateral and production schedules must be coordinated and any legal product licensing, terms and conditions, and warranties must be finalized. Manufacturing forecasts for product builds must be estimated based on expected demand and pre-orders from the channel.

Another activity to keep on the radar screen is internal communications. You'll want to get your company revved up about the product launch. It's a good idea to keep interested parties in the loop with progress and status updates to create internal excitement and interest. Email updates, internal posters, or other awareness and communication activities can go a long way to creating a cohesive and positive launch for both direct launch team members and other interested employees.

Although the product is not yet out the door, the post-launch sustaining marketing plan must be created. Chapter 9 covers key concepts that can help frame the thinking and focus for marketing in the post-launch environment. Finally, the important topic of engaging the direct sales force in the pre-launch time frame must be addressed.

FIGURE 8-18: Illustrative International Engagement Model

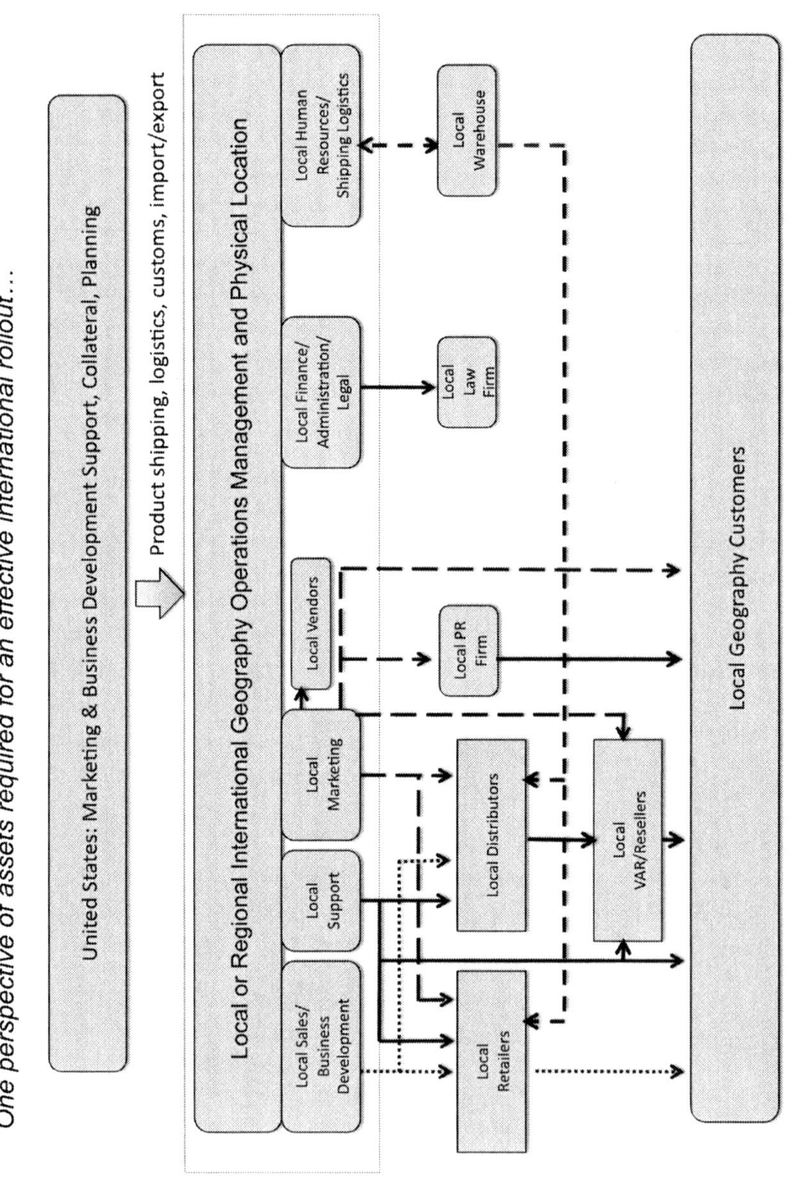

Engaging the Field Sales Force

Early in the launch cycle and on an increasingly ramping rate of interaction, the direct field sales force must be engaged and brought into the product launch. The primary pre-launch focus areas for this engagement include creating awareness of the product and the launch throughout the field, communication regarding launch progress, and sales force readiness to arm, enable, and assist the field sales force to sell the product once it's launched.

To properly support these focus areas there are a number of "Do's" for the product marketing team or the launch team. These may have a positive impact on making the engagement with the sales force a smooth, productive, and all-around win for stakeholders involved in a launch.

Do Get Sales Input Into the Rollout Plan: Engaging sales force management for input on the right sales model and structure to pursue as part of the rollout plan is one activity that sales should plug into right from the beginning. Generating and validating post-launch fiscal year revenue goals is another planning input that sales should provide in the pre-launch time frame.

Do Provide Early Technical Sales Education: Early on in the product development cycle, get the technical sales force and/or your firm's consulting staff up to speed. If you do have a consulting arm, begin the process of building a technical consulting practice and competencies around the product if the product warrants this. The earlier you can build technical competency in the field around your product the better. As you move into later phases of the launch, this competency will be an especially critical asset to drive the first few large customer wins, such as the EAP customers. These early customers will be highly demanding of your resources in trade for their early adoption and deployment of your product, and a strong technical field sales team can help meet these demands.

Do Include Sales in Pre-Launch Customer and Partner Programs: The sales force should play an integral role and involvement in programs such as the Technology/Product Adoption Program, the EAP, customer councils, partner councils, and partner summits. Involvement in these programs will act as one leg of the sales force readiness efforts. Including sales in these programs also has the benefit of avoiding mistakes that negatively affect the sales/marketing relationship and adversely impact the business. For example, when approaching customer or partner accounts to engage in pre-launch customer programs, first discuss your intent with the sales team before contacting the customers if these accounts are directly managed by sales account managers. The account manager has an established relationship with the key folks in the customer or partner account and is aware of current customer/partner issues, sensitivities, and situations.

Understanding the landscape before approaching the customer or partner can help create a successful outcome and avoid making an existing problematic or iffy customer/partner situation worse. For example, a customer may feel like they are being overused by your company for customer references or product feedback, and approaching them to do a case study or join your customer council may not be well received. A good account manager will understand this and provide the heads up that this is not the right account to pursue. Or the account manager may be in a particularly sensitive negotiation to re-up an existing, but expiring, purchase contract for other products. Approaching the customer or partner at the wrong time, or saying the wrong thing may negatively impact the negotiation at hand.

Do Establish a "Sales Champs" Email Alias: This provides the field direct out-bound communication from the product marketing group or launch team about product news, program updates, opportunities, and status. This is an opt-in email alias for field sales personnel that are interested in the product. One reason to have an opt-in alias vs. solely an internal launch website is that the field folks that opt-in will be the most easily identifiable and most engaged sales people for the product. This will help build relationships with the key sales people that will be helpful resources when you need to identify potential pre-launch customer program candidates, sales opportunity referrals, and customer contacts for research or case studies.

Do Establish a "Push" Email Alias: This is an email alias for in-bound questions from the field to the launch team owners for both technical and sales/marketing questions. Having such an alias ensures that a standard and reliable communication path into the launch team is available. Be sure to assign someone to regularly monitor the alias and be the point person to get questions answered in a timely fashion.

Do Establish Shared Goals and Metrics: Both product marketing and sales teams should have revenue, unit, and customer wins as part of their key performance objectives. Not establishing shared goals and metrics can create a huge disconnect between the sales and marketing teams and foster inappropriate behavior and activities.

Do Act as a Sales Resource, Especially in the Early Stages, But Also Ongoing: The product marketing team should be committed and prepared to call on potential customers with the sales team at the customer site (or at your headquarters if customers are being brought in) as the "corporate" representative to present the corporate plans/strategy/direction around your product. This is especially critical during early customer engagements when the sales force may not be quite as up to speed on the product, business, and plans as are the product marketing and launch teams.

Do Get Feedback From the Sales Force on Effective Sales Tools and What Tools They Require to Successfully Sell the Product: This should be one feedback stream that shapes the requirements for the marketing BOM. Provide the right collateral and sales tools in a timely fashion and keep the key pieces regularly updated based on new learning and knowledge.

Do Establish a Campaign Rollout Communication and Coordination Process With the Sales Team: Make sure that there is agreement for standard and sufficient lead times for the various pre-launch activities.

Do Visit the Sales Districts Regularly: Get to know the key sales people in the various regions in person, and establish a personal relationship. Provide regular updates on the product during the visits and take feedback.

Do Produce and Maintain a Living Rude Q&A or Objections & Response Document: As the launch progresses, questions will come in and be answered. Capturing this knowledge in one place can act as a resource for the sales team to see questions and answers from prior communications to speed up the knowledge transfer process.

The relationship between sales and marketing is one of the most important relationships to get right during a product launch. To maximize the success of a launch, this relationship must be tight and positive. Unfortunately, this is not always the case, as there will be some unavoidable tension between the marketing and sales teams. This is natural. The tension is partly because the sales team has a sales quota and goals, and this puts pressure on them whether they are selling to end-customers directly or have responsibility to ensure that certain indirect channels are meeting quota.

If the product launches, goals are being met, and everything is rosy, there will be less tension between marketing and sales. However, when post-launch problems develop, the sales team may need a scapegoat (e.g., marketing) if product sales quota and goals are not quickly and easily being met. This can lead to sales teams blaming the lack of marketing support for poor sales performance. Or the sales team uses perceived (but perhaps not real) deficiencies in sales tools, messaging, lead quality, or partner quality as an excuse to push the blame for poor sales performance to another group.

On the marketing side, it is not helpful that some marketing teams take a mindset that once the product is out the door, their responsibility comes to an end, and they place the burden for product revenue and unit goal attainment solely on the sales team. I have also seen marketing teams that do not effectively and transparently communicate plans with the sales team and that completely discount any sales input.

In these situations, neither the sales nor the marketing team are ever blameless, but they are both wrong. It is completely counterproductive to pass blame. The sales and marketing management teams must ensure that these scenarios and perspectives do not occur. Mitigating and managing the inevitable sales vs. marketing tension is a key pre-launch management responsibility. Whether they organizationally fall under one unifying executive or are in entirely separate organizations, the VP or Director of the sales organization and of the marketing organization must be tightly in synch and coordinating with one another on pre- and post-launch planning and execution. These leaders will set the example by which the sales and marketing teams interact. A positive, tight, and coordinated sales and marketing relationship will reflect these same characteristics in their management and throughout the actions of their teams.

9

It's Not Over: Post-Launch Marketing

The product is out the door, the launch event and activities were successful, and everyone is enjoying a post-launch glow as the soon-to-be successful product enters the market. The sustaining marketing phase of the launch has now begun. Until now, the pressure of actually starting to fulfill on some of the promises and commitments made in the business and rollout plans has not been faced. Now the market share, revenue, and units that were committed to in these plans must be acquired. To do so, you need a sustaining marketing plan that will shift from launching the product to the nuts and bolts of marketing execution to drive the product success in-market.

To shift into sustaining marketing execution, there are a few key goals and focus areas that need attention as the post-launch marketing plan is executed, including:

- Engaging the sales force and ramping sales
- Converting any pre-launch customers, such as beta, trial, or product preview customers to paying customers
- Driving and managing the channel and your partners to sell and market your product effectively, while growing and training your core partner base
- Leveraging early customer wins for collateral, PR, selling material, and sales references
- Maintaining and continuing to develop new sales tools and collateral as you continue to learn through market experience

- Gathering product feedback from customers, press, analysts, and customer support
- Continuing to drive sustaining post-launch momentum and buzz through positive PR and strong analyst support
- Driving market awareness and demand generation throughout your target customer segments, and generating leads

The specific execution elements, success factors, and tactical detail of implementing these key focus areas in a sustaining marketing plan will vary by industry, product, and target audience. For example, if the product is a software product and the channel to market is through value-added resellers, the post-launch partner focused activities will consist of different specific tactics than if the product is a consumer goods packaged product and the channel to market is through retailers.

Given the tactical variations that are possible, this chapter will provide general foundational concepts underlying effective post-launch marketing that can be used to shape the sustaining marketing plan—a plan that incorporates the appropriate marketing tactics specific to the recently launched product, industry, and target audience.

These foundational concepts are summarized within three categories:

- **Planning:** Developing and defining strategic marketing levers and pillars, defining offers, and defining the customer life cycle marketing process
- **Driving Marketing ROI (MROI) via Execution Excellence:** Defining and developing a closed loop marketing process, creating an integrated marketing environment, and establishing relationship/loyalty marketing
- **Managing the Business:** Keeping an eye on key post-launch metrics, customers, and channels

To hit the ground running at the time the product is generally available to the market, you should start developing the sustaining marketing plan, incorporating these foundational concepts, at least six months before launch. The plan should address at least the key post-launch focus areas and goals mentioned above. This leaves adequate time for long-lead items like campaign materials to be created and to put marketing programs and processes into place before general product availability.

To develop the strongest possible post-launch sustaining plan, the first step is to understand the foundational planning concepts that should drive your plan.

PLANNING CONCEPTS

The manner in which the sustaining marketing plan is structured will form the backbone of the go-to-market process. A few key planning concepts will help you think through the plan structure. Two of these concepts are strategic marketing levers and customer relationship management (which includes the underlying customer contact and offer strategies).

The first of these concepts, strategic marketing levers, provides a perspective on structuring the plan strategies, goals, and tactics seamlessly together.

Strategic Marketing Levers: Linking Business Strategy and Marketing Tactics

It is unreasonable to assume that you can successfully execute a large number of high-level marketing goals having equal priority with a limited budget and resources. There can be a lot of goals, but you should focus money and resources on the key goals that will have the most significant impact on overall success, which likely means driving revenue.

WHAT ARE STRATEGIC LEVERS?

Bank the marketing strategy on those few key strategic goals that, when executed correctly, most strongly and directly affect successful execution of the business strategy and objectives. These key goals, the strategic levers, comprise the core marketing goals, and are the foundational link between the business goals and tactical marketing execution. They should drive the overall marketing focus, investment, and tactical execution. The strategic levers will also enable the launch and marketing teams and the rest of the company to converge on a common go-to-market focus that inspires and clearly states the strategic marketing focus required to drive success.

MAPPING LEVERS TO STRATEGY AND TACTICS

Figure 9-1 is an example of linking business goals to tactics with strategic marketing levers and is one format for generating a top-level summary of a sustaining marketing plan. In the example, there are a few key business goals focused on revenue and share. These reflect the goals in the rollout plan (Chapter 3). For each business goal, there are a couple of strategic

FIGURE 9-1: Mapping Strategic Marketing Levers to Business Plan and Tactical Activities

Strategic marketing levers are the foundational link between business goals and marketing tactics…

(Business Goals) ← → (Tactical Execution)

Top business goals…	Business goals achieved with marketing focus on key levers…	Lever success rests upon…	And specifically we're going to…	Success will be measured by…
Key Business/Strategic Goals	**Key Aspirational/Strategic Marketing Levers**	**Marketing Sub-goals (Support the Levers)**	**Marketing Tactics**	**Key Marketing Metrics**
Drive incremental revenue through new product launch in existing market	Win customer mindshare	•Create significant customer awareness •Drive competitive wins	•"Tell-em-quick" blitz campaign •Competitive selling collateral •Award quest •Web microsite with comparisons	•5 PR placements •100k impressions •2 new "best of" industry awards •Positive Sales force collateral feedback •10k unique website users
	Capture the high-end installed base	•Convert top 20% of high-end customers •Create lead pipeline for sales closure	•Discount incentive •Closed loop demand generation	•50% incentive take-up in first 6 months •15k qualified leads to sales
Expand and take share leadership position in strategic new markets	Market share leadership in healthcare vertical	•Drive pilot trials into top 1000 accounts	•Reseller pilot program	•200 resellers signed-up/engaged
	Increase breadth and depth of reseller channel	•Sign top 3 healthcare distributors •Acquire shelf space for lead SKU in top retailers	•New contract/ incentives •New packaging	•Contract completion •3 signed w/in 12 months •Stocking by top 10 retailers

marketing levers that are supported by market data, are broad and aspirational in nature, and that clearly map to supporting the business goal. Winning customer mindshare and capturing the high-end installed base are the example's highest priority, and are the most effective strategic market levers to pull to drive incremental revenue.

Based on the strategic levers chosen, sub-goals are derived to put the levers into effect. For example, winning customer mindshare will be made real if significant customer awareness can be created and competitive wins occur. To actualize and execute against the sub-goals of awareness and competitive wins, the plan calls for running the "Tell-em-quick" blitz campaign, creating new and effective competitive selling tools to arm the sales force, and attempting to win industry awards. Of course, each of these different marketing campaigns will require a full plan for execution success—Figure 9-1 simply indicates a top-line summary. Finally, quantifying success of these tactics requires defining specific metrics around PR placements, impressions, and the other indicated metrics.

Measuring success means measuring the impact made to advance the cause driven by the strategic levers. The key marketing metrics in Figure 9-1 are specifically designed to quantify the tactics being implemented, but offer nothing specific about the impact on the strategic lever. For example, it's great to have five PR wins and 100k impressions supporting the lever of winning customer mindshare, but have those success metrics moved the mindshare bar? The only way to know is to have a measurement system in place before beginning to execute, baselining the mindshare metric against some specific criteria, and later re-measuring to see the net impact. It's easier to measure success against capturing the high-end installed base, but you still need a measurement system in place to track it.

Correctly identifying and forming the strategic levers drives the business in the right direction, simplifies marketing budget allocation decisions, focuses people and priorities, and clarifies communications to other stakeholders.

CHOOSING THE RIGHT LEVERS

Choosing the right strategic levers can make or break the marketing strategy. Some key aspects for defining these levers as thinking and plans are formulated follow.

Is the Strategic Lever Highly Aspirational in Nature? Microsoft forms strategic levers around goals that can motivate the team and form a rally point. Why not give people a quest that inspires (from a business perspective) and a big goal to shoot for? It's not just a marketing campaign, it's a mission! Creating big goals sets a high bar and pushes a team to think broadly and take bold steps. Some examples of aspirational vs. non-aspirational marketing levers include:

- Highly Aspirational:
    - Win the IT Professional mindshare.
    - Win the hearts and minds of developers.
    - Be the first brand in a customer's mind for the product category.
    - Excite our customers with buzz, awareness, and demand.
- Somewhat Aspirational:
    - Upgrade the high-end installed base.
    - Increase breadth and depth of reseller channel.
    - Achieve market share leadership in the healthcare vertical.
- Non-Aspirational:
    - Drop 10,000 emails to reach our target customer base.
    - Implement a PR strategy to create awareness.
    - Generate interest in the target segment.

Does the Lever Map To and Support the Business Strategic Goals? Someone could create a goal that clearly has nothing to do with driving the business strategy. Or the goal may make business sense, but not in the context of the specific business problem being addressed. In any case, the strategic lever will drive the tactical marketing execution; if the lever does not link to the business goal, any tactics executed will not help achieve the business goals.

Are the Levers Chosen Supported by Data? Even if they recognize what a strategic lever is, many marketers will simply use their intuition or just plain guesswork when defining their strategic levers. They are either playing internal politics and setting the strategy based on gamesmanship, or they don't have a solid, in-depth understanding of the market and customer space. These are both poor approaches to take for such a critical link in the marketing process. The choices must be justified and supported by market data and information. If questioned, the choices must be defended with solid factual evidence, not just "feeling" it's the right thing to do. If the market data to defend the levers does not yet exist, get it.

Are They the Right Levers? It's likely that you can identify several potentially viable strategic levers that can support specific business goals. However, which should you focus on? How do you know? Some indicators to guide correct choices are:

- Market and research fact-based data support the choices.
- The chosen levers provide a higher ROI and will generate more revenue, profit, or market share relative to the alternatives.
- You have adequate resources and funding to invest in effectively pursuing the levers of choice.
- There is prior positive experience with similar levers or analogies from other successful marketing strategies inside or outside the company.
- There is consensus about the chosen levers throughout the organization.
- Partners are happy with the focus.
- The tactics derived from the levers will clearly drive the business goals.
- The choices are within the organizational span of control to effectively execute against with the directly available resources.
- Results and impact are measurable.

With the right levers defined, in place, and linked to the proposed marketing tactics, the chance of market success rises. However, how these marketing tactics are pursued will also significantly affect potential in-market success. A customer relationship strategy should be in place to form the basis and methodology for the sustaining marketing programs and tactics. This strategy should define the execution paradigm for the sustaining marketing activities. Customer relationship marketing, including its implementation, is the second foundational planning concept for developing a sustaining marketing plan.

Customer Relationship Management: Mapping the Sustaining Marketing to the Customer Life Cycle

Once the product is launched and generally available, activities and focus shift from launch preparation work to a programmatic approach for driving the business through marketing activities. A good way to approach post-launch sustaining marketing and to execute against the strategic marketing levers is to be mindful of the phases or states in which a potential customer may exist (from the marketer's perspective). A potential customer might exist in various mindsets at any given point in time. Some customers will not know the product at all, others may have heard about it and want to learn more, and others may be ready to purchase. Recognize the reality that customers move through a life cycle comprised of varying states of awareness, product knowledge, and readiness to purchase. Some call this marketing approach "Customer Relationship Management." It incorporates a customer life cycle perspective into the marketing plans and execution activities.

DEFINING THE CUSTOMER LIFE CYCLE PHASES

Figure 9-2 visually lays out the customer life cycle phases, with the primary phases as follows.

Awareness and Consideration: The focus here is on creating awareness of the product and its benefits to bring customers not yet exposed to the product one step closer to purchase. In essence, pursue awareness activities to get the product into the game, moving it into the consideration set for a potential customer. If the product is not even in the game, there's no chance to ever score. Awareness activities are crucial to establish the product's presence in the customer's mind. Some marketing activities that can help drive awareness include case studies, direct mail, advertising, PR, whitepapers and other collateral, your website, and speaking opportunities.

Trial and Evaluation: At this point, the customer is aware of the product and you are providing a more tactile or real experience to move them toward purchase. Trial samples, evaluation software, and web-based Flash demos are some activities that can drive trial and evaluation.

Purchase: In this phase, customers are ready to, or are considering, making a purchase. The goal here is to make the purchase process as clearly defined and as easy to pursue as possible. For example, in the software world, there are many potential purchase options or paths. Customers could buy at retail, purchase from a partner, or purchase direct. Clearly explaining the options and directing the potential customer to the appropriate one removes unnecessary purchase barriers. The purchase phase is also where special deals are offered, like discounts or other purchase incentives, which help move the customer to final purchase.

FIGURE 9-2: Marketing via the Customer Life Cycle

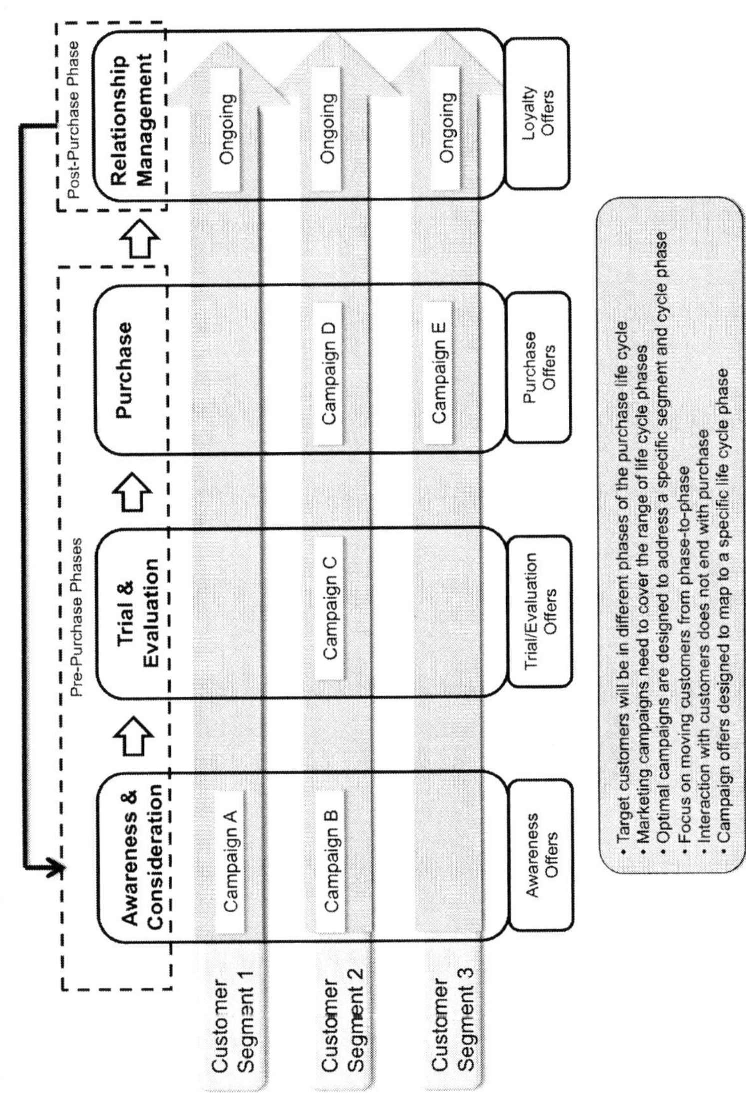

Post-Purchase Relationship Management: Once a potential customer actually purchases the product, they become a real customer. At this point, many firms will simply log the customer purchase information into their database, provide some toll-free number for questions or support, and move on. This is a mistake. To develop reliable repeat business, develop customer loyalty to the product and brand, and get product recommendations you must establish a deeper relationship with the customer. This generally means regular customer communication and continuing to add value in the post-purchase time frame. Loyalty programs are examples of relationship programs that many firms use to build and nurture a sustaining relationship with customers and add incremental value to the relationship. Microsoft has built a number of these programs targeted at different customer segments. Examples include TechNet for IT Professionals, MSDN for Developers, Small Business Plus for small businesses, Momentum for mid-size businesses, and Executive Circle for high-level business decision makers. American Express has its rewards program, where customers earn points when they use their cards. You are not a customer with Amex, you're a Member of the Club. Program benefits are tied to the continued and loyal use of their product, providing a method to continually add perceived value to their cardholders, and a reason to regularly communicate with them.

MOVING CUSTOMERS THROUGH THE LIFE CYCLE

These individual customer life cycle phases, while discrete unto themselves, also form a continuous looping process that should be recognized. The marketer's goal is to move customers through the various life cycle phases into purchase, then into a sustaining relationship in which activities are designed to re-enter these customers into the awareness and consideration phases for incremental sales. This starts the customer life cycle process anew.

The target customer base will likely exist in varying phases of the life cycle. Some will be in the awareness phase, others may be ready to purchase, and others will be existing customers in a masterfully managed ongoing relationship. However, it is not necessarily clear what phase any given customer is in when approaching them via marketing outreach. You can take a scattershot approach and guess what phase the targeted customers are in. This approach may be necessary for marketing to a broad non-business audience like consumers. However, it's always best to make the outreach efforts as targeted as possible to maximize effectiveness. The more that is known about the customers, the more interaction history and data will be available, making it easier to glean their life cycle phase and to effectively target them.

Acquiring deep customer knowledge is where the benefits of database marketing are truly enabled. Tracking the various customer interactions in a well-designed database, making smart inferences from the data, and leveraging these inferences into action will increase marketing success rates. Examples of valuable data include:

- Prior customer purchase data
- Website page view or download data
- Customer support inquiry data
- Salesperson customer visit/call and account reports
- Prior marketing campaign interaction (e.g., event attendance, direct mail recipient, email recipient, and webcast attendee)

DEFINING MARKETING CAMPAIGNS USING THE LIFE CYCLE

Marketing campaigns following the life cycle model must be designed to address the customers in the phase in which they exist. Be aware of these potential differences when you apply the model to different customer segments:

- Different customer segments may follow a different distribution of members within that segment across the customer life cycle. For example, one segment may have a large majority of potential customers requiring awareness and consideration activities because that specific segment has not previously been addressed. Another segment may have had two years of marketing contact, so these potential customers are likely aware of the product and would be candidates for trial and evaluation activities. A newer company with minimal sales probably will not have much of a customer base in the relationship management phase; however, a longer-lived firm with a large installed customer base can target customers in that phase.
- The types of marketing activities pursued in any given life cycle phase could differ among segments. If Segment A was hospital administrators and Segment B was medical doctors, you would use different outreach mechanisms to address these segments, with different messaging, and,

perhaps, different offers in the awareness and consideration phase. If the real purchase decision makers were the hospital administrators, you would focus on this segment for the purchase phase marketing activities, avoiding purchase phase activities directed to the medical doctors.

- The intensity of investment required in any given phase can vary depending on the segment. It is driven by such factors as how dispersed or fragmented the segment is, how reachable it is, inherent predilection to accept and internalize marketing messaging and outreach mechanisms, how closely mapped the solution or product is to the segment customer needs, and how urgently the product is needed.
- Offers may need to be different or changed according to segment or life cycle phase. In the awareness and consideration phase the hospital administrator segment may respond better than the doctor segment to a whitepaper offer touting the value of a product's ability to reduce hospital overhead costs.

Figure 9-2 provides some hypothetical examples of how to approach marketing via the customer life cycle model. In these examples, Customer Segment 1 is a new, yet-to-be addressed segment for your company. Perhaps this segment was only recently identified, or previously there was insufficient money, time, or resources available to address it. These customers exist in the awareness phase of the life cycle. Assuming that resources now exist, the first step is to create awareness of the recently launched product. Campaign A is designed to create awareness throughout the segment, which knows little, if anything, about the product. Of course, Campaign A will appropriately align the outreach messages, marketing mix elements, and offers for the awareness phase.

Customer Segment 2 was identified as a high priority segment, so a lot of money will be spent on it. An awareness campaign (Campaign B) was designed to reach out to the uneducated masses, following-up via Campaign C, with a trial offer for the product to both those that respond to the initial awareness campaign and to other ongoing outreach mechanisms. Finally, once the time is right, the final campaign will be initiated with an unbeatable purchase offer via Campaign D, again targeting prior campaign responders, now an educated segment. Campaign timing, tracking, and follow-up are key to success in this approach.

Via these sequenced campaigns, you make an effort to actively move the targeted customers from one phase of the life cycle to the next, culminating with purchase. It is not necessarily a complicated process to implement sequential campaigns, but it does take up-front forethought and planning to tie them together.

Finally, Segment 3 is an existing customer segment that's been marketed to for years—these customers know your firm's prior product lines and have been tempted to purchase, if they haven't already done so. They are in the purchase phase of the cycle. So give them their chance, and provide a killer offer to incent purchase of the newly released product using Campaign E. Maybe the same purchase offer created for Campaign D could be re-used, perhaps customizing the offer to this particular segment's specific needs and desires. In any case, the campaign will again leverage the most segment-appropriate messaging, hot buttons, and outreach mechanisms to convey the offer.

As these campaigns are running, the ongoing customer relationship and loyalty program continues to execute for existing customers. Campaigns and outreach do not end with purchase, so creating, fostering, and nurturing a vibrant customer-installed base will pay dividends.

These examples illustrate how and why one might think about marketing campaigns targeted at various segments and implemented using the customer life cycle as the model. Such a model and process must be adapted and shaped to address your firm's unique product, marketing offers, and customer knowledge into an effective execution model.

Another aspect of life cycle marketing is the potential customers that find themselves on the public product website. Given the likely anonymity of these visitors, the website should be designed to capture visiting customers existing in any phase and drive them through the life cycle. If a visitor should land on the site knowing nothing about the product, there should be clear opportunity for them to learn about the product and its benefits. Messaging and educational content should be appropriately designed to address a customer in the awareness phase. Awareness creation offers could include invitations to attend local events to learn more, or to download an informative whitepaper.

If a website visitor is looking for a good deal on the product (being in the purchase phase), the site should provide purchase information (where to buy, partners or salespersons to contact) and clearly identify existing purchase offers. The site should be designed to be a self-contained marketing campaign and capture customers in any life cycle phase, providing a mechanism to move them to the next step.

DEFINING MARKETING OFFERS BY CUSTOMER LIFE CYCLE PHASE

Formulating offers to map to the different phases is critical. In general, a strong, solid offer will greatly increase the odds of achieving the desired action. Weak offers can fail a marketing campaign and fail to elicit the desired customer response. The offers must be both strong and appropriate to the customer's life cycle phase. If customers are in the awareness phase, with no real knowledge of your product, how likely will they be to respond to a "Buy Now–20% Off" direct mail piece? Unlikely, since a discount offer is not appropriate to the mindset of that specific customer or customer segment, and so is ineffective. If customers are already keenly aware of the product's value, and they see a web ad touting "Learn More–Click Here–Free Information" whitepaper, the odds of them clicking that ad are minimal, since the offer does not map to the state they exist in. The whitepaper offer would be more appropriate for either a trial and evaluation offer to move them to the next phase, or a "Buy Now–20% Off" offer to take them directly to purchase.

Figure 9-3 summarizes the concepts for designing offers by life cycle phase and provides examples. When thinking of offers consider both the end-customers and partners (if your firm has a partner channel). This classifies target audiences for offers into three primary categories:

- To-customer: offers you present to end-customers.
- Through-partner (then to the customer): offers you develop for a partner to deliver to the end-customer.
- To-partner: offers you develop that are specific to your partner channel and are not end-customer focused.

To-customer offers are those most folks think of when the term "offer" comes to mind. These offers are common because most companies run to-customer marketing campaigns to affect sales directly, whether the actual purchase takes place direct from the manufacturer or indirectly through resale channels. Whether delivered via newspaper coupons, physical mail, email, or on the Internet, to-customer offers like product discounts, special pricing, and "buy one get one free" help get the end-customer to take some action and move toward purchase.

Apply your personal experience as an end-customer or business purchaser and you will see that the attractive offers will be determined by your life cycle state. If you are unaware of a product, perhaps an informational piece such as a video, whitepaper, or seminar to learn more will attract you.

FIGURE 9-3: Offers and the Customer Life Cycle

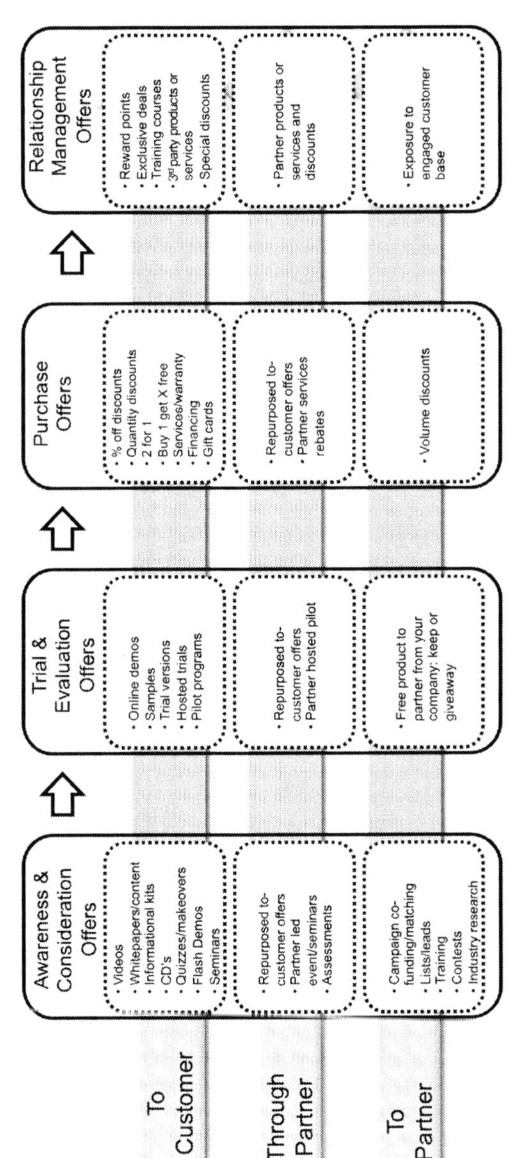

Creative offers such as taking quizzes can also incent you to take action in a less direct manner.

End-customers can be brought further down the life cycle path via a more hands-on experience after they've been made aware of the product and it is in their consideration set. With the Internet it is much easier to provide a virtual hands-on experience using an online demonstration or product walk-through. Samples or, in the case of software, crippled evaluation versions, can also provide physical trial and evaluation. The ubiquitous "30-day money-back guarantee" offer is essentially a trial and evaluation offer with some good stick to it, i.e., most customers who take up this offer will not generally return the product.

Purchase offers such as price and quantity discounts and bundles are the most well-known type of offers. Less typical in some industries are service and warranty offers (free or discounted maintenance, repair, or support) or financing offers. These offers are pervasively used for expensive consumer appliances and electronics, automobiles, and financial industries. However, these concepts can still be leveraged and applied to your product to create compelling offers and drive demand.

Leveraging the power and reach of your partner channel as an offer distribution mechanism using through-partner offers might also make sense. If your firm goes to market with partners, any to-customer offers can likely be re-used or repurposed for use as through-partner offers the channel can use. For example, if an information kit has been created to drive product awareness, why not provide the kit or a subset of the kit's materials to the channel to distribute via their marketing activities? Perhaps the kit content can be slightly modified to allow the partners to add customized content sections or special offers they create to incent product purchase. If a Flash demo has been created, why not syndicate this demo and allow partners to host it on their own website, perhaps allowing them to custom brand it?

EXECUTION EXCELLENCE: MAXIMIZING POST-LAUNCH MARKETING ROI

Given the right strategic levers and a well-developed customer relationship management strategy, the framework for marketing success is in place. Execution efficacy within that framework is where success or failure is achieved. Of course, success is the goal, and success typically means generating the planned and expected revenue numbers. To generate revenue efficiently, marketing execution excellence is required.

Marketing Return on Investment

A key measure of efficiency and execution excellence is termed Marketing Return on Investment (MROI). MROI can be defined as a ratio: the Actual Revenue Achieved/Campaign Cost. If $100 was spent on a marketing campaign, and achieved $1000 in actual sales revenue, MROI would be $1000/$100 = 10. In this case a 10x (10 times or 10x) MROI has been achieved. Clearly, a higher MROI reflects more effective campaign implementation, more revenue accrued, more efficient implementation of marketing tactics, and higher leverage accrued from each marketing dollar spent.

MROI calculations should be disconnected from accounting and revenue recognition issues. If a customer generates $1000 in revenue, an MROI calculation should disregard any timing issues on when the revenue will be recognized from a Generally Accepted Accounting Principles (GAAP) perspective. From a GAAP perspective, the rules may state that revenue from a sale can be recognized today or require that revenue recognition be spread out over a number of years. Regardless, MROI calculations should be independent of those revenue recognition rules. If marketing dollars generate a $1000 return, then $1000 should be included as revenue in the MROI calculation.

Benchmarks for a good MROI will depend on the type of product, its price per unit or average deal size, customer segment type, market maturity, and marketing and sales efficacy. Typically, MROI measurements will fall into the range of 5-20, with five an acceptable number, and 20 extremely high. An MROI lower than five could indicate execution problems in the marketing mix; changes should probably be made. An MROI higher than 20 is unrealistic in most cases and somewhat suspicious; although it is not unheard of at Microsoft, it is not common. Shooting for an 8-12 MROI benchmark, and consistently achieving it, will indicate good success and marketing efficacy. Data from the Direct Marketing Association's 2005 Economic Impact study indicates that across all industries, a $1 direct marketing or advertising spend will return on average $11.49 in incremental revenue, or an MROI of 11.49.

Push vs. Pull Marketing and MROI

Typically, a company will make marketing investments to drive revenue both directly to the end-customers and through any available distribution or partner channels. Channel marketing investments are generally termed "push" marketing, as the product is being "pushed" through the channel to the end-customers. Marketing directly to end-customers is generally referred to as "pull" marketing, in which awareness and demand is being created to "pull" the customers into a sale.

Different types of marketing investments are required for push and pull marketing tactics, and a balance must be struck to maximize MROI with both approaches. Figure 9-4 indicates investment considerations for both push and pull marketing. For example, push marketing generally requires account management heads to manage the reseller channel relationship and drive the marketing activities. Funds known as "Market Development Funds," which are marketing dollars dedicated to co-marketing with channel partners, need to be allocated and spent. Channel support, training, and sales tools need to be budgeted for and created to enable an efficient sales process through the channel. As these spends are made, the resulting revenue from the channel should be evaluated to determine the MROI of these investments. The same is true for pull marketing activities, although different investments are made when pursuing a pull approach. In any case, MROI should be evaluated for both push and pull marketing investments, with both types of investments holistically analyzed, and a consolidated MROI determined.

Intent of Marketing Efforts Drives the Approach

At a high level, driving marketing excellence and efficiency is also tied to the underlying intentions for the marketing activities in place, the tactics used to pursue the intentions, and the execution vehicles used. Figure 9-5 illustrates this point. For example, if the key marketing intent is to build a brand, or generate general awareness for a firm, broad air cover marketing using pull mechanisms might be the correct approach (e.g., PR, business websites, and radio or television advertising). If the intent is to execute marketing campaigns through a partner channel (through-partner marketing), direct tactics (e.g., direct mail, email, and events) via a push approach may be the model to pursue.

Regardless of intent, the model chosen (push, pull), or the specific execution elements employed, the question to be asked is, "How to optimize the marketing spend to maximize results and MROI?" When properly implemented, three concepts can have a dramatic effect on increasing MROI:

- Creating an integrated marketing process
- Creating and managing an efficient and effective pipeline
- Driving down marketing costs

FIGURE 9-4: MROI and Push/Pull Marketing

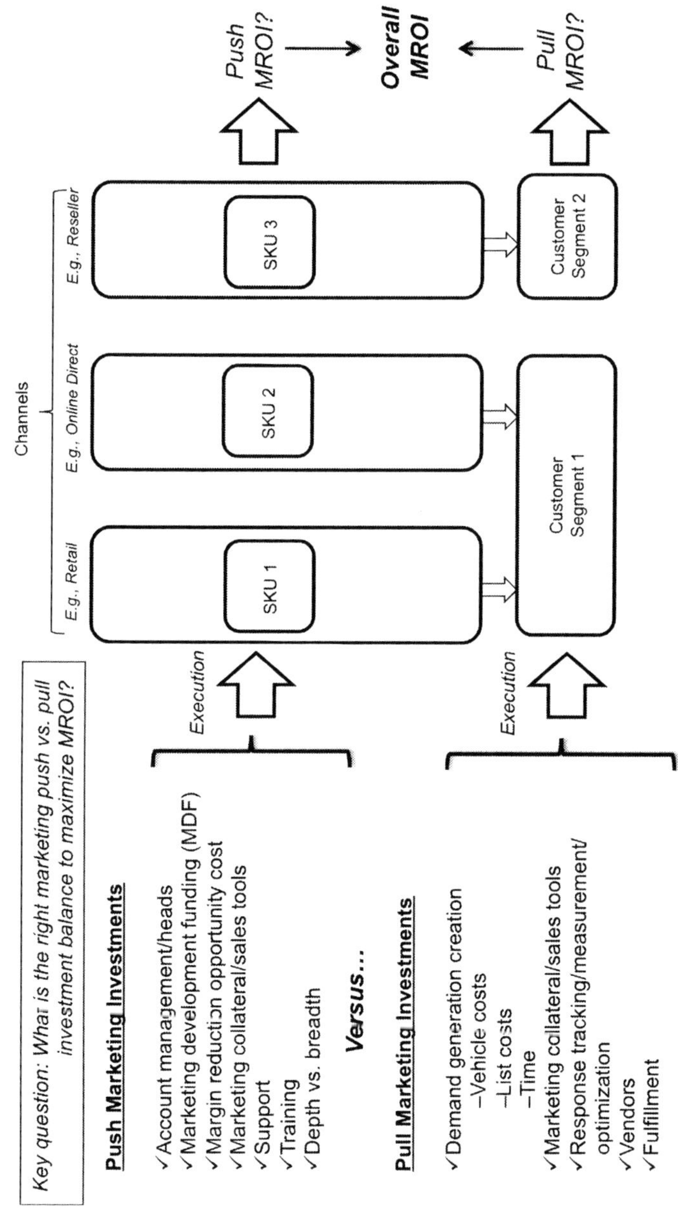

FIGURE 9-5: Key Intent Drives Marketing Approach

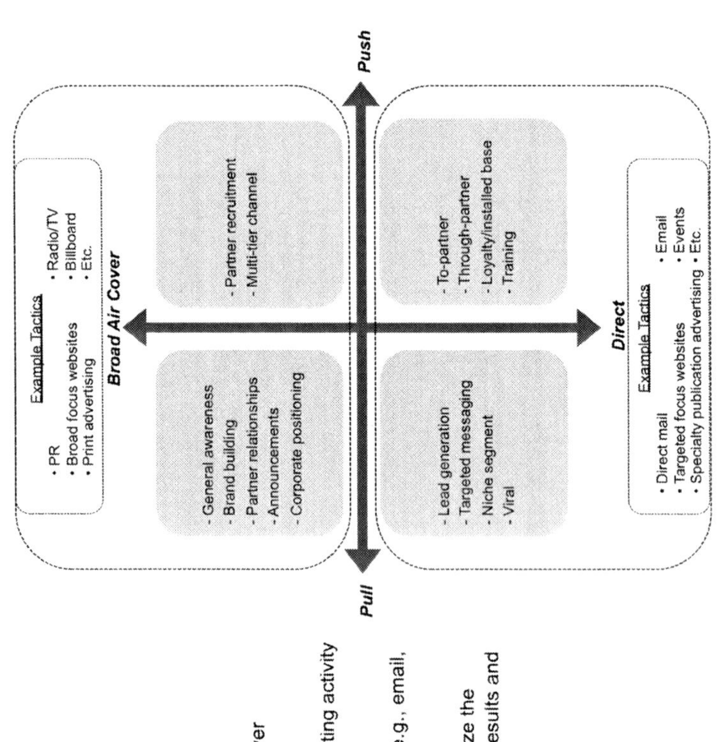

Integrated and Connected Marketing: Another Foundational Concept

One area where Microsoft marketing has made significant strides is in the area of integrated, or connected, marketing. This means defining and executing marketing and customer outreach campaigns that are coordinated and integrated within a given time frame. Campaigns implemented without integration and coordination (i.e., disconnected) typically generate poor results and can cause many problems.

For example, many product marketing groups at Microsoft used to create, define, and execute their own marketing campaigns in isolation. These campaigns would target the same customer segments, often with conflicting messages and solutions. Worse, many times the marketing would take place on an ad hoc and non-integrated basis. For example, a direct mail campaign touting a particular solution or product might occur without having previously informed the field sales force. When customers contacted their Microsoft sales representative, or called Microsoft telesales in response to the campaign, these folks had to manage an embarrassing situation, since they had no knowledge of the campaign.

At the same time the direct mail was in market, a press release or an email campaign might have been executed touting a completely different solution from what was addressed in the direct mail piece. Of course, the product website content wasn't up-to-date to reflect the messages or offers expressed in any of these outreach mechanisms, or, worse, customers responding to the outreach found conflicting information on the website.

Meanwhile, the Microsoft partners were even less informed or armed with information about the campaign, and had to hold similarly embarrassing conversations with their customers. The results from such campaigns were not overly positive, either from a marketing metrics or customer and partner satisfaction perspective.

Microsoft marketing has come a long way since the days these types of situations were commonplace. Not that it doesn't happen anymore or upon occasion, but with far, far less frequency. Why is that the case? Because Microsoft finally realized the negative consequences of such a marketing execution paradigm and moved toward a more coordinated and integrated approach to marketing, an approach that is still evolving. The core principle of the approach is basic, although as usual the devil is in the execution details, especially once a company reaches Microsoft size.

So what is the core principle? In a word—alignment. Alignment and coordination of campaign outreach elements, alignment of the campaign efforts in conjunction with the partner channel and sales force, and alignment of internal efforts and resources so they don't conflict, allowing in-market activities to be coordinated and prioritized holistically across the company.

One method Microsoft uses to create this alignment for marketing execution is called a customer campaign (previously known as a GTM, or go-to-market campaign). These are typically defined in a top-down manner. Key executives and lieutenants across the company meet to decide the next year's key focus areas and priorities for each customer segment.

The key focus areas chosen are good examples of strategic marketing levers. For example, for the enterprise customer segment, they may decide that one key focus area should be helping IT Professional customers save money and time by becoming more operationally efficient when using Microsoft products and solutions. Thus the "Operational and Efficiency Customer Campaign" is born. Many of these large-scale, company-wide, global campaigns can (and are) identified to meet the diverse marketing needs across Microsoft. Once defined, the multiple campaigns go through a rationalization process, with money and responsibility allocated to various groups to execute against these campaigns in the defined time frames.

Once the planning is done, it is execution time. Virtual teams representing various stakeholders from across the company are formed around each customer campaign. These stakeholders may include product groups, U.S. and non-U.S. subsidiary marketing members, creative agency representatives, partner marketing, and field sales representatives. Together these teams develop the messaging frameworks, marketing BOM content, and campaign offers based on feedback and input from stakeholders. As of 2007, Microsoft subsidiaries in different countries have responsibility to execute customer campaigns by leveraging the materials created for the campaigns by the virtual team and augmenting with their own marketing materials as necessary to meet local needs.

For you, your product, and your company, it is important to realize that when it gets down to the execution level, where the rubber hits the road, alignment becomes necessary. One can plan and plan again, but if the execution is bad the entire effort is wasted. During campaign execution, alignment among demand generation, through-partner marketing, offers, and sales activities becomes critical to the campaign success, as illustrated in Figure 9-6. All key activities must be aligned and coordinated to enable a successful marketing campaign.

Tactics and deliverables *within* each high-level activity (demand generation, through-partner marketing, offers, sales force) also must be

FIGURE 9-6: Integrated Marketing

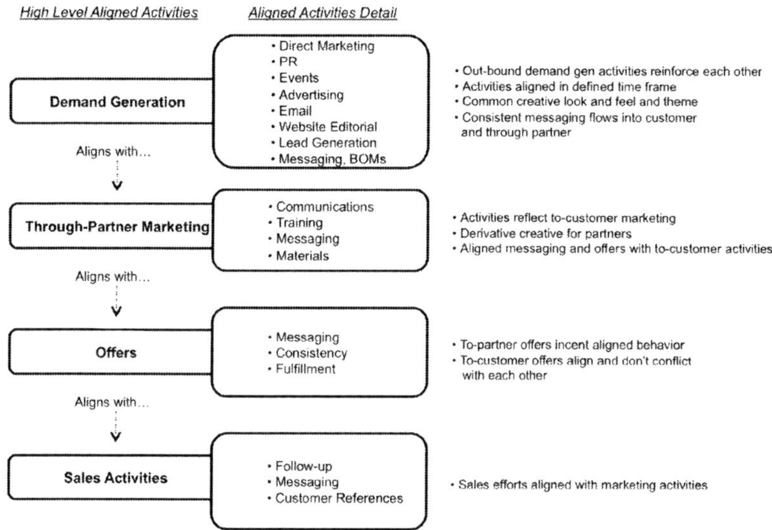

aligned. For example, demand generation activities and materials all must reinforce each other to maximize their effectiveness. This means content pieces like direct mail, advertising, and website content must deliver a consistent set of messages in the same time frame, while pushing the same offers. PR activities should fall into line with any press releases or media outreach focused on the same set of messages as the rest of the out-bound activities.

The look and feel of the campaign is another factor in connecting demand generation activities. For a given campaign, it's important to make sure all the pieces share a branded look: similar and consistent graphics, color, design, and visuals. This visually reinforces the campaign in the customer's mind and reinforces the individual touches through associative recall. The campaign deliverables provided to the partner channel should be based on the to-customer deliverables, reflecting the same messaging and offers. This helps scale up the distribution and communication of the campaign messages and offers. If the information being delivered by partners is inconsistent with the to-customer information, a large disconnect is created that can cause both customer and partner confusion and detract from the overall effectiveness of the campaign. The visual look and feel of the through-partner marketing materials should also reflect the to-customer materials delivered directly to end-customers. A derivative look for partner materials enables an increased partner connection to the campaign while reinforcing the relationship your firm has with them to the end-customer. This also holistically ties the campaign together.

Connecting partners to campaigns involves much more than simply delivering content. Communication and training delivered to partners well in advance of the campaign execution dates is highly desirable and will be much appreciated. These communications should clearly describe and explain the campaign, detail what value the partners will get from participating, describe opportunities for business or technical training that might be required, and note any partner deliverables or asks required for participation. If through-partner offers are being provided, be sure to indicate how to order or deliver the offers (e.g., a kit or an informational CD), and any quantity restrictions or timing expectations.

The direct sales force deserves the same level of up-front communication and campaign notification provided to partners. It's a good idea to leverage the same advance communications and training opportunities provided partners to ensure that the sales force will actively execute against the upcoming campaign(s), delivering consistent messaging and offers.

A key benefit to ensuring alignment for marketing execution is maximizing the potential for a high MROI. Campaign critical mass can be achieved if a campaign is aligned across demand generation, partners, offers, and sales. All the elements of the campaign will reinforce one another with a consistent presentation to the target audience. Regardless of outreach vehicle (email, partner, web, PR), the customer will receive the intended message, offer, content, or evidence points. Each repetitive and consistent touch then maximizes the opportunity to elicit the desired customer response. Partners and the direct sales force will be properly focused, executing in tandem with the overall marketing efforts, magnifying and intensifying these efforts.

Pipeline Creation: Putting It All Together With Connected Closed-Loop Marketing

Together strategic levers, relationship marketing using the customer life cycle, and integrated marketing form and influence effective marketing activities. Strategic marketing levers link business goals to tactical marketing activities. Tactical marketing activities are implemented via campaigns based on customer life cycle phases. Campaign messaging and offers are oriented to address specific customer segments and life cycle phase. Demand generation, through-partner activities, offers, and sales efforts are all connected and in alignment via integrated marketing. Finally, outbound customer reach activities, such as PR, direct mail, email marketing, and partner marketing, map together and reinforce each other.

It is important to not lose sight of the end goal of selling product and generating revenue and profit. The final leg of the process is via a "pipeline" process, as illustrated in Figure 9-7, which connects marketing activities to the sales activities where revenue generation occurs. The pipeline process moves the customers from the awareness generated by marketing activities through a funnel-like process that further qualifies and motivates a customer to eventually purchase.

There are four major stages in the pipeline model in Figure 9-7: impressions, unqualified leads or responses, qualified leads or responses, and lead follow-up and engagement. At Microsoft, this pipeline process and definition of stages, and the corresponding requirements and criteria to place a prospect in a defined stage, are based on a technique called the Solution Selling Process. That model breaks these four general stages into 10 stages, which are somewhat more refined than the general model in Figure 9-7. There are reference books available that overview that particular sales methodology.

FIGURE 9-7: Connecting Marketing and Sales

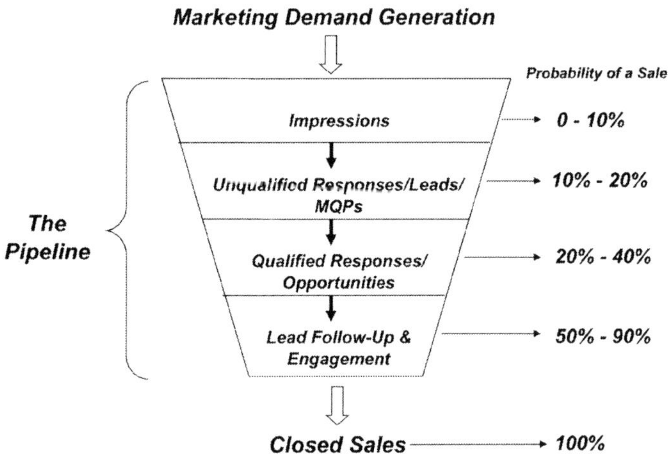

As a potential customer (the prospect) moves through the pipeline funnel and hits each stage, there is an increasing probability of purchase. Figure 9-7 indicates the general probabilities for a purchase at each stage. For example, if a prospect has reached the qualified lead stage, there is a 20-40% chance that this prospect will eventually purchase. This means that if 1,000 prospects have reached this stage, chances are that 200-400 will eventually become paying customers. The exact probabilities at each stage may vary depending on the specific product and business, but the Figure 9-7 numbers are a useful starting point until specific campaign results provide data to refine them. A pipeline process always starts with marketing-generated customer impressions, then selectively whittles down the number of customers in each stage, moving them through the process and ending in a sale.

Customer impressions are a consequence of demand generation activities. As integrated marketing campaigns execute, awareness is generated within the target customer base. Each time a potential customer is exposed to advertising, receives a direct mail piece, gets a newspaper or magazine containing an article generated via PR activities, receives an event invitation, or is exposed to messaging and offers through another marketing mechanism, an impression is created. Creating impressions, and lots of them, is the first step to moving the customer to purchase and into the pipeline. Different marketing vehicles provide varying levels of impression creation ability and carry differing creation costs. Balancing the reach and cost trade-off for each marketing vehicle is an important exercise. The cost of creating impressions by different marketing vehicles is one element that drives MROI and should be closely tracked.

Quantifying the number of impressions created by a particular marketing vehicle can present difficulties. It is relatively easy to quantify impressions created through a direct mail campaign, since you know the exact number of pieces mailed (assuming the addresses are good and each person actually receives and looks at the direct mail piece). Print or web ads are less measurable, although print vehicles have circulation numbers, and many websites can count unique users. It's more difficult to quantify PR activities, though it's possible to count article placements and mentions, and, knowing their associated circulation numbers or web traffic users, it's possible to approximate the impression count.

With partner marketing, it is much more difficult to quantify impressions, since most typically do not share this information willingly, or don't know. Retail is a good example: how many people actually saw and/or read that shelf-talker or end-cap display? It's difficult to quantify exactly what percentage of the foot traffic actually passes by and reads the in-store marketing materials.

Unqualified leads come from the pool of prospective customers that have been exposed to and acted on the marketing message. Examples are prospects that click on a web ad, call a phone number, respond to an email, and register for an event. They are considered unqualified because although they have expressed interest in what is being offered they have not yet been assessed as potential purchasers. In the Microsoft parlance, these prospects are referred to as "Marketing Qualified Prospects," or MQPs. Typically, only 10-20% of MQPs will become a closed sale. The goal is to move them from the MQP stage into qualified prospects via the pipeline process.

Qualified prospects, also called "Opportunities," have been further assessed through a qualification and screening process and determined to actually be viable and real customer prospects. This screening process applies specific criteria to determine whether the MQP is truly an opportunity. Examples of such criteria include the definitive knowledge that they are in fact the purchase decision maker, they have budget allocated for purchase, they are actively seeking to learn more about your product, or they are willing to receive a follow-up visit from a sales rep or one of your partners. The specific criteria applied to rate a prospect as "qualified" will depend on the business model and needs.

Whatever criteria is used, be sure that the filter created is tight enough so that truly unqualified prospects do not slip through to the next level. This is important for measuring the effectiveness of the pipeline processes—unqualified prospects will lower the pipeline quality and negatively impact pipeline conversion metrics and MROI. If a good job is done applying the qualification criteria, expect that 20-40% of these opportunities will eventually turn into customers. If, after tracking actual pipeline metrics, there is not a 20-40% close rate from qualified customers, tighten up the opportunity qualification criteria.

Once a customer is qualified as an opportunity, they move into the lead follow-up and engagement. This is the stage where core selling activities will occur. Once you have fully engaged a prospect at this stage, 50-90% close rates are the norm.

The pipeline approach can be applied no matter what the business. The main element that will vary between businesses is how the various pipeline stages are defined. For example, in the retail world you might define impressions as those created via the Sunday newspaper circular inserts, unqualified responses as those that come into the store based on those impressions, qualified responses as those that visit or call the store and have talked to a floor salesperson, and lead follow-up and engagement as the delivery of in-store sales activities, pitches, and any up-sell/cross-sell that occurs. In the Microsoft world, one might define impressions as website exposures to web-based advertising, unqualified responses as those that actually click on the ad and visit the website, and qualified responses as those visiting the website that accept an offer (e.g., order a kit from the website), with these leads then pursued via a telemarketing phone call, sales visit, or partner visit.

As the pipeline process is executed, a key concept to keep in mind is "pipeline velocity." This is the rate at which prospects move through the pipeline stages. If you have many customers at the 10% stage, and they stay at that stage for months, then prospects are not moving efficiently through the pipeline—something is wrong, and the pipeline is stuck. The same issue can occur in later pipeline stages. For example, it may have been a great success to move many customers to the 50-90% sales probability level, but these customers just aren't converting to final sales. Is the problem pricing? Is it the partner or sales force skill set? Is it the contract transaction terms? Watching for and solving these pipeline roadblocks is crucial to effectively moving customers through the process and generating revenue.

MANAGING AND IMPLEMENTING THE PIPELINE PROCESS

Conceptually moving a customer through the various pipeline stages is straightforward. In reality the implementation details become a bit more complicated. Figure 9-8 reviews these details and provides a model that can be used to implement a pipeline process.

There are three typical response mechanisms for customer prospects to respond to a marketing touch: visit a website, respond by phone, or mail a physical response. Responding prospects are the "unqualified leads" or MQPs that start the pipeline process, becoming the targets to develop into "qualified" prospects or opportunities. Qualification involves the prospects providing information to your firm about themselves. The most important information to get is customer contact information (name, phone number, email address, and mailing address). Without this it is impossible to take a prospect through the pipeline process.

Customers will generally provide this level of information, especially when it is a prerequisite to receiving an offer they feel has value. Providing contact information in exchange for the offer is a value trade-off; it requires that the offer itself is valuable enough for customers to "pay" for it by providing their contact information.

FIGURE 9-8: Lead Creation and Processing Infrastructure

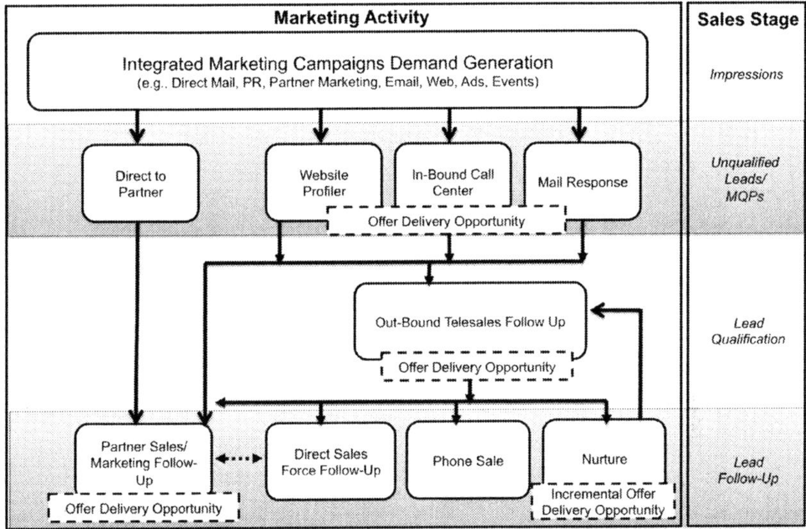

The mechanisms for gathering customer contact information depend on the response mechanism. If the contact capture point is on a website, you create a customer profile page or form for the prospect to fill out for offer fulfillment. If a telephone call to your business is the response mechanism, set up the in-bound call center to capture the contact information. For postal mail backs, the collateral the customer mails back should contain this information. In each case, the contact information should be entered into a customer lead and sales transaction database. This database is a crucial element to managing prospects through the pipeline process, and forms the basis of implementing the marketing activities using the customer relationship life cycle model.

Once the customer contact information is captured and the offer is fulfilled, there is now a chance to further qualify these MQPs and turn them into opportunities. At Microsoft, lead qualification is usually via an out-bound telemarketing group. Customer contact information from campaign respondents is pulled from the prospect database and fed into the telesales group for follow-up phone calls.

A telesales follow-up is a good way to re-touch a prospect, as it is a personal touch and allows direct customer engagement. A telesales call can help overcome the perception that a company is distant, unreachable, or impersonal. The follow-up phone call can also be the mechanism by which the offer is delivered: if customers want that great free information kit being offered, they supply their contact information and the telesales representative (a "telerep") calls to validate it, initiating the offer delivery process and providing an opportunity for further qualification. Telesales qualification is an efficient method to scale and handle a large number of leads.

The key focus of the telesales call is to further qualify the prospect. To hold informed conversations with customers the telereps must be adequately trained to understand the details of the campaign and offer, the product features/benefits and key value propositions, typical customer product usage scenarios, and customer hot buttons; they also need a list of the key lead qualification questions. The answers are then used to qualify the prospect.

There are three outcomes from the follow-up telesales call process: prospects are qualified and become opportunities, they are unqualified, and/or they are "nurture" candidates. Qualified customers meet the filtering criteria and lead qualification questions as defined and become opportunities. They can be sent directly to a partner or company sales representative for follow-up, or the telerep could close the sale on the call. A lead tracking system should be put into place to enable reporting and tracking of leads and opportunities, their close rates, and the resulting sales revenue.

Unqualified customers should be identified by the lead qualification screening questions. Perhaps the respondents simply enjoy receiving free offers, did not realize the product or solution does not match their needs, or do not fit the targeted market segment profile. Effective demand generation activities, tightly targeted, with effective and on-point messaging will help lower the percentage of unqualified customers.

It is also possible that campaign respondents may be just the right type of prospect and could almost be considered a qualified lead, but they are just not quite there. Perhaps they require more product information, or are waiting for budget, or they aren't ready to move forward though they meet all qualification criteria. These prospects become nurture prospects. Dropping these nearly qualified customers and treating them like unqualified prospects is the wrong move. These folks take a bit more care and feeding to eventually move up to a qualified lead status. For that a programmatic nurture process should be put into place that regularly reconnects, retouches, and reengages with these prospects and provides the opportunity to deliver incremental offers and value-add. For example, the nurture process could include a follow-on phone call a few months later to see if their situation has changed. A nurture process might also send the prospect new product information on a regular basis to keep your product and company top of mind. Perhaps your firm is hosting a seminar in their geographic area, and an invitation might help move them along to a qualified status.

As the pipeline process proceeds, and assuming demand generation has been on target, the nurture candidates will likely become a relatively large percentage of the pipeline. Over time, the conversion rate to a sale from these prospects may actually be higher than conversion rates from other qualified leads.

Implementing a telesales lead qualification process can be highly effective but expensive on a large scale. The costs must be weighed relative to the return. It may be more cost-effective in some cases to outsource a telesales process instead of hiring in-house staff. Generally, higher-priced products will provide a more positive MROI because the response and conversion rates won't need to be as high to generate net positive results.

If the cost of telesales qualification is too high, another option is to simply send the unqualified leads (MQPs) directly to partners, which is simpler. Many leads can be generated for partners in this way. A direct pass-through of the lead also allows partners an opportunity to deliver the campaign offer themselves, reinforcing the close partner relationship to the customer. However, pursuing this path means the level of lead qualification will be unknown, since it will not have been rigorously screened and filtered up front (web profiling does not count as rigorous and accurate profiling). If the leads passed on are no good, the partners will eventually feel they are wasting their time and will stop following up on them.

As a final alternative, the MQPs could be sent directly to the direct sales force for further qualification or follow-up. This has the same pitfalls as sending unqualified leads directly to partners, except the time you're wasting also directly hits your company's bottom line and can negatively affect sales force productivity. Most sales compensation schemes involve quotas and bonuses for exceeding quotas, and spending time pursuing unqualified leads is unproductive.

MAXIMIZING THE MROI OF PIPELINE AND DEMAND GENERATION ACTIVITIES

Driving good business results through connected marketing is a lot like driving a race car—to get the maximum performance and driving experience all the parts need to work together seamlessly. At the heart of the car is the engine, enabled by the fuel flow. The more fuel flowing into the car's engine, the faster it will go. By analogy, a pipeline process is the engine that drives business success, with the fuel being the MQPs. The more efficient and effective the process to generate MQP fuel for the pipeline engine, the higher the MROI will be.

Driving MROI higher depends on some key measures that impact overall pipeline efficacy. Taking a slightly different perspective of the pipeline process, Figure 9-9 provides an example with additional pipeline process detail and some key metrics that must be tracked, monitored, and tweaked as sales and marketing activities occur.

Any marketing campaign comes with a budget allocation. The budget should reflect the actual costs expected for a particular campaign. In the example, $1,000,000 is allocated for the illustrative campaign. It will be spent on demand generation activities: PR, direct marketing through direct mail/email/web, advertising, and events. This generates impressions, from which come the initial customer responses to the campaign (MQPs).

In Figure 9-9, 500,000 impressions are created by the $1,000,000 marketing campaign, so the cost per impression is $2 ($1,000,000 spend/500,000 impressions). Whether this is a good number depends on the type of out-bound marketing activities that generated the responses. A lower cost per impression should be expected for online marketing activities and PR, and a higher cost from direct mail, events, and other higher-cost demand generation activities. The cost and quality of the impression are equally important. A $2 web-ad cost per impression may seem cheap compared to a $10 direct mail piece cost per impression. However, having a large number of $2 impressions that fail to convert to sales vs. a smaller number of higher-quality $10 impressions that do convert at a high rate might make the higher cost per impression worth it.

As impressions are created by the out-bound marketing activities, the hope is that responses will emerge from targeted customers. These responses are referred to as initial responses. Assume the call-to-action from the out-bound demand generation activities focuses on driving people to a website to receive a special offer, and 25,000 initial responses are generated. That is, from the 500,000 impressions created, 25,000 prospects responded and visited the website, which is a 5% initial response rate (25,000 initial responses/500,000 impressions) and a cost per initial response of $40 ($1,000,000 spend/25,000 initial responses).

So far so good—the campaign has captured the direct interest of 25,000 prospects. These customers have taken an action to further investigate what

FIGURE 9-9: Driving MROI Through Pipeline Metric Tracking and Management

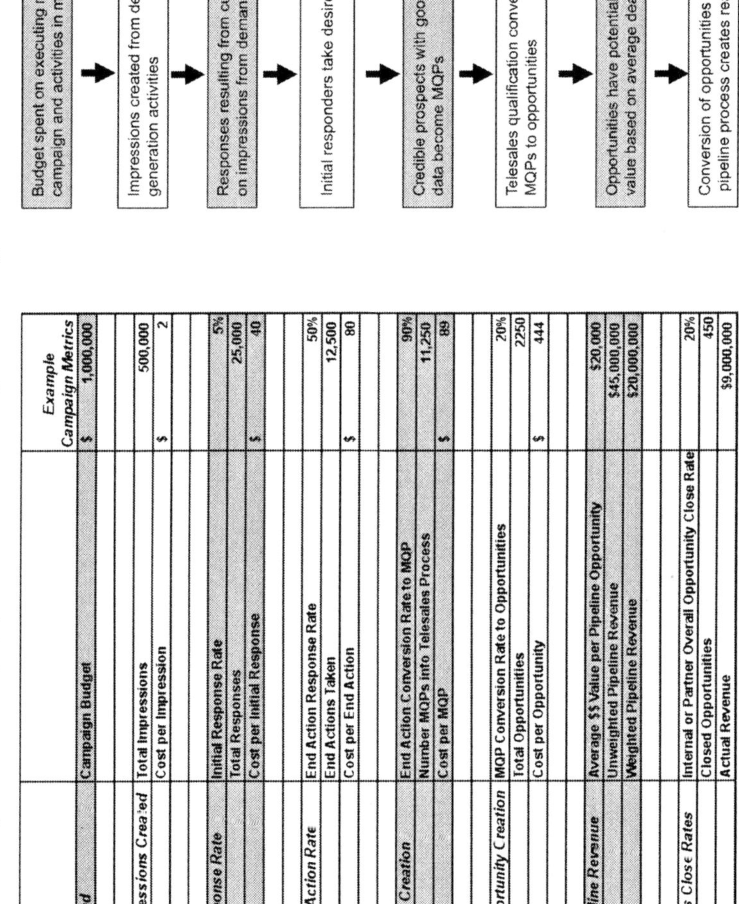

Driving MROI through pipeline metric tracking and management…

		Example Campaign Metrics
Spend	Campaign Budget	$ 1,000,000
Impressions Created	Total Impressions	500,000
	Cost per Impression	$ 2
Response Rate	Initial Response Rate	5%
	Total Responses	25,000
	Cost per Initial Response	$ 40
End Action Rate	End Action Response Rate	50%
	End Actions Taken	12,500
	Cost per End Action	$ 80
MQP Creation	End Action Conversion Rate to MQP	90%
	Number MQPs into Telesales Process	11,250
	Cost per MQP	$ 89
Opportunity Creation	MQP Conversion Rate to Opportunities	20%
	Total Opportunities	2250
	Cost per Opportunity	$ 444
Pipeline Revenue	Average $$ Value per Pipeline Opportunity	$20,000
	Unweighted Pipeline Revenue	$45,000,000
	Weighted Pipeline Revenue	$20,000,000
Sales Close Rates	Internal or Partner Overall Opportunity Close Rate	20%
	Closed Opportunities	450
	Actual Revenue	$9,000,000

A 9:1 MROI generated in this example

is being offered. Now the task is getting them to take the key step of actually doing what you want them to do—provide their contact information to receive the special offer. Initial responders that actually take action on the website to receive the offer are considered to have taken the desired "end action." Not every initial responder hitting the website in response to the demand generation will actually complete the end action. Those that do become the MQPs needed to feed and fuel the pipeline engine. In the example, 50% of the initial responders decided to take up the compelling offer (12,500 end actions taken/25,000 initial responses). This translates to an $80 cost per end action.

Not all customer prospects that take the end action will move on to further stages of the pipeline. For example, sometimes goofballs will provide nonsensical contact information on the web form, the email address or mailing address will be invalid, or the required telephone number won't be provided. Some drop-off should be expected. Our fictional example campaign assumes that 90% of those that take an end action will be valid, so these become MQPs that can be fed into the pipeline engine. This drop-off increases the cost per MQP to $89, but provides 11,250 MQPs to feed into the pipeline engine.

At this point it's in the hands of the telereps to move the MQPs further through the pipeline process, placing the out-bound phone calls to qualify the customers. At Microsoft, a customer that passes the qualification process is considered to be at the 20% stage of the pipeline process, where an MQP is converted into an opportunity. The Figure 9-9 example assumes 20% of the MQPs get converted into opportunities, providing 2250 opportunities generated from the budgeted campaign spend. This translates to a cost per opportunity of $444 ($1,000,000 spend/2250 opportunities).

During the lead qualification process, the potential value of the prospective customer is generally assessed, with an estimate on how much money a sale might generate. This revenue estimate is considered "un-weighted" for calculating pipeline revenue, because it assumes there is a 100% probability that that sale will occur, and is not "weighted" by the real probabilities based on the pipeline stages.

To get a true picture of the real potential pipeline revenue, a weighted approach is necessary. To illustrate, assume there is a three-stage pipeline with stage sale probabilities of 25%, 50%, and 75%. If there are 100 prospects at the 25% stage, 50 prospects at the 50% stage, and 10 prospects at the 75% stage, the formula for weighted pipeline revenue (WPR), which includes average revenue per sale (ARS), is:

WPR = 100*.25*ARS + 50*.50*ARS + 10*.75*ARS

In the Figure 9-9 example, you'll note that unweighted revenue is much higher than weighted revenue, which is expected, since unweighted revenue is reduced by the pipeline stage sale probabilities. Use weighted pipeline revenue numbers to track the size and growth of the pipeline potential and to forecast revenue.

After the MQP is converted into an opportunity, it can then be handed off to partners participating with your company in the campaign or to the direct sales force. In either case, it is now up to those folks to continue moving the opportunities through the pipeline via the various sales activities and tactics being executed. Finally, at the end of the process, opportunities have been converted into actual sales. The sales closure rate will have a significant impact on actual revenue from the campaign. In the example campaign, 450 sales were actually closed from the opportunities generated. This implies a 20% sales closure rate against opportunities (450 closed deals/2250 opportunities), generating $9,000,000 total in actual revenue for the campaign.

With a $1,000,000 marketing investment generating $9,000,000 in revenue, the campaign has achieved a 9:1, or 9X, MROI. This is in line with the 8-12 MROI range previously referenced, so it was a good campaign and should be a candidate for replication and scaling up with larger marketing investments.

This particular example campaign was successful, but that's not always the case. As a campaign executes, and the results start coming in, monitoring the various cost and response rate metrics indicated in Figure 9-9 will help ensure campaign success. If the campaign metrics seem headed in the wrong direction, there may be opportunities to take corrective action even as the campaign executes.

Driving Marketing Costs Down to Increase MROI

A good marketer will focus on increasing marketing efficiency over time, learning what does and does not work. A good way to learn with minimal risk is to use pilot programs to test marketing ideas. Piloting campaigns to try new approaches should be ingrained into the standard marketing modus operandi at any company; Microsoft does this. Pilot campaigns can change offers, messages, targeted segments, and execution tactics and provide a venue to try new things. You should implement them with minimal investments to learn which campaigns work. When one is discovered that

FIGURE 9-10: Increasing MROI

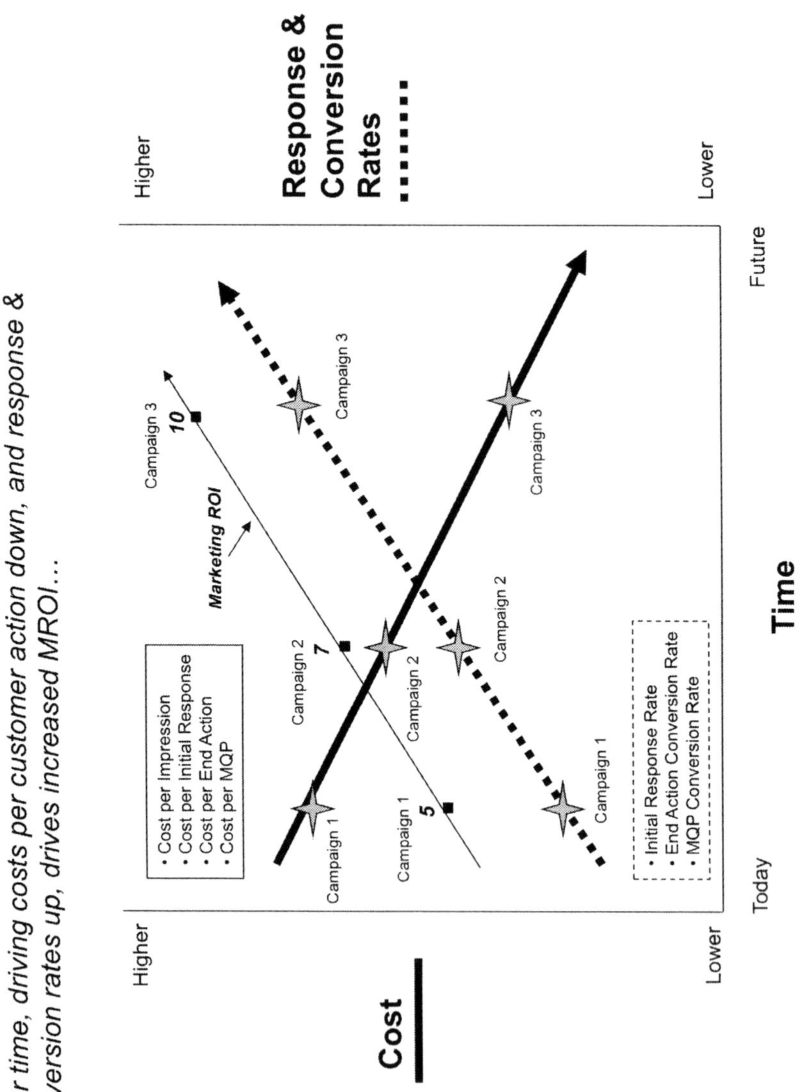

is successful and delivers the desired MROI, it creates an opportunity to replicate the campaign investment, scaling it up to drive more significant levels of revenue.

The process of becoming a more efficient marketing machine also mandates that, as various campaigns and pilots run, you must closely track results to make changes to increase efficacy and MROI. To increase MROI, you must become more efficient at driving down the various marketing cost drivers and increase response and conversion rates throughout the pipeline process. Figure 9-10 visually illustrates this—MROI will increase as the costs per impression, cost per end action, and cost per MQP decrease, while initial response rates, end action conversion rates, and MQP conversion rates increase. In this example, for each successive campaign, fine-tuning based on previous campaign learning improved marketing efforts from Campaign 1 to Campaign 3. Costs went down and response and conversion rates went up for each of the key metrics in the successive campaigns, doubling the campaign MROI from 5 to 10.

If the MROI results sought are not occurring, and the cost and conversion curves for campaign results don't look like the Figure 9-10 curves, look for several problems. First double-check that proper reporting is occurring across the entire marketing pipeline. If the campaign result data is incorrect, the campaign metrics being calculated will be inaccurate. Beyond checking reporting accuracy and resolving any issues that may appear, Figure 9-11 outlines some of the more common issues that can drive marketing costs up and lower MROI.

For each major cost driver category, a number of possible symptoms and causes are listed that, if present, will tend to drive marketing efficiency and MROI down, delivering less than optimal campaign results. The main causes of inefficient marketing generally are not getting the expected number of impressions, getting low response rates to customer contact vehicles, generating low customer uptake for desired end actions, and poor conversion of leads to opportunities and sales. The potential causes for each of these issues are listed in Figure 9-11. For example, a low response rate can occur if the customer offer is weak or it is the wrong offer for customers in a particular life cycle phase. If the telesales team is not converting leads to opportunities, the quality of the leads may be poor, or the telereps are inadequately trained and skilled to effectively move a customer to the next level in the pipeline. Whatever the case, it is important to ensure that campaign results and metrics are adequately captured, tracked, and monitored so negative indicators can be flagged and evaluated.

FIGURE 9-11: Drivers of Increased Marketing Costs and Decreased MROI

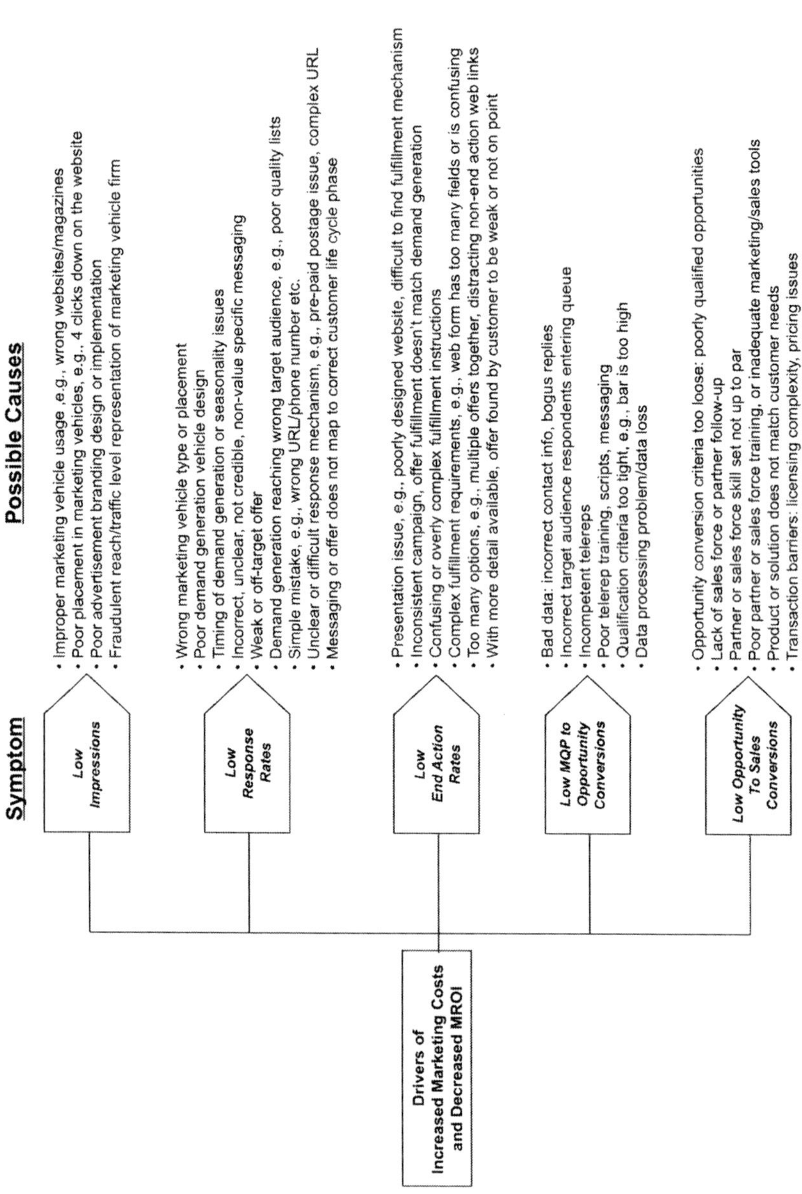

MANAGING THE BUSINESS: STAYING ON TOP OF THINGS POST-LAUNCH

In the post-launch marketing execution environment, campaigns are launched, tracked, and optimized. Don't take your eyes off the big picture. It is easy to acquire tunnel vision, getting deep into the MROI evaluations, executing and managing specific campaigns, and analyzing sales data. However, remember the overall business plan and rollout strategy. Given all the marketing and sales activities that happen post-launch, what is the progress against the rollout plan and goals? It's great if things are going well, revenue goals are being met, campaigns are achieving stellar MROI, and the product market share in the product category is growing. However, problems may develop, especially if no one is looking. Figure 9-12 indicates some potential post-launch problems and their possible causes. Once the product is in market, revenue or profitability, product or execution, or unit volume issues could occur.

FIGURE 9-12: Market Share vs. MROI

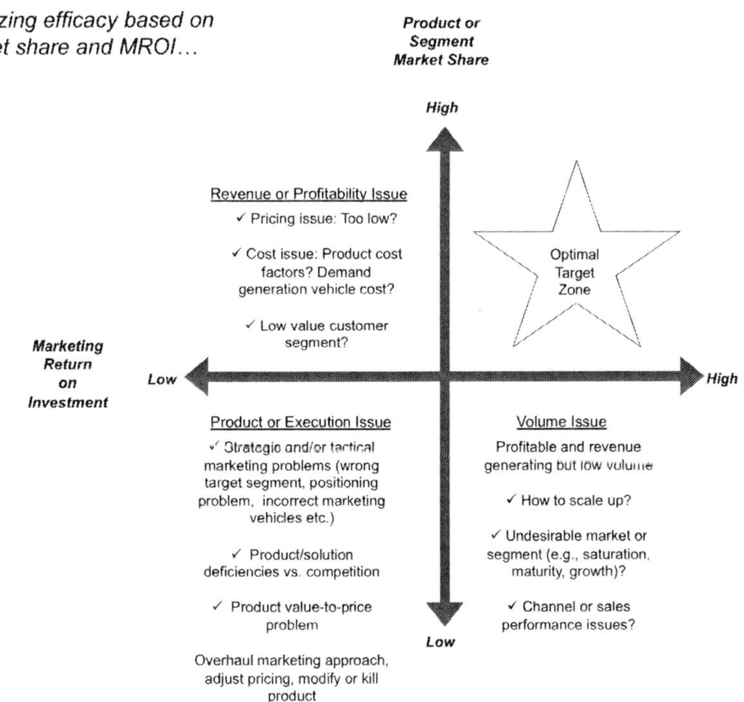

Revenue or Profitability Issue: Achieving high MROI and high market share is optimal. However, if MROI is low but market share looks good and many units are being sold it could indicate a low revenue acquisition or insufficient profitability situation for the business. Is there a potential pricing problem? Is the product price too low, average deal revenue too small, or transactions overly discounted? Are product factor costs driving down sale profitability, resulting in low profitability and decreased MROI? Perhaps the customer segment being targeted is comprised of low value customers, the expected demand in the segment is just not there, or the segment customers are overly price sensitive.

Product or Execution Issue: If MROI and market share are both low possible culprits are: a product or execution issue caused by ineffective marketing; the product is not competitive on a feature basis; or the perceived product value-to-price ratio is low. If the problem stems from the product itself, there is not a lot that marketing can do to fix the situation except to insist on a modified or new product. Poor marketing execution can be fixed, but the right analysis must be performed to determine the issues and correct them.

Volume Issue: A high MROI but low market share situation could imply a volume issue or a marketing or sales strategy inadequately designed and executed to enable scaling up to sell enough unit volume to take share. Low marketing efficiency, an undesirable customer segment, or even channel and partner performance could also be the underlying causes.

Several post-launch analysis activities can help minimize the development of these potential problems and help drive the business forward, including:

- Assessing customer revenue and profitability scenarios
- Assessing channel efficacy
- Dynamically managing and growing more effective partners
- Actively promoting customer loyalty and satisfaction

Evaluating Customers to Drive Revenue and Profitability

As sales come in it can be illuminating to develop a sense of the customer installed base makeup and segment contributions to the business. Figure 9-13 indicates one form of analysis that is useful in understanding which customers or segments are generating revenue and profit. In this example, there are low-value and high-value customers. The low-value customers, making up 50% of the customer installed base by number, are generating only 20% of the product revenue and 10% of the profits.

Half the customer base is generating only 10% of the profits! Why would a business want customers who deliver little or no value to the business? Why are they becoming customers in the first place? Are the wrong segments being targeted, is the messaging incorrect, or are certain channels or partners responsible? Low-value customers will drag down your MROI and waste marketing dollars.

What a business really needs are more high-value customers. In the example, high-value customers make up only 10% of the customer base by number but are generating 60% of the product revenue and 40% of the profits. How are these customers being acquired? What are their characteristics? How can the business get more of them?

This type of analysis can identify the truly desirable customer types and help direct changes in the strategy and marketing/sales efforts to acquire more high-value customers, minimizing the potential for revenue or profitability problems.

FIGURE 9-13: Analyzing Customer Installed Base Contributions

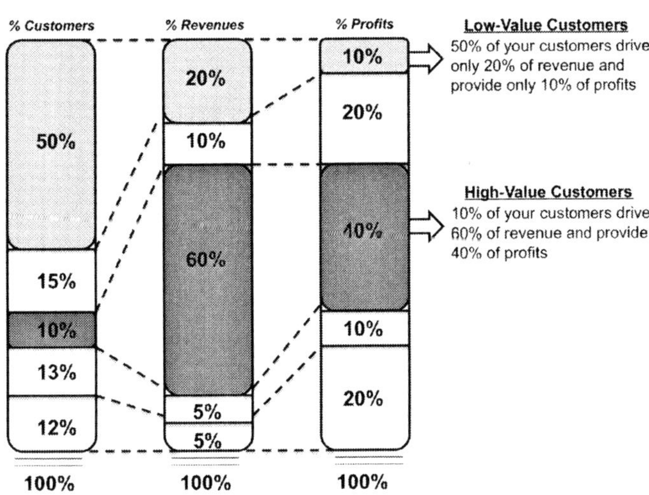

Evaluating Channels to Drive Reach

To acquire high-value customers it is important to go deep to understand existing customer makeup. It is also important to evaluate distribution and reseller channels to understand channel efficacy, inform the go-forward strategy and marketing activities to avoid or correct potential unit volume problems, and take advantage of new opportunities.

Choosing the right channels and driving sales through them is an important go-to-market lever that can help achieve unit volume goals. Channel MROI can be a key component of overall MROI. Investing in the right channels and getting the optimum return are important. You must regularly analyze this to ensure it.

Figure 9-14 is an example of an analysis applied to distribution channels. There are four major distribution categories through which the product flows: retail, OEM, resellers, and distributors. Data is analyzed by customer segment showing the channel reach, or share, channel growth rate, and percentage of product channel sales. Putting such information side-by-side may produce interesting insights. For example, a large part of the product sales (50%) is being generated by the retail channel, which has a 40% penetration in the Enterprise IT Professional customer segment, but is also the slowest growth channel. Thus there seems to be a significant overreliance on a slow-growth channel which could limit future revenue growth. (This is an example and clearly not real: retail is *not* generally a good channel to reach IT Professionals in large companies.) This company may also be missing an opportunity within the distributor channel which is accruing a 50% growth rate into the target customer segment. This channel's high growth rate could indicate an opportunity to shift channel marketing dollars to distributors to drive up MROI.

In the second customer segment—mid-market business decision makers—the retail channel again stands out. It has a huge reach into the customer segment, and is on par with other channels for growth, but only 10% of product revenue comes from the retail channel. This may indicate that investment in this channel for that customer segment is not high enough, given the large implied under-penetration based on the percent of market sales. Distributors in this case may also be problematic, since that channel has only a 10% reach into the target customer segment, but constitutes 30% of product sales. Perhaps the distribution channel is highly efficient in selling your product. However, given its low penetration in the target customer segment, any upside may be limited and become a business risk if product sales are too dependent on a channel with such limited reach.

FIGURE 9-14: Analyzing Channel Contributions

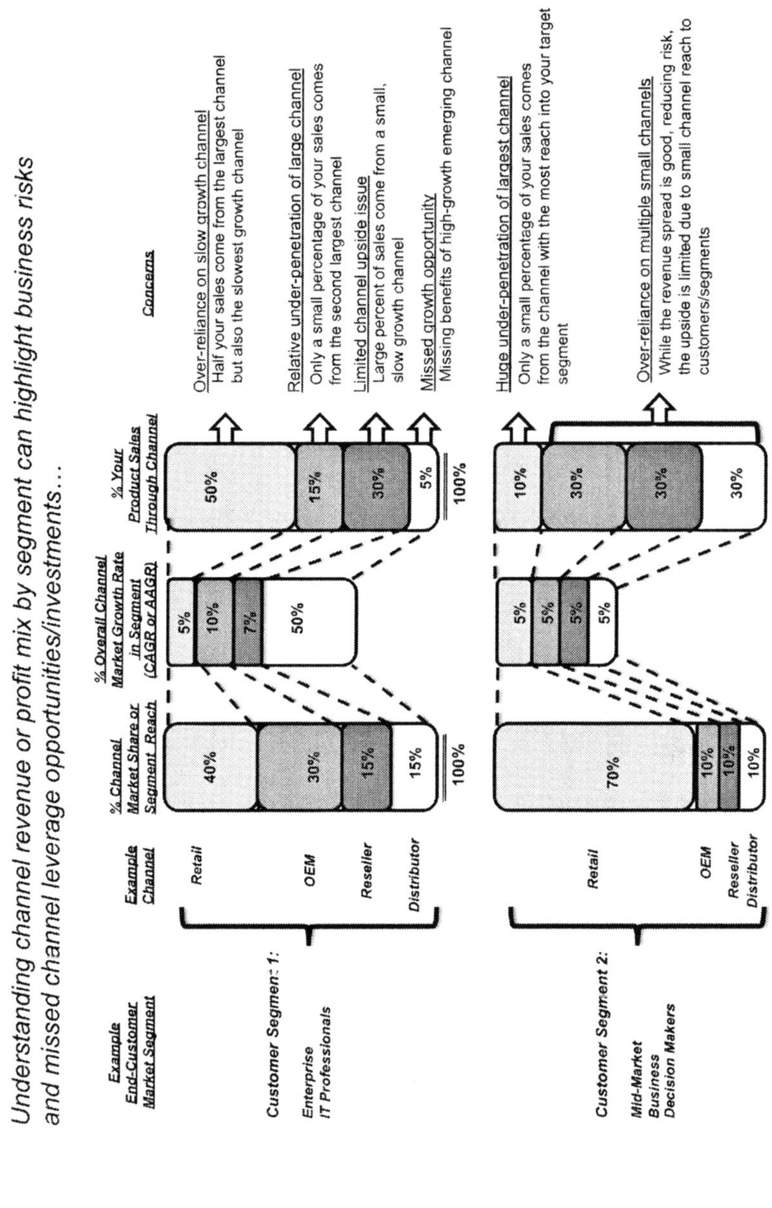

Understanding channel revenue or profit mix by segment can highlight business risks and missed channel leverage opportunities/investments…

Example End-Customer Market Segment	Example Channel	% Channel Market Share or Segment Reach	% Overall Channel Market Growth Rate in Segment (CAGR or AAGR)	% Your Product Sales Through Channel
Customer Segment 1: Enterprise IT Professionals	Retail	40%	5%	50%
	OEM	30%	10%	15%
	Reseller	15%	7%	30%
	Distributor	15%	50%	5%
		100%		100%
Customer Segment 2: Mid-Market Business Decision Makers	Retail	70%	5%	10%
	OEM	10%	5%	30%
	Reseller	10%	5%	30%
	Distributor	10%	5%	30%
		100%		100%

Concerns

Segment 1:

Over-reliance on slow growth channel
Half your sales come from the largest channel but also the slowest growth channel

Relative under-penetration of large channel
Only a small percentage of your sales comes from the second largest channel

Limited channel upside issue
Large percent of sales come from a small, slow growth channel

Missed growth opportunity
Missing benefits of high-growth emerging channel

Segment 2:

Huge under-penetration of largest channel
Only a small percentage of your sales comes from the channel with the most reach into your target segment

Over-reliance on multiple small channels
While the revenue spread is good, reducing risk, the upside is limited due to small channel reach to customers/segments

Dynamically Managing and Sustaining Partner Engagement

Staying on top of the business post-launch also requires effectively managing partner engagements. You need a solid understanding of partner strengths, weaknesses, and business desires to understand how best to activate partners and aid their sales and marketing effectiveness. For example, in the high-tech world, many partner firms were founded by folks that are highly technically skilled. They understand the technological aspects of the product, sometimes as well as your firm's own engineering staff. However, these partners may not be strong marketers. There is a good chance they grew their business by one-on-one selling, not through marketing. In retail, partners may have an excellent grasp on moving inventory and keeping product flowing and maximizing sales by understanding customer traffic patterns. However, the floor salespeople may lack experience or knowledge about the products and have difficulty expressing key product value propositions and benefits to customers.

In the sustaining marketing phase, when making investment decisions and trade-offs for money and resource investments for getting partners to market and sell, you might consider framing such decisions along the lines of Figure 9-15. It classifies partners around their inclination to grow relative to their level of active involvement with your product or business. Analyzing the partner base and categorizing the partners this way will identify the partners most appropriate for sustaining investment. There is never an infinite budget, so clearly identifying the partners that will generate the largest bang for the channel buck is important to maximize MROI. Generally, the most active partners will be prime candidates for higher investment levels. While defining an active partner is subjective, it might include the criteria that they:

- Consistently generate increasing sales revenue around the product and maintain a solid *partner-initiated* customer prospect pipeline.
- Sell a significant variety of your firm's product SKUs.
- Generate a significant and growing percentage of their overall revenue from your firm's product lines.
- Use the partner website, collateral, and training materials provided in the channel partner BOM.
- Regularly provide product, competitive, and market feedback.
- Regularly participate in partner events.
- Bring customers for case studies and testimonials.

FIGURE 9-15: Partner Growth Inclination and Engagement Level

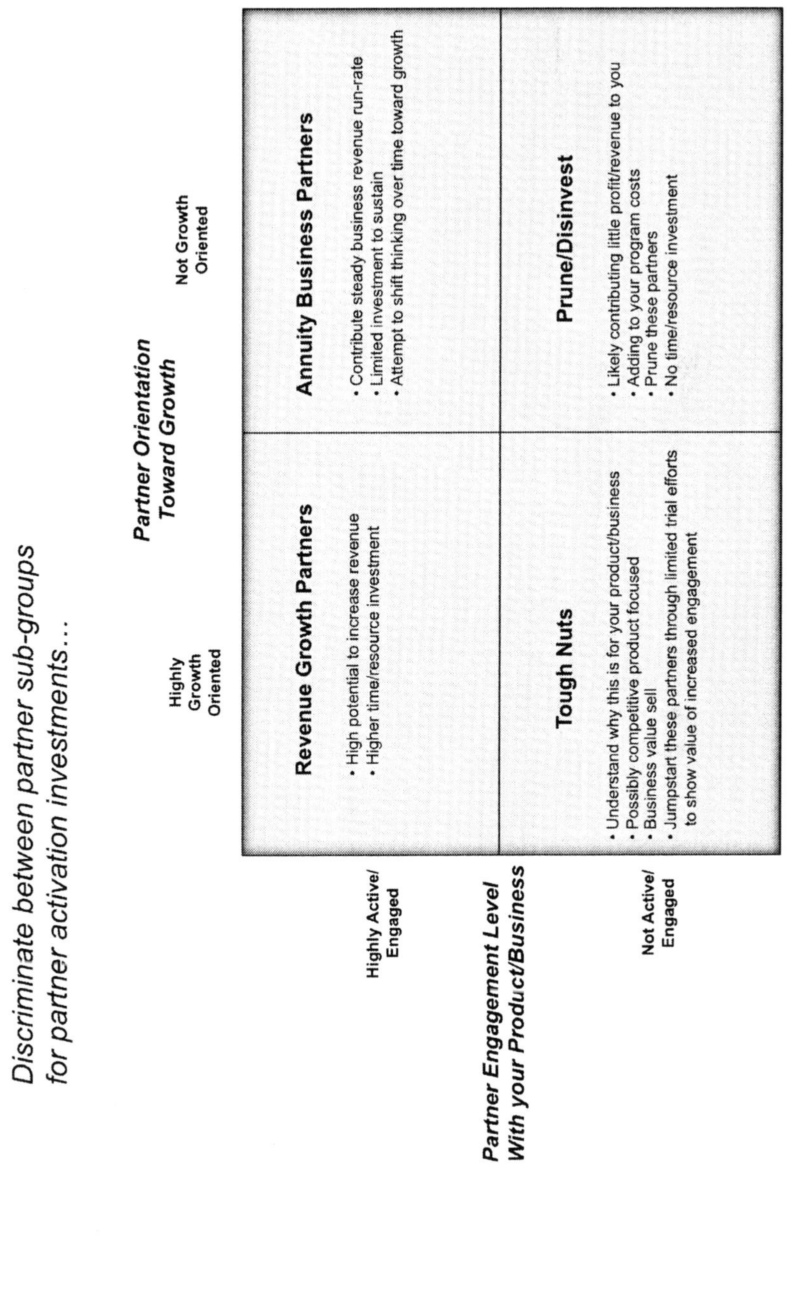

Discriminate between partner sub-groups for partner activation investments…

		Partner Orientation Toward Growth	
		Highly Growth Oriented	**Not Growth Oriented**
Partner Engagement Level With your Product/Business	**Highly Active/ Engaged**	**Revenue Growth Partners** • High potential to increase revenue • Higher time/resource investment	**Annuity Business Partners** • Contribute steady business revenue run-rate • Limited investment to sustain • Attempt to shift thinking over time toward growth
	Not Active/ Engaged	**Tough Nuts** • Understand why this is for your product/business • Possibly competitive product focused • Business value sell • Jumpstart these partners through limited trial efforts to show value of increased engagement	**Prune/Disinvest** • Likely contributing little profit/revenue to you • Adding to your program costs • Prune these partners • No time/resource investment

There will also be active partners that are happy with the size of the business they have with the product and do not wish to further grow revenue. Mom and Pop resellers fit this mold—they choose a work/life balance or lifestyle choice over growing their businesses. Others are hungry to grow. The best partners are those that are highly actively engaged with the product and want to grow their business revenue.

Assuming a reasonable level of competency, these "Revenue Growth Partners" are those where investment is most appropriate and that offer the most upside for generating increasing product revenue. These are the likely candidates for the largest monetary channel investment.

The "Annuity Partners" are the actively engaged but non-growth oriented partners who will supply you with a steady but non-growing revenue stream. A moderate sustaining investment in these partners is required to keep them active.

The toughest set of partners to handle is the "Tough Nuts," those who are growth oriented but not actively engaged with selling and marketing your product. These partners must have once had some level of interest in your product or company or they would not have joined the partner program. You must determine why they are not active and, if possible, re-engage them with limited co-marketing activities. This will remind them of how beneficial the relationship with your company can be and perhaps reactivate them.

The worst partners are those that are neither actively engaged nor have any wish to grow their business. They add cost and overhead to the partner program and offer nothing in return. They should be identified and removed from the program or receive no significant dollar or resource investment.

Once you know which partners to focus time and money on, you must put a process into place to manage and grow them and their businesses, which also grows the business around your product. Figure 9-16 illustrates one way to view such a process.

Partner recruitment must continue on an ongoing basis. The partners recruited pre-launch got your firm to and through the launch, but recruiting should not stop post-launch. There is always an opportunity to find great partners that can help drive the business forward. Continue the to-partner recruitment marketing activities to build up the breadth partner program and grow the number of partners. This is important to grow the business and mitigates against partner loss because of natural attrition and churn, or pruning/disinvestment. To attract these new partners, and to maintain the existing good partners, you should make sustaining investments into the breadth partner program to continually provide new program benefits, leads, marketing and sales collateral, and sales tools.

The breadth partners in the partner program are the focus of the active engagement/growth classification analysis. Once the "revenue growth partners" have been identified as growth prospects, you need a process to actively manage and invest in these partners to help build their businesses. This could mean assigning a partner account manager headcount to each partner to help execute sales and marketing activities, build a business plan, provide increased lead opportunities, and provide more training to increase skill sets and competencies.

The ultimate goal is to continually refine the list of growth partners to find the real gems—the partners that could become strategic market-making partners. The process of finding and growing these high-potential partners takes place in parallel to ongoing business development activities (Chapter 2), where your firm is continually seeking additional strategic market-making partners.

FIGURE 9-16: Managing Sustaining Partner Engagements

Continue to recruit new partners into the partner program and invest in those with significant growth potential, while continuing to develop new strategic partner accounts...

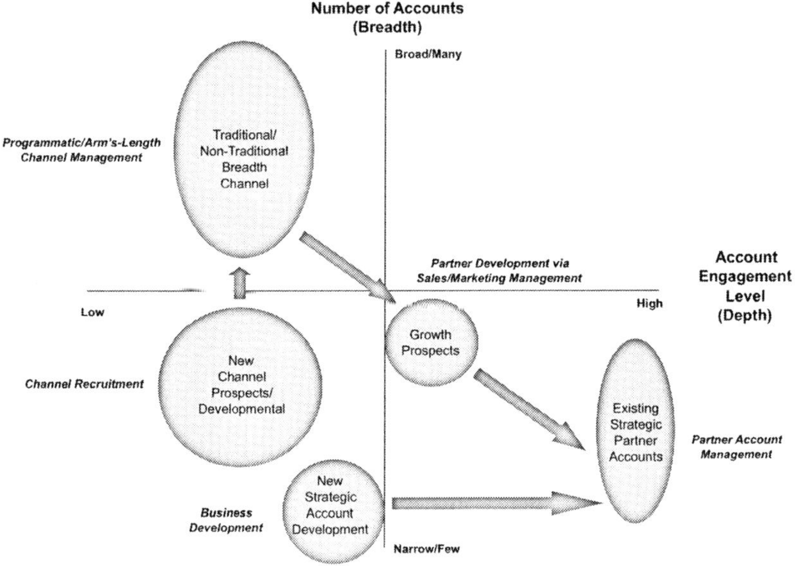

Post-Launch Relationship and Loyalty Marketing

Recall again the pipeline process: after a prospect becomes an opportunity, and the opportunity is converted into a sale, the prospect becomes an actual customer. At this point, a new phase of the customer life cycle begins as relationship management. There is tremendous opportunity to derive long-term economic value from the existing customer base. Developing an ongoing relationship program with customers to drive post-purchase satisfaction, loyalty, and follow-on sales is good way to maximize your customers' long-term economic value to your firm.

The underlying premise is that a close, positive, and ongoing relationship will make them happier customers who are more satisfied, less likely to switch, and will provide a communication channel between company and customer to enable follow-on, up-sell, and cross-sell sales. Thus, there is likely a direct link between effectively managing customer relationships and future revenue. A strong relationship and loyalty program can create a competitive advantage for your company.

Some businesses or situations naturally lend themselves to tight-knit customer relationships. Small businesses are generally closer to their customers and more prone to have direct relationships and fewer customers overall. Service businesses like consulting, legal, and medical are also more tightly bonded to their customers. In a large business like Microsoft, there are business pockets that tend to have a strong, direct customer relationship. One such pocket is found in the business-to-business space, where companies maintaining a direct sales force sell to other medium and large businesses. This relationship pivots around the interaction between a long-term salesperson or account manager and the decision makers in the customer business. The customer's perception of its supplier's business and customer satisfaction levels is largely driven by the personal relationship between the salesperson and the customer.

However, these engagements are not typical business-to-customer interactions. If a business has hundreds, thousands, tens of thousands, or millions of customers, how can it create and maintain a strongly bonded relationship with its customers? What about businesses that sell through partner channels like retailers or distributors, and so are several steps removed from the end-customer? How can they build a relationship with the end-customer to drive loyalty? Although many businesses sell through partners and view them as their customers, it is the end-customers who make the final purchase decision and who will or will not remain loyal to a product or brand. Thus, it is the end-customers who are the target for a relationship and loyalty program.

Microsoft has put a number of end-customer relationship programs into place over the years, and most of them have been reasonably successful. The common elements that worked well across all of them are candidates for replication in your program. These commonalities are:

- The Internet is a key program interaction mechanism that allows the program to reach end-customers and to scale up; however, offline interaction mechanisms should also be in place.
- Regular and targeted two-way communications are in place and enabled.
- Customer profile information is captured and maintained; the customers are known, not anonymous, and activities to move customers from anonymous to known are in effect. New customer profile information is actively sought and added, and customer privacy is maintained. The information is actually used and acted upon to create incremental economic value, allowing personalization and targeted cross-sell/up-sell opportunities.
- Added-value program enhancements and offers for the customer are continually created and evolved as incentives to engage and remain engaged.
- The program becomes a central point of interaction between the customer and the company, and the program value propositions and benefits are designed to meet the ongoing and evolving needs and pain points of the customer.
- The program value and benefits are only available to those who opt in and join the program—program added-value is exclusive and unavailable to non-members to avoid diluting the program's value.
- A mechanism exists for the company to actively incorporate and respond to customer feedback, if that is promised.
- Customer satisfaction levels grow over time, and these eventually become the company's most satisfied customers.

To implement a successful relationship program you need to build a structured program comprised of some basic building blocks, including:

- The program website, where value is delivered and consumed
- Business development activities, where incentives are created
- Customer acquisition activities, to attract customers
- Sustaining relationship management activities to maintain and engage customers and to derive economic value from them

Figure 9-17 visually highlights these main building blocks and presents key activities for each.

The program hub is the website. To efficiently and cost-effectively scale a program to thousands of customers, you need a web-based interaction and delivery platform. The website itself is the repository for exclusive content for the relationship program members. It could include informative training content, video, access to special webcasts, offers, or other creative, exclusive member content. The program website is one element of a relationship program that should enable cross-sell/up-sell opportunities that can drive incremental economic value. For example, the site could serve up personalized offers or content relevant to the customer based on known customer profile information. The more personalized and relevant the offers and information, the more likely the customer will take the desired action.

To use a Microsoft example, if the relationship program customer database indicated a particular customer had purchased Microsoft Office, and their business title was Lead Project Manager, one could reasonably assume the customer is familiar with and knowledgeable about Office and their job revolves around managing projects. Given this, the website portal could serve up information, offers, or other content that could expose the

FIGURE 9-17: Relationship Program Components

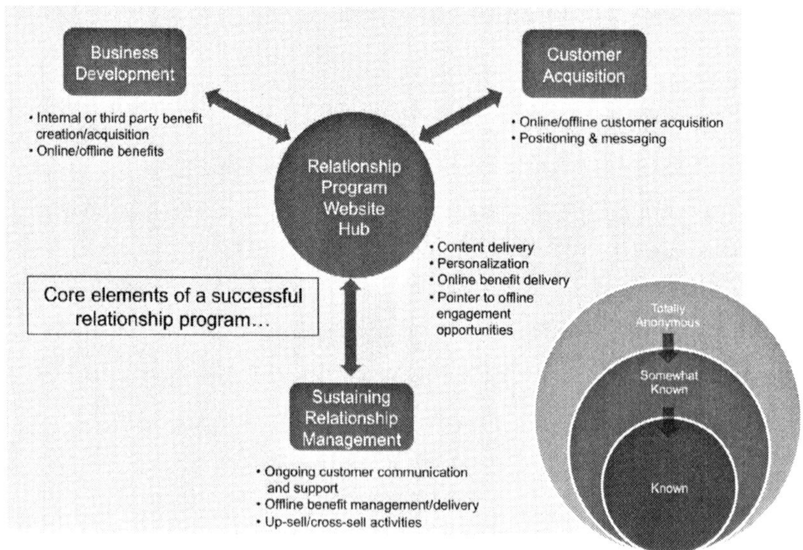

customer to a project management solution such as Microsoft Project (a member of the Office product line), creating awareness and a cross-sell opportunity.

Serving up personalized information in this manner is the first step to take a customer into the awareness phase of the life cycle. If website usage and activity can be tracked and matched to that customer, and they act on the content or information being served up about Microsoft Project, they have definitely moved into the awareness phase. Updating the program database shows that the customer has acted on the awareness offer, deepening what is known about them. The next time that customer logs into the site they might be provided a trial offer of Microsoft Project to move them from awareness and into the trial/evaluation phase of the life cycle. Assuming the customer then trials the product (which would be captured in the program customer database), a further offer including a purchase incentive could be made, potentially generating a sale. If a sale is made, a successful cross-sell has occurred and incremental economic value created from the initial investment to acquire that customer.

The ability to be effective in deriving ongoing incremental economic value depends on the quality and scope of the information available about the customers. This is why it is important to move a customer from a totally anonymous state, where no information is known, to a state where much information is known and can be effectively used to generate more revenue. This is how businesses like Amazon.com and others generate cross-sell revenues using pitches like the "Others that have bought this title also liked to read..." feature.

It is important that the customer database be regularly updated with additional customer information acquired through the program website. There are many methods to capture such incremental information beyond the initial registration data captured when the customer signed up for the relationship program. These include incremental data capture via forms when a customer downloads content, sign-up data for an exclusive member service, survey research data into the membership installed base, and site click and time tracking.

Obviously, there is significant technical implementation planning required to design the optimal user experience and the customer database, and to create the required business rules. Regardless of the technology issues, the key business issue is to acquire more detailed information about the customer in an acceptable, balanced manner, which means:

- There is a value trade-off customers must make to decide if they are willing to provide incremental personal information relative to the value of the offering. Customers will provide the level of information proportional to the value of the content, information, service, or product being offered.

- A user experience balance must be met on requiring incremental information from a customer to gain access to a program offer, information, or service. If the customer begins to feel "nickel-and-dimed," or inconvenienced by providing personal information, the program is unbalanced and will suffer. It's critical to get the balance right between when and if to ask for customer information, and how much information to ask for.

The web portal also links various value elements of the relationship program, providing a mechanism or path to get to those elements, whether they are delivered online or offline.

Acquiring the portfolio of program value elements is the responsibility of the business development function of the marketing group owning the relationship program. This involves identifying the right program benefits to include in the program and developing them with internally available assets or creating any necessary third-party relationships. Various types of benefits can be included in a relationship program that add significant value to the customers in the program and help incent new customers to join.

Figure 9-18 includes some examples that have proven valuable in Microsoft programs. For example, the Product Benefits category could include free or low-cost product enhancements or extensions to products the customer already owns. For example, if a customer owns Microsoft Office, free templates using the various Office products such as Excel, Word, or PowerPoint could be made available exclusively to those customers in the program. If the product is a consumer goods food product, discount coupons for additional or similar items could be provided.

Complementary benefits for a product the customer owns are another opportunity. An example is developing exclusive third-party offers for the membership base. There are likely a large number of third-party vendors that could provide additional product or services value to the program participants. If your firm is selling computer hardware, you could offer discounted or free third-party installation services. If your firm sells financial software, a complementary offer from a local bank could be arranged (e.g., six months free business account). If customers are primarily business owners, a deal with FedEx or Kinko's offering discounted shipping or business services could add value.

FIGURE 9-18: Exclusive Relationship Program Offers

Ensure that a relationship program contains exclusive offers available only to members...

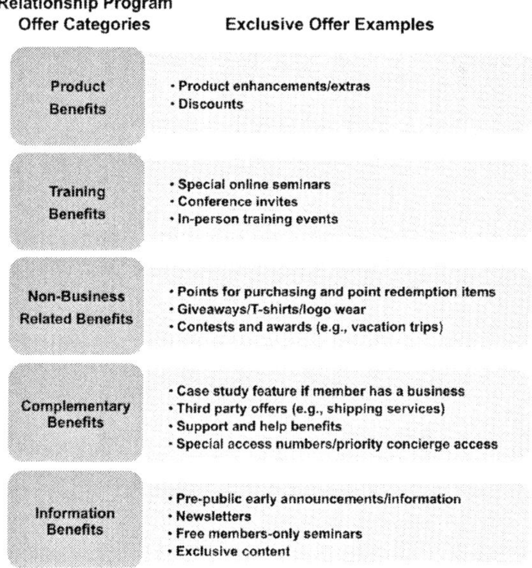

These deals provide business value for all: your company gets a great and compelling benefit to provide to existing program members and an additional incentive for new members to join. The partner gets access to new customers that may drive incremental revenue, and program members can take advantage of valuable third-party offerings. Another great benefit is a premier level of customer service, where customers go to the front of the queue for support calls or have a special access line to personalized service.

The best way to decide which benefits to incorporate in the program is to research the customer base and ask them what they want, what they value, and what would incent them to join. The second best way is to make educated assumptions about what the best benefits would be, put them out there, and hope it works, fine-tuning as the program evolves and customer feedback or uptake patterns are analyzed. I would choose the "asking the customers first" option to ensure that the initial spend to get the program up and running will result in adequate customer acquisition and use of program benefits. Continually get feedback from customers on what is and is not working, regularly add new program benefits to keep things fresh, modify benefits that need fine-tuning, and drop program benefits that are not being used or valued.

Once the program value and benefits are defined and ready and the website is up and running, customer acquisition and sustaining relationship marketing for the program take the stage. Customer acquisition marketing is the primary feeding mechanism to build program membership. Obvious targets for recruiting customers into the program include the installed base of existing, long-lived customers and more recently acquired customers. Since the installed base is the target, the contact information for these customers should be readily available for awareness creation activities via email, direct mail, or the corporate website. Developing the proper positioning for the program, defining value propositions, and clearly communicating are tasks for acquisition marketing. A positioning framework (Chapter 4) should also be created for the relationship program to ensure clarity of communication across all customer acquisition activities, demand generation vehicles, and website content.

Maintaining regular contact with program members via a regular email newsletter update is also highly recommended. Reasons include:

- To provide a customer touch and keep your firm top of mind.
- To remind customers of the valuable program benefits and encourage their use. Non-engaged customers will limit the cross-sell/up-sell opportunities and limit the upside in customer satisfaction potential.
- To provide a regular opportunity to cross-sell/up-sell with special offers.

It's important to understand that the program website, business development, customer acquisition, and relationship management activities must be synchronized and executed in tandem—they cannot operate independently. For example, the website needs to be current with program offers that business development has brought in, and program positioning and messaging must keep current with the latest value offerings. Otherwise customers have a poor experience.

A successful relationship program brings potential long-term incremental revenue from existing customers and can help acquire new customers if the program value proposition is compelling. For example, you could use the program itself as an offer to acquire a new customer (e.g., "Buy the product today and get your FREE membership in WeRelateToYou, our rewarding membership program that gives you the following great benefits…."). In addition, over time the program will host many satisfied customers, which creates a built-in pool of potential positive customer testimonials to use on websites, for PR and analyst purposes, and for case studies to assist in acquiring new customers. Other possible uses include the opportunity to include the partner channel members and allow them to provide exclusive offers. It's a win-win all around.

Staying on Top of Customer and Partner Satisfaction

In the end, satisfied customers will continue to drive the business. You can gain new customers over time, but if there is low customer satisfaction with your company or product, there will be no repeat business or cross-sell/up-sell opportunities. If there is low partner satisfaction, engagement levels and resale revenue will fall off. These situations initiate a downward spiral. Maintaining satisfied customers and partners is important. A solid customer relationship program firing on all cylinders and a robust and attentive partner program will help.

Defining customer and partner satisfaction can take various forms, and there are different ways to measure these statistics. Whatever measure is used, the important thing is that a measure *is used* and tracked over time so that course corrections can be made if there is a fall-off in the satisfaction ratings. Tracking over time requires that a satisfaction baseline be developed to measure against. Immediately post-launch, the only customers to baseline will be the pre-launch time frame customers and partners, and these may not be an appropriate baseline. It is best to wait until there are enough post-launch customers and partners with enough product experience to produce a valid customer and partner satisfaction baseline.

Approaches to getting the satisfaction data include:

- Perform a broad customer and partner satisfaction survey several times a year.
- Incorporate satisfaction surveys into the sales cycle. When a direct sales person closes a deal, they should follow-up within a certain time frame and ask the end-customer to take the satisfaction survey.
- If the deal was partner led, or involved a partner, it is appropriate to ask the end-customer for feedback. Your firm's sales representative could also follow-up later regarding satisfaction with partners.

As in any feedback or survey, there are many questions that could be asked or data points gathered. Satisfaction data and surveys are no different. However, two key data points that must be captured and tracked as the core of the satisfaction tracking effort are the number of secured customers in the customer base and the number of very satisfied and very dissatisfied customers in the installed base.

Secured customers are defined in Figure 9-19. In essence, these customers fit three specific criteria:

- They are very satisfied with your product.

FIGURE 9-19: Measuring Customer Satisfaction

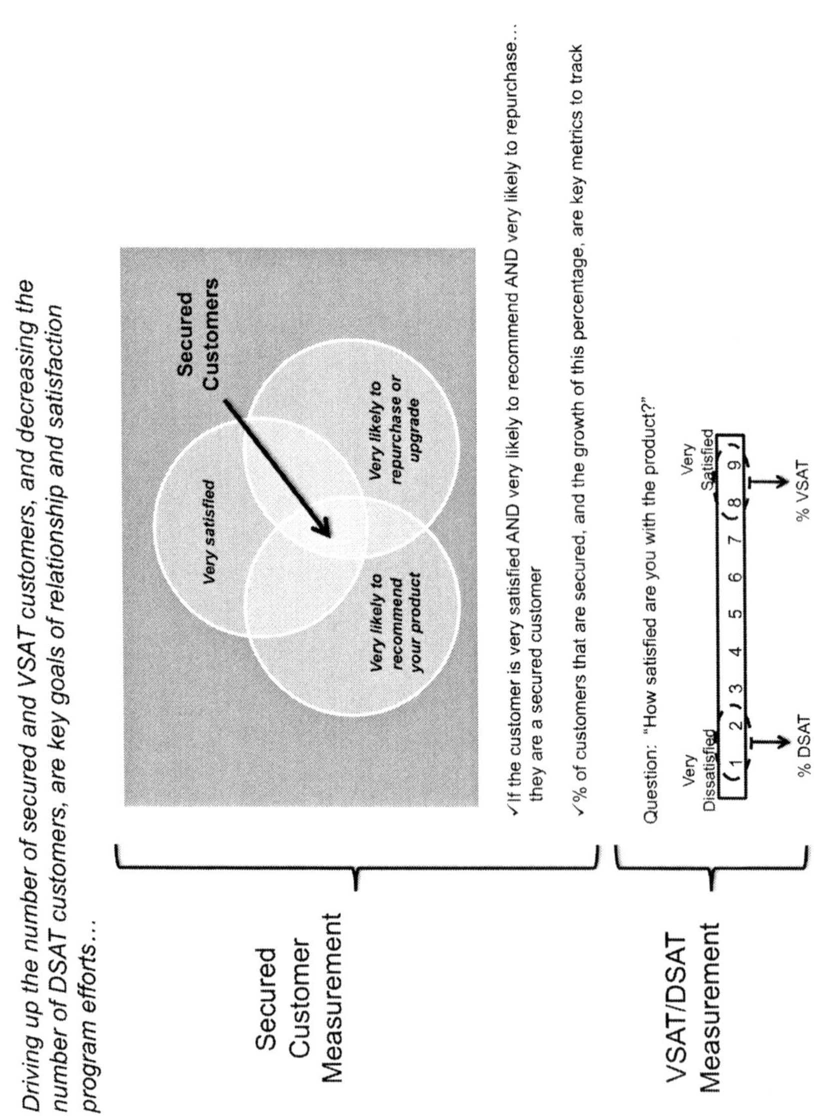

- They are very likely to recommend your product.
- They are very likely to repurchase your product or upgrade.

These customers have a low probability of being lost to a competitor. Minor changes to these questions can enable a similar measure to be applied to partner channel members to quantify a secured partner metric.

Another satisfaction measurement is the percentage of very satisfied and very dissatisfied customers in the installed base. On a 9-point scale, the percentage of very satisfied (VSAT) customers would be those that indicated an 8 or 9 (top two scores) on a survey question asking how satisfied they are. Similarly, a 1 or 2 score (bottom two scores) would indicate the percentage of very dissatisfied (DSAT) customers. The game is to move the DSAT customers up and decrease their percentage in the installed base, and to increase the number of VSAT customers by keeping them and moving some of the in-the-middle customers up to VSAT levels.

The trick to getting more secured customers, more VSAT customers, and fewer DSAT customers is identifying the key levers that can affect these changes and putting the plans and programs into place to make the changes happen. The typical barrier for programs designed to increase customer or partner satisfaction is not knowing the correct levers to pull because the right data does not exist or has not been gathered. To change customer or partner satisfaction, it is not enough to simply know the numbers and percentages; you must also identify the underlying rationale and drivers for VSAT, DSAT, and secured or unsecured customers. For example, what is driving the percentage of dissatisfied customers—service problems, product security issues, lousy support, or inadequate access to company personnel? Once identified, those underlying causes can be addressed via specific programs. The same is true for the VSAT numbers—identify the drivers that create high satisfaction and make investments to keep these drivers performing well.

10

It Never Ends

The first nine chapters of this book covered a lot of ground. At the start, we discussed that change is the rule for a product launch, the product life cycle, and the importance of the qualitative aspects of a launch such as leadership, planning, perseverance, and flexibility. Ensuring an in-depth understanding of the customer is important, since understanding the target customers and their characteristics underlies all launch activities. Actionable segmentation, research, scenarios, and personas were indicated as some tools that enable this understanding.

Launch strategy and rollout planning was then addressed, focusing on key launch planning issues like integrated plans, revenue opportunity analysis, SKUs, strategy trade-offs between long- and short-term goals, channels, and more. These topics formed the basis for developing an integrated rollout plan. After launch strategy and rollout plans, we reviewed the development of positioning statements and value propositions using a positioning framework. The importance of getting positioning correct cannot be overstated.

At that point it became execution time for the launch. Since most companies cannot bring a product to market completely independently, you must identify, prioritize, and acquire key market-making partners. Effectively creating and managing these relationships can make or break a launch.

PR activities and their importance were also addressed. Important topics included understanding and interacting with editors and analysts, key PR launch activities, planning, and creating buzz. PR can be one of the most effective marketing tools for a launch. Remember to make sure that what you communicate via your PR activities is truly newsworthy.

Rolling out important pre-launch customer and partner programs followed. Effective pre-launch engagement with these audiences through these programs creates awareness for the product and helps fine-tune and hone the product, the key communication points, and the go-to-market process and activities.

The nuts and bolts of a launch were presented as the block and tackle activities. Marketing BOMs, events, channel sell-in, customer service, and the importance of effectively engaging the field sales force were highlighted as key.

Finally, a framework for post-launch marketing was addressed. Planning with strategic levers, executing programs via a customer relationship management model, maximizing MROI by connecting marketing to sales with integrated marketing, and effectively managing a pipeline were some important post-launch activities noted. Don't forget about staying on top of the business post-launch by analyzing your customers and channels, implementing some sort of customer relationship loyalty program, and tracking and managing customer satisfaction.

While that summarizes this book, if you think that's it, the end, then think again. Will your customer or partner councils stop after the launch? Will there never be new product SKUs to create? Will event attendance simply end? Does product positioning remain static over time? Do market-making partners simply disappear? Of course the answer is no. These and many other activities put into place during the pre-launch time frame will continue post-launch.

Finally, a viable company continually conceptualizes, designs, and introduces new products into the market. Each of these products must be taken through some sort of launch process, whether they are product updates, revisions, extensions, or new versions. Depending on the scope of the new products, and their importance to the firm, they will require different levels of launch activity scope and breadth. Product releases of lesser scope and importance may not require an investment across the full range of launch activities covered in this book. Or they may require all of them executed in a lightweight manner. However, broad scope products of great importance warrant the full rigor of the launch concepts and tactics. While all this occurs, the current product must be actively marketed and sold.

Once you've completed a launch, you should feel really good about that accomplishment. It's a huge investment in time and energy to take a product to launch. Not everyone gets to experience that, so enjoy it. Hopefully, you will have (or had) fun during the launch process. The big launch event is always something to look forward to as well, so enjoy that when you are living it. Another fun tip—try to get your executives to commit to doing something crazy if you meet a major milestone or make the planned launch date without slipping (or even just get the product out the door). It's like when a football team wins the big game and the coach gets Gatorade or water dumped on him—the big cheese takes one for the team. At Microsoft, I've seen executives commit to shaving their heads, getting fully dunked into one of the various water fountains and pools on the Microsoft campus, and eating dog food (no, I am not kidding). Those are always amusing activities to watch and participate in—just keep in mind that this same person may be overseeing your next launch!

With all that in mind, it should be clear that a product launch is only the beginning of a road that never really ends. Have fun, learn something, and enjoy. Good luck.

Index

About the Author

James Mastan is a highly regarded marketing and business strategy expert, speaker, and founder of Blue Rain Marketing LLC, a premier Northwest business and marketing strategy and program execution consulting firm. Mastan has 14 years of Microsoft marketing and launch experience, and over 20 years of overall experience creating effective business and marketing strategies and programs that have delivered significant business value to his clients. His experience and knowledge span small business, mid-size, and enterprise markets in a wide range of industries and products, including computer software and hardware products, information services, medical devices, software as a service, automotive, home networking, uninterruptible power supplies, search technologies, project management, aerospace, speech recognition, and computer networking. At Microsoft, Mastan led or was involved in numerous product launches, including developer oriented programming tools, desktop productivity software, server software, subscription products, e-learning, emerging technologies, and books.

Mastan holds a Bachelor of Science degree in computer science/ mathematics from UCLA and an MBA in marketing and corporate strategy from the Ross School of Business at the University of Michigan, Ann Arbor. He currently resides in Washington state with his wife, Kim, and his two darling and sometimes mischievous daughters, Nicole and Meagan.

To contact James, email him at **inquiries@bluerainmarketing.com** or visit the Blue Rain Marketing website at **www.bluerainmarketing.com**. For book feedback and suggestions, email **bookfeedback@bluerainmarketing.com.**